Fiona Patterson · Lara Zibarras
Editors

Selection and Recruitment in the Healthcare Professions

Research, Theory and Practice

palgrave
macmillan

Editors
Fiona Patterson
Work Psychology Group
Derby, UK

Lara Zibarras
Department of Psychology
City, University of London
London, UK

ISBN 978-3-030-40472-7   ISBN 978-3-319-94971-0 (eBook)
https://doi.org/10.1007/978-3-319-94971-0

Library of Congress Control Number: 2018946800

Cover illustration: Ohata Yoki/EyeEm/gettyimages

This Palgrave Macmillan imprint is published by the registered company Springer Nature Switzerland AG
The registered company address is: Gewerbestrasse 11, 6330 Cham, Switzerland

Selection and Recruitment in the Healthcare Professions

Preface

Overview

The ways in which we recruit and select people to become healthcare professionals is high stakes because their jobs are challenging and can—in many cases—significantly impact the public. There is a duty to understand how best to select for these roles, and to ensure that the way in which we choose our future clinicians is sound, and fair to all who apply.

To select and then train the right people, organizations must first define *what attributes and values make a competent and compassionate healthcare worker*, and use "evidence-based" methods to assess these reliably. This moves away from hiring decisions that are based on intuition, gut feel and potentially flawed data. An evidence-based approach can ensure more effective selection decisions for a high-quality healthcare workforce. A good quality recruitment and selection system will improve an organization's ability to identify those people with the greatest chance of success in a role.

Drawing upon many years of experience in researching, designing and evaluating selection systems for healthcare, alongside our co-authors, our book takes a comprehensive look at the issues surrounding selection into healthcare roles. We outline the latest research relating to the key stages of designing an effective selection system, from role analysis, to the identification of relevant selection methods, through to broader issues in selection systems design.

We present research, theory and evidence that reviews a range of selection methods currently used in professional healthcare roles, at different stages of selection (e.g. student, postgraduate training and senior roles). We bring together a collection of international case material that demonstrates some of these issues in practice. We also highlight the key contemporary issues in this area, for example: technology in recruitment and selection; fairness; selecting for values; diversity and widening access; taking a modular approach to selection; and coaching. Each chapter is authored by experts in their field of research and practice, and includes international practical case material to bring the topic to light.

Why read this book?

Given that regulators within the healthcare profession internationally now demand that all education providers demonstrate evidence of good quality selection practices, this text can inform a wide range of selection practices across the globe. Furthermore, widening access to medical and healthcare roles is increasingly important internationally, not only in terms of fairness but also in terms of making sure the workforce is representative of the population they serve.

Nevertheless, there are many complex challenges ahead and several areas of uncharted territory to explore which makes selection and recruitment thought-provoking topics for further research. This book is intended as a platform to promote further debate between colleagues across the globe on these issues.

Who will benefit from this book?

This book is intended for academics, admission tutors, researchers, educators working in the field of selection and recruitment (in healthcare education and otherwise) and students. Professionals in a variety of areas, especially human resources or personnel, may find this book useful. It should be particularly helpful to those new to the recruitment and selection topic within healthcare.

Derby, UK Fiona Patterson
London, UK Lara Zibarras

Acknowledgements

We thank the Palgrave Editorial staff for their help with the manuscript, from inception, support, guidance, and through to completion. We are also enormously grateful to the many authors who contributed to this book, and our collaborators who provided case material to bring the theory to light. We would also like to thank the numerous friends and colleagues who have—in their various ways—contributed to our thinking and the development of the ideas, theory and practice to advance the field. Lastly, we are hugely indebted to Sarah Stott whose help was essential during the final stages of the book.

Contents

Notes on Contributors

Kirsty Alexander is a doctoral candidate at the Centre for Healthcare Education Reseach and Innovation (CHERI), University of Aberdeen, Scotland. Kirsty's Ph.D. research investigates how the medical school admissions process is understood and negotiated by those within in it—by medical schools, secondary school teachers and potential applicants. She is particularly interested in the influence these perceptions may have on initiatives to widen access to medicine. Before starting the Ph.D. Kirsty completed an M.A. at the University of St Andrews, and after graduating worked in a widening access role at two different UK universities, which sparked her interest in this fascinating area.

John Barratt is a teaching fellow in Occupational Psychology at University of Leicester and has a Master's degree in Work Psychology and Business. His research interests focus on recruitment and selection practices in the UK adult health and social care sector. He has a particular interest in the role of personality in relation to job performance and satisfaction, and is a registered qualified psychometric test user.

Jennifer Cleland is John Simpson Chair of Medical Education Research, and Director of the Centre for Healthcare Education

Research and Innovation (CHERI), University of Aberdeen, Scotland. With nearly 200 peer-reviewed journal articles and book chapters, she has published widely in a broad range of journals including the *BMJ* and *Medical Education*.

Jen's particular research interests are selection and widening access, assessment and performance, and medical careers decision making. Her research spans the continuum of undergraduate, postgraduate and continuing medical education and training.

Jan Corstjens is Ph.D. candidate at the Department of Personnel Management and Work and Organizational Psychology at Ghent University, Belgium. He obtained his Bachelor's degree in Cognitive Psychology (2011) and his Master's degree in Work and Organizational Psychology (2012) from Maastricht University, the Netherlands. His research interests are positioned in the field of selection and assessment. Specifically, he focuses on selection procedures that assess academic and non-academic constructs, and how cognitive-motivational processes affect test performance.

Rachel Driver is a business psychologist specializing in Organizational Psychology and with interests in talent assessment and development in high-stakes settings, and diversity and inclusion. Her M.Sc. thesis investigated the impact of two SJT response formats on performance across candidate subgroups.

Helena Edwards is a Senior Consultant at Work Psychology Group. She specializes in the design and delivery of bespoke assessment and development solutions grounded in psychological theory with the aim of improving organizational effectiveness. Her work has ranged from ensuring that the development of Values-Based Recruitment (VBR) frameworks are informed by the latest research evidence, through to coordinating the delivery of development centers for one of the largest providers of residential care homes in the UK. Helena holds an M.Sc. in Occupational Psychology from the University of Nottingham and is a Chartered Member of the British Psychological Society (BPS).

Eamonn Ferguson is Professor of Health Psychology at the University of Nottingham. He is a Chartered Health and Occupational Psychologist, a Fellow of the Royal Society for Public Health, an Associate Fellow of the British Psychological Society, and co-founding President of the British Society for the Psychology of Individual Differences (www.bspid.org.uk/). He was recently made a "Distinguished International Affiliate" of the division of Health Psychology of the American Psychological Association. His current theoretical work focuses on the integration of theory and models from psychology, in particular personality theory, with behavioral economics, to address questions focusing on (i) the overlap of personality and pro-social preferences, (ii) understand blood and organ donor behavior, (iii) resource allocation and, (iv) subjective wellbeing and emotion processing. He has published 180 peer reviewed journal articles to date (including in *BMJ*, *Psychological Bulletin*, *Annals of Behavioral Medicine*, *Health Psychology*, *BMC Medicine*; *Psychosomatic Medicine*, *Journal of Personality*, *Personality* and *Social Psychological Bulletin*) with his work funded by the HSE, ESRC, and DEFRA, ARUK amongst others.

Charlotte Flaxman is a Consultant at Work Psychology Group, with expertise in selection and development for high stakes professions, organizational change and evaluation. Specifically, Charlotte has been involved in role analyses and the development of competency frameworks for multiple roles within healthcare, utilizing best practice methodology and informed by the latest research. Charlotte's key area of interest includes utilizing the outputs of a role analysis to inform assessments for selection and development. Charlotte holds an M.Sc. in Organizational Psychology from Manchester Business School.

Gail Fleming is a registered Pharmacist and Pharmacy Dean for the London and South East area for Health Education England. Within this role Gail leads the strategic development of the Pharmacy workforce. She is also the professional lead for the development and delivery of the National Pre-registration Pharmacist Recruitment Scheme for England and Wales. Gail works as an accreditor of M.Pharm. degrees for the General Pharmaceutical Council which provides a good insight to the breadth of pharmacy undergraduate experience across the UK.

Barbara Griffin is an endorsed Organizational Psychologist and Professor in the Department of Psychology at Macquarie University,

Australia. Her research investigates person-environment fit and adjustment processes across the employee career cycle, including projects on selection, culture assessment, maladaptive behavior, and career transition. Within the field of medical education, Barbara has developed selection systems for undergraduate and graduate medical programs in Australia, led several major longitudinal studies of medical student outcomes, and collaborated on large multi-institutional studies. Her published research includes articles on predictive validity, MMI interviews, commercial coaching, and widening participation.

Wolfgang Hampe is Professor for Biochemistry at the University Medical Centre Hamburg-Eppendorf. He has completed a Master's degree in Medical Education and is responsible for the development and implementation of the student admission tests.

Johanna Hissbach is a Psychologist and trained Psychotherapist. She was responsible for the introduction of MMIs to the University Medical Centre Hamburg-Eppendorf and has a particular interest in reliability and feasibility aspects of MMIs.

Maureen E. Kelly has research interest in selection and widening diversity in the medical profession. Arising from her Ph.D. work she is recognized as a national and international expert on selection of medical students. She is regularly sought to speak on selection matters and advise on national policy. She is the NUI Galway representative on the National Research Group Evaluating Entry and Selection to Medical Schools, a member of the International Network for Researchers in Selection into Healthcare (INReSH), an Associate Editor of BMC Medical Education and author of several peer reviewed papers on selection.

Máire Kerrin is a Director of the Work Psychology Group, a leading provider of research in healthcare education, specializing in assessment of non-academic attributes and evaluation. She has worked in collaboration with the Department of Health (UK and Australia), Health Education England (in Medical, Dental and Pharmacy training), Medical Schools Council, General Medical Council, Nursing and Midwifery Council and various UK Medical Royal Colleges. Previous to her current role, she was a Senior Lecturer in Organizational

Psychology at City University, London, and Lecturer at the University of Nottingham, UK. She remains a Visiting Lecturer at Cass Business School, City University of London.

Tom Kinirons is a Psychologist at Work Psychology Group. Tom's role involves leading and supporting on a range of projects within the healthcare sector with a particular focus on the design and implementation of Situational Judgement Tests for both selection and development purposes. He is proficient in a range of qualitative research methods and quantitative statistical techniques and supports the Research and Development activities within Work Psychology Group. Tom holds an M.Sc. in Organizational Psychology from Manchester Business School, as well as an M.Sc. in Applied Psychology from Trinity College Dublin, Ireland.

Mirjana Knorr is a Psychologist with a special interest in work and organizational psychology. Her Ph.D. thesis focuses on reliability and validity aspects of the Hamburg multiple mini-interview for the selection of medical students.

Filip Lievens is the Lee Kong Chian Professor of Human Resources at the Lee Kong Chian School of Business of Singapore Management University. He is also an Honorary Professor at the University of Cape Town and a Visiting Professor at Ghent University, Belgium, where he also obtained his Ph.D. in 1999. He has published over 160 articles in the areas of selection, assessment, and recruitment. His research interests deal with talent assessment, situational judgement, intra-individual variability, personality, and organizational attractiveness. His articles have appeared among others in the *Annual Review of Psychology*, *Journal of Applied Psychology*, *Personnel Psychology*, and *Journal of Management.*

Emma Morley is a Senior Consultant at Work Psychology Group and has a wide range of experience in the area of selection into the healthcare professions, with particular expertise in the development and delivery of competency frameworks. Emma's role involves her key area of interest; designing and evaluating bespoke and innovative assessment solutions, informed by the latest research literature and intention to disseminate key learnings. Emma is a Graduate Member of the British

Psychological Society (BPS) and holds an M.Sc. with distinction in Occupational Psychology from the University of Sheffield.

Liz Mossop was formerly Professor of Veterinary Education at the University of Nottingham, School of Veterinary Medicine and Science, and is now Deputy Vice Chancellor at the University of Lincoln. Liz has particular interests in professionalism and the teaching and assessment of professional skills. Her research focuses on defining professionalism and attitudes to challenging situations such as errors and ethical dilemmas. Liz is a qualified Veterinary Surgeon and holds a Ph.D. and Masters in Clinical Education. She is an HEA National Teaching Fellow and has received many awards for her teaching and student engagement initiatives.

Lazaro M. Mwandigha focused his Ph.D. project on developing and extending statistical methods for adjusting the attenuation of predictive validity estimates associated with aptitude tests due to selection. He has also been involved with work relating to the DREAMS network led by Dr. Paul Tiffin.

Sandra Nicholson is Professor of Medical Education and Head of the Centre for Medical Education at the Institute of Health Sciences Education, Queen Mary University of London. She has a sustained interest over many years of having worked and published in medical selection and widening participation. Sandra's own Ph.D. thesis examined the academic experiences of medical students from lower socio-economic backgrounds.

Fiona Patterson is the founding Director for Work Psychology Group, a research-led consulting practice located in the UK and Australia, providing advice to organizations internationally. She is a Visiting Researcher at the University of Cambridge, London, Nottingham and Aberdeen. In recognition of her work in medical selection she was awarded an Honorary Fellowship of the Royal College of General Practice, which is the highest award a College can bestow. In 2013, she was the first woman to win the annual British Psychological Society's Academic Contribution to Practice award. In 2014, Fiona established a new international research network for selection for the healthcare professions with contributions from around the globe. In 2017, she won an International Women in Business award sponsored by HSBC.

Paul A. Tiffin focused his academic work on eliciting and measuring individual differences (psychometrics) and linking these to outcomes. His research is focused on the 'educational epidemiology' of the healthcare workforce and is recognized for his expertise in exploiting large, routinely arising datasets in clinical education. As lead for the DREAMS network (Developing and Researching the Economics and Mathematics of Selection) he has been facilitating a collaboration developing new approaches to understanding and communicating the effectiveness of personnel selection methods.

Stephen A. Woods is Professor of Work and Organizational Psychology at Surrey Business School, University of Surrey. He is known for his research on psychometric and personality trait assessment, personality and vocational development, and recruitment and selection. Steve is a Registered Practitioner Occupational Psychologist in the UK and works with businesses and organizations globally in the areas of HR assessment and development.

Lara Zibarras is Senior Lecturer in Organizational Psychology at City, University of London. As a Chartered Occupational Psychologist and Associate Fellow of the British Psychological Society. Lara has conducted extensive selection assessment research in high-stakes settings, focusing on the applicants' perspective, diversity and use of innovative assessment methods. She has published widely in academic journals and consulted for public and private sector organizations in the areas of selection, training, development and psychometric assessment.

List of Figures

List of Tables

List of Case Studies

1

Designing and Evaluating Selection and Recruitment in Healthcare

Fiona Patterson

Selecting competent and compassionate healthcare workers is an increasingly important issue internationally. There is over a century's worth of research literature exploring how best to select a person for a given role, but historically less attention has centred on selection into the healthcare professions. This picture is changing rapidly however, and here we present the research evidence with a view to supporting recruiters, researchers, educators and students in understanding the design and evaluation issues to further inform selection policy and practices in future.

In this opening chapter, the context of healthcare is explored and the implications for how to approach the design of selection methods and processes. The key principles in designing selection processes are presented and various evaluation criteria used to judge the quality of selection practices are offered. From here, the key topics addressed in this book are introduced, categorized into three parts including (i) the

---

F. Patterson (✉)
Work Psychology Group, Derby, UK
e-mail: f.patterson@workpsychologygroup.com

F. Patterson and L. Zibarras (eds.), *Selection and Recruitment in the Healthcare Professions*, https://doi.org/10.1007/978-3-319-94971-0_1

effectiveness of different selection methods, (ii) designing selection systems and (iii) issues in recruitment. In each part, there is a collection of chapters authored by leading researchers in their field. They present the research evidence, alongside international case material to showcase the practical application of these findings.

Context of Selection and Recruitment in Healthcare

Selection into the healthcare professions remains highly competitive for some professions such as medicine and dentistry, whereas other healthcare professions struggle to recruit, such as in nursing in the UK. Furthermore, within professions, the picture can look very different; for example, recruitment into medical school is highly competitive internationally, yet there are recruitment shortages into postgraduate training in specialties such as psychiatry and general practice (family physicians). In this book, we explore designing selection methods and systems in both highly competitive settings and in settings where there are workforce shortages which tend to focus more on recruitment and attraction issues. It must also be acknowledged that most of the previous research has focused on medical education, although the learning from this evidence base has strong relevance for many other healthcare professions.

Traditionally, most research on selection in healthcare has focused on exploring the quality of different selection methods using largely student populations (those entering education programmes in healthcare such as medical school admissions; see Hecker & Norman, 2017). In the past five years, the field has progressed to potentially more complex topics, including selection policies and systems design, methodological concerns (beyond psychometric issues), diversity and fairness issues, new evaluation frameworks, and developments in theory (Patterson et al., 2018).

Practically, selection and recruitment are often resource-intensive, so a key consideration is efficiency. Where there are a high-volume number of applicants, a key consideration is how to 'manage the numbers'; for example, how one constructs short-listing procedures and interview processes are important real-world problems. Drawing upon international case material, we also explore the increasing use of technology to deliver selection tests and interviews which we review in detail in our closing chapter (Chapter 13).

Key Principles in Selection Research and Evaluation

Two main principles underlie the role that selection procedures play in healthcare settings. The first principle is that there are individual differences between people in aptitudes, values, skills and other personal qualities. This simple principle leads to the very important conclusion that people are not equally suited to a career in healthcare and suggests that procedures for selecting healthcare workers have important implications for patient safety and good-quality patient care. Historically, research has tended to focus mainly on academic capability as the main criterion for selection in healthcare, but more recently, the field has progressed to focus more on how best to select for various non-academic attributes and values (see Chapter 3 on personality assessment, Chapter 4 on situational judgement tests (SJTs), Chapter 5 on interviews, Chapter 11 on values-based recruitment and Chapter 12 focusing on altruism and pro-sociality in selection).

The second principle is that future behavior is, at least partly, predictable. The goal of selection activities is to match people to roles and ensure the best possible levels of future performance (both as a trainee and a practicing clinician). The belief that *future performance* can be estimated is an important facet of the second principle mentioned above. The essential function of selection methods and processes is to provide means of estimating the likely future performance of candidates and wherever possible, linked to health outcomes.

In evaluating professional exams, the *reliability* of the assessments is viewed as the 'gold standard'; to ensure that a trainee is safe for subsequent independent practice. In selection, the *predictive validity* of the assessments has traditionally been the gold standard, as students and trainees enter supervised education, and recruiters wish to appoint those most likely to succeed in training. Selection research in healthcare has largely focused on reliability issues (e.g. how many stations are required for a multiple mini-interview to be reliable), and here, we remind readers that it is quite possible to be *reliably wrong*, such that greater attention should be paid to establishing the predictive and construct validity of selection systems. Furthermore, the field is moving beyond relatively simple linear and regression-based approaches to judging the validity of selection practices to acknowledge that selection is a complex, multi-level, dynamic phenomenon and as such has recently been characterised as a 'wicked problem' (see Cleland, Patterson, & Hanson, 2018).

This shift in emphasis beyond psychometric issues is reflected in a new international consensus statement on selection and recruitment to the healthcare professions (developed at the 2018 Ottawa-ICME Joint Conference on the Assessment of Competence in Medicine and the Healthcare Professions and reviewed in more detail in Chapter 13). The statement was developed by a specially convened group of international researchers with expertise in selection and recruitment, assessment, curriculum and educational theory to critically appraise the literature and develop a consensus statement (see Patterson et al., 2018). In addition to dealing with the latest evidence on selection methods, the statement pays attention to the issues surrounding *selection philosophies and policies*, a topic that has received relatively little attention until now. The statement suggests that "*individual institutions define their selection philosophy and uniquely enact a selection policy (or policies) within the context of their national or state-based regulations, their own history, mission and goals, and stakeholder organizations, by choosing and implementing a combination of specific methods from the range available to them*". This is a helpful framing for understanding the breadth of approaches to selection practices across the globe (for example, in dealing with diversity and widening access issues, a lottery system is culturally acceptable in some countries, but not in others). By drawing upon international case-study material throughout this book, we encourage the reader to reflect on the issues. We return to the topic of selection philosophy alongside the international consensus statement recommendations in Chapter 13.

How Effective are Selection Methods?

Drawing upon recent reviews of the research literature (e.g. Ferguson & Lievens, 2017; Patterson et al., 2016; Rees et al., 2016; Roberts et al., 2018), there exist some clear messages about the comparative reliability, validity and effectiveness of various selection methods. The research evidence for different selection methods is summarized in Table 1.1.

The first part of this book focuses on reviewing selection methods for which there is a relatively large evidence base. Various authors present

Table 1.1 Summary of the research evidence and implications for different selection methods (Patterson et al., 2016, 2018; Roberts et al., 2018)

Selection method	Research evidence and implications
Academic achievement	There is a high level of consensus regarding predictive validity but concerns that the discriminatory power is diminishing as increasing numbers of students achieve top high school grades. Moreover, comparability across different types of schools and school systems is frequently questioned. Academic records can negatively impact widening access if school systems are socially selective
Aptitude tests	Different tests are located on a continuum between pure ability and pure knowledge tests. Reliability tends to be favourable. The knowledge parts especially in the natural sciences predict study performance. Evidence is mixed on the fairness of aptitude tests, specifically regarding predictive validity, so each tool requires evaluation in its own right. Knowledge tests are also often used for postgraduate selection and demonstrate in this context also favourable reliability and validity
Personal statements and CVs	Candidate acceptability is high, but susceptibility to coaching and plagiarism is also high. There is very little evidence for predictive validity. For postgraduate recruitment, CVs are often used as part of an interview but usually in a non-standardized format
References and letters of recommendation	Little research supporting validity or reliability and high costs for scoring. However, use of references remains widespread and candidate reactions are positive. References might be used to flag up problematic applicants

(continued)

Table 1.1 (continued)

Selection method	Research evidence and implications
Situational Judgement Tests (SJTs)	Improved validity over other high-volume selection tools for non-academic characteristics (e.g. personality tests) and can be mapped to organizational values. Although SJTs can be relatively costly to design, they can be machine-marked and delivered online, producing cost savings in high volume selection. Flexibility in format from text-based to multi-media item presentations. Susceptibility to coaching can be minimised through appropriate design
Personality assessment	Some personality traits have been linked to in-training performance (e.g. Conscientiousness), although depending on the personality tool used, the evidence can be mixed. Where there is a high risk for susceptibility to faking or coaching, personality assessment might be used to drive more focused questioning at interviews (rather than as a standalone instrument without verification)
Interviews/Multiple Mini Interviews (MMIs)	Traditional unstructured interviews perform poorly, whereas structured interviews based on a role analysis, with standardised questions, trained interviewers and appropriate scoring, can be reliable and valid methods. MMIs are the most structured type of interviews. They typically comprise six or more interview stations, which broadens the sampling of performance to enhance reliability. MMIs are relatively expensive to design and implement but can offer favourable validity and positive candidate reactions. All types of interviews create the opportunity for a live interaction with applicants which makes them resource-intensive to deliver, but offers other advantages such as enabling a more personal connection between applicant and programme. Candidates prefer interviews to other methods
Selection Centers (SCs) using work samples and simulations	Multi-station SCs are relatively expensive to design and implement as they involve a range of simulations (e.g. group exercises, in-tray tasks, presentations, interactive exercises with role players). They offer a similar multi-sampling approach as MMIs. SCs have been used in postgraduate selection and further evidence of the predictive validity of SCs in undergraduate medical selection is required

the latest research in relation to aptitude tests (Chapter 2), personality assessments (Chapter 3), situational judgement tests (Chapter 4) and interviews (Chapter 5) and review each method for their suitability for selection in healthcare.

Although selection systems differ internationally, prior academic attainment has been traditionally the primary basis for selection into educational healthcare programmes and in postgraduate settings and is usually assessed at an initial screening stage. Prior academic attainment of candidates remains a universal feature of selection policies internationally and the strength of evidence for this remains strong. However, students from less advantaged backgrounds tend to have less strong academic records than those students from more privileged backgrounds and therefore diversity is a key consideration if there is over-reliance on prior academic attainment as the main selection method.

Many recruiters have turned to using aptitude tests (tests designed to determine a person's suitability to enter a career in healthcare) to address diversity concerns (explored in detail in Chapter 2), which usually focus on 'academic readiness' for training programmes and comprise measures of scientific knowledge and general cognitive ability. However, the evidence for the use of aptitude tests is less clear due to the large number of aptitude tests and the differences between currently available aptitude tests; the diverse outcome measures against which performance on aptitude tests is compared (to assess validity), the multiple ways in which aptitude tests are implemented; the mixed nature of the evidence on the effectiveness of aptitude testing in healthcare. There is also some evidence that some aptitude tests may favour certain types of candidates, which may have implications for fairness and widening access issues. However, such a conclusion may be supported in future for specific aptitude tests and for specific outcome measures, should further good quality research evidence become available.

In recent years, there has been increasing recognition that competent clinical practice requires a range of other non-academic attributes (empathy, teamwork, integrity, creativity and resilience) which has sparked a strong research interest in not just which of these attributes are most important in healthcare, but what selection methods can test these reliably. It is argued that designing effective selection methods for important personal attributes is generally more challenging than testing for clinical knowledge or academic attainment (Patterson, Cleland, & Cousans, 2017; Reiter, 2017). In testing for personal attributes, research shows that structured interviews/multiple-mini-interviews (MMIs; an interview format that uses many short independent assessments, typically in a timed circuit), SJTs and SCs (a combination of different selection tools such as simulations, interviews and group exercises) are relatively effective methods and generally fairer than unstructured interviews, references, letters of recommendation and personal statements (a written description of one's achievements, interests, etc., included as part of an application for a job or a place at university). When judging the quality of different tools, it is important to note that structured interviews, SJTs and SCs are measurement methods and within each category comprise a multitude of different design parameters. For example, when evaluating MMIs and SJTs, the construction and content of the interview or test can vary significantly. Depending on the design, this may significantly alter the quality of the instrument to the extent that each needs to be individually evaluated before reaching conclusions about its effectiveness. Although results from meta-analytic studies can indicate the quality of different selection methods in general, local validation studies are required to determine the effectiveness of any given selection system.

Research shows that SJTs and MMIs are more valid predictors of inter- and intra-personal (non-academic) attributes such as empathy and integrity than personal statements or references. SJTs and MMIs are complimentary: while SJTs can measure a broader range of constructs efficiently as they can be machine marked, by contrast, MMIs are a face-to-face encounter. Although expensive, this allows applicant responses to be probed further and in more depth.

In demonstrating the practical implications of these issues, Case Study 1.1 presents recent developments in selection practices for medical school admissions in Indonesia. Case Study 1.1 describes how selection traditionally focused on prior academic attainment, whereas recently there has been a shift towards exploring non-academic attributes using MMIs and SJTs in addition.

Case Study 1.1: Moving from Academic Merits-Based Selection to a Comprehensive Selection System for the Undergraduate Medicine Entry in Indonesia

Diantha Soemantri, ***[1)]Senior Lecturer in the Department of Medical Education, [2)]Member of the assessment team for Medical Education Unit, Faculty of Medicine Universitas Indonesia***

For a long time, medical student selection to enter public medical schools in Indonesia has been based only on academic merit. The entry examination to public medical schools consists of an aptitude test, chemistry, biology and mathematics. It is conducted by a national committee and applies to all candidates for natural sciences subjects. Private universities and some prominent public universities are allowed to design their own selection system; however, most systems are still based only on academic attributes. In 2017 there were 83 public and private medical schools in Indonesia (Ministry of Research, Technology and Higher Education, 2017). The level of competition to enter medical schools is very varied. For a few prominent medical schools, such as Universitas Indonesia, the competition ratio can be up to 1:100 (Faculty of Medicine Universitas Indonesia, 2015). Indonesia is an archipelagic country with the distance from east to west of 5271 km (Nations Encyclopaedia, 2017) with a lot of inequality, especially of income and wealth. These demographic and geographic challenges may pose some problems in ensuring fair selection methods since disparities relating to primary and secondary educational qualities are quite significant in different regions. Therefore, an invitation (non-test) stream for high performing high school students throughout the country was opened.

The need to expand the selection system to also include non-academic attributes has existed for some time. In 2004–2008 the Health Workforce Service (HWS) Project (Director of Learning and Student Affairs, Directorate of Higher Education, Ministry of Education and Culture, 2013) from the Ministry of Higher Education developed a psychometric test to assess candidates' suitability to become medical doctors, however, this particular test was never used. There are also some initiatives to use traditional or multiple mini interview (MMI) for undergraduate selection, although this is confined to several established medical schools. Therefore, in line with the Act of Medical Education number 20 year 2013, there is an urgent need to develop selection instruments that consider candidates' non-academic attributes important for medical doctors, yet accessible for all potential candidates throughout Indonesia. However, maintaining the standards of MMI to be used as a national entry exam can be very challenging since it requires a high number of trained interviewers and multiple sites with the same standards throughout the country.

In 2015 Faculty of Medicine Universitas Indonesia (FMUI) developed a Situational Judgement Test proposed as a subset of selection instruments of undergraduate medical education. A series of item writing sessions and pilot studies have been conducted to establish the validity of UI's SJT as a testing tool. Medical teachers of FMUI developed the SJT items in Indonesian language by considering the local values, norms and cultural context, both in the learning and clinical settings. The item writing process has not only been fruitful to produce a testable SJT, but also to provide opportunities for medical teachers to further examine the expected learning outcomes of medical students, specifically from affective and behavioural perspectives. The UI's SJT is now being proposed to the national committee for university undergraduate selection to become an additional specific selection examination only for medical school candidates.

Designing Selection Systems

The second part of this book explores key issues in selection system design and evaluation. Figure 1.1 provides a summary of the main elements of designing and implementing a selection process. This starts by defining appropriate selection criteria and conducting an analysis of the relevant knowledge, skills, abilities and attitudes associated with performance in the target role (see Chapter 6 on role analysis). This information is used to construct a person specification (and job description where appropriate) and used to decide which selection methods will elicit applicant information related to the identified selection criteria. Outputs from this analysis should detail the responsibilities in the target role and provide information about the attributes and characteristics required of the job holder. In Chapter 6, Kerrin et al. (2018) present research insights in conducting job analysis studies and provide case material to show that this has been applied within a variety of healthcare professions.

In deciding to apply for a post (or a place at University), applicants engage in *self-selection* where they make an informed judgement about whether the role suits their skills, abilities and values. Once selection decisions are made and accepted applicants enter training, the trainees' performance on the original selection criteria should be used to examine the predictive validity of the selection methods (i.e. to what extent are

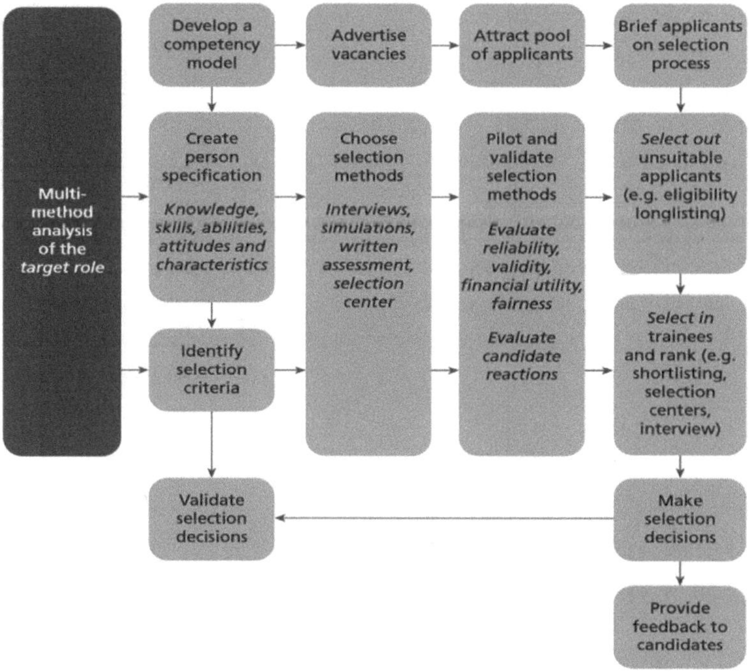

Fig. 1.1 Outline of the selection process

scores at selection associated with assessment of in-training and subsequent work performance?).

Selection is a 'two-way' process. To attract the best trainees, both universities and hospitals have become increasingly aware that candidates' reactions to the selection process are important particularly in relation to perceptions of fairness, a topic reviewed in detail in Chapter 8.

The rudiments of designing selection processes are clear, yet research shows that two elements in the process are often not conducted effectively. First, many organizations do not conduct sufficiently robust job analyses to identify the key knowledge, skills and behaviors associated with competent performance in target roles (in the present and in the future). This is particularly important when exploring potential differences between healthcare specialties (see Patterson, Ferguson, & Thomas, 2008). Second, validation studies are rarely conducted in organizations as they are time-consuming and difficult to administer. It often means tracking trainees' performance over several years, from university selection through to senior posts. In medical education and training, far more validation research has occurred in undergraduate selection, exploring the predictive validity of various cognitive factors (prior academic performance or knowledge tests) with respect to subsequent exam performance (Prideaux et al., 2011). The criteria used to judge performance at medical school are more readily observed, as there are standardized assessments involved, such as examinations. By contrast, the research literature has been relatively sparse when considering selection for either postgraduate training or non-academic factors, although this picture is changing as evidenced by recent systematic literature reviews (Roberts et al., 2018).

Evaluation Criteria to Judge the Quality of Selection Practices

Table 1.2 offers twenty criteria for judging the 'quality' of selection practices to be reviewed as part of the design and implementation process. In overview, when choosing the selection method(s), it is important that the output (score) is consistent/stable (*reliable*) and relevant/accurate (*valid*), and that the method is *objective*, *standardized*, administered by trained professional(s) and monitored. Evaluation of the system is essential to ensure that selection methods used are also *fair*, *defensible*, *cost-effective* and *feasible*. Feedback is used to make continual improvements to the selection system to enhance accuracy and fairness. For postgraduate training, there are legal reasons for ensuring that accurate selection procedures are used, as it is usually essential for compliance with employment law.

The sheer number of evaluation criteria involved demonstrates that designing good-quality selection methods and recruitment systems is complex with many different factors to consider. Furthermore, it is important to note that recruiters will need to decide which evaluation criteria are priorities because by meeting some criteria (e.g. cost efficiency) this may be at the expense of others (e.g. validity). For example,

Table 1.2 Evaluation criteria to judge the quality of selection and recruitment process

Category	Evaluation criteria	Description	How can this be evidenced?
Accuracy and effectiveness	1. Evidence of reliability	A selection method is reliable if it is consistent in how it assesses candidates under varying conditions	• Psychometric evaluation
	2. Evidence of validity	The selection tool measures what it claims to measure, it should be relevant, precise and accurate	• Psychometric evaluation
	3. Arrangements for initial & ongoing validation, evaluation & development are in place	After selection has taken place, the predictive validity of various selection tools can be evaluated. Results from validity studies are used to review the selection criteria and choice/design of selection methods to make improvements and to optimise selection decisions	• Appropriate data is collected • Validation data is analysed by experts in selection
	4. Susceptibility to coaching	The extent to which access to coaching taken to improve a candidate's selection score and unduly advantage a candidate's standing in the selection process	• Comparison group studies
	5. Fairness, promotes diversity/widening access	This is based on three principles; (1) valid selection criteria; (2) accurate and standardized administration by trained staff; (3) monitored outcomes. Meets equalities impact assessments	• Evaluation questions posed to candidates. • Analysis of sub-group differences
	6. Legality	The extent to which the design of a selection process and the decisions generated is legally defensible. Selection processes that are perceived as unfair are more likely to result in legal case initiation	• HR experts in employment law

(continued)

Table 1.2 (continued)

Category	Evaluation criteria	Description	How can this be evidenced?
Cost and efficiency	7. Scalability for high-volume recruitment	The extent to which a selection process can be scaled up or down and remains efficient and effective for different volumes of applicants	• Data modelling with costs of implementation and validity of selection methods
	8. Efficiency	The costs involved, and the time taken in developing and implementing the selection tool(s)	• Analysis of costs by recruiters and employers
	9. Utility	The costs involved, and the time taken to develop more accurate adequate procedures need to be balanced with the potential benefits (e.g. improved performance)	• Statistical analysis of the predictive validity of a selection tool compared to the costs to implement the tool (using established utility calculation methods)
	10. Generality of use	The degree to which a selection tool used in one context can be transferred/tailored for use in another context or role	• Judgement by recruiters
Implementation issues	11. Practicality	The procedures should be acceptable within the organization and capable of being implemented effectively. The overall process should be efficient at each stage. Those responsible for administering the procedures may need to be trained	• Recruiter's and administrator's judgements
	12. Expertise required for analysis and interpretation of information generated by the tool	Some selection tools (for example personality tests) require an appropriately trained individual to administer, score and provide feedback. Similarly, assessors in SCs must also be appropriately trained in how to evaluate a candidate in a work sample test for example	• For psychometric tools there are specific licensure guidelines (e.g. from the British Psychological Society)

(continued)

Table 1.2 (continued)

Category	Evaluation criteria	Description	How can this be evidenced?
	13. Ease of interpretation	The degree to which the information generated by the selection tool provides clear and appropriate information relating to a candidate's competence and aptitude for the role	• Judgement by recruiters and stakeholders
Stakeholder acceptance and feedback	14. Positive employee/trainee/student perceptions	The extent to which employees/trainees/students react positively to the selection process and each selection method within that process	• Evaluation questionnaires of candidate perceptions
	15. Generates appropriate feedback	When using selection tools, it is good practice to ensure that candidates receive appropriate and useful feedback	• Evaluation questionnaires of candidate perceptions • Recruiter's judgements
	16. Educational impact/value	The extent to which candidates obtain useful information to inform their future education, learning and development	• Evaluation of candidate, educators and employer perceptions
Operational issues and administration	17. Management of complaints	The extent to which there is an appropriate complaints procedure and that any complaints are dealt with effectively and in a timely manner	• Evaluation of complaints procedures and incidence of complaints
	18. Externality	The extent to which there is appropriate lay involvement and trainee involvement in the design and implementation of the selection process	• Evaluation questionnaires of candidate perceptions • Recruiter's judgements

(continued)

Table 1.2 (continued)

Category	Evaluation criteria	Description	How can this be evidenced?
	19. Assessor/ Interviewer training	The extent to which assessors and interviewers are trained appropriately and the methodology is designed to ensure they are calibrated effectively	• Evaluation of assessor/ interviewer training • Calibration studies
Values-based recruitment	20. Values are assessed within the recruitment process	The extent to which there are robust assessments of values that are aligned to the espoused organizational values	• Evaluation of the extent to which the recruitment process targets the values identified

in using personal statements for short-listing purposes, this may lead to positive candidate reactions, but the evidence for validity is poor, and susceptibility to coaching is high. In addition, by focusing heavily on academic attainment as the main selection criterion, there may be good validity, but this may negatively impact on widening access and diversity. Practically, it is unlikely that all evaluation criteria will be fully met, and it is clear that there is no 'one best way' of designing selection systems—thus organizations must first review their selection policy to decide upon the design priorities for their purpose and locality.

Validation Studies in Selection

No single validation study will provide a definitive answer regarding the validity of a selection method. Each validation study is conducted on a sample of relevant people at a point in time, using a specific selection method, or combination of selection methods (see Gale et al., 2010 for an example validation study for selection into postgraduate training in Anaesthesia). A specific challenge, especially for validating selection methods that focus on non-academic selection criteria, is in identifying appropriate outcome variables, as many researchers have tended to use subsequent exam performance which rarely focus solely on non-academic attributes. Here, it is recommended that researchers ensure that the selection criteria are appropriately matched to the criteria underpinning the outcome markers (see Sackett & Lievens, 2008 for a review of predictor–criterion matching in selection). However, certain factors such as the sampling, the methods, the timing of the study and so on, will influence the results in some way. The ultimate goal might be to link selection procedures to important health outcomes, but practically, this is very difficult to achieve—a topic that we revisit in Chapter 13.

Applying statistical models such as generalizability theory allows for the contribution of selection method components to the overall effect size to be estimated (e.g. see O'Neill, Korsholm, Wallstedt, Eika, & Hatvigsen (2009) for an example). To estimate the validity of a selection method, more than one study design is needed, to minimize the error. Most selection systems combine several predictors (selection methods), such as an applicant's score on an interview and academic achievements. In this respect, a major challenge in validity research for selection is that different institutions tend to weight selection methods in different ways and so conducting large-scale longitudinal validation studies (rather than smaller scale single-site studies) can be problematic.

In validation studies, a key question is: how much does adding another predictor (i.e. selection method) increase the predictive power of the selection process? This is known as *incremental validity*. Specifically, recruiters may want to know how accuracy is improved, for example, due to using a personality assessment rather than relying solely on interview scores. Information on the incremental validity of a specific selection method is valuable, as it allows organizations to conduct a cost–benefit analysis of using additional tools. Table 1.3 provides a list of the different forms of validity in selection research for reference.

Table 1.3 Different types of validity in selection

Faith validity	This is 'blind' faith that a selection method works because someone plausible said so
Face validity	The selection tool content appears relevant to the target role (determined by the applicants)
Content validity	The content of the selection tool is judged to be directly relevant to the target role by subject matter experts
Criterion validity: *Concurrent*	A form of criterion-related validity in which data on the predictor and criterion are obtained at the same time. High correlations between predictor and criterion scores indicate concurrent validity
Criterion validity: *Predictive*	This is the extent to which a predictor measure (e.g. a selection test score) is correlated to a criterion measure (e.g. work performance). High predictive validity indicates that a selection measure gives an accurate indication of candidates' future performance on the criterion
Incremental validity	This is an empirical issue to determine how much additional value using another assessment provides
Construct validity	An indication of the extent to which the test or procedure measures the construct that it is intended to measure (such as empathy, clinical expertise)
Political validity	An indication of the extent to which various stakeholders and stakeholder groups (such as employers, parents, government departments, society, the regulator) consider the tool(s) to be appropriate and acceptable for use in selection

Traditionally, researchers examining the validity of selection have tended to focus on evaluating selection procedures as a whole. In Chapter 7, Lievens and colleagues propose a new approach to conceptualizing selection processes and reviewing their effectiveness. This so-called 'modular approach' breaks down selection processes into their basic underlying measurement components to advance theory, research, and design. Thus, unlike previous meta-analytic studies (e.g. Schmidt & Hunter, 1998), rather than reviewing selection procedures as a whole, the effects of key measurement components that make up these selection procedures are evaluated. In this way, the approach provides more information to evaluate the effects of these measurement components on criterion-related validity, amongst other aspects (e.g. subgroup differences and applicant perceptions).

Predictive Validity and the 'Criterion Problem' in Selection

The way to collect criterion-related validity data, i.e. how well scores on the selection method predict some future outcome or criterion, is to use a predictive (or follow-up) design. This design involves collecting predictor information (e.g. interview ratings, test scores) for candidates and then following up for performance data (e.g. during their first year of employment or exams at medical school). Predictive validity is assessed by examining the correlation between scores at selection (Time 1) and criterion data collected at Time 2 (perhaps through relevant work-based assessments, examinations, etc.). However, it is important to note that it is unusual in field studies to obtain validity coefficients over $r = 0.5$ (see Arnold & Randall, 2016).

Conducting validation studies in practice presents various problems. As referred to earlier, one major problem regards accessing the appropriate criterion (outcome) data to validate the selection process. Often, the criteria used to measure performance in the job role do not match the criteria used for selection (see above regarding predictor–criterion matching). Conversely, sometimes the criterion and predictor are very similar (e.g. using a knowledge-based selection test to predict subsequent knowledge-based exam performance), which may lead to common method variance issues and content overlap. Ideally, predictor scores should only be used to make selection decisions *after* a predictive validation study has been conducted. Practically, this is difficult to achieve, so piloting is essential to conduct an appropriate validation. Various sources of error are important to consider when conducting validation studies in selection, including sampling, measurement precision, restriction of range issues, selection bias, reverse causation and missing variable problems (for example, see Van Iddekinge & Ployhart, 2008). In dealing with these complexities, we return to these issues in Chapter 13 to explore how validation studies might be conducted in future.

Current Issues in Healthcare Recruitment

Acknowledging that the primary focus of previous selection research in healthcare has tended to focus on the quality of selection methods, in the third part of our book, various authors look beyond these issues and explore broader topics relating to recruitment.

Selection methods used are frequently driven by stakeholder acceptance issues (see Kelly, Patterson, O'Flynn, Mulligan, and Murphy (2018) for a review on stakeholder acceptance). Patterson, Lievens, Kerrin, Zibarras, and Carette (2012) suggested that the *political* validity is important, which refers to the acceptance of selection practices by a range of stakeholders. This includes the reactions of applicants and recruiters, along with reactions from wider stakeholders, such as government, regulatory bodies and the general public, which play an important role in decision-making at the policy level. Perceptions of 'fairness' can vary considerably between different stakeholder groups and from a candidate perspective, there is a significant risk of litigation if the method is viewed as 'unfair'. In Chapter 8, Zibarras takes a closer look at the latest research insights accounting for *candidate perceptions* when designing selection systems and methods. Here, Zibarras reviews the increasing use of technology in delivering selection and the impact this has on candidate perceptions, which provides important information on how best to design selection procedures in future.

Another functional reality of designing selection systems (especially in highly competitive settings) is the influence of *coaching*. In many parts of the globe, there exists a 'commercial coaching industry' and very little research exists to inform recruiters of how best to mitigate against susceptibility to coaching and to inform applicants who may part with significant sums of money in the belief that purpose-built coaching will improve their chances of success. In Chapter 9, Griffin presents the very latest research in exploring access to, and the potential influence of, commercial coaching in selection.

A key topic internationally is how best to construct selection methods and systems to ensure a 'level playing field' for applicants. Previously, there was a dearth of research literature to help recruiters address how best to design a selection system to promote *widening access and diversity*, especially within medicine. In Chapter 10, Cleland, Alexander and Nicholson present a state-of-the-art review of the issues and provide case material within medicine specifically, demonstrating a significant gap between the research evidence and policy enactment.

Although much attention is now being paid to diversity issues regarding socio-economic status (especially in medicine), less attention has been paid to address issues regarding diversity and ethnicity in selection, especially regarding causal factors. Diversity and ethnicity in selection is a complex issue and to demonstrate this, our second case study (Case Study 1.2) presents the challenges in addressing diversity in medical school admissions in South Africa, which has a relatively unique demographic profile.

Case Study 1.2: Selection for Demographic Representation in South Africa

South Africa has a legacy of race-based differential access resources, including to higher education and training in medicine. Despite the repeal of legislation that removed the legal basis for racial classification in South Africa, the country still includes self-identifying questions about race in surveys, to monitor progress in eradicating this previous dispensation.

The South African population of 56 million people is grouped into Black African (80.5%), Coloured (8.8%), White (8.2%) and Indian or other Asian people (2.5%). However, across South Africa, students at medical schools have historically not reflected this demographic distribution. Analysis in 2009 of the students enrolled for medicine at Stellenbosch University, showed undergraduate medical students were distributed as follows Black African (13%), Coloured (30%), White (46%) and Indian or other Asian people (11%). To redress differential racial access, Stellenbosch University developed a strategy which aimed to select a more representatively diverse body of students. By 2017 this had shifted to Black African (24%), Coloured (34%), White (31%) and Indian or other Asian people (11%).

Annually, 4000–5000 school leavers compete for 320 places in medicine. A selection factor (SF) for each applicant is calculated from academic performance (AP) achieved on leaving school, the national benchmark test (NBT) mark, and a non-academic merit (NAM) score as follows:

$$AP\ (45\%) + NBT\ (30\%) + NAM\ (25\%) = SF$$

All applicants are ranked according to their selection factor. The selection process to reach a total of 320 then takes place as follows:

- The top 110 ranked applicants.
- A further 170 applicants in order of selection factor ranking that are Black African and Coloured applicants from all the provinces in the country, and all Indian or Asian applicants from our neighbouring provinces—provided that they meet the minimum admission requirements. This action takes place until the 280 places have been filled.
- An additional 40 Black African applicants are selected, provided that they meet the minimum admission requirement of school academic performance.

The university's history and its situation in the Western Cape present challenges to shifting the demographics of students who apply to Stellenbosch University. The Western Cape population has a far greater proportion of people who identify as Coloured (50%) and a far lower proportion of people who identify as Black African (33%) than the national average. Historically this was a White, Afrikaans speaking university. Both these factors contribute to challenges in attracting more Black African students and more students whose home language is not Afrikaans.

While demographic redress is improving in terms of selection, we continue to be challenged by the shifts that need to occur in the institution to ensure that previously under-represented students are met by a welcoming culture and have access to whatever psychosocial support they need in order to be successful.

Proportions of different ethnical groups selected into medicine at Stellenbosch University, the province in which the university is located in South Africa

		African Black	Coloured	White	Indian and other Asian
National	%	81	9	8	2
Western Cape		33	50	17	1
Stellenbosch University	2009	13	30	46	11
	2017	24	34	31	11

Authors: Alwyn Louw, Advisor in Centre for Health Professions Education at the Faculty of Medicine and Health Sciences, Stellenbosch University in South Africa

Alwyn is a senior lecturer in Higher Education mostly involved in Health Professions education where he teaches at under graduate as well as post graduate level.

Julia Blitz, Vice-Dean: Learning and Teaching; Faculty of Medicine and Health Sciences, Stellenbosch University in South Africa

Julia is a Family Physician by clinical background. Her current job as Vice-Dean includes a responsibility in selecting students for access and success. She has a strong interest in health professions education.

Compassion, benevolence, respect and dignity are important for any healthcare professional to ensure the provision of high-quality care and patient outcomes. In Chapter 11, Edwards, Kinirons and Patterson introduce values-based recruitment (VBR) practices, which involves attracting and recruiting students, trainees and employees based on the extent to which their values align with the values of the healthcare organization in which they work. This concept has international relevance, and in the UK has been explored extensively following government enquiries which highlighted major concerns about compassionate care (or lack thereof) within some pockets of the UK. The workforce plays a vital role in delivering safe and compassionate care, and values are important in facilitating this. The purpose of VBR is to ensure that people are recruited who have the right skills, and the right values to support effective delivery of high-quality patient care and outcomes. In Chapter 11, Edwards et al. present the theory underlying values-based recruitment with relevant case material demonstrating how recruiters have re-aligned their selection systems to focus on values amongst other attributes. Furthermore, in Chapter 12, Ferguson provides fresh theoretical insights in selection for important attributes in healthcare such as altruism and pro-sociality. Alongside practical examples, Ferguson draws upon inter-disciplinary research to explore how theoretical models from behavioural economics can be applied to selection in healthcare. Such paradigms are so far under-researched and Ferguson suggests how these may be useful in informing the preferences of individuals entering a career within healthcare and, in turn, the implications for future recruitment and training are reviewed.

Summary

Over 100 years of research on selection and recruitment has yielded many advances for various occupational groups, especially in understanding the quality of different selection methods. However, the field continues to present challenging and complex issues, especially within selection and recruitment for healthcare. The chapters in this book review recent advances in designing, implementing and evaluating selection methods and selection systems and tackles broader issues in recruitment for healthcare. In our closing chapter (Chapter 13), we re-visit these issues and draw together key insights, discuss areas where practice lacks an evidence base, and provide directions for future research.

References

Arnold, J., & Randall, R. (2016). *Work Psychology* (6th ed., pp. 1–848). Harlow, UK: Pearson.

Cleland, J., Patterson, F., & Hanson, M. (2018). To what extent are selection and widening access complex and wicked problems? *Medical Education* (in press).

Director of Learning and Student Affairs, Directorate of Higher Education, Ministry of Education and Culture. (2013). *Presentation on the national policy of medical students selection.*

Faculty of Medicine Universitas Indonesia. (2015). *Local admission data.* Accessed December 2017.
Ferguson, E., & Lievens, F. (2017). Future directions in personality, occupational and medical selection: Myths, misunderstandings, measurement, and suggestions. *Advances in Health Sciences Education, 22*(2), 387–399.
Gale, T. C. E., Roberts, M. J., Sice, P. J., Langton, J. A., Patterson, F. C., Carr, A. S., …, Davies, P. R. F. (2010). Predictive validity of a selection centre testing non-technical skills for recruitment to training in anaesthesia. *British Journal of Anaesthesia, 105*(5), 603–609.
Hecker, N., & Norman, G. (2017). Have admissions committees considered all the evidence? *Advances in Health Sciences Education, 22*(2), 573–576.
Kelly, M. E., Patterson, F., O'Flynn, S., Mulligan, J., & Murphy, A. W. (2018). A systematic review of stakeholder views of selection methods for medical schools admission. *BMC Medical Education, 18*(1), 139.
Ministry of Research, Technology and Higher Education. (2017). *Higher education response data.* Retrieved from https://forlap.ristekdikti.go.id/.
Nations Encyclopaedia. (2017). *Indonesia.* Retrieved from http://www.nationsencyclopedia.com/geography/Indonesia-to-Mongolia/Indonesia.html.
O'Neill, L., Korsholm, L., Wallstedt, B., Eika, B., & Hartvigsen, J. (2009). Generalisability of a composite student selection programme. *Medical Education, 43,* 58–65.
Patterson, F., Cleland, J., & Cousans, F. (2017). Selection methods in healthcare professions: Where are we now and where next? *Advances in Health Sciences Education, 22*(2), 229–242.
Patterson, F., Ferguson, E., & Thomas, S. (2008). Using job analysis to identify core and specific competencies: Implications for selection and recruitment. *Medical Education, 42*(12), 1195–1204.
Patterson, F., Knight, A., Dowell, J., Nicholson, S., Cousans, F., & Cleland, J. (2016). How effective are selection methods in medical education? A systematic review. *Medical Education, 50*(1), 36–60.
Patterson, F., Lievens, F., Kerrin, M., Zibarras, L., & Carette, B. (2012). Designing selection systems for medicine: The importance of balancing predictive and political validity in high-stakes selection contexts. *International Journal of Selection and Assessment, 20*(4), 486–496.
Patterson, F., Roberts, C., Hanson, M., Hampe, W., Eva, K., Ponnamperuma, G., …, Cleland, J. (2018). The Ottawa 2018 consensus statement on selection and recruitment to the healthcare professions. *Medical Teacher* (in press).

Prideaux, D., Roberts, C., Eva, K., Centeno, A., Mccrorie, P., Mcmanus, C., …, Wilkinson, D. (2011). Assessment for selection for the health care professions and specialty training: Consensus statement and recommendations from the Ottawa 2010 Conference. *Medical Teacher, 33*(3), 215–223.

Rees, E. L., Hawarden, A. W., Dent, G., Hays, R., Bates, J., & Hassell, A. B. (2016). Evidence regarding the utility of multiple mini-interview (MMI) for selection to undergraduate health programs: A BEME systematic review: BEME Guide No. 37. *Medical Teacher, 38*(5), 443–455.

Reiter, C. D. (2017). A research agenda for establishing the validity of non-academic assessments of medical school applicants. *Advances in Health Sciences Education, 22*(2), 559–563.

Roberts, C., Khanna, P., Rigby, L., Bartle, E., Llewellyn, A., Gustavs, J., …, Lynam, J. (2018). Utility of selection methods for specialist medical training: A BEME (best evidence medical education) systematic review: BEME Guide No. 45. *Medical Teacher, 40*(1), 3–19.

Sackett, P. R., & Lievens, F. (2008). Personnel selection. *Annual Review of Psychology, 59,* 419–450.

Schmidt, F. L., & Hunter, J. E. (1998). The validity and utility of selection methods in personnel psychology: Practical and theoretical implications of 85 years of research findings. *Psychological Bulletin, 124*(2), 262.

Van Iddekinge, C. H. V., & Ployhart, R. E. (2008). Developments in the criterion-related validation of selection procedures: A critical review and recommendations for practice. *Personnel Psychology, 61*(4), 871–925.

2

Aptitude Testing in Healthcare Selection

Maureen E. Kelly, Paul A. Tiffin and Lazaro M. Mwandigha

Overview

This chapter describes the development and use of aptitude testing in healthcare selection. First, the historical context of aptitude tests is outlined. This is followed by a detailed exploration of what aptitude tests measure, including examples of those that test "fluid" as compared to "crystallized" intelligence. Issues of fairness are explored, along with the predictive validity of aptitude tests, and future possibilities. Two case studies of aptitude tests are presented, one from the UK and one from Ireland.

M. E. Kelly (✉)
National University of Ireland (NUI) Galway, Galway, Ireland
e-mail: maureen.kelly@nuigalway.ie

P. A. Tiffin
University of York, York, UK
e-mail: paul.tiffin@york.ac.uk

L. M. Mwandigha
Imperial College London, London, UK
e-mail: l.mwandigha@imperial.ac.uk

F. Patterson and L. Zibarras (eds.), *Selection and Recruitment in the Healthcare Professions*, https://doi.org/10.1007/978-3-319-94971-0_2

By the end of this chapter, you should:

- Understand the background to and rationale for the development of aptitude testing.
- Recognize what aptitude tests are designed to measure.
- Understand the potential for test bias.
- Understand the evidence for predictive validity of these tests.

What are Aptitude Tests?

Aptitude tests are defined as "*standardized tests designed to measure a person's ability to develop skills or acquire knowledge*" (Patterson & Ferguson, 2010, p. 359). They are widely used internationally, across a range of healthcare professions, largely due to their feasibility and ease of administration. They can be designed to measure a broad range of abilities including verbal, numerical and knowledge components (Cleland, Dowell, McLachlan, Nicholson, & Patterson, 2012). Aptitude tests, used for healthcare selection, can be broadly classified into those that include a knowledge-based component, usually measuring basic scientific knowledge, termed "crystallized intelligence" and those testing applicants' "fluid intelligence" which is mental processing, reasoning and decision making without testing underlying background knowledge.

Aptitude Tests of Fluid Intelligence

Fluid intelligence is the ability to solve new problems using logical reasoning. An example of a (practice) item from the *abstract reasoning* subtest of the UK Clinical Aptitude Test (UKCAT) is provided in Fig. 2.1. This type of item involves an understanding of the rules underlying each of the two sets of patterns displayed. Candidates must choose which set a test item presented belongs to. In the example, in set 'A', if there is a black circle to the right of a square, then in the next square down the diagonal line is the previous one rotated by 90° *clockwise.* Conversely in Set 'B', it is rotated 90° *anticlockwise.* Therefore, the correct answer, in this example, is that the test shape belongs to set 'A'. In such tests, practice

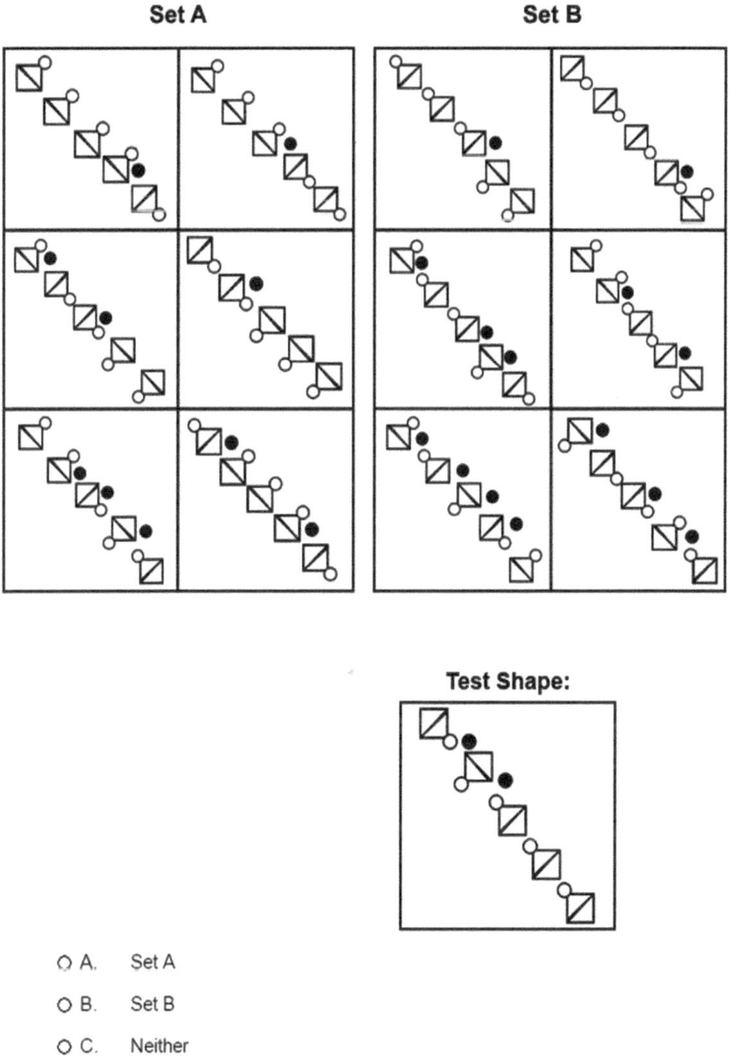

Fig. 2.1 Sample UKCAT item, testing fluid intelligence (reproduced with permission from UKCAT)

effects increase candidates' performance on average by approximately one third of a standard deviation (Puddey, Mercer, Andrich, & Styles, 2014). Nevertheless, the ability to deal with similar, though novel problems, especially in a time-limited test will tap into a testee's fluid intelligence to a greater degree than tests of knowledge or even learnt procedural skills.

Aptitude Tests of Crystallized Intelligence

'Crystallized intelligence' is conceptualized as the ability to apply and use previously acquired knowledge and experience (Cattell, 1971). A number of commonly used aptitude tests used in medical and healthcare selection, such as the Biomedical Admissions Test (BMAT) and the Medical College Admission Test (MCAT), include tests of crystallized intelligence. For example, at the time of writing, the latest version of the MCAT includes a section relating to knowledge of 'Biological and Biochemical Foundations of Living Systems' which could be considered a test of crystallized intelligence.

A Brief History of the Development of Aptitude Testing in Healthcare Selection

Aptitude tests are amongst the most common tests of general mental ability used for selection to the health professions. They were first introduced in the early twentieth century, at a time when standardized aptitude tests were beginning to be used for admission to other college courses in North America.

Standardized **tests for college entrance** were introduced largely in response to the enormous variation amongst colleges, with respect to the level of subject matter proficiency they required from successful applicants. One writer noted that the introduction of standardized tests was an attempt "*to introduce order into an educational situation approaching an anarchy*" (McCandless, 1967, p. 45). In 1901, the College Entrance Examination Board held its first written examination. The "**College Board**" was subsequently modified and ultimately replaced in 1926 with the "**Scholastic Aptitude Test**" (**SAT**), a test that was designed to be "*an easily scored, multiple-choice instrument for measuring students' general ability or aptitude for learning*" (Lemann, 1999, as cited in Atkinson & Geiser, 2009, p. 21). This change reflected a significant shift away from solely basing selection on evidence of ***achievement***, to including evidence of ***aptitude*** for college. The shift was heavily influenced by public and academic interest, in standardized psychological tests. Data from large-scale testing of World War I soldiers had led to the development of tests of intelligence quotient (IQ) most notably the Army Alpha and Beta tests (Yerkes, 1921). Experience with these tests gave rise to the assumption that "*a student with good mental ability or intelligence (original nature) will do well in school or college and receive good marks*" (Burtt & Arps, 1920, p. 289). It was hoped that the SAT would be a test that could be administered relatively cheaply, to large groups of applicants and that it would help identify applicants from disadvantaged backgrounds, who despite lower academic grades, were deserving of admission to college. The extent to which the SAT, and similar ability tests, have delivered on these aims, from educational and socio-political perspectives, remains debatable (see Chapter 10 in this book, Cleland et al.).

The situation within the health professions courses was similar. In the 1920s, medical schools across North America were struggling to cope with a surge in applications due to a general increase in college application numbers post World War I; reduced opportunities for work because of economic depression and the closure of several medical schools. There were widespread problems with high dropout rates, with up to 25% of entrants failing to graduate (Kandel, 1940). Furthermore, most applicants to medical schools had completed 2–4 years of pre-medical courses, but there were wide variations in the standard of education and examinations relating to these. In response to these factors, and at the urging of the Flexner Report (Flexner, 1910), many medical schools believed a test to determine 'medical aptitude' should be included in the selection of medical students.

The earliest version of an aptitude test for medicine—the "**Scholastic Aptitude Test for Medical Schools**"—was developed by Dr. F. A. Moss

(School of Medicine, George Washington University) and adopted for widespread use by the Association of American Medical Colleges (AAMC) in 1930. The "**Moss Test**", as it became known, was a combination of true/false and multiple-choice questions. It was designed to measure scientific vocabulary, pre-medical information, memory for verbal content of a medical nature, recall of names of parts on an anatomical diagram, reading comprehension and logical reasoning (Erdmann, Mattson, Hutton Jr., & Wallace, 1971). Since the 1930s, the Moss test has undergone several well-documented iterations and modifications, ultimately becoming the "**Medical Colleges Admission Test**", still in use in North America and elsewhere today (Erdmann et al., 1971; McGaghie, 2002; Schwartzstein, Rosenfeld, Hilborn, Oyewole, & Mitchell, 2013).

Records confirm that, between the 1930s and 1950s, aptitude testing became established as a method of selection by a range of other health professions, in North America. For example, in nursing, the "**Pre-Nursing and Guidance Test Battery**" and later the "**Pre-Admission and Classification Examination**" were overseen by the National League for Nursing Education and the National League for Nursing respectively (Meadow, 1964; Shaycoft, 1951). The **Pre-Nursing and Guidance Test Battery** test consisted of five tests that measured achievement in the basics of maths, natural sciences and social studies, as well as quantitative reasoning, and reading comprehension. Nowadays, nursing schools in North America utilize a variety of different nursing aptitude tests including the Test of Essential Academic Skills (TEAS); the National League for Nursing Pre-Admission Examination and the Nurse Entrance Test, amongst others (Schmidt & MacWilliams, 2011).

In the 1940s, the Dental Admission Testing Programme began to experiment with a variety of aptitude tests. Out of this experimental program, the "**Dental Aptitude Test Battery**" was born. It was designed to measure abilities in mathematics, verbal reasoning, reading comprehension in the sciences, academic achievement in the natural sciences, as well as object visualization and chalk carving (Hinshaw, Krawczak, Tsai, & Vanek, 2011; Travers & Wallace,

1950). The latter was a test of hand and finger dexterity, whereby applicants were provided with a knife and required to carve a piece of chalk, according to specific dimensions. For several reasons including practicality and cost, the chalk carving test was replaced with the Perceptual Motor Ability Test, although chalk carving still forms part of selection to dentistry in various institutions today (Ballard, Hagan, & Cheramie, 2015). From 1950 onwards the test, known as the "**Dental Admission Test**" (DAT), was administered nationally, overseen by the American Dental Association. Its use continues to this day, with a separate version, the "**Dental Aptitude Test**" available in Canada.

In the field of veterinary medicine, the late 1940s saw the development, validation and use of the **Veterinarian Aptitude Test** in the USA, by Owens and colleagues (Owens, 1950). It comprised four subtests: two subsets measured achievement in chemistry and zoology, while the third and fourth tests measured reading comprehension and verbal memory respectively. Later, the **Veterinary College Admission Test** was used; however, nowadays, most accredited veterinary professional programs within the US, employ the Graduate Record Examination (GRE), as the standardized test of choice (Kogan, 2002).

Today, aptitude tests are widely used internationally across a range of healthcare professions including: graduate entry medicine (Australian Council for Educational Research (ACER), 2017a), pharmacy (American Association of Colleges of Pharmacy, 2017), optometry (Association of Schools and Colleges of Optometry, 2017), occupational therapy and speech and language therapy students (Australian Council for Educational Research (ACER), 2017b) and other allied health professions (Insight Assessment, 2017). The past twenty years have seen the addition of several newer aptitude tests developed for selection to medicine in Europe and Australia. Table 2.1 lists a sample of tests from across the various professions. Case Study 2.1 describes test sections and provides examples of typical test items from one of these newer tools, the Health Professions Admission Test-Ireland.

Table 2.1 Examples of aptitude tests used in the selection by a range of health professionals

Name of test/URL	Use	Brief description
DAT http://www.ada.org/en/education-careers/dental-admission-test	Selection to dentistry programs in USA and Canada (separate Canadian version, the Dental Aptitude Test available)	First used in 1950, the DAT is overseen by the American Dental Association and administered by Prometric. Its four sections are: Survey of the Natural Sciences, Perceptual Ability, Reading Comprehension, and Quantitative Reasoning
Graduate Medical School Admissions Test (GAMSAT) https://gamsat.acer.org/	Selection to graduate entry medicine in Australia, Ireland, UK and elsewhere. Also used by some veterinary, physiotherapy and other health professions	Developed and administered by the Australian Council for Educational Research, GAMSAT has been used since 1995. It has three sections: (1) reasoning in humanities and social sciences; (2) written communication and (3) reasoning in biological and physical sciences
Health Science Reasoning Test (HSRT) https://www.insightassessment.com/Products/Products-Summary/Critical-Thinking-Skills-Tests/Health-Sciences-Reasoning-Test-HSRT	Selection to some health sciences education—including nursing programs in North America and internationally	Used since 1994, the HSRT is a multiple-choice test designed and administered by Insight Assessment, specifically for use in health professions. An overall critical thinking score and five subscale scores are reported: inference, induction, deduction, analysis, and evaluation

(continued)

Table 2.1 (continued)

Name of test/URL	Use	Brief description
MCAT https://students-residents.aamc.org/applying-medical-school/taking-mcat-exam/	Selection to medical schools and some veterinary schools in USA and Canada	First used in 1928, MCAT is developed and overseen by the American Association of Medical Colleges. It currently consists of four sections: Biological and Biochemical Foundations of Living Systems; Chemical and Physical Foundations of Biological Systems; Psychological, Social, and Biological Foundations of Behavior; Critical Analysis and Reasoning Skills
Pharmacy College Admission Test (PCAT) http://www.pcatweb.info/	Selection to the majority of pharmacy programs in USA, and some Canadian colleges	First used in 1974, PCAT is a computer-based test, endorsed by the American Association of Colleges of Pharmacy and administered by Pearson PLC. It consists of five subtests: Writing; Biological Processes; Chemical Processes; Critical Reading and Quantitative Reasoning
The UKCAT https://www.ukcat.ac.uk/	Selection to the majority of UK undergraduate medical and dental schools	Developed by the UKCAT Consortium in 2006, and administered by Pearson Vue, the UKCAT is a computer-based test with five sections: Verbal Reasoning, Decision Making, Quantitative Reasoning, Abstract Reasoning and Situational Judgement

Case Study 2.1: The Health Professions Admission Test-Ireland (HPAT-Ireland)

HPAT-Ireland (https://hpat-ireland.acer.org/) is a multiple-choice test, developed and administered by the Australian Council for Educational Research (ACER). Since 2009, HPAT-Ireland is a requirement for school leaver admission to all Irish medical schools. Results are used in a standardised way according to nationally agreed criteria. It is also used in selection to some Occupational Therapy and Speech and Language therapy courses. A separate version, HPAT-Ulster is used in Northern Ireland for admission to a variety of health professions programmes including Podiatry, Physiotherapy and Dietetics.

There are three timed sections described by ACER as follows: (Australian Council for Educational Research (ACER), 2017b).

Section 1: Logical reasoning and problem solving consists of 44 questions. Applicants are required to analyze and logically reason through the information presented. Time 65 minutes.

Section 2: Interpersonal Understanding, consists of 36 questions. Applicants have to identify, understand, and infer the thoughts, feelings and behaviours of the people represented in the situations. Time 45 minutes.

Section 3: Non-Verbal Reasoning consists of 30 questions based on recognition of patterns and sequences of shapes, to test applicants' abstract and non-verbal reasoning. Time 40 minutes. (Questions in this section are similar to the "Bongard Problem" described later in this chapter.)

An additional fourth section "Written English" is required for admission to some of the therapy programmes. Time 60 minutes.

Sample Section 1 Question

Out of 28 cases of people who have been found guilty of an offence and then subsequently proved innocent by evidence from DNA testing, 24 had been positively identified in police line-ups or 'mug shots' as being the criminals concerned. Which of the following is best supported by this information?

A. *DNA testing is a very inexact science.*
B. *People's memories of what took place at crime scenes are far from reliable.*
C. *DNA testing should be restricted to confirming or denying the remembered evidence of eye-witnesses.*
D. *If people are found guilty of a crime through the evidence of DNA testing, it is not necessarily true that they committed the crime.*

Sample Section 2 Question

Below is one woman's perspective of recovering from *depression*:

Looking back, I think the road to recovery started one day some years ago when I took myself to yet another doctor. My thoughts as I sat down in the waiting room were of fear, apprehension and uncertainty. But somewhere inside myself I still had hope. I confided in the doctor and told her I felt like a silly, neurotic woman. I told her I should be able to help myself and not need to come to her. Just pick myself up with the help of family and friends. She sat back in her chair and said, 'I don't think you are a silly woman and I don't expect you to do it on your own'.

The doctor's response is best described as

A. *Supportive.*
B. *Insensitive.*
C. *Ambiguous.*
D. *Challenging.*

Answers

Question 1- B *Correct* **Question 2- A *Correct***

Sample questions reproduced with permission from ACER

Aptitude Tests and Academic Attainment

Academic attainment has been the mainstay of selection in healthcare internationally (Patterson & Ferguson, 2010). Thus, aptitude testing must be discussed in this context. Prior academic achievement is one of the strongest and consistent predictors of future academic performance across the healthcare disciplines (Kreiter & Kreiter, 2007; Patterson et al., 2016; Salvatori, 2001). In medical selection, past academic achievement has been conceptualized as the "academic backbone", with each level of achievement providing scaffolding for further learning. A meta-analysis with almost 12,000 participants showed that, in virtually all cases, the last level of academic achievement predicted the next, throughout medical school and higher professional training (McManus, Woolf, Dacre, Paice, & Dewberry, 2013).

Typically, previous academic attainment is used as a threshold, whereby applicants are required to demonstrate a certain level of academic attainment, prior to being included in the next round of selection. This approach, however, is not without its critics (Patterson, Cleland, & Cousans, 2017). Despite being a strong predictor of future performance, past academic record accounts for only between 23 and 65% of variance in future academic performance, leaving a sizeable degree of variance unaccounted for (Ferguson, James, & Madeley, 2002; McManus, Woolf, et al., 2013). Secondly, grade inflation means that it is increasingly difficult to distinguish between applicants based on academic scores alone. An example is the UK-based school leaving test (General Certificate of Education Advanced Level (A-level)) where the numbers of applicants achieving the maximum three A level grades became a significant challenge to medical school admissions committees (McManus, Dewberry, Nicholson, & Dowell, 2013; Parry et al., 2006). Thirdly, academic record is associated with patterns of social exclusion whereby students from professional backgrounds, fee-paying, private or selective schooling and white ethnicity achieve higher scores compared to the general population (Cleland et al., 2012; James, Yates, & Nicholson, 2010; Tiffin, McLachlan, Webster, & Nicholson, 2014). Therefore, the real value of aptitude testing in selection is where it demonstrates significant incremental validity over academic attainment, tests a broader range of relevant abilities than those tested by school examinations and exhibits less susceptibility to socioeconomic influences. These issues are explored in more detail in the following sections.

Fairness Issues

The potential for bias in aptitude testing is important to consider for two main reasons. Firstly, it is important that tests are fair, and do not unfairly disadvantage certain groups. Such potential 'adverse impacts' may be a barrier to widening access to the healthcare professions. Secondly, if aptitude tests are used as an important component in admission decisions, then the results will influence the demographics of the profession being selected. There is considerable existing literature on the sensitivity of cognitive tests to sociodemographic factors, such as gender and socioeconomic status (Jensen, 1980; Suzuki, Short, & Lee, 2011). Thus, it is unsurprising that aptitude tests show similar patterns of association between performance and personal characteristics. It should also be noted that there is a long and contentious history in relation to performance on cognitive tests and ethnicity in the field of individual differences research (Rushton & Jensen, 2005). Moreover, there has also been recent concerns about differential attainment in postgraduate medical education and ethnicity (Woolf, McManus, Potts, & Dacre, 2013; Woolf, Potts, & McManus, 2011; Woolf, Rich, Viney, Needleman, & Griffin, 2016). We will not enter into a detailed discussion about these controversies at this point, but rather would like to highlight that ethnicity is best regarded as a social, rather than a genetic, construct.

When considering such effects it is important to distinguish between "item impact" and "differential item functioning". In *item impact* higher average scores in certain groups, such as men versus women, are due to absolute differences in the level of trait or ability being assessed (Ackerman, 1992). Where items, with known item impact, are used in selection decisions, it is essential that the trait being measured is relevant to future on the job performance.

Differential item functioning (DIF) should be carefully avoided in selection tests. In DIF, the performance of candidates on a particular item, or set of items, is influenced by factors other than that intended to be evaluated. Thus, if the content or wording of the question appealed to a certain group of the population, then they may tend to perform better in that particular item, even if their overall ability was the same as candidates from another group. A contrived example might be a quantitative reasoning question which was based on Jazz music. Groups interested in this type of music may find the question intuitively easier to answer compared to those who did not, even if they had the same underlying level of overall quantitative reasoning ability. It is relatively straightforward to evaluate for DIF and a number of statistical tests exist for this purpose (Zumbo, 2007). It is clearly undesirable to have test items which show substantial levels of DIF as they will advantage or disadvantage certain candidates unfairly. For this reason, DIF in relation to major socio-demographic groups are routinely tested for by organizations that deliver such aptitude tests, so that items can be eliminated or modified accordingly.

Validity of Aptitude Tests in Healthcare

A recent systematic review of selection methods in medical education concluded that "*Mixed evidence exists among researchers on the usefulness of aptitude tests in medical student selection and findings largely depend on the specific aptitude test studied*" (Patterson et al., 2016). The authors also noted that there were, at that time, no published reports relating to the cost-effectiveness of aptitude tests in medical selection. It is well known that the correlation between a selection test score and an outcome in those (successful) candidates who are selected can be a poor guide to the effectiveness of a test. This is because there are several factors which can work to attenuate the relationship between test scores and outcomes in a selection context. These include 'restriction of range' (e.g. outcomes cannot be observed in unsuccessful [lower scoring] candidates), as well as the imperfect reliability of a test. These issues have previously been highlighted in the case of medical selection (McManus, Dewberry, et al., 2013). There are several approaches to correct for these effects which are beyond the scope of this chapter. The degree of correlation between the test score and another variable of interest will also vary according to the outcome selected, as well as the sub-population of entrants chosen (e.g. graduate versus 'school-leaver'). Range restriction and imperfect reliability contribute to the mixed findings regarding the predictive validity of aptitude tests (Patterson et al., 2016). For example, some studies have found that both the UKCAT and HPAT-Ireland possess high levels of predictive validity and are thus useful for the selection of medical school students (Halpenny, Cadoo, Halpenny, Burke, & Torreggiani, 2010; McManus, Dewberry, et al., 2013; Tiffin et al., 2016). Others have reported evidence of poor predictive validity, suggesting the resultant scores add little (if any) value in the selection process of medical students (Kelly & O'Flynn, 2017; Kelly et al., 2013; Lynch, MacKenzie, Dowell, Cleland, & Prescott, 2009; Yates & James, 2013). In general, aptitude test scores tend to predict academic, knowledge-based, undergraduate performance most strongly with 'like predicting like'. In addition, studies generally report 'raw' predictive validity but do not always correct or control for the effects of other selection measures, such as prior educational attainment. Thus, it is not always clear from the existing literature the extent to which such tools add incremental value within the selection process.

How are Aptitude Test Scores used by Recruiters?

Whatever the psychometric properties of a selection test are, the impact that scores make on the demographics of a student population will depend on how the assessment is implemented. There is evidence that the manner of implementation influences the predictive validity of a medical selection test (Albanese, Farrell, & Dottl, 2005; Hissbach, Klusmann, & Hampe, 2011; Zhao, Oppler, Dunleavy, & Kroopnick, 2010). Oftentimes, aptitude tests are taken prior to applying to medical, dental or veterinarian school. Thus, a candidate's score may influence their decision to apply to certain universities. In the UK, for example, medical schools often set their UKCAT requirements after receiving the applications. This means that sometimes candidates have to guess or estimate what those requirements may be, and how it may affect their possibilities of obtaining a place at that particular institution. In the US, it may be that candidates who obtain low MCAT scores are encouraged to apply to medical schools outside of North America. Medical and dental schools in the UK predominantly use the UKCAT as part of the selection process. A smaller number use BMAT and some institutions also use the GAMSAT for graduate applications. Case Study 2.2, describes how one medical school in the UK utilizes the UKCAT in the selection process for medical students, and how this has been modified over years.

Case Study 2.2: The Use of UK Clinical Aptitude Test (UKCAT) at Hull York Medical School (HYMS)

HYMS was in the first wave of universities to implement the UKCAT in 2006. Initially the test consisted of four cognitive subtests: *Verbal reasoning*—a test of verbal comprehension; *Quantitative reasoning*—numerical problems; *Abstract reasoning*—identifying sequences and patterns in shapes (see Fig. 2.1), and; *Decision analysis*—making inferences from a set of codes. In 2016, the decision analysis sub-test was replaced by a different 'decision making' scale. This involves making inferences from presented information, such as graphs. A Situational Judgment Test (SJT) was also introduced in 2013 but the scores were not used in selection until the following year.

HYMS initially introduced the test relatively cautiously. The UKCAT was attractive as it provided a metric that could discriminate between a homogenous group of high performing candidates, many of whom were expected to achieve maximum school grades. It was also hoped that using the test would help widen access to medicine. Initially the total test scores were used as a factor accounting for 16% of the ranking score allocated to the decision to invite for interview. This was raised to a maximum of 50% for the 2012 application round and has been reduced to approximately 40% in subsequent years. Alongside the 'factor' approach, in the applications rounds from 2009 to 2012, applicants also had to score above threshold scores on the UKCAT to reach the interview. Using such thresholds can be attractive as they are considered a defensible way of screening out otherwise strong candidates, given that there are finite resources to carry out interviews.

However, thresholds changed from year to year. The threshold approach was abandoned after 2012 as there were concerns that candidates who achieved lower scores than if they had sat the test the preceding year may be discouraged from applying to universities with previous high thresholds. This issue can also lead to institutions appearing to have relatively low competition ratios for their courses. Currently at HYMS applicants are assigned a score based on the candidate's UKCAT decile achieved, with a weight of 40% attributed to this for the applicant's ranking as part of the decision to interview. The remaining 60% is composed of previous educational attainment (30%), SJT score (15%) and 'contextual' (socioeconomic) markers (15%).

The perceived impact of using the UKCAT has been admission of some students who performed well on the UKCAT but may not have been selected on the basis of traditional criteria. Many have proved to be high performing students. As elsewhere, an impact on the gender imbalance was observed: approximately 40% of the entrants were male in 2007–2008, but this rose to approximately 50% for 2013–2014. This may be due to the relatively large weight that total UKCAT scores place on non-verbal ability (with one verbal versus three non-verbal scales). Thus, HYMS plans to use a balanced form of the total score with the non-verbal scores averaged.

An unintended consequence of placing increasing weight on aptitude test scores may be the homogenization of the health professions. Moreover, anecdotally at least, there may be those high scorers who receive several offers from several institutions and lower scorers who fail to secure even a single interview. This may pose planning challenges for admissions teams. This could lead to too many or few offers being made for the number of available places. Generally, universities use the total UKCAT score, rather than basing decisions on individual subtest performance. In practice, this means that a disproportionate amount of weight may be placed on non-verbal performance. This is because the total score comprises the scores from three non-verbal subtests and one test of verbal reasoning. This could contribute to the observed gender patterns in UK medical schools given that males tend to outperform females on tests of non-verbal reasoning. It has previously been suggested that this issue could be addressed by averaging the scores on the three non-verbal subtests and then adding the verbal reasoning scores, providing a more balanced metric of cognitive ability (Tiffin, 2013).

One of the key problems is in establishing 'true' predictive validity. A previous study has used data simulation techniques to create plausible values for UKCAT candidates where no outcomes at medical school could be observed (Tiffin et al., 2016). The study explored the concept of the UKCAT total score being used as a sole, crude screening test for selection, to try and avoid entrants who were likely to fail at least one end-of-year exam at medical school. The findings suggested that for every 'poor' candidate screened out using a threshold score, approximately one 'good' candidate would also have been rejected on this basis. In this instance, 'poor' and 'good' meant candidates unlikely to pass all their undergraduate exams at first sitting. This ratio was designated the *Number Needed to Reject* (NNR) and was intended to serve as a metric of effectiveness of a selection test. With data simulation techniques improving and being more easily implemented, it is likely that more sophisticated ways of evaluating the effectiveness of such aptitude tests will develop. In particular, it is notable that a mathematical framework has been proposed in order to evaluate both the effectiveness of selection tests, as well as their potential adverse impact on underrepresented groups (De Corte, Sackett, & Lievens, 2011). To date, this has not been applied to aptitude tests and the case of medical selection.

Future Possibilities

Advances in technology enable testers to evaluate a wider range of traits more accurately as well as streamline assessment processes. For example, given the well-documented socio-economic bias of even 'pure' cognitive aptitude tests, it may be that a *dynamic testing* approach is required to identify potential in candidates from disadvantaged backgrounds. In dynamic testing a learning environment is created within the test itself (Beckmann, 2014). Thus, a candidate may get feedback after giving an incorrect answer. Candidates who can learn from this feedback are then allowed to increase their scores as their learning potential allows. Dynamic testing can also be used to evaluate cognitive flexibility. Cognitive flexibility is important in the modern health service, where adaptability is important. Within a dynamic testing environment, candidates may be presented with logical problems, such as those shown in Fig. 2.1. Subsequent items may appear similar, but there may be different rules underlying the pattern. Candidates must therefore show cognitive flexibility and be able to recognize new rules, not getting "stuck" on the previous patterns to achieve higher scores. Computer adaptive testing (CAT) is also being used to make testing more efficient. By ongoing calibration of the difficulties of test items to a candidate's estimated ability (which will change as testing proceeds), much shorter tests can achieve the same precision as conventional assessments.

Given the generally fierce competition for places on health professions programs in the Western world, most candidates are very academically able. Therefore, even well-designed 'aptitude' tests that focus on fluid intelligence are unlikely to add substantial amounts of value within the selection system, above and beyond conventional academic attainment. Thus, it is likely that there will be a continued and increasing focus on personal, non-academic qualities that are essential to professionalism and effective practice within the healthcare workplace. Such characteristics are more challenging to measure than traditional concepts of cognitive ability. Both Virtual Reality and Augmented Reality (VR and AR respectively) offer environments where such traits can be evaluated. VR is already being used in clinical training and offers an immersive experience in which professional or personal scenarios can be created so that candidate responses can be recorded, coded and scored (Ruthenbeck & Reynolds, 2015). In contrast, AR can be used to present candidates with such scenarios by mixing computer-generated and live images (Zhu, Hadadgar, Masiello, & Zary, 2014). There have also been some attempts to use machine learning (the basis of artificial intelligence) in staff selection (Campion, Campion, Campion, & Reider, 2016). Where prediction, rather than explanation, is the focus of a task, machine learning offers some advantages over conventional statistical approaches. For example, developing an expert scoring key for an SJT is resource-intensive and challenging. Machine learning has previously been used in organizational psychology to side-step this issue by predicting subsequent supervisor ratings from raw response patterns in candidates (Guenole, Weekley, & Ro, 2016). It is possible that such approaches will prove useful in linking aptitude test score patterns to future performance in applicants to the health professions.

Conclusion

Aptitude tests have been widely implemented within healthcare staff selection. However, their use has not gone unchallenged. Emerging evidence suggests that tests of fluid intelligence predict future academic performance and that this ability is at least modestly incremental to that offered by traditional metrics of educational attainment. The ability of such assessments to mitigate the disadvantage faced by certain under-represented groups is less certain, and it may be that newer and less academically focused tests may have more impact in this area.

References

Ackerman, T. A. (1992). A didactic explanation of item bias, item impact, and item validity from a multidimensional perspective. *Journal of Educational Measurement, 29*(1), 67–91.

Albanese, M. A., Farrell, P., & Dottl, S. (2005). Statistical criteria for setting thresholds in medical school admissions. *Advances in Health Sciences Education, 10*(2), 89–103.

American Association of Colleges of Pharmacy. (2017). *The Pharmacy College Admission Test (PCAT)*. Retrieved 12/10, 2017, from https://www.pcatweb.info/About-the-PCAT.php.

Association of Schools and Colleges of Optometry. (2017). *The Optometry Admission Test (OAT)*. Retrieved 12/10, 2017, from http://www.ada.org/en/oat.

Atkinson, R. C., & Geiser, S. (2009). Reflections on a century of college admissions tests. *Educational Researcher, 38*(9), 665–676.

Australian Council for Educational Research (ACER). (2017a). *Graduate Medical School Admissions Test*. Retrieved 12/10, 2017, from https://gamsat.acer.org.

Australian Council for Educational Research (ACER). (2017b). *Health Professions Admission Test (HPAT)-Ireland*. Retrieved 12/10, 2017, from https://hpat-ireland.acer.org/.

Ballard, R. W., Hagan, J. L., & Cheramie, T. (2015). Relationship between hand-skill exercises and other admissions criteria and students' performance in dental school. *Journal of Dental Education, 79*(5), 557–562.

Beckmann, J. F. (2014). The umbrella that is too wide and yet too small: Why dynamic testing has still not delivered on the promise that was never made. *Journal of Cognitive Education and Psychology, 13*, 308–323.

Burtt, H., & Arps, G. (1920). Correlation of Army Alpha Intelligence Test with academic grades in high schools and military academies. *Journal of Applied Psychology, 4*(4), 289.

Campion, M. C., Campion, M. A., Campion, E. D., & Reider, M. H. (2016). Initial investigation into computer scoring of candidate essays for personnel selection. *Journal of Applied Psychology, 101*(7), 958.

Cattell, R. B. (1971). *Abilities: Their structure, growth, and action*. New York: Houghton Mifflin.

Cleland, J., Dowell, J., McLachlan, J. C., Nicholson, S., & Patterson, F. (2012). *Identifying best practice in the selection of medical students*. London: General Medical Council.

De Corte, W., Sackett, P., & Lievens, F. (2011). Designing Pareto-optimal selection systems: Formalizing the decisions required for selection system development. *Journal of Applied Psychology, 96*, 907–926.

Erdmann, J. B., Mattson, D. E., Hutton, J. G., Jr., & Wallace, W. L. (1971). The Medical College Admission Test: Past, present, future. *Academic Medicine, 46*(11), 937–946.

Ferguson, E., James, D., & Madeley, L. (2002). Factors associated with success in medical school: Systematic review of the literature. *British Medical Journal, 324*(7343), 952–957.

Flexner, A. (1910). *Medical education in the United States and Canada bulletin number four* (The Flexner Report). New York: The Carnegie Foundation for the Advancement of Teaching.

Guenole, N. R., Weekley, J. A., & Ro, S. (2016). Scoring Keys and Measurement Models Not Required? SJT Predictions of Job Performance by Recursive Partitioning and its Variations. Oral conference presentation given at the 2016, 31st Annual Conference of the Society for Industrial and Organizational Psychology, held at Anaheim, CA. The presentation was given on 15th April 2016 and is listed on page 111 of the Conference Abstract Booklet.

Halpenny, D., Cadoo, K., Halpenny, M., Burke, J., & Torreggiani, W. (2010). The Health Professions Admission Test (HPAT) score and leaving certificate results can independently predict academic performance in medical school: Do we need both tests? *Irish Medical Journal, 103*(10), 300–302.

Hinshaw, K. J., Krawczak, J., Tsai, T.-H., & Vanek, C. A. (2011). *Dental Admission Testing Programme-User manual.* Chicago, IL: D. o. D. T. Services (Report 3).

Hissbach, J. C., Klusmann, D., & Hampe, W. (2011). Dimensionality and predictive validity of the HAM-Nat, a test of natural sciences for medical school admission. *BMC Medical Education, 11*(1), 83.

Insight Assessment. (2017). *Health Sciences Reasoning Test (HSRT).* Retrieved 5/12, 2017, from https://www.insightassessment.com/Products/Products-Summary/Critical-Thinking-Skills-Tests/Health-Sciences-Reasoning-Test-HSRT.

James, D., Yates, J., & Nicholson, S. (2010, February 16). Comparison of A level and UKCAT performance in students applying to UK medical and dental schools in 2006: Cohort study. *British Medical Journal, 340*, c478. https://doi.org/10.1136/bmj.c478.

Jensen, A. R. (1980). *Bias in mental testing.* New York: The Free Press.

Kandel, I. L. (1940). *Professional aptitude tests in medicine, law, and engineering.* New York: American Book-Stratford Press Inc.

Kelly, M. E., & O'Flynn, S. (2017). The construct validity of HPAT-Ireland for the selection of medical students: Unresolved issues and future research implications. *Advances in Health Sciences Education, 22*(2), 267–286.

Kelly, M. E., Regan, D., Dunne, F., Henn, P., Newell, J., & O'Flynn, S. (2013). To what extent does the Health Professions Admission Test-Ireland predict performance in early undergraduate tests of communication and clinical skills?—An observational cohort study. *BMC Medical Education, 13*, 68, 11 pages.

Kogan, L. R. (2002). *A comparison of subjective and objective procedures in the admissions process of veterinary students.* S. Hamilton, ProQuest Dissertations Publishing.

Kreiter, C. D., & Kreiter, Y. (2007). A validity generalization perspective on the ability of undergraduate GPA and the medical college admission test to predict important outcomes. *Teaching and Learning in Medicine, 19*(2), 95–100.

Lynch, B., MacKenzie, R., Dowell, J., Cleland, J., & Prescott, G. (2009). Does the UKCAT predict Year 1 performance in medical school? *Medical Education, 43*(12), 1203–1209.

McCandless, S. A. (1967). *A brief description of historical background and current status of the testing programs of the College Entrance Examination Board.* New York: United States Department Health, Education & Welfare.

McGaghie, W. C. (2002). Assessing readiness for medical education: Evolution of the medical college admission test. *Journal of the American Medical Association, 288*(9), 1085–1090.

McManus, I., Dewberry, C., Nicholson, S., & Dowell, J. (2013). The UKCAT-12 study: Educational attainment, aptitude test performance, demographic and socio-economic contextual factors as predictors of first year outcome in a collaborative study of twelve UK medical schools. *BMC Medicine, 11,* 244.

McManus, I., Woolf, K., Dacre, J., Paice, E., & Dewberry, C. (2013). The Academic Backbone: Longitudinal continuities in educational achievement from secondary school and medical school to MRCP(UK) and the specialist register in UK medical students and doctors. *BMC Medicine, 11,* 242.

Meadow, L. (1964). Assessment of students for schools of practical nursing. *Nursing Research, 13*(3), 222–229.

Owens, W. A. (1950). An aptitude test for veterinary medicine. *Journal of Applied Psychology, 34*(5), 295.

Parry, J., Mathers, J., Stevens, A., Parsons, A., Lilford, R., Spurgeon, P., & Thomas, H. (2006). Admissions processes for five-year medical courses at English schools. *British Medical Journal, 332*(7548), 1005–1009.

Patterson, F., Cleland, J., & Cousans, F. (2017). Selection methods in healthcare professions: Where are we now and where next? *Advances in Health Science Education, 22*(2), 229–242.

Patterson, F., & Ferguson, E. (2010). Selection for medical education and training. In T. Swanwick (Ed.), *Understanding medical education: Evidence, theory and practice* (p. 359). Oxford: Wiley Blackwell.

Patterson, F., Knight, A., Dowell, J., Nicholson, S., Cousans, F., & Cleland, J. (2016). How effective are selection methods in medical education? A systematic review. *Medical Education, 50*(1), 36–60.

Puddey, I. B., Mercer, A., Andrich, D., & Styles, I. (2014). Practice effects in medical school entrance testing with the undergraduate medicine and health sciences admission test (UMAT). *BMC Medical Education, 14*(1), 48–63.

Rushton, J. P., & Jensen, A. R. (2005). Thirty years of research on race differences in cognitive ability. *Psychology, Public Policy, and Law, 11*(2), 235.

Ruthenbeck, G. S., & Reynolds, K. J. (2015). Virtual reality for medical training: The state-of-the-art. *Journal of Simulation, 9*(1), 16–26.

Salvatori, P. (2001). Reliability and validity of admissions tools used to select students for the health professions. *Advances in Health Sciences Education, 6*(2), 159–175.

Schmidt, B., & MacWilliams, B. (2011). Admission criteria for undergraduate nursing programs: A systematic review. *Nurse Educator, 36*(4), 171–174.

Schwartzstein, R. M., Rosenfeld, G. C., Hilborn, R., Oyewole, S. H., & Mitchell, K. (2013). Redesigning the MCAT exam: Balancing multiple perspectives. *Academic Medicine, 88*(5), 560–567.

Shaycoft, M. F. (1951). A validation study of the pre-nursing and guidance test battery. *The American Journal of Nursing, 51*(3), 201–205.

Suzuki, L., Short, E., & Lee, C. (2011). Multicultural perspectives of racial and ethnic group differences on intelligence in the United States. *Cambridge Handbook of Intelligence*. Cambridge: Cambridge University Press.

Tiffin, P. A. (2013). *Understanding the dimensionality and reliability of the cognitive scales of the UK Clinical Aptitude Test (UKCAT): Summary version of the report.* Retrieved June 25, 2017, from https://www.ukcat.ac.uk/media/1182/understanding-the-dimensionality-and-reliability-of-the-cognitive-scales-of-the-ukcat.pdf.

Tiffin, P. A., McLachlan, J. C., Webster, L., & Nicholson, S. (2014). Comparison of the sensitivity of the UKCAT and A Levels to sociodemographic characteristics: A national study. *BMC Medical Education, 14*, 7.

Tiffin, P. A., Mwandigha, L. M., Paton, L. W., Hesselgreaves, H., McLachlan, J. C., Finn, G. M., & Kasim, A. S. (2016). Predictive validity of the UKCAT for medical school undergraduate performance: A national prospective cohort study. *BMC Medicine, 14*(1), 140.

Travers, R. M., & Wallace, W. L. (1950). Inconsistency in the predictive value of a battery of tests. *Journal of Applied Psychology, 34*(4), 237.

Woolf, K., McManus, I., Potts, H., & Dacre, J. (2013). The mediators of minority ethnic underperformance in final medical school examinations. *British Journal of Educational Psychology, 83*, 135–159.

Woolf, K., Potts, H. W. W., & McManus, I. C. (2011). Ethnicity and academic performance in UK trained doctors and medical students: Systematic review and meta-analysis. *British Medical Journal, 342*, d901. https://doi.org/10.1136/bmj.d901.

Woolf, K., Rich, A., Viney, R., Needleman, S., & Griffin, A. (2016). Perceived causes of differential attainment in UK postgraduate medical training: A national qualitative study. *British Medical Journal Open, 6*(11), e013429.

Yates, J., & James, D. (2013). The UK clinical aptitude test and clinical course performance at Nottingham: A prospective cohort study. *BMC Medical Education, 13*, 32. https://doi.org/10.1186/1472-6920-13-32.

Yerkes, R. M. (1921). *Psychological examining in the United States Army* (Ed. R. M. Yerkes, Vol. 15). Washington, DC: US Government Printing Office.

Zhao, X., Oppler, S., Dunleavy, D., & Kroopnick, M. (2010). Validity of four approaches of using repeaters' MCAT scores in medical school admissions to predict USMLE Step 1 total scores. *Academic Medicine, 85*(10), S64–S67.

Zhu, E., Hadadgar, A., Masiello, I., & Zary, N. (2014). Augmented reality in healthcare education: An integrative review. *PeerJ, 2*, e469.

Zumbo, B. D. (2007). Three generations of DIF analyses: Considering where it has been, where it is now, and where it is going. *Language Assessment Quarterly, 4*(2), 223–233.

3

Personality Assessment in Healthcare and Implications for Selection

Stephen A. Woods and John Barratt

Overview

Personality traits matter for performance and effectiveness in healthcare settings, and therefore offer potential benefits in recruitment and selection in those settings. This is the key proposition built and elaborated in this chapter, which reviews the evidence for the scope of impact of personality in medical training and beyond, and discusses the mechanisms by which this evidence may be put to work.

Our chapter commences with an orientation to contemporary personality trait psychology and psychometrics, followed by a review of key evidence across many different settings that traits can predict effectiveness at work. This evidence is used to frame a conceptual approach

S. A. Woods (✉)
Surrey Business School, University of Surrey, Surrey, UK
e-mail: s.a.woods@surrey.ac.uk

J. Barratt
University of Leicester, Leicester, UK
e-mail: jmb92@le.ac.uk

F. Patterson and L. Zibarras (eds.), *Selection and Recruitment in the Healthcare Professions*, https://doi.org/10.1007/978-3-319-94971-0_3

to understanding the potential application of personality measurement in healthcare settings specifically.

The literature on personality and outcomes in healthcare education, and practice is reviewed initially, with four key themes emerging: effects on GPA; training and performance; specialty choice; and attrition, burnout, and well-being. Implications and practical steps for integrating personality assessment into recruitment and selection practice are then discussed, alongside two case examples.

By the end of the chapter you will:

- Understand the background research on personality traits and their measurement.
- Know how personality traits affect outcomes for students and clinical practitioners in healthcare.
- Be able to apply research on personality traits in healthcare settings to the selection and recruitment assessment practice.
- Understand how you could use personality trait assessment to support and potentially improve recruitment and selection in healthcare settings.

Orientation and Introduction to Personality Traits and Psychometrics

Personality has been defined as people's characteristic patterns of behavior, thought, and emotion, combined with the processes, hidden or not, behind those mechanisms (Funder, 2001). Personality traits represent the typical ways that people behave, think, and feel. Research on personality traits in multiple independent studies (e.g., McCrae & Costa, 1997; Goldberg, 1990) has factor-analyzed participant ratings of personality inventory item sets and converged on the conclusion that there are five broad domains of personality: Extraversion, Agreeableness, Conscientiousness, Emotional Stability, and Openness. These domains are described more fully in Table 3.1.

This 'Big Five' model of personality has catalyzed the emergence of a huge body of literature on the effects of personality traits in various aspects of life. For example, a significant volume of research indicates

Table 3.1 Five domains of personality

Extraversion	The extent to which a person is outgoing and sociable versus quiet and reserved
Agreeableness	The extent to which a person is warm and trusting, versus cold and unfriendly
Conscientiousness	The extent to which a person is organized and dependable, versus impulsive and disorganized
Emotional stability	The extent to which a person is calm and stable, versus neurotic and anxious
Openness/Intellect	The extent to which a person is imaginative and open to new experiences, versus narrow-minded and unimaginative

effects of traits on performance at work (Barrick & Mount, 1991; Salgado, 1997). The personality trait Conscientiousness has been shown to be a significant correlate of long-term health across the lifespan (Hampson & Friedman, 2008), reflecting responsible health behavior.

With so much accumulated evidence of the criterion effects of the Big Five, researchers in personality psychology have sought to develop further understanding of the structure of personality traits (Woods & Anderson, 2016). Underneath the Big Five are narrower personality constructs referred to as 'facets'. These generally represent a primary domain of the Big Five, plus a substantive secondary domain (for example the facet *warmth* would be a blend of Extraversion and Agreeableness). Facet models are variously defined and linked to personality measurement (see Woods & Anderson, 2016 for a review).

Measuring Personality Traits

Personality traits are most commonly measured by self-report questionnaires or personality inventories, which comprise lists of items or statements, and require people to indicate the extent to which they agree or disagree with the statements. In psychometric methodology, each trait or dimension measured by a particular inventory has a number of items associated with it, collectively referred to as scales. The bipolar nature of personality traits means that items are designed to tap into both poles of the dimension. So, for example, a scale measuring Extraversion will contain items that refer to characteristics associated with Extraversion (e.g., is the life of the party) and Introversion (e.g., has little to say). From the items, are derived scores for each of the scales (i.e., dimensions being measured).

There is a plethora of different personality inventories that are available commercially and in the research literature (see e.g., Woods & Anderson, 2016; Woods & Hardy, 2012). However, not all are equal. The quality and scientific robustness of personality inventories is represented in empirical psychometric evaluations, which at a minimum should test the following properties:

- Reliability: indicated by the internal consistency of the scales items, and test–retest correlations over a period of time.
- Content Validity: a critical qualitative review of the item content by subject experts.
- Construct Validity: tests of the factorial structure and scale intercorrelations, plus ideally correlations with other personality scales to test convergence.
- Criterion Validity: examination of the predictive effects of the scales with non-test criteria (e.g., education attainment, attitudes, and career preferences).

If you are considering using personality assessment as part of healthcare education provision, or selection, it is essential that you seek information on the psychometric properties of any instrument that you consider purchasing.

Development of digital methods and new technology for capturing assessment data are bringing new innovations and enabling fast adaptation to suit different recruitment and selection needs (Ahmed & Woods, 2018). A future challenge for assessment specialists will be to maintain scientific robustness of methodology whilst ensuring its currency in the digital economy.

A Final Note on Accuracy

One of the implications of measuring personality traits in this way is that we essentially rely on the people's judgments about traits and behavior. Funder has examined the accuracy of these judgments in a number of studies and articles (e.g., Funder, 1995). Evidence for the accuracy of personality judgments is found in studies that show that people agree to an extent in their judgments of others (Funder, 1995) and that self-ratings of personality tend to correlate with ratings of others (so peoples' self-perceptions are a good indicator of how they are seen by others). Agreement between self- and other-perceptions is higher for visible traits such as those related to Extraversion than for less visible traits like Openness/Intellect.

Nevertheless, the implications of personality assessments typically being operationalized through self-report methods should be kept in mind. On one hand, measurements of traits using solely self-reports may predict performance less effectively compared to combined self-reports and observer-reports (Mount, Barrick, & Strauss, 1994). On the other hand, self-reports can be susceptible to socially desirable responding (Paulhus, 2002), reducing the quality and utility of data collected. We return to this issue later in the discussion of applying personality assessment in recruitment settings.

Personality and Effectiveness in Training and at Work

Personality traits have been associated with training performance in several meta-analyses across many different occupational settings (e.g., Barrick & Mount, 1991; Blume, Ford, Baldwin, & Huang, 2010; Colquitt, LePine, & Noe, 2000). Personality traits have the potential to affect individuals' training proficiency because they can influence motivation, participation, attitudes, and attention to training, which can all impact how much they learn (Gully & Chen, 2010). Blume et al. (2010) showed meta-analytic associations of Conscientiousness and Neuroticism with intentions to apply training. In a longitudinal study, Dean, Conte, and Blankenhorn (2006) reported that Conscientiousness, Openness and Extraversion predicted simulation-based training outcomes. Cullen, Muros, Rasch, and Sackett (2013) reported that Conscientiousness and Extraversion were correlated with post-training declarative and procedural learning under certain training conditions.

In a medical setting, using a pre- and post-test methodology to test the effectiveness of training in self-awareness, Woods, Patterson, Koczwara, and Sofat (2016) showed that highly Conscientious employees were more likely to learn more and retain that learning at follow-up.

Personality traits have been found to be associated with an array of organizational and other behaviors (see Ozer & Benet-Martinez, 2006). Traits have been found to predict various forms of job performance. Barrick and Mount (1991) examined the prediction of job performance from the Big Five, reporting that Conscientiousness was particularly important for a variety of performance outcomes (e.g., general job performance, training outcomes). Subsequent meta-analyses were reviewed by Barrick, Mount, and Judge (2001), who concluded that Conscientiousness predicted job performance to some extent in all occupations. Emotional Stability and Extraversion also emerge as important predictors of performance in some, but not all occupations (Ozer & Benet-Martinez, 2006). Hogan and Holland (2003) applied methods of job analysis (see e.g., Woods & Hinton, 2017) to consider which traits might be relevant for performance in particular jobs. In their study, the correlations appear to be higher, suggesting that specific personality traits are more or less important in different jobs.

Theoretical Frame for Applying Personality in Healthcare Recruitment and Selection

The decision to include personality assessment as part of recruitment and selection practices should be informed by theory about how and in what ways traits are likely to influence effectiveness in the target job. There are two relevant theoretical models that help to understand these issues.

The first is Trait Activation Theory (TAT; Tett & Burnett, 2003). In TAT, the pathway from traits to performance is elaborated, and the role of situation and context is underlined, with job, social, and organizational contextual factors positioned as activators of personality traits. For example, interpersonal situations activate Extraversion and Agreeableness. Once activated, traits are expressed in behavior.

To the extent that behavior is consistent with job demands, it can be conceptualized as *performance* behavior. The key implication of TAT is to understand the context of the job being recruited, and the typical demands that are placed on the job holder. From this, relevant traits can be identified, and more importantly, the trait scores that would give rise to effective performance can be determined. TAT tells us that different traits will be important in different selection processes, and it is important to prioritize what we seek to measure in assessment.

The second model is the Dynamic Developmental Model of personality and work (DDM; Woods, Lievens, DeFruyt, & Wille, 2013). In the DDM, job demands are conceptualized as dynamic rather than static. The demands that jobs place on people in the first months of their tenure are different from those that they will encounter in later years of their tenure for example. Combining with TAT, the implication is that traits that may not be important for performance when a person starts their job can lie 'dormant' until later job demands activate them. The result is that those traits will, at that time, impact performance. This model is especially relevant for selection in healthcare and medical settings, where there is good evidence already for the differential impact of traits in different years of medical training (see Sect. "Personality in Healthcare Education and Practice"). The key conclusion from the DDM for selection is that it is important to consider the impact of traits in the short- and long-term.

A final point from the DDM concerns the reciprocal influence of work on personality traits. Although traditionally considered to be stable characteristics, more and more research points to the potential for traits to develop over time, with work experiences being a key source of that development. The likely slow rate of development and change means that while personality assessment for selection decision making remains a justifiable evidence-based strategy, retesting personality throughout a person's tenure would be informative for making personnel and other decisions about their potential through the course of their employment. In the case of medical education especially, where people undertake extensive directed development, there is a lack of data upon which to draw conclusions about personality stability versus change (Ferguson & Lievens, 2017).

Personality in Healthcare Education and Practice

Personality trait assessment has been applied to the field of healthcare education and healthcare settings more generally and has returned important findings that can be used to inform and enhance the recruitment and selection process within healthcare education. In this section, we review relevant studies and commentaries in this area, relating to four key areas of healthcare education and career development: Grade Point Average (GPA) and academic performance; training and clinical performance; specialty choice; and attrition, burnout, and well-being.

Personality and GPA (Grade Point Average) and Academic Performance

In relation to personality being applied to medical education, research has identified a relation between the personality of an individual and their performance on medical education in the form of their GPA scores and academic performance. This link demonstrates a timely need to consider how personality assessment is best used within healthcare education selection systems. Indeed, research has shown the predictive utility of personality traits is on par with that of general mental ability, and therefore warrants inclusion in assessment and selection practices (Lievens, Ones, & Dilchert, 2009).

Lievens et al. (2009) emphasize the importance of admission and personnel decisions relying on stable predictor–criterion relationships. Their longitudinal research examined the Big Five personality traits validity in predicting academic performance across multiple years of medical school. They reported that personality factors became increasingly able to predict academic success as the students advanced through the medical curriculum. The traits Extraversion, Openness and Conscientiousness and their facets particularly showed increased validity for predicting GPA over time. Conscientiousness (and facets) especially is identified as highly influential in medical students with respect to academic attainment (Ferguson, James, O'Hehir, Sanders, & McManus, 2003; Lievens, Coetsier, De Fruyt, & De Maeseneer, 2002; Lievens et al., 2009). The Big Five traits have been found to correlate with and explain 14% of the variance in GPA, and therefore be influential in candidate academic performance (Komarraju, Karau, Schmeck, & Avdic, 2011; Vedel, 2014).

Beyond the Big Five, the trait anxiety has been found to negatively correlate with GPA in medical students (Grover & Smith, 1981); whilst research in Australia using the Hogan Developmental Survey over three cohorts found 'Moving away' syndrome (borderline personality characteristics) and 'Moving against' syndrome (schizoid personality characteristics) negatively related to academic grades, whereas 'Diligent' syndrome positively related (Knights & Kennedy, 2006). This supports the Conscientiousness finding, as diligent syndrome is associated with a tendency to be attentive and good with details, orderly, rational, careful and well organized. These are similar characteristics to those of the Big-Five Conscientiousness trait. However, the complexities of the expression of traits in behavior mean that the implications of any trait dimension score or profile overall are not simplistic, being rather a blend of positive and negative, often determined by situation or context (Ferguson et al., 2014).

A crucial consideration when utilizing personality assessment is that the relative importance of each trait depends upon the particular requirements of a given course. For example, although Extraversion and Openness yielded little initial benefit with respect to GPA in early years of medical school, Lievens et al. (2009) found that as later curriculum involved clinical practice, these traits took on an increasing importance. Extraversion especially showed the biggest change across years. Coupled with this, Ferguson et al. (2003) reiterate this point and reported Conscientiousness to be positively related to preclinical performance but negatively related to clinical grades. This can be seen to relate to trait activation theory whereby individuals express and experience trait-relevant benefits when presented with trait-relevant situational cues (Tett & Burnett, 2003).

Training and Clinical Performance Outcomes

One fundamental argument to utilizing personality assessment within healthcare assessment and selection is the association personality traits have with training outcomes and performance. Trait assessment could help to identify those candidates both better suited to the role in terms of performance; as well those who are more likely to engage with and consequently benefit from training. By extension, these can be used to inform the selection of candidates onto educational courses within the healthcare professions, as they will help in identifying candidates most likely to thrive during training and in their subsequent career.

Woods, Patterson, Koczwara, et al. (2016) examined the big five personality traits of medical practitioners in postgraduate training in relation to their self-reported learning following participation in a self-awareness training course. They reported Conscientiousness to associate with pre-learning, learning straight after training, and again at one-month follow-up. These findings demonstrate the role of personality with respect to engagement with training as well as the consequential implications for performance. It suggests those high in Conscientiousness are more likely to work hard to acquire job related skills through engagement in training practices, and this in turn has potential to enhance their subsequent performance.

Indeed, further research on medical physicians has identified the importance of Conscientiousness in relation to training outcomes. Hassan, Bashir, and Mussel (2015) propose this can be explained through Conscientiousness' relationship to epistemic curiosity. They also identify openness to experience to indirectly impact on learning through epistemic curiosity. This once again demonstrates the potential importance of assessing relevant personality traits during selection due to the impacts traits have on subsequent training performance once in a healthcare post.

More directly perhaps, personality traits and facets have been shown to have an association with the clinical performance of medical and healthcare trainees and professionals. It has been proposed that personality can have a more useful predictive potential on clinical performance than cognitive ability (Gough & Hall, 1975; Shen & Comrey, 1997;

Spiegel, Smolen, & Hopfensperger, 1986; Turner, Helper, & Kriska 1974). Personality traits have been found to add incrementally to the predictive validity of traditional admission tools with respect to course performance of medical students. However, crucially personality traits have also been found to predict clinical performance, where more traditional methods do not (McLarnon, Rothstein, Goffin, & Mestdagh, 2017). Personality assessment therefore has the potential to enhance the selection process and to increase the likelihood of identifying high performers in healthcare. Goffin et al. (2011) undertook research with medical students concerning the development of a personality-oriented job analysis process to enhance the choosing of job-related personality traits. They found that the traits that received the highest personality-oriented job analysis ratings tended to predict the performance of medical students on related job tasks. This reiterates the utility and validity of personality traits in relation to performance, and also the need to identify the specific traits required for a role.

Traits related to Agreeableness have been shown to correlate with clinical performance, the most prominent being empathy, which has been shown to predict clinical performance of anesthesiology residents (Gough, Bradley, & McDonald, 1991; Shen & Comrey, 1997). This is due to these individuals having the ability to sense the needs of their patients and medical teams. Doherty and Nugent (2011) highlight the main trait consistently identified as relating to training and performance as Conscientiousness, followed by sociability (i.e., extraversion, openness, self-esteem, and neuroticism), particularly in the applied medical environment. Doherty and Nugent describe how personality traits take on increasing importance and link stronger to performance as the candidate progresses through medical training.

Beyond the Big Five, research on care workers of challenging clients has identified Honesty–Humility as a sixth dimension of personality. Johnson, Rowatt, and Petrini (2011) found this trait to correlate with supervisor ratings of employees' job performance with regards to workers who provide care for challenging clients. Furthermore, a three-year study on medical students in the US found that sociability linked to clinical competency ratings (Hojat, Callahan, & Gonnella, 2004).

Medical Specialty Choice

A further argument for the inclusion of personality assessments in the selection of candidates onto healthcare courses reflects the differences in personality trait profiles of firstly those undertaking medicine as a career (i.e., compared to the general population), but also secondly between the different medical specialties (Lievens et al., 2002). For example, students undertaking medicine courses score high on Extraversion and Agreeableness from the Big Five personality traits; compared to for example students of the arts, humanities and psychology who score higher on Neuroticism and Openness (Vedel, 2016). It is therefore possible to firstly consider the fit of a student's preferences to study healthcare and medicine, and secondly to consider the particular specialty of medicine and healthcare to which they may be best suited. Research has utilized the RIASEC model (*Realistic, Investigative, Artistic, Social, Enterprising, and Conventional*) to map and identify the occupation environment differences between specialties. The RIASEC model argues that people with corresponding interests and traits are more likely to fit and be satisfied with particular occupation environments. For example, administrative medicine is considered a more 'enterprising' specialty, involving the need to manage. Whereas laboratory medicine is deemed a more 'conventional' specialty, because pathologists and other laboratory specialists have to develop, implement, and follow complex systems (Petrides & McManus, 2004). Further examples Petrides and McManus provide are: Surgery (Realistic)—as surgeons work with their hands and tools, needing high levels of technical proficiency, craftsmanship and practical skills; Hospital Medicine/internal medicine (Investigative)—as physicians investigate patients' symptoms; Psychiatry (Artistic)—as psychiatrists have to interpret the problems or ideas that a patient expresses; and Public Health (Social)—as this is not individual patients. The consequence being each role specialty has its own specific demands, and therefore each role requires its own particular trait profile dependent on these demands, which has implications for selection into postgraduate training.

Woods, Patterson, Wille, and Koczwara (2016) examined the role of personality in occupational specialty choice, with the aim of better understanding how and in what ways personality traits might influence vocational development after a person has chosen a career. They assessed the Big Five traits in combination with Holland's RIASEC profiles of their specialty.

They reported that junior doctors' Agreeableness (with social) and Neuroticism (with realistic, artistic and enterprising) were the main predictors of the RIASEC profiles of their specialty selections. The implication of this being that personality traits influence specialty selection in a predictable way, and differently compared to occupational choice. Moreover, that different occupations and specialties activate different traits in workers. This demonstrates traits influence not only occupational choice, but also specialty choice. This reiterates the need to include personality assessment in postgraduate recruitment and selection to identify candidates more suited to each specialty.

More widely, research has consistently demonstrated that workers in different medical specialties have different trait profiles. For example, Borges and Savickas (2014) identified that medical students who went into internal medicine scored higher on measures involving working with people (rather than ideas and things), compared to students who went into careers in surgery or anesthesiology. Moreover, students who opted for careers in obstetrics or gynecology also scored higher on working with people than those students entering anesthesiology. Coupled with this, Rotge, Lemongne, and Jouvent (2015) research revealed differences between traits in different medical specialties. They reported that high Openness and low Extraversion were associated with laboratory workers; low Neuroticism linked to the roles anesthesia and emergency and intensive care workers; high Neuroticism with medicine; high Extraversion, low Agreeableness, and low Neuroticism with surgery workers; and, high Extraversion, high Agreeableness and high Openness with psychiatry. This demonstrates for example that an introverted individual, who has a tendency to prefer to be quiet and less talkative, would be better suited to a role such as that of a laboratory worker that involves less interaction with other people. This shows how the traits of an individual relate and could be considered in selection with respect to specialty choices in healthcare and in careers counseling.

Furthermore, retrospective research by Borges and Gibson (2005) identified personality differences between person-oriented specialists (patient oriented) and technique-oriented specialists (body oriented with special technical skills). They broadly found that the trait 'Agreeableness' predicted differences between the two specialties. More specifically, they report person-oriented physicians often need to possess traits associated with Agreeableness such as trust, altruism, and cooperation. This is because they relate to the continuity of care and interpersonal relationship aspects associated with person-oriented specialty areas. Their findings extend research comparing personality differences between the person-oriented specialty of family practice and the technique-oriented specialties of anesthesiology and general surgery.

Relatedly, research has identified that person-oriented specialists differ on two core factors: rule-consciousness and abstractedness (Borges & Osmon, 2001). Indeed, family practitioners were more likely to be strict followers of rules and more imaginative and ideal-oriented compared to anesthesiologists and general surgeons. Linked to this, Taber, Hartung, and Borges (2011) examined personality traits in relation to predicting medical specialty choice. They found that personality traits predicted person- or technique-oriented medical specialty choice. For example, medical students who entered person-oriented specialties tended to be more sensitive, display more warmth, be more rule conscious, and be more apprehensive. This once again demonstrates how the traits of an individual influences the specialty they are suited.

Specifically focusing on the personality of surgeons, differences have been examined with other clinical specialties. Compared to other specialties, surgeons are found to score significantly higher on the traits Conscientiousness and Extraversion but lower on Agreeableness (Drosdeck et al., 2015).

Hoffman, Coons, and Kuo (2010) compared traits among surgery residents (using the five-factor model) with medicine residents, medical students, and community norms. They found surgery residents scored higher on Conscientiousness, Extraversion, and Emotional Stability, and scored lower on Openness when compared with community norms. They were also found to obtain higher scores than medical students and pediatric residents on the trait Conscientiousness, as well as greater Extraversion scores and lower Openness scores when compared with first-year medical students. Linked to this, further research utilizing the Big Five has shown that when contrasting surgical trainees (postgraduate) from medical students specifying surgical career intent (undergraduate), Neuroticism was the only personality trait to differ significantly between the two groups. Specifically, medical students scored significantly higher than surgical trainees (Preece & Cope, 2016), consistent with the findings of Woods, Patterson, Wille, and Koczwara (2016).

This body of research suggests an inherent difference between the trait profiles of medical specialties, clearly between surgeons and other clinical specialties. This implies that utilizing personality assessment may be beneficial during the selection process for applicants deciding on specialties. Likewise, it could be especially fruitful in candidate's career choice decisions.

Attrition, Burnout, and Well-Being

A benefit of implementing the use of personality assessment into the selection and assessment process in healthcare is the relationships that have been established between personality and potential negative outcomes at work, such as attrition, unprofessional behavior, and burnout versus well-being of individuals in a medical and healthcare setting.

Firstly, with regards to attrition, Lievens et al. (2009) identified that low Conscientiousness and high Openness associated with attrition in the early years of medical school. Moreover, as students progressed into latter years, the traits low Conscientiousness and Agreeableness became the core traits associating with medical school attrition. The utility of this is the identification of those candidates at a heightened risk of attrition. The consequence being prevention strategies can be implemented and targeted at those candidates at heightened risk of attrition. However, responsibility and socialization (which assess primarily Conscientiousness and Agreeableness) were found to negatively relate to medical school attrition (Gough & Hall, 1975). This raises questions over whether specific facets of traits link to attrition, or whether the discrepancy with Lievens et al. findings is due to the use of different trait instruments.

Research has identified personality traits associated with unprofessional behavior of medical students. Hodgson, Teherani, Gough,

Bradley, and Papadakis (2007) had medical students complete the California Personality Inventory (CPI). They found significant differences between individuals who had demonstrated unprofessional behavior and those who had not on the CPI subscales for responsibility, communality, well-being, rule respecting, and for total score. Their findings help in identifying those candidates most as risk of partaking in unprofessional behavior, and this once again enables the proactive development of intervention strategies to prevent this occurring.

When considering the well-being of those in healthcare, it has been shown to associate with the clinical performance of anesthesiology residents (Gough et al., 1991), and is therefore an area of importance from both the worker perspective but also all those impacted by their subsequent performance. Furthermore, research on undergraduate medical students has identified that Agreeableness and Openness are negatively related to depressive symptoms, whereas Neuroticism is positively related (Shi, Liu, Yang, & Wang, 2015). Shi et al. also report self-esteem to act as a mediator between Agreeableness, Openness, Neuroticism, and depressive symptoms. The implication of these findings is that through identifying students at risk of depressive symptoms it becomes possible to undertake intervention strategies.

Linked to well-being is research relating to the stress and the susceptibility of healthcare workers. McManus, Keeling, and Paice (2004) conducted a 12-year longitudinal study across five UK medical schools to examine the relation between personality traits and stress post-graduation. They found that high Neuroticism and low Extraversion and low Conscientiousness mediate between the doctors' approaches to work and learning styles, in turn, leading to stress. This research is important, as it enables identification of workers at risk of stress, which is crucial as stress has been shown to link to underperformance and errors in doctors and medical settings (British Medical Association, 2004; Fahrenkopf et al., 2008).

Similarly, Hojat, Gonnella, Erdmann, and Vogel (2003) also reported differences between the personalities traits of those classed 'resilient' to stress and those deemed as 'frail' and 'intermediate'. Their findings showed that resilient candidates scored lower than the other groups on all 'negative' aspects of personality such as general and test anxiety, depression, Neuroticism, and the intensity of loneliness scales. They concluded that the 'resilient' medical students presented a more positive personality profile than their other classmates.

In addition to this evidence of personality and stress, research on medical students in Norway examined Extraversion, Neuroticism, and Conscientiousness in the context of personality types (combinations of traits) in relation to stress over six years of medical training. Results indicated 'brooders' (individuals who are high on Neuroticism and Conscientiousness and low on Extraversion) demonstrate high level of perceived stress, whereas 'hedonists' (individuals with low Neuroticism and Conscientiousness and high Extraversion) had lower perceived stress levels (Tyssen et al., 2007). The core findings are that an individual with a combination of high Neuroticism and high Conscientiousness is at particularly high risk of stress. This therefore needs to be acknowledged in the selection of candidates onto medical course and throughout their subsequent training.

Lee, Choi, and Chae (2017) found that personality might account for the level of burnout experienced by individuals in medical education. They found higher harm avoidance and lower self-directedness and cooperativeness on the Cloninger's Temperament and Character Inventory, predicted the subscales of academic burnout in medical students.

Summary

This section has provided an overview of the evidence base for including personality assessment into the selection process of candidates onto healthcare education courses such as medicine, and in medical selection into practice. Traits have been shown in scientific studies to predict GPA and academic performance, training, and clinical performance, the specialty doctors pursue within medicine, and attrition, well-being, and burnout during medical careers. Having reviewed the evidence to support the use of personality assessment in recruitment and selection contexts, the final part of this chapter discusses some potential practical steps in doing so, taking into consideration what we know about personality traits in general and specifically in medical practice.

Applying Personality Assessment in Selection onto Healthcare Programs and into Clinical Practice

Evidence provides a compelling rationale for the application of personality assessment in medical school selection. Robust psychometric profiling could be added to a stagewise application process for prospective students. In typical recruitment and selection processes, techniques of assessment are deployed sequentially with key criteria being used to efficiently 'select-out' applicants, and more in-depth techniques such as interviewing being used to differentiate and 'select-in' candidates (Woods & West, 2014).

Great care is needed in the application of personality assessment in screening and 'select-out' stages. Given what we know about some of the limitations of self-report methodology, to use personality assessment as a *sole* means of rejecting an applicant would not be justified, yet the additional insights do give screeners and recruiters the means to differentiate applicant potential. Research into the application of personality at select-out stage indicates that the methodology should focus on screening out applicants who are a clear misfit to a career in healthcare, or the focal role being recruited, rather than providing any form of pre-interview rank-ordering (see Mueller-Hanson, Heggestad, & Thornton, 2003).

Personality profiling could be used effectively as a 'select-in' strategy, with candidates having met relevant entry requirements being asked to complete a psychometric personality assessment to be used as part of an interview process. It is good practice in recruitment for specific elements of an individual's personality profile to be discussed with them in a structured interview (see for example, Case Study 3.1 for senior clinician selection in this chapter). In such an interview, questioning could focus on the traits which appear to represent a risk for performance in training, burnout, or attrition (such as low Conscientiousness, and Neuroticism), to establish if an applicant is suitable for a career in healthcare. A Big Five based assessment would seem to be most relevant (i.e., covering the Big Five domains, but with facets scored underneath each).

Case Study 3.1: Using Trait Assessment to Support Selecting Clinical Leaders into Hospital Trusts

In this chapter, we have shared the value of using personality trait assessment for the selection of healthcare professionals, and in particular for doctors into practice roles where an assessment of more than clinical proficiency is needed. This case centers around the use of a personality instrument—the Trait personality inventory (Aston Business Assessments, 2011)—for selection of consultants into hospital trusts in the UK National Health Service.

The Trait assessment measures thirteen facets of personality, each relevant for different aspects of working style and performance (for example, Sociability, Orderliness, Leadership, Optimism, Cooperation, Stability, and Calmness). Based on research on the criterion validities of personality traits and performance-related trait composites (e.g., Woods & Anderson, 2016), the inventory also provides assessment of potential in nine competency areas (e.g., Working with Others, Leading Others, Coping with Pressure).

The assessment has been used in three hospital trusts in the UK to assess more than 1000 candidates for roles as senior clinicians (consultants) across a wide variety of practice specialties. The HR teams in the hospitals position the assessment post-screening, prior to interview, and use the profiling results to help develop relevant structured questions for each candidate. The impact for selectors is to provide important insights into the non-clinical competencies of candidates. For example, when discussing the impact of the assessment, HR professionals share:

> "Our interview panel is formed of senior Managers and Medical Directors. Trait (assessment) saves them time by highlighting the areas that will matter the most and suggesting relevant questions. For the respondent, it helps to ensure a good match with the team".

> "We use personality trait assessment as part of a formal assessment process. The reports prompt our Recruiting Managers with the most relevant questions and enhances their understanding of how a person matches our competency framework. It helps us to make a better-informed choice over candidates".

Beyond initial selection, there are also obvious potential advantages for embedding personality assessment into the ongoing education and development of students. For example, profiles of traits could indicate potential challenges later in the training for individual students. Those low on Extraversion may find later stages in practice settings more challenging. Educational interventions, early in the curriculum, could be initiated to make them ready to overcome such challenges to mitigate the risk of experiencing difficulty in training and in practice. The extensive literature on traits and specialty choice also underlines the relevance of personality assessment in career guidance. Selecting a specialty for which the student is a good fit is likely to bring benefits for the student themselves in terms of well-being and satisfaction, and long-tenure within the profession.

Returning to the earlier theoretical positioning around the Dynamic Developmental Model, a further implication is that the experience of medical training may result in development for the student. A logical recommendation would be to repeat assessments through the medical training so that decisions are taken and vocational guidance given based on up-to-date trait profiles (e.g., to assess annually, or at key milestones each 2 or 3 years).

For more senior-level clinical appointments, it is possible to also use trait-based assessment to understand how medical practitioners might cope with future challenges, especially in recruitment for senior leadership roles. In selecting senior consultants for example, it would be important to assess a candidate's potential for impacting on the development, performance and well-being of others. Traits of effective management and leadership could be examined when promoting practitioners into such roles or selecting into them externally.

Another example is the potential for burnout and stress. There is strong evidence of the link between key traits such as Neuroticism with doctors' stress and potential to burn out. It is also justifiable to suppose that although most medical settings bring pressure and stress of some form, there are those where the psychological load is significantly more acute. Given that doctors' stress is related to potential for error, exploring such issues using personality assessment within an interview process could prove an effective approach. Psychometric results can be discussed and evaluated in face-to-face interviewing or may help to confirm or challenge evidence acquired in interviews of work samples. Moving a step further, the process of on-boarding could also make use of assessment results, in planning development and assignment of new recruits to duties and roles.

Summary and Conclusion

Accumulated research evidence points to the impact that personality assessment can make in selection in healthcare settings. In particular, trait assessment can play a crucial role in identifying individuals better suited and more likely to succeed in healthcare roles, as well as identifying those who may be more susceptible to stress and attrition. It can help place individuals in specialties their traits will be best suited to, and this can in turn enhance the satisfaction of the individual. Moreover, through utilizing personality assessment in combination with accurate job analysis within healthcare selection it addresses calls to assess attributes beyond clinical knowledge and academic achievement. This is with respect to ensuring doctors train and work within a specialty for which they have a particular aptitude (Patterson, Ferguson, & Thomas, 2008), and likely preference (Woods, Patterson, Wille, & Koczwara, 2016).

There are key practical considerations in realizing these potential benefits, especially in the methodology by which personality tools are included within a selection process. From our discussion of these issues, it is clear that personality inventories need to be embedded and used in combination with other methods of assessment to build a representative profile of potential. With careful application in this way, personality tools may enhance decision-making at different selection stages, leading to better outcomes for education providers, healthcare employers, and recruits.

Practice Points

- Personality traits provide a relevant context around which to explore and understand people's potential, career trajectories and specialty preferences in healthcare.
- For recruitment and selection, assessment of personality traits may provide insights to help decision making about candidate suitability in a variety of healthcare contexts.
- Personality assessments can be deployed at different stages of selection:

- At select-out, combination of personality assessments might provide insights to complement other applicant data to identify where candidates are a clear *misfit* to career or role requirements.
- At select-in, personality assessments can provide important information on potential, and effectively highlight areas for questioning and exploration at interview.

References

Ahmed, S., & Woods, S. A. (2018). New technology in selection. In *Proceedings of the AOM Specialized Conference: Big Data and Managing in a Digital Economy*, Guildford, Surrey.

Aston Business Assessments Ltd. (2011). *Trait: Manual and user guide.* Birmingham UK.

Barrick, M. R., & Mount, M. K. (1991). The Big Five personality dimensions and job performance: A meta-analysis. *Personnel Psychology, 44*(1), 1–26.

Barrick, M. R., Mount, M. K., & Judge, T. A. (2001). Personality and performance at the beginning of the new millennium: What do we know and where do we go next? *International Journal of Selection and Assessment, 9*(1–2), 9–30.

Blume, B. D., Ford, J. K., Baldwin, T. T., & Huang, J. L. (2010). Transfer of training: A meta-analytic review. *Journal of Management, 36*(4), 1065–1105.

Borges, N. J., & Gibson, D. D. (2005). Personality patterns of physicians in person-oriented and technique-oriented specialties. *Journal of Vocational Behavior, 67,* 4–20.

Borges, N. J., & Osmon, W. R. (2001). Personality and medical specialty choice: Technique orientation versus person orientation. *Journal of Vocational Behavior, 58,* 22–35.

Borges, N. J., & Savickas, S. (2014). Work style preferences among medical specialties. *Journal of Vocational Behavior, 84*(3), 303–306.

British Medical Association. (2004). *Underlying causes of doctors' disciplinary problems: Survey results*. London: BMA.

Colquitt, J. A., LePine, J. A., & Noe, R. A. (2000). Toward an integrative theory of training motivation: A meta-analytic path analysis of 20 years of research. *Journal of Applied Psychology, 85*(5), 678.

Cullen, M. J., Muros, J. P., Rasch, R., & Sackett, P. R. (2013). Individual differences in the effectiveness of error management training for developing negotiation skills. *International Journal of Selection and Assessment, 21*(1), 1–21.

Dean, M. A., Conte, J. M., & Blankenhorn, T. R. (2006). Examination of the predictive validity of Big Five personality dimensions across training performance criteria. *Personality and Individual Differences, 41*(7), 1229–1239.

Doherty, E. M., & Nugent, E. (2011). Personality factors and medical training: A review of the literature. *Medical Education, 45*(2), 132–140.

Drosdeck, J. M., Osayi, S. N., Peterson, L. A., Yu, L., Ellison, E. C., & Muscarella, P. (2015). Surgeon and non-surgeon personalities at different career points. *Journal of Surgical Research, 196,* 6–66.

Fahrenkopf, A. M., Seetish, T. C., Barger, L. K., Sharek, P. J., Lewin, D., & Chiang, V. W. (2008). Rates of medication errors among depressed and burnt-out residents: Prospective cohort study. *British Medical Journal, 336,* 488–491.

Ferguson, E., James, D., O'Hehir, F., Sanders, A., & McManus, I. C. (2003). Pilot study of the roles of personality, references, and personal statements in relation to performance over the five years of a medical degree. *British Medical Journal, 326*(7386), 429–432.

Ferguson, E., & Lievens, F. (2017). Future directions in personality, occupational and medical selection: Myths, misunderstandings, measurement, and suggestions. *Advances in Health Sciences Education, 22*(2), 387–399.

Ferguson, E., Semper, H., Yates, J., Fitzgerald, J. E., Skatova, A., & James, D. (2014). The 'dark side' and 'bright side' of personality: When too much conscientiousness and too little anxiety are detrimental with respect to the acquisition of medical knowledge and skill. *PLoS ONE, 9*(2), e88606.

Funder, D. C. (1995). On the accuracy of personality judgment: A realistic approach. *Psychological Review, 102*(4), 652.

Funder, D. C. (2001). Personality. *Annual Review of Psychology, 52,* 197–221.

Goffin, R. D., Rothstein, M. G., Rieder, M. J., Poole, A., Krajewski, H. T., Powell, D. M., ... & Mcstdagh, T. (2011). Choosing job-related personality traits: Developing valid personality-oriented job analysis. *Personality and Individual Differences, 51*(5), 646–651.

Goldberg, L. R. (1990). An alternative "description of personality": The big-five factor structure. *Journal of Personality and Social Psychology, 59*(6), 1216–1229.

Gough, H. G., Bradley, P., & McDonald, J. S. (1991). Performance of residents in anesthesiology as related to measures of personality and interests. *Psychological Reports, 68,* 979–994.

Gough, H. G., & Hall, W. B. (1975). An attempt to predict graduation from medical school. *Journal of Medical Education, 50,* 940–950.

Grover, P. L., & Smith, D. U. (1981). Academic anxiety, locus of control, and achievement in medical school. *Journal of Medical Education, 56,* 727–736.

Gully, S., & Chen, G. (2010). Individual differences, attribute-treatment interactions, and training outcomes. In S. W. J. Kozlowski & E. Salas (Eds.), *SIOP organizational frontiers series. Learning, training, and development in organizations* (pp. 3–64). New York, US: Routledge/Taylor Francis Group.

Hampson, S. E., & Friedman, H. S. (2008). Personality and health: A lifespan perspective. In O. P. John, R. W. Robins, & L. A. Pervin (Eds.), *Handbook of personality: Theory and research* (pp. 770–794). New York, NY: Guilford Press.

Hassan, M. M., Bashir, S., & Mussel, P. (2015). Personality, learning, and the mediating role of epistemic curiosity: A case of continuing education in medical physicians. *Learning and Individual Differences, 42,* 83–89.

Hodgson, C. S., Teherani, A., Gough, H. G., Bradley, P., & Papadakis, M. A. (2007). The relationship between measures of unprofessional behaviour during medical school and indices on the California Psychological Inventory. *Academic Medicine, 10*(Suppl), 4–7.

Hoffman, B. M., Coons, M. J., & Kuo, P. C. (2010). Personality differences between surgery residents, non-surgery residents, and medical students. *Surgery, 148,* 187–193.

Hogan, J., & Holland, B. (2003). Using theory to evaluate personality and job-performance relations: A socioanalytic perspective. *Journal of Applied Psychology, 88*(1), 100–112.

Hojat, M., Callahan, C. A., & Gonnella, J. S. (2004). Students' personality and ratings of clinical competence in medical school clerkships: A longitudinal study. *Psychology, Health, and Medicine, 9*(2), 247–252.

Hojat, H., Gonnella, J. S., Erdmann, J. B., & Vogel, W. H. (2003). Medical students' cognitive appraisal of stressful life events as related to personality, physical well-being, and academic performance: A longitudinal study. *Personality and Individual Differences, 35,* 219–235.

Johnson, M. K., Rowatt, W. C., & Petrini, L. (2011). A new trait on the market: Honesty–humility as a unique predictor of job performance. *Personality and Individual Differences, 50,* 857–862.

Knights, J. A., & Kennedy, B. J. (2006). Medical school selection: Impact of dysfunctional tendencies on academic performance. *Medical Education, 41*(4), 362–368.

Komarraju, M., Karau, S. J., Schmeck, R. R., & Avdic, A. (2011). The Big Five personality traits, learning styles, and academic achievement. *Personality and Individual Differences, 51*(4), 472–477.

Lee, S. J., Choi, Y. J., & Chae, H. (2017). The effects of personality traits on academic burnout in Korean medical students. *Integrative Medicine Research, 6*(2), 207–213.

Lievens, F., Coetsier, P., De Fruyt, F., & De Maeseneer, J. (2002). Medical students' personality characteristics and academic performance: A five-factor model perspective. *Medical Education, 36*(11), 1050–1056.

Lievens, P., Ones, D. S., & Dilchert, S. (2009). Personality scale validities increase throughout medical school. *Journal of Applied Psychology, 94*(6), 1514–1535.

McCrae, R. R., & Costa, P. T., Jr. (1997). Personality trait structure as a human universal. *American Psychologist, 52*(5), 509.

McLarnon, M. J. W., Rothstein, M. G., Goffin, R., & Mestdagh, T. (2017). How important is personality in the selection of medical school students? *Personality and Individual Differences, 104,* 442–447.

McManus, I. C., Keeling, A., & Paice, E. (2004). Stress, burnout and doctors' attitudes to work are determined by personality and learning style: A 12-year longitudinal study of UK medical graduates. *BMC Med 2*, 29.

Mount, M. K., Barrick, M. R., & Strauss, J. P. (1994). Validity of observer ratings of the Big Five personality factors. *Journal of Applied Psychology, 79*(2), 272–280.

Mueller-Hanson, R., Heggestad, E. D., & Thornton III, G. C. (2003). Faking and selection: Considering the use of personality from select-in and select-out perspectives. *Journal of Applied Psychology, 88*(2), 348–355.

Ozer, D. J., & Benet-Martinez, V. (2006). Personality and the prediction of consequential outcomes. *Annual Review of Psychology, 57,* 401–421.

Patterson, F., Ferguson, E., & Thomas, S. (2008). Using job analysis to identify core and specific competencies: Implications for selection and recruitment. *Medical Education, 42,* 1195–1204.

Paulhus, D. L. (2002). Socially desirable responding: The evolution of a construct. In H. I. Braun, D. N. Jackson, & D. E. Wiley (Eds.), *The role of constructs in psychological and educational measurement* (pp. 49–69). Mahwah, NJ: Erlbaum.

Petrides, K. V., & McManus, I. C. (2004). Mapping medical careers: Questionnaire assessment of career preferences in medical school applicants and final-year students. *BMC Medical Education, 4,* 18.

Preece, R. A., & Cope, A. C. (2016). Are surgeons born or made? A comparison of personality traits and learning styles between surgical trainees and medical students. *Journal of Surgical Education, 73*(5), 768–773.

Rotge, J. V., Lemogne, C., & Jouvent, R. (2015). Relationship between personality dimensions and medical specialty in 1661 residents. *Journal of Psychosomatic Research, 79,* 331–332.

Salgado, J. F. (1997). The five factor model of personality and job performance in the European community. *Journal of Applied Psychology, 82*(1), 30–43.

Shen, H., & Comrey, A. L. (1997). Predicting medical students' academic performances by their cognitive abilities and personality characteristics. *Academic Medicine, 72,* 781–786.

Shi, M., Liu, L., Yang, Y. L., & Wang, L. (2015). The mediating role of self-esteem in the relationship between Big Five personality traits and depressive symptoms among Chinese undergraduate medical students. *Personality and Individual Differences, 83,* 55–59.

Spiegel, D. A., Smolen, R. C., & Hopfensperger, K. A. (1986). Medical student stress and clerkship performance. *Journal of Medical Education, 61,* 929–931.

Taber, B. J., Hartung, P. J., & Borges, N. J. (2011). Personality and values as predictors of medical specialty choice. *Journal of Vocational Behavior, 78,* 202–209.

Tett, R. P., & Burnett, D. D. (2003). A personality trait-based interactionist model of job performance. *Journal of Applied Psychology, 88*(3), 500–517.

Turner, E. V., Helper, M. M., & Kriska, S. D. (1974). Predictors of clinical performance. *Journal of Medical Education, 49,* 338–342.

Tyssen, R., Dolatowski, F. C., Røvik, J. O., Thorkildsen, R. F., Ekeberg, O., Hem, E., ..., Vaglum, P. (2007). Personality traits and types predict medical school stress: A 6-year longitudinal and nationwide study. *Medical Education, 41*(8), 781–787.

Vedel, A. (2014). The Big Five and tertiary academic performance: A systematic review and meta-analysis. *Personality and Individual Differences, 71,* 66–76.

Vedel, A. (2016). Big Five personality group differences across academic majors: A systematic review. *Personality and Individual Differences, 92,* 1–10.

Woods, S. A., & Anderson, N. R. (2016). Toward a periodic table of personality: Mapping personality scales between the five-factor model and the circumplex model. *Journal of Applied Psychology, 101*(4), 582–604.

Woods, S. A., & Hardy, C. (2012). The higher-order factor structures of five personality inventories. *Personality and Individual Differences, 52*(4), 552–558.

Woods, S. A., & Hinton, D. P. (2017). What do people really do at work? Job analysis and design. In N. Chmiel, F. Fraccaroli, & M. Sverke (Eds.), *An introduction to work and organizational psychology: An international perspective* (3rd ed.). London: Wiley Blackwell.

Woods, S. A., Lievens, F., De Fruyt, F., & Wille, B. (2013). Personality across working life: The longitudinal and reciprocal influences of personality on work. *Journal of Organizational Behavior, 34,* S7–S25.

Woods, S. A., Patterson, F. C., Koczwara, A., & Sofat, J. A. (2016). The value of being a conscientious learner: Examining the effects of the Big Five personality traits on self-reported learning and training. *Journal of Workplace Learning, 28*(7), 424–434.

Woods, S. A., Patterson, F. C., Wille, B., & Koczwara, A. (2016). Personality and occupational specialty: An examination of medical specialties using Holland's RIASEC model. *Career Development International, 21*(3), 262–278.

Woods, S. A., & West, M. A. (2014). *The psychology of work and organizations.* Cengage Learning EMEA.

4

Situational Judgement Tests (SJTs)

Fiona Patterson and Rachel Driver

Introduction

Situational judgement tests (SJTs) are increasingly used for assessing important non-academic attributes in healthcare selection. In this chapter, we explore the latest research in the design and development of SJTs alongside some practical case studies to illustrate their application. First, we examine the design principles of SJTs, including their theoretical underpinning, and then outline the evidence for the effectiveness of SJTs as a selection method. Specifically, the evidence for using SJTs in healthcare selection will be explored, focusing on reliability, validity, fairness, and susceptibility to coaching. Second, we explore the practical aspects of developing SJTs, including practical guidelines for item structure, format, response options, and scoring. We also provide

F. Patterson (✉) · R. Driver
Work Psychology Group, Derby, UK
e-mail: f.patterson@workpsychologygroup.com

F. Patterson and L. Zibarras (eds.), *Selection and Recruitment in the Healthcare Professions*, https://doi.org/10.1007/978-3-319-94971-0_4

several illustrative examples and two case studies alongside some comments about future SJT research and implications for practice in education and training. Finally, we explore the implications of the research findings for policy and practice in healthcare and present an agenda for future research.

By the end of this chapter, you should have an understanding of:

- the SJT measurement methodology
- the theoretical underpinning of SJTs
- how SJTs can be used in selection processes
- considerations relevant to different SJT design elements
- the challenges to be addressed in further research and development.

What are SJTs?

Overview

SJTs are a measurement methodology designed to assess non-academic attributes relevant to a target role. Importantly, we emphasize that SJTs are best considered as a measurement method (instead of a single style of assessment) as the format and appearance of a specific test itself can vary significantly according to specific elements of SJT design (such as response instructions and approaches to scoring).

Typically, SJTs present candidates with hypothetical text or video-based scenarios describing a work-relevant situation. For each scenario, candidates are asked to indicate the effectiveness of corresponding response options from a predefined list of alternatives (see Fig. 4.1 for an example). Candidates' responses are scored using a predetermined scoring key advised by subject matter experts.

A single SJT is likely to comprise several scenarios so that a broad range of constructs can be measured efficiently. An SJT's content, format, and test length are designed to fit the role, the selection criteria, and specification requirements for the test (Lievens, Peeters, & Schollaert, 2008). SJTs have been used in assessment for over 50 years

Example SJT item for post-graduate medical education.	On the morning ward round, your registrar/specialty trainee said that Mrs. Anderson is medically fit following her knee replacement and could be discharged if Occupational Therapy feel it is appropriate. The occupational therapist has assessed Mrs. Anderson and believes it is safe for her to go home with a care package that has been arranged. It is now 4 p.m. and the nurse informs you that Mrs. Anderson is demanding to see a doctor, as she does not feel that she is ready to go home yet. An elective admission is waiting in the day room for Mrs. Anderson's bed. *Rank in order the appropriateness of the following actions in response to this situation (1 = Most Appropriate; 5 = Least Appropriate).* A. Ask Mrs. Anderson about her concerns. B. Ask a senior colleague to speak with Mrs. Anderson. C. Ask the bed manager if he can find another bed for the elective patient. D. Explain to Mrs. Anderson that the bed has already been allocated and she has to go home. E. Ask the occupational therapist to come and speak to Mrs. Anderson with you.
Example SJT item for selection into specialty training.	You are reviewing a routine drug chart for a patient with rheumatoid arthritis during an overnight shift. You notice that your consultant has inappropriately prescribed methotrexate 7.5mg daily instead of weekly. Rank in order the appropriateness of the following actions in response to this situation. A. Ask the nurses if the consultant has made any other drug errors recently. B. Correct the prescription to 7.5mg weekly. C. Leave the prescription unchanged until the consultant ward round the following morning. D. Phone the consultant at home to ask about changing the prescription. E. Inform the patient of the error.

Fig. 4.1 Two examples of SJT items used in healthcare selection settings, from Patterson, Zibarras, and Ashworth (2015)

across a broad range of occupational contexts in public and private sectors (Chan, Schmitt, Sacco, & DeShon, 1998; Ployhart, Weekley, Holtz, & Kemp, 2003), and more recently have been applied to roles in medicine and other healthcare professions—see Patterson, Knight, Dowell, et al. (2016) for a systematic review.

Theory Underpinning SJTs

SJTs are based on two key theoretical propositions. First, SJTs are derived from the *behavioral consistency* theory, where the central principle is that current behavior allows the prediction of future (i.e., in-role) behavior (Motowidlo, Hooper, & Jackson, 2006; Wernimot & Campbell, 2009).

Second, research literature presents a growing consensus that SJTs measure prosocial Implicit Trait Policies (ITPs), and depending on the job level, specific job knowledge, as in postgraduate selection (Motowidlo & Beier, 2010; Patterson, Prescott-Clements, et al. 2015). ITP theory proposes that individuals develop beliefs about the effectiveness of certain behaviors, relating to their inherent tendencies or traits, in different contexts. These beliefs guide behavior by evaluating the benefits of expressing these traits in a given situation (Golubovich et al., 2017).

Evidence suggests that SJTs are effective predictors of job performance because SJTs measure procedural understanding about effective behavior in a given situation (including domain-based knowledge where appropriate (Lievens & Patterson, 2011; Motowidlo et al., 2006). For example, individuals reporting higher levels of agreeableness (as measured by the NEO personality inventory) tended to respond favorably to SJT items measuring Agreeableness ($r=0.31$, $p<0.01$), indicating Agreeableness ITPs. Further, individuals with Agreeableness ITPs also demonstrated agreeable behaviors in a simulated work situation (Motowidlo et al., 2006).

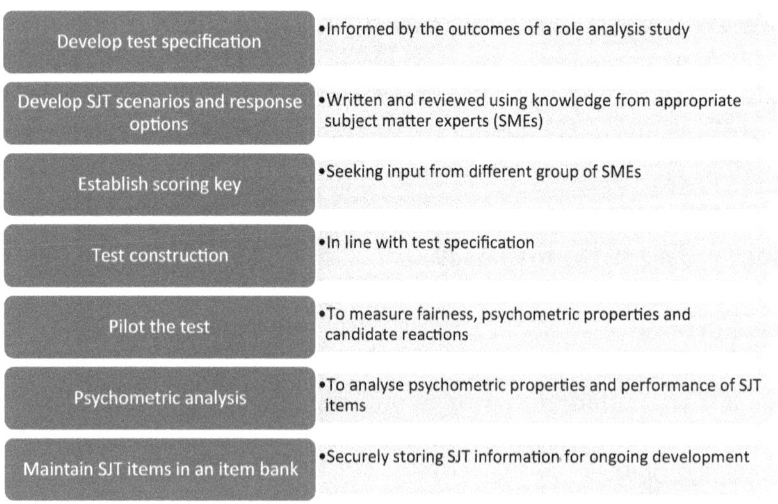

Fig. 4.2 Overview of SJT design

SJT Design Process

Designing a good-quality SJT requires thorough development and validation processes. The key steps to the design of an SJT are summarized in Fig. 4.2. For a detailed, step-by-step description of this recommended process, see Patterson, Aitkenhead, et al. (2015). Each step ensures an SJT is relevant to the specific role for which it has been developed, and optimizes the likelihood that an SJT is reliable, valid, and fair. An example of SJT design is detailed in Case Study 4.1.

Case study 4.1: Pre-registration Pharmacy SJT, Charlotte Flaxman and Vicki Ashworth, Work Psychology Group, UK

In England and Wales, pharmacy graduates who successfully complete their education and training must apply for a role as a Pre-registration Pharmacist, before they are eligible to work towards becoming a fully qualified pharmacist. Approximately 2500 candidates apply each year for Pre-registration Pharmacy roles, and it is a high-stakes environment. Until recently, there was no standardised procedure or methodology for selecting pre-registration candidates into these roles: pharmacies across England and Wales used various selection methods to select candidates.

A team of Organisational Psychologists from Work Psychology Group (www.workpsychologygroup.com) worked in collaboration with the client, a governing body for Pre-registration Pharmacist training, to design and deliver an SJT to be used in a national selection process. Following best practice, a test specification was agreed, including test length, level of difficulty (i.e. suitable for 4th year pharmacy students applying to pre-registration pharmacy roles) and format (i.e. ranking and multiple choice). The SJT aimed to measure four key attributes (multi-professional working and leadership, person-centred care, professional integrity and ethics and problem-solving, clinical analysis and decision-making), as defined in the professional attributes, framework for Pre-registration Pharmacists. (*The competency framework was designed using role analysis: for further detail on this role analysis work, please refer to* Chapter 6 *in this book.*)

Workshops were held with SMEs (including incumbent Pre-registration Pharmacists, trainers and supervisors) to write SJT items. Resulting items were reviewed by the consulting team and SMEs to ensure consistency in fairness, appropriateness and relevance. Before delivering the SJT live, items were piloted with incumbent pharmacy–students. Analyses of pilot responses identified items that could reliably differentiate between candidates' performance ranging from poor to excellent. Items that performed well were included in the final test.

Preliminary analyses showed the SJT to have favourable internal reliability ($\alpha > 0.70$), and no significant differences between candidate subgroups, indicating fairness to candidates. This SJT was first used in operational selection processes for Pre-registration Pharmacists in England and Wales in 2017.

Response Instructions and Format

Within high-stakes settings, such as medicine, response instructions for SJTs typically fall into one of two categories: knowledge-based (i.e., what is the best option) or behavioral tendency (i.e., what would you be most likely to do). Evidence from validity studies indicates that knowledge-based response instructions have a lower risk of susceptibility to coaching (Patterson, Knight, Dowell, et al., 2016).

As well as response instructions, a variety of response formats can be used. These include: *ranking* responses in order (i.e., from most to least appropriate), *rating* each response independently (i.e., in terms of appropriateness), *choosing the three best* responses from a larger number of options (multiple choice), or choosing the *best and/or worst* responses. Some researchers have developed a single-response SJT format, whereby only one response is selected (Martin & Motowidlo, 2010; Motowidlo, Crook, Kell, & Naemi, 2009). See Fig. 4.3 for examples of response formats.

How Reliable, Valid, and Fair are SJTs? Evidence from Research in Healthcare

Reliability

There are several ways to ensure that an SJT is reliably measuring constructs in a consistent way. These include *internal consistency*, which assesses whether items measuring the same construct produce similar

Choose three format	Ranking response format	Best single response format
You review a patient on the surgical ward who has had an appendicectomy performed earlier in the day. You write a prescription for strong painkillers. The staff nurse challenges your decision and refuses to give the medication to the patient. *Choose the THREE most appropriate actions to take in this situation.* A. Instruct the nurse to give the medication to the patient. B. Discuss with the nurse why she disagrees with the prescription. C. Ask a senior colleague for advice. D. Complete a clinical incident form. E. Cancel the prescription on the nurse's advice. F. Arrange to speak to the nurse later to discuss your working relationship. G. Write in the medical notes that the nurse has declined to give the medication. H. Review the case again.	You are looking after Mr. Kucera who has previously been treated for prostate cancer. Preliminary investigations are strongly suggestive of a recurrence. As you finish taking blood from a neighboring patient, Mr. Kucera leans across and says, 'Tell me honestly, is my cancer back?' *Rank in order of appropriateness the following actions in response to this situation.* A. Explain to Mr. Kucera that it is likely that his cancer has come back. B. Reassure Mr. Kucera that he will be fine. C. Explain to Mr. Kucera that you do not have all the test results, but you will speak to him as soon as you do. D. Inform Mr. Kucera that you will chase up the results of his tests and ask one of your senior colleagues to discuss them with him. E. Invite Mr. Kucera to join you and a senior nurse in a quiet room, get a colleague to hold your 'bleep' then explore his fears.	Patient: So, this physiotherapy is really going to help me? Physician: Absolutely, even though in the first days it might still be painful. Patient: Yes, I suppose it will take a while to start working. Physician: That is why I am going to prescribe a painkiller. You should take 3 painkillers per day. Patient: Do I really have to take them? I have already tried a few things. First, they don't help me. And second, I'm actually opposed to taking any medication. I'd rather not take them. They are not good for my health. *What is the best way for you (as a Physician) to react to this patient's refusal to take the prescribed medication?* A. Ask her if she knows something else to relieve the pain. B. Give her the scientific evidence why the painkillers will help. C. Agree not to take them now but stress the importance of the physiotherapy. D. Tell her that, in her own interests, she will have to change her attitude.

Fig. 4.3 Example SJT items in different response formats. Adapted from Patterson, Ashworth, Zibarras, et al. (2012)

score patterns; *test–retest reliability*, which indicates whether a measure is stable over a given time period; and *parallel forms reliability*: two versions of the same test should correlate sufficiently (Rust & Golombok, 1999).

Traditional SJTs have been described as a construct heterogeneous at the item level (McDaniel & Whetzel, 2007; Whetzel & McDaniel,

2009) since they rarely measure one single dimension, which implies an inherent difficulty in accurately estimating internal consistency, and risks underestimating their reliability (Catano, Brochu, & Lamerson, 2012; McDaniel & Whetzel, 2007; Whetzel & McDaniel, 2009). Early results from a meta-analysis of 39 different studies found Cronbach's alpha coefficients ranging from $\alpha = 0.43$ to 0.94 (McDaniel, Morgeson, Finnegan, & Campion, 2001). Construct-driven SJTs designed to measure a specific construct (i.e., unidimensionality) is likely to produce more favorable reliability (Lievens, 2017).

As SJT research has developed, in line with the view that SJTs measure a core situational judgement construct, internal consistency of SJTs used in medical and dental contexts (Koczwara et al., 2012; Patterson, Aitkenhead, et al., 2015; Patterson, Ashworth, Mehra, & Falcon, 2012) have been found to consistently approach or exceed $\alpha = 0.70$, the accepted value indicating good internal consistency (Kline, 2000). SJTs have also shown good levels of internal consistency for selection into radiology ($\alpha = 0.84$; (Patterson, Knight, Mcknight, & Booth, 2016) and Pre-registration Pharmacy ($\alpha < 0.70$, see Case Study 4.1), and for measuring resilience in palliative care workers (Pangallo, Zibarras, & Patterson, 2016). A recent systematic review of 25 studies found strong support for SJTs reliably assessing non-academic attributes in healthcare (Patterson, Knight, Dowell, et al., 2016).

Some researchers argue that test–retest or parallel forms reliability may be a more accurate approach to examining the reliability of an SJT since internal consistency is more appropriate for unidimensional (construct homogenous) tests (Catano et al., 2012; Lievens et al., 2008; McDaniel & Nguyen, 2001). Research shows a range of values for test–retest reliability of SJTs, from $r = 0.20$ to $r = 0.92$ (Pangallo et al., 2016; Ployhart & Ehrhart, 2003; Ployhart et al., 2003), dependent upon the quality of test construction, and good levels of parallel forms reliability, for example: $r = 0.76$ (Chan & Schmitt, 2002) and $r = 0.66$ (Lievens, Buyse, & Sackett, 2005).

In summary, the research shows that well-designed SJTs have moderate-to-good levels of reliability. Since SJTs are a measurement method and there is no one single type of SJT, it is important to evaluate each test independently to judge reliability.

Validity: How Well do SJTs Measure the Constructs they are Intended to Measure?

As with other assessment tools, there are multiple approaches to evaluate the validity of an SJT. Best-practice guidance recommends measuring criterion-related validity (i.e., evaluating the extent to which scores on an SJT predict subsequent performance in the target role); incremental validity (i.e., does the SJT predict variance in outcome criteria beyond other tools); and construct validity (i.e., the extent to which a tool is measuring what it is designed to measure, Patterson, Zibarras, et al., 2015).

Criterion-Related Validity

When assessing criterion-related validity for any selection method it is important to consider what the method is intended to measure, and for both predictors and criterion (outcome) measures when assessing relationships between the two (Lievens et al., 2005). Additionally, whereas measures of academic performance target *maximal* performance, SJTs can be designed to target *typical* performance; so, criterion measures that reflect this (e.g., in-role measures of performance) are useful (Cousans, Patterson, Edwards, McLaughlan, & Good, 2017; Patterson, Knight, Dowell, et al., 2016; Whetzel & Reeder, 2016).

We would expect SJTs to predict performance on criterion-matched outcomes, such as interpersonal skills courses, educational supervisor ratings of empathy and integrity or communication stations in an Objective Structured Clinical Examination (OSCE).

Indeed, Cousans et al. (2017) found that the SJT used for selection into the UK Foundation Programme predicted supervisor ratings of performance in physicians' first role in clinical practice to a greater extent than did academic performance (Cousans et al., 2017). Similarly, Oswald, Schmitt, Kim, Ramsay, and Gillespie (2004) found that an SJT predicted performance for leadership and perseverance, but not grade point average, and Libbrecht, Lievens, and Carette (2014) found that an SJT measuring emotional intelligence predicted performance in courses on communication and interpersonal sensitivity in medical school, beyond cognitive ability and Conscientiousness.

Meta-analytic studies show favorable criterion-related validity for SJTs compared to other selection methods: Christian, Edwards, and Bradley (2010) found corrected operational validity coefficients of $r = 0.25–0.47$, and McDaniel et al. (2001) estimated a criterion-related validity of $r = 0.34$. SJTs have also demonstrated comparable or increased predictive validity over academic performance (Cousans et al., 2017), structured interviews (McDaniel, Whetzel, Schmidt, & Maurer, 1994), selection centers (Gaugler, Rosenthal, Thornton, & Bentson, 1987) and cognitive ability tests (Buyse & Lievens, 2011; Clevenger, Pereira, Wiechmann, Schmitt, & Harvey, 2001; Corstjens, Lievens, & Krumm, 2017). For a summary of recent research investigating the comparative benefits of SJTs for predicting future performance, see Patterson, Knight, Dowell, et al. (2016).

Regarding medical education specifically, one study showed an SJT used in selection for postgraduate training in the UK predicted subsequent in-training performance and end-of-training competence after three years, with large effect sizes (Patterson, Lievens, Kerrin, Munro, & Irish, 2013). Longer term studies also show that the SJT predicts performance in training in relation to educational supervisors' ratings (Lievens & Patterson, 2011) and performance in clinical skills licensing OSCEs (Patterson, Lievens, Kerrin, Zibarras, & Carette, 2012). Positive results are also found in Belgium: three longitudinal, multiple cohort studies in Belgium found that an SJT used within medical school admissions predicted several assessments at different points throughout training, in addition to job performance in all three studies: $r = 0.27$ (Buyse & Lievens, 2011), $r = 0.22$ (Lievens & Sackett, 2012) and $r = 0.15$ (Lievens, 2013).

In summary, SJTs have been found to have good levels of predictive validity across healthcare education and training. Methodologically, it is important to ensure that appropriate outcome criteria and measures are identified in order to meaningfully assess the validity of SJTs.

Incremental Validity

It is important to establish whether an SJT has predictive validity over and above other selection methods, such as cognitive ability, personality and job knowledge tests, to assess the value added using an SJT in a selection system. Incremental validity can support the cost-effectiveness and efficiency of SJTs, and their theoretical rationale.

Incremental validity of SJTs has been widely demonstrated in the literature across numerous populations, including healthcare. For example, in sales, an SJT was found to predict sales success, above and beyond logical reasoning and personality (Stemler, Aggarwal, & Nithyanand, 2016). Within healthcare, in a study looking at the predictive validity of core medical training (CMT) selection methods on trainees' performance on their exams for Membership of Royal College of Physicians (MRCP(UK)), SJTs explained variance in performance over and above other selection methods (Patterson et al., 2017).

In the context of medicine specifically, Lievens et al. (2005) found that an SJT assessing interpersonal awareness for entry into medical schools in Belgium had incremental validity over the cognitive measures for components of the curricula that had an interpersonal skills component. Patterson, Baron, Carr, Plint, and Lane (2009) showed that an SJT used for selection in postgraduate general practice training had substantial incremental validity over scores from an application form (17%) and a job-knowledge test (14%). Similar findings have been demonstrated for an SJT into CMT in the UK (Patterson, Carr, et al., 2009; Patterson, Ashworth, Zibarras, et al. 2012). SJTs have also demonstrated incremental validity over and above multiple mini-interviews (MMIs) for postgraduate GP training in Australia (Patterson, Rowett, et al., 2016).

In summary, evidence in healthcare and beyond indicates that SJTs provide added value over other selection methods for predicting job performance. That said, not all SJTs demonstrate good predictive validity and therefore we recommend that each is judged in their own right.

Considerations in Assessing the Predictive Validity of SJTs

Research suggests that the predictive validity of measures of non-academic attributes tends to be lower early in the curriculum and higher when students enter clinical practice. We propose that this is because during the classroom-based, didactic learning environment of the early years of a medical degree, the focus is more on cognitive indicators and academic attainment. However, as students move into clinical practice and beyond, the necessity for interpersonal skills comes to the fore because the team-based working and patient contact are key indicators of competence (Ferguson et al., 2014). This is highlighted by the findings in Case Study 4.2, where performance on the UKCAT SJT predicted tutors' ratings of performance at a later point.

This proposition is supported by other researchers (Lievens et al., 2008; McDaniel & Whetzel, 2007) and reiterates the importance of choosing both appropriate outcome criteria and collecting outcome data at the appropriate time. For example, longitudinal research has demonstrated that in trainee physicians, performance on an SJT at selection was predictive of performance on licensing exams ($r=0.37$–0.40, Patterson et al., 2017). Another longitudinal study also supported SJTs' predictive validity for postgraduate training for GPs in Australia (Patterson, Rowett, et al., 2016). Similarly, in a recent study of applicants to the UK Foundation Programme, applicants' SJT scores were correlated with in-role supervisor ratings of performance; additionally, those with low SJT scores were significantly more likely to receive remedial action (Cousans et al., 2017). SJTs also demonstrate predictive validity in other healthcare disciplines, for example, performance on SJTs are reported to significantly predict dental school performance in the UK and Belgium (Buyse & Lievens, 2011; Patterson et al., 2017), and has been correlated with the Medical Qualifying Examination in Canada (Dore, Reiter, Kreuger, & Norman, 2017a, b). Besides performance, Pangallo et al. (2016) found that scores on an SJT measuring resilience predicted sickness absence in palliative care workers.

Emerging evidence from the medical education literature in the UK indicates that SJTs may have greater predictive validity at the lower end the performance distribution. For medical trainees in their first year working in clinical practice, lower scores on the SJT correlated more strongly with in-role performance than for those who had scored highly on the SJT (i.e., low, $r=0.33$ compared to high, $r=0.11$) (Cousans et al., 2017). In addition, applicants lacking prosocial ITPs are less likely to perform well on an SJT. Further research both internally and in broader healthcare contexts is required to replicate and extend these findings.

In summary, it is important to take into consideration the point in a healthcare education or training pathway that outcome data is collected, to accurately assess the validity of an SJT. Emerging evidence suggests that SJTs may be best used to 'select out' candidates as they are potentially better predictors at the lower end of the distribution of scores; however, evidence for this is still in its infancy.

Case Study 4.2: UKCAT: Using SJTs to Widen Access to Medical Schools in the UK and Predict Performance (Lievens, Patterson, Corstjens, Martin, & Nicholson, 2016)

Over 25,000 candidates apply for entry into medical and dental schools in the UK annually. Until recently, selection into medical education and training in the United Kingdom focused on academic attainment (Cleland, Nicholson, Kelly, & Moffat, 2015). However, research shows that doctors also require important non-academic attributes (e.g., integrity and compassion) to deliver good quality patient care (e.g. Powis, 2014). High-stakes selection into medicine is now aiming to assess attributes in prospective medical students (Lievens et al., 2016). Additionally, to widen access to medical professions and increase cultural competence, it is crucial selection methods do not disadvantage candidates from diverse subgroups i.e. females, ethnic minorities, and low socio-economic status candidates.

To create a reliable, valid and fair way of assessing candidates likely to succeed, a role analysis was undertaken to clarify the attributes essential to effective performance as a medical student. Using the resultant attribute framework and following best practice, an SJT was designed in collaboration to measure key competency domains: integrity, perspective taking, and team involvement (Lievens et al., 2016). For full details on the development process, see Lievens et al. (2016).

Since its first operational use in the selection process in 2013, the UKCAT SJT has been used to successfully sift candidates applying for medical schools in the UK. Candidates' performance on the SJT is predictive of performance later as rated by their tutors (corrected $r=0.34$, Lievens et al., 2016). Additionally, the SJT has shown favourable reliability ($a=0.75$–0.79), candidate reactions, and minimal differences between candidate subgroups (i.e., between gender, ethnicity, or socio-economic-status groups). For example, socio-economic status had a lower effect on performance for the SJT compared to scores on the UKCAT cognitive test.

This has had significant impact nationally by enabling universities to sift applicants who lack the requisite non-academic skills to deliver quality healthcare, in a way that is reliable, validated, cost-efficient, favourable and supportive of social mobility.

Construct Validity

As SJTs represent a methodology rather than a specific test, scenarios and responses can be designed to assess a range of different attributes or constructs. Consequently, a candidate's response may represent a combination of their ability, personality, and experience (Lievens & Motowidlo, 2016; Lievens et al., 2008). There is ongoing debate regarding construct validity.

Traditional SJTs designed using specific role-relevant content and based on real scenarios can therefore be heterogeneous in nature, measuring a range of behavioral constructs. On the other hand, construct-driven SJTs are designed to measure specific constructs, whereby response options all relate to a specific construct (e.g., Agreeableness), and vary in the degree to which it is reflected (Guenole, Chernyshenko, & Weekly, 2017; Lievens, 2017).

McDaniel et al.'s (2001) review shows that SJTs generally correlate with *cognitive ability*, although the magnitude of the relationship depended on several factors: SJTs based on a job analysis correlated more highly with cognitive ability ($r=0.50$) than those that were not ($r=0.38$), and SJTs which contained more detailed questions were more highly correlated with cognitive ability ($r=0.56$) than those less detailed ($r=0.47$). As might be expected, SJTs that are cognitively oriented (such as those involving planning, organizing, and problem-solving) tend to correlate higher with cognitive ability than those focused on interpersonal issues such as empathy. In postgraduate medical selection, Koczwara et al. (2012) found that an SJT correlated significantly with cognitive ability tests, suggesting that they measure overlapping constructs. Recent research also found correlations between cognitive ability tests performance and performance on an SJT requiring cognitive ability (Golubovich et al., 2017). Other research found no correlation between SJT performance and cognitive ability (Clevenger et al., 2001; Escudier, Flaxman, Cousans, Woolford, & Patterson, 2015). Golubovich and colleagues (2017) concluded that SJTs correlate with cognitive ability to the extent that the SJT contains cognitive demand in reading, understanding, and integrating several pieces of information. As such, the evidence indicates that the extent to which SJTs measures cognitive ability varies, depending on the specific design of each individual SJT.

In relation to *personality*, research on traditional SJTs has found mixed associations between various personality traits and SJT performance. For example, a meta-analysis found that SJT scores had a corrected correlation of $r=0.25$ with Agreeableness; $r=0.31$ with Emotional Stability, $r=0.26$ with Conscientiousness, $r=0.06$ with Extraversion and $r=0.09$ with Openness (McDaniel & Nguyen, 2001). McDaniel, Hartman, Whetzel, & Grubb (2007) found similar results, indicating that SJTs correlate most highly with Agreeableness and Conscientiousness, i.e., cooperation, forgiveness and a tendency to defer to others in interpersonal conflict; and achievement striving, leadership skills and organization, respectively (McCrae & Costa, 2008). Recent studies have found an SJT measuring behavioral perception correlated with Openness, but no other traits (Golubovich et al., 2017), and an SJT designed to assess the five-factor personality traits (Openness, Agreeableness, Conscientiousness, Extraversion, and Neuroticism) correlated with the NEO measure of personality traits across all five factors (Mussel et al., 2016).

These varied associations between SJT scores and personality may be due to the relationship between personality and ITPs (described earlier; see Motowidlo & Beier, 2010). This can be explained by the notion of *dispositional* fit; that is, some individuals' dispositions (i.e., their personalities) are more appropriate for handling challenging social situations than others'. Dispositional fit specifies that people develop beliefs consistent with their personality traits about how best to handle difficult situations. Situations encountered in any given role are believed to vary in the extent to which they require behavioral responses that are expressive of a given trait. When individuals' beliefs about the appropriate behavioral responses to a situation correspond to the type of response actually required by the situation, those individuals possess greater knowledge because their beliefs are correct (Graziano, Jensen-campbell, & Hair, 1996). For example, individuals high on Agreeableness may have a greater level of knowledge on the effectiveness of Agreeableness compared to individuals lower on Agreeableness. An SJT relating to Agreeableness will therefore likely differentiate between candidates who have differing levels/ITPs for Agreeableness, with those higher on that trait more likely to discriminate accurately between SJT response options, according to the level of Agreeableness expressed by each response option; thereby achieving higher scores on an SJT (Lievens & Motowidlo, 2016).

The literature has not yet converged on the association between SJTs and *role knowledge*. Some research has suggested that SJTs may measure role-specific procedural knowledge (Schmidt, 1994), while others suggest that since experience is multifaceted, different operationalizations of experience will result in different relationships between experience in a role and performance on an SJT. Motowidlo and Beier (2010) posit that the type of experience that leads to the development of ITPs (i.e., general experience) is different from the type of experience that allows individuals to develop specific knowledge about a particular role. More recently Lievens and Motowidlo (2016) conceptualize SJTs as a form of general domain knowledge. They argue that the ITPs and specific role knowledge combine to produce the procedural knowledge measured by an SJT, but they have independent effects on role performance. Moreover, some SJTs are more strongly related to general experience (ITPs) than to highly role-specific experience. This implies that SJT design may need to differ for undergraduate selection (where applicants have no specific job knowledge or experience) versus postgraduate selection (some specific job knowledge and experience). In fact, more recently, research has considered construct-driven SJTs, designed to assess one trait by measuring responses across different levels of the trait in question. This may allow for more direct or pure measurement of the intended attributes, that is, besides role knowledge (Lievens, 2017).

In summary, since SJTs can be designed to assess a range of different attributes, research regarding their construct validity has been mixed. Research identifies that SJTs can correlate with cognitive ability, personality, and knowledge, depending on the specification and design of the SJT.

Fairness

Fairness issues in selection represent a challenge globally, and it is becoming an increasingly important consideration (Patterson, Knight, Dowell, et al., 2016). Medical education and training providers are tasked with identifying selection methods that select individuals with the required attributes and abilities, and also admit a diverse pool of individuals into healthcare education and training positions, to ensure that the healthcare workforce is representative of society (British Medical Association, 2009; Cleland et al., 2015; Patterson, Ashworth, Mehra, et al., 2012). For an in-depth discussion of these issues see the Chapter 10 on diversity issues in this book (Cleland, Alexander, & Nicholson).

Research allows only tentative conclusions to be drawn about different selection methods regarding their impact on widening participation (Lievens et al., 2016; O'Neill, Vonsild, Wallstedt, & Dornan, 2013); however, emerging evidence suggests that SJTs may not follow socioeconomic trends often observed in some aptitude test scores and measures of prior academic attainment (Wakeford, Denney, Ludka-Stempien, Dacre, & McManus, 2015; Whetzel, McDaniel, & Nguyen, 2008; Woolf, Potts, & McManus, 2011), where White candidates from the higher socioeconomic classes tend to outperform Black and minority ethnic (BME) candidates and those from lower socioeconomic backgrounds, and males outperform females.

A meta-analysis by Whetzel et al. (2008) reported that White test takers did marginally better than other ethnic groups on the SJT, with a small effect size. Regarding gender, research generally suggests that females score marginally higher on SJTs than males (Lievens, 2013; Luschin-Ebengreuth, Dimai, Ithaler, Neges, & Reibnegger, 2015; O'Connell, Hartman, McDaniel, Grubb, & Lawrence, 2007; Whetzel et al., 2008), consistent with other forms of non-academic assessment (e.g., oral communication in a selection center, Anderson, Lievens, van Dam, & Born, 2006). In addition, Lievens et al. (2016) found that in comparing the performance of applicants undertaking the UKCAT medical school entry assessment, smaller subgroup differences were found for the SJT compared to the cognitive ability tests. In summary, research suggests that SJTs have less adverse impact regarding ethnicity and gender compared to other selection tools (see also Chapter 2 on Aptitude Tests).

Candidate Perceptions

When SJT scenarios are highly contextualized, the face validity of SJTs is higher, and therefore, SJTs are generally perceived positively by candidates. Studies assessing candidate perceptions have shown that SJTs tend to receive more positive candidate reactions than several other selection methods (i.e., cognitive ability tests, Koczwara et al., 2012; Luschin-Ebengreuth et al., 2015), although less so when compared to interviews. SJTs have two key advantages that contribute to positive reactions compared to ability tests: first, candidates usually prefer assessments perceived as job-relevant (i.e., face validity, see, for example, Lievens et al., 2008). A greater focus on the constructs being measured rather than the scenarios/contexts in SJTs may produce less favorable candidate reactions, due to the perceived loss of job relevance (Chen, Fan, Zheng, & Hack, 2016); on the whole, candidates tend to prefer high-fidelity SJTs (Lievens et al., 2008). Please refer to Chapter 8 for further exploration of the issues surrounding candidate reactions in selection.

Considerations for Application in High-Stakes Healthcare Selection

Technology Considerations

SJTs have traditionally been conducted in a written format, requiring candidates to read text-based scenarios and response options. However, like in many areas of selection, there is a growing interest in how technology can improve aspects of the process. Further, in today's increasingly mobile world, technological advancements can improve accessibility of SJTs for candidates. Advancements in SJTs using technology have involved delivering traditional tests using a computer screen, or using audio- or video-based scenarios (Dore et al., 2017a, b; Golubovich et al., 2017). Additionally, interest and use of technologies such as video conferencing, game-based assessment and Virtual Reality (VR) is increasing. Such technologies may be used to improve the presentation of scenarios to candidates or measure candidates' responses to scenarios. For example, research with police candidates in the Netherlands has demonstrated that video conferencing can be used to measure responses to scenarios (Lievens, De Corte, & Westerveld, 2015).

Using these technologies may allow richer, detailed, and more realistic scenarios to be presented, which is associated with more favorable candidate perceptions and greater face validity (Chan & Schmitt, 1997; Kanning, Grewe, Hollenberg, & Hadouch, 2006; Lievens et al., 2008). It may also have positive implications for widening access, for example lowering cognitive demand by reducing the reading required in each scenario (Chan & Schmidt, 1997; Weekley & Jones, 1999; Whetzel & McDaniel, 2009). However, given that Golubovich et al. (2017) found their video-based SJT correlated with performance on a cognitive ability test, video formats may still induce cognitive demand, so again each SJT needs to be evaluated in its own right.

Text-based SJTs are still more frequently used than high-fidelity formats such as video (Campion, Ployhart, & MacKenzie, 2014), which may be due to the greater costs in development (Whetzel & McDaniel, 2009) and limited evidence concerning added validity and reliability. Research to date is mixed: some report SJTs that utilize technology have greater validity than written SJTs to measure interpersonal qualities (Christian et al., 2010; Patterson, Knight, Mcknight, et al., 2016; Whetzel & Reeder, 2016), while others report lower validity and reliability when measuring cognitive ability (Campion et al., 2014; Kasten & Freund, 2016; Whetzel & Reeder, 2016). The potential practical applications of digitally delivered SJTs are plenty, but it is important that psychometric properties, such as reliability and validity, and group differences in performance (e.g., via differing cognitive loads), are considered carefully.

Coaching Effects

Overall, the research on coaching effects and impacts relating to SJTs is mixed. Some studies suggest that coaching significantly improves performance: Stemig, Sackett, and Lievens (2015) found that medical school applicants unsuccessful on their first attempt who undertook commercial coaching, significantly improved their performance on the SJT at their second attempt (by 0.5 standard deviations). However, the SJT in this study employed a 'single best answer' format and covered two competency domains (relationship building and communicating information); these features would increase susceptibility to coaching. Therefore, it may be advisable to use more cognitively loaded formats if the risk of coaching effects is substantial. Other research shows that coaching has no impact on the operational validity of SJTs used in healthcare selection (Simon, Walsh, Paterson-Brown, & Cahill, 2015; Stemig et al., 2015).

It is important to highlight the distinction between coaching candidates to simply 'pass the test' and learn test-taking strategies versus coaching to actually learn or develop the skills measured. For example, coaching candidates on test-taking strategies tends to focus on the short-term aim of passing the test and does not address the development of knowledge about effective behaviors in the context of the target role the SJT refers to. Conversely, training for skill development in domains such as communication or teamwork would be expected to improve a candidate's understanding of the effectiveness of those skills in the longer term, and in fact SJT performance *should* improve in line with an improvement in skills (Patterson, Ashworth, Kerrin, & O'Neill, 2013).

The issues and challenges around coaching for selection assessments are explored in more detail in Chapter 11.

Cross-Cultural Applications

Increasing globalization has resulted in an increased need for selection processes to be used cross-culturally. While there is evidence that SJTs can be developed and effectively used in various countries and cultures (Banki & Latham, 2010; Lievens, Corstjens, et al., 2015; Stemler et al., 2016), despite a call for research looking into the cross-cultural generalizability of SJTs over a decade ago (Ployhart & Weekley, 2006), research looking at whether developed SJTs can be transported and used in other countries/cultures remains limited. As SJTs are highly contextualized, they may be more prone to cultural differences than other assessment methods. Issues such as use of colloquial language, differences in the suitability of responses, and an adverse impact on validity due to items and responses having different associations with constructs are all proposed as possible barriers to cross-cultural transferability (Lievens, Corstjens, et al., 2015). Recent research has revealed that an SJT developed in the USA could be successfully applied in a Spanish context: most scenarios were considered realistic, and most of the responses converged on the original scoring keys (Lievens, Corstjens, et al., 2015). This finding is positive; however, caution is advised in assuming transferability of SJTs across cultural contexts, as it is important to note that the USA and Spain are both Western, Individualistic cultures. It would be useful for future research to build on this by investigating SJT transferability across Western/Eastern cultures and Individualistic/Collectivist cultures.

Summary and Future Directions for Research and Practice

In overview, SJTs represent a measurement methodology, rather than a specific measure per se. Given that each SJT may be constructed differently, they have the potential to vary significantly in terms of their robustness, reliability and validity. Therefore, good-quality SJTs require expertise to design and develop them appropriately. SJTs can be resource-intensive to design in the short term but can be efficient to screen large numbers of applicants as they can be computer-delivered and scored.

On balance, substantial evidence from research indicates well-designed SJTs offer a reliable, valid, and fair method that is likely to be perceived positively by candidates and that selects candidates who are likely to perform well in the target role. Further, SJTs can be cost-effective and scalable (i.e., through online delivery and machine marking), enabling efficient delivery across large numbers of candidates.

With the view to improving the functionality and versatility of the SJT as a method, there are several avenues of research that would be valuable to develop.

Understanding Group Differences

The evidence from research suggests that well-designed SJTs can create smaller subgroup differences compared to traditional selection methods such as cognitive ability tests. Although a growing body of research has focused on unpicking group differences in SJT performance, more research in this area is needed.

Technology

There is limited research investigating the various benefits and disadvantages of technological applications such as video and audio modes of delivery. Further research could systematically compare video-based and text-based SJTs to more adequately elucidate the advantages and disadvantages of each approach. Table 4.1 summarizes some of the latest thinking on different delivery formats.

Use for Education and Training and Development Purposes

Future areas of enquiry may include the use of SJTs as a diagnostic tool to identify individuals' training needs. This has the potential to be supplemented by education interventions to provide training in the non-academic skills required for the target role, and so accelerate time to competence in preparation for entry into clinical practice. Although

Table 4.1 Descriptions of various SJT formats

Modality	Description	Strengths	Limitations
Written with audio	Written SJTs supported by audio files	This approach might help reduce group differences that relate to reading levels and is more engaging than text-based	Unclear whether it would add substantial value over and above text-based
Written with 'flat' imagery	Use appropriate scenario-related images to support the scenario	Candidates find this more engaging than text only and the face validity is thus increased Some text could be removed (i.e., won't need to say the patient has a broken arm)	In this instance, the initial investment is higher than text-based. Identifying the appropriate image in some instances may be challenging
Written with 'moving' imagery	As 'flat' imagery but the design goes a step further. For example, a depiction of a telephone as a 'flat' image, for the 'moving' image the telephone may be being picked up	Potentially more engaging to candidates	Unclear if there would be any benefit to the validity. Likely to be more costly than flat
Animated SJTs	Rather than having actors play out the scenario, a cartoon version of the scenario is created. Dialogue would be heard (and could be displayed also)	This is likely to be superior to images, as it provides a more realistic and engaging alternative	For professional animation, the cost is likely to be high

(continued)

Table 4.1 (continued)

Modality	Description	Strengths	Limitations
Video	Video-based SJTs operate in the same way as the text-based SJTs but rather than presenting the candidate with a paragraph of text to read, they are provided with a video where the written scenario is acted out on screen. Candidates are still required to respond to a series of statements about the scenario	Very engaging. Likely to have the highest face validity, particularly in a high-stakes context Although potentially longer to watch, can easily contain information that would need to be explicit in written format (e.g., who is there, their emotions/expressions) Likely to have less redundancy than written due to reduced ambiguity in content	Expensive to make; can date quickly. Videos could introduce extraneous, potentially unhelpful information which might reduce reliability
Avatar	Use computer-animated instead of video	Likely to be regarded as innovative with high face validity. In the long term, they are easier to update than videos, as avatar clothing could be changed for example	Initial investment likely higher than video

more traditionally used in selection contexts, extending the application of SJTs to training and development may provide a beneficial resource in monitoring and training relevant non academic attributes as individuals progress through a given role or training program. For example, Pangallo et al. (2016) successfully used an SJT to assess resilience in palliative care workers and significantly influenced prediction of important work-related well-being factors such as turnover intention and psychological well-being (Pangallo et al., 2016). The current authors are also applying this methodology in development programs for medical students in the UK, using SJT scenarios and responses to facilitate learning sessions focused on specific constructs such as resilience and human factors (i.e., self-awareness, decision making, and conflict management).

Further longitudinal research studies are required to evaluate the extent to which SJTs effectively predict performance throughout the medical education pathway, from medical school admissions through to independent clinical practice, and beyond. This is especially relevant, given the emerging evidence that SJTs have different predictive validity at different stages during medical education, training, and practice. More research is also required to confirm initial findings that SJTs are more predictive of performance at the lower end of score distributions than at the top end (i.e., by identifying individuals who lack the appropriate values and attributes to be suited to a career in healthcare).

Conclusion

In conclusion, as SJTs continue to be increasingly developed and used in healthcare selection, and delivered by a growing variety of mediums, research must strive to clarify important questions raised. While the evidence to date suggests SJTs can be effective methods by which to select students into healthcare education, continued developments in research (particularly longitudinal) will further unpick the mechanisms involved so that selection methods can be designed in accordance with best practice design principles, to reliably measure the target attributes/constructs in a way that delivers robust predictions of future performance.

Practice Points

- SJTs are a measurement methodology (rather than a single test).
- SJTs provide a reliable method for measuring non-academic attributes (e.g., empathy, integrity, and teamwork) that are important for education, training, and practice in healthcare roles.
- SJTs measure prosocial Implicit Trait Policies (ITPs)—beliefs about the cost or benefits of certain behaviors (e.g., showing compassion) in a given situation.
- When designed appropriately, SJTs are generally reliable, valid, fair, and positively received by candidates.
- Good-quality SJTs can be expensive to design, but once developed, are a cost-effective selection tool, as they can be delivered and marked electronically.

Explore Further

- For a practical guide of the design and development of SJTs: F. Patterson, L. Zibarras, and V. Ashworth (2015). Situational judgement tests in medical education and training: Research, theory and practice: AMEE Guide No. 100. *Medical Teacher*, *0*(0), 1–15. https://doi.org/10.3109/0142159X.2015.1072619
- For the latest in research on SJT development and use in healthcare education: https://www.smu.edu.sg/faculty/profile/153991/LIEVENS,-Filip—Filip Lievens research on SJTs, or https://www.researchgate.net/profile/Fiona_Patterson for Professor Fiona Patterson's latest research on SJTs and other selection methods for high-stakes healthcare.

References

Anderson, N., Lievens, F., van Dam, K., & Born, M. (2006). A construct-driven investigation of gender differences in a leadership-role assessment center. *Journal of Applied Psychology, 91*(3), 555–566. https://doi.org/10.1037/0021-9010.91.3.555.

Banki, S., & Latham, G. P. (2010). The criterion-related validities and perceived fairness of the situational interview and the situational judgment test in an Iranian organization. *Applied Psychology: An International Review, 59*(1), 124–142.

British Medical Association. (2009). *Equality and diversity in UK medical schools*. London: BMA.

Buyse, T., & Lievens, F. (2011). Situational judgment tests as a new tool for dental student selection. *Journal of Dental Education, 75*(6), 743–749.

Campion, M. C., Ployhart, R. E., & MacKenzie, W. I., Jr. (2014). The state of research on situational judgment tests: A content analysis and directions for future research. *Human Performance, 27*(4), 283–310.

Catano, V., Brochu, A., & Lamerson, C. (2012). Assessing the reliability of situational judgment tests used in high-stakes situations. *International Journal of Selection and Assessment, 20*(3), 333–346.

Chan, D., & Schmitt, N. (1997). Video-based versus paper-and-pencil method of assessment in situational judgment tests: Subgroup differences in test performance and face validity perceptions. *Journal of Applied Psychology, 82*(1), 143–159.

Chan, D., & Schmitt, N. (2002). Situational judgment and job performance. *Human Performance, 15*(3), 233–254.

Chan, D., Schmitt, N., Sacco, J. M., & DeShon, R. P. (1998). Understanding pretest and posttest reactions to cognitive ability and personality tests. *Journal of Applied Psychology, 83*(3), 471–485.

Chen, L., Fan, J., Zheng, L., & Hack, E. (2016). Clearly defined constructs and specific situations are the currency of SJTs. *Industrial and Organizational Psychology, 9*(1), 34–38.

Christian, M. S., Edwards, B. D., & Bradley, J. C. (2010). Situational judgment tests: Constructs assessed and a meta-analysis of their criterion-related validities. *Personnel Psychology, 63*, 83–117. https://doi.org/10.1111/j.1744-6570.2009.01163.x.

Cleland, J. A., Nicholson, S., Kelly, N., & Moffat, M. (2015). Taking context seriously: Explaining widening accesspolicy enactments in UK medical

schools. *Medical Education*, 25–35. Retrieved from http://www.gmc-uk.org/Identifying_best_practice_in_the_selection_of_medical_students.pdf_51119804.pdf.
Clevenger, J., Pereira, G. M., Wiechmann, D., Schmitt, N., & Harvey, V. S. (2001). Incremental validation of situational judgment tests. *The Journal of Applied Psychology, 86*(3), 410–417. https://doi.org/10.1037/0021-9010.86.3.410.
Corstjens, J., Lievens, F., & Krumm, S. (2017). Situational judgement tests for selection. In *The Wiley Blackwell handbook of the psychology of recruitment, selection and employee retention, 1* (pp. 226–247). Wiley.
Cousans, F., Patterson, F., Edwards, H., McLaughlan, J., & Good, D. (2017). Evaluating the complementary roles of a situational judgement test and academic assessment for entry into clinical practice. *Advances in Health Sciences Education Special Issue, 22*(2), 401–413.
Dore, K. L., Reiter, H. I., Kreuger, S., & Norman, G. R. (2017a). CASPer, an online pre-interview screen for personal/professional characteristics: Prediction of national licensure scores. *Advances in Health Sciences Education, 22*(2), 327–336. https://doi.org/10.1007/s10459-016-9739-9.
Dore, K. L., Reiter, H. I., Kreuger, S., & Norman, G. R. (2017b). Correction to: CASPer, an online pre-interview screen for personal/professional characteristics: Prediction of national licensure scores. *Advances in Health Sciences Education, 22*(5), 1321–1322. https://doi.org/10.1007/s10459-017-9798-6.
Escudier, M., Flaxman, C., Cousans, F., Woolford, M., & Patterson, F. (2015). Pilot results from a new assessment of professionalism. *Proceedings of the AMEE Conference 2015; Glas. UK.*
Ferguson, E., Semper, H., Yates, J., Fitzgerald, J., Skatova, A., & James, D. (2014). The 'dark side' and 'bright side' of personality: When too much conscientiousness and too little anxiety are detrimental with respect to the acquisition of medical knowledge and skill. *PLoS ONE, 9*(2), 1–11.
Gaugler, B. B., Rosenthal, D. B., Thornton, G. C., & Bentson, C. (1987). Meta-analysis of assessment center validity. *Journal of Applied Psychology, 72*(3), 493–511.
Golubovich, J., Seybert, J., Martin-raugh, M., Naemi, B., Vega, R. P., & Roberts, R. D. (2017). Assessing perceptions of interpersonal behavior with a video-based situational judgment test. *International Journal of Testing, 17*(3), 191–209. https://doi.org/10.1080/15305058.2016.1194275.
Graziano, W. G., Jensen-campbell, L. A., & Hair, E. C. (1996). Perceiving interpersonal conflict and reacting to it: The case for agreeableness. *Journal of Personality and Social Psychology, 70*(4), 820–835.

Guenole, N., Chernyshenko, O. S., & Weekly, J. (2017). On designing construct driven situational judgment tests: Some preliminary recommendations. *International Journal of Testing, 17*(3), 234–252. https://doi.org/10.1080/15305058.2017.1297817.

Kanning, U. P., Grewe, K., Hollenberg, S., & Hadouch, M. (2006). From the subject's point of view: Reactions to different types of situational judgment items. *European Journal of Psychological Assessment, 22,* 168–176.

Kasten, N., & Freund, P. A. (2016). A meta-analytical multilevel reliability generalization of Situational Judgment Tests (SJTs). *European Journal of Psychological Assessment, 32*(3), 230–240.

Kline, P. (2000). *Handbook of psychological testing* (2nd ed.). London: Routledge.

Koczwara, A., Patterson, F., Zibarras, L. D., Kerrin, M., Irish, B., & Wilkinson, M. (2012). Evaluating cognitive ability, knowledge tests and situational judgement tests for postgraduate selection. *Medical Education, 46*(4), 399–408. https://doi.org/10.1111/j.1365-2923.2011.04195.x.

Libbrecht, N., Lievens, F., & Carette, B. (2014). Emotional intelligence predicts success in medical school. *Emotion, 14*(1), 64–73. https://doi.org/10.1037/a0034392.

Lievens, F. (2013). Adjusting medical school admission: Assessing interpersonal skills using situational judgement tests. *Medical Education, 47,* 182–189. https://doi.org/10.1111/medu.12089.

Lievens, F. (2017). Construct-driven SJTs: Toward an agenda for future research. *International Journal of Testing, 17,* 269–276. https://doi.org/10.1080/15305058.2017.1309857.

Lievens, F., Buyse, T., & Sackett, P. R. P. (2005). The operational validity of a video-based situational judgment test for medical college admissions: Illustrating the importance of matching predictor and criterion construct domains. *The Journal of Applied Psychology, 90*(3), 442–452. https://doi.org/10.1037/0021-9010.90.3.442.

Lievens, F., Corstjens, J., Angel, M., Olea, J., Ponsoda, V., & Jos, F. (2015). The cross-cultural transportability of situational judgment tests: How does a US-based integrity situational judgment test fare in Spain? *International Journal of Selection and Assessment, 23*(4), 361–372.

Lievens, F., De Corte, W., & Westerveld, L. (2015). Understanding the building blocks of selection procedures: Effects of response fidelity on performance and validity. *Journal of Management, 41*(6), 1604–1627.

Lievens, F., & Motowidlo, S. J. (2016). Situational judgment tests: From measures of situational judgment to measures of general domain knowledge. *Industrial and Organizational Psychology, 9*(1), 3–22. https://doi.org/10.1017/iop.2015.71.

Lievens, F., & Patterson, F. (2011). The validity and incremental validity of knowledge tests, low-fidelity simulations, and high-fidelity simulations for predicting job performance in advanced-level high-stakes selection. *The Journal of Applied Psychology, 96*(5), 927–940.

Lievens, F., Patterson, F., Corstjens, J., Martin, S., & Nicholson, S. (2016). Widening access in selection using situational judgement tests: Evidence from the UKCAT. *Medical Education, 50*(6), 624–636. https://doi.org/10.1111/medu.13060.

Lievens, F., Peeters, H., & Schollaert, E. (2008). Situational judgment tests: A review of recent research. *Personnel Review, 37*(4), 426–441. https://doi.org/10.1108/00483480810877598.

Lievens, F., & Sackett, P. R. (2012). The validity of interpersonal skills assessment via situational judgment tests for predicting academic success and job performance. *Journal of Applied Psychology, 97*(2), 460–468. https://doi.org/10.1037/a0025741.

Luschin-Ebengreuth, M., Dimai, H. P., Ithaler, D., Neges, H. M., & Reibnegger, G. (2015). Situational judgment test as an additional tool in a medical admission test: An observational investigation. *BMC Research Notes, 8*(1), 81.

Martin, M., & Motowidlo, S. (2010). A single-response SJT for measuring procedural knowledge for human factors professionals. In *Poster Session Presented at 25th Annual Meeting of the Society for Industrial Organizational Psychology*.

McCrae, R. R., & Costa, P. (2008). Empirical and theoretical status of the five-factor model of personality traits. In *The Sage handbook of personality theory and assessment* (pp. 273–294). https://doi.org/10.4135/9781849200462.n13.

McDaniel, M., Hartman, N., Whetzel, D., & Grubb, W. (2007). Situational judgment tests, response instructions, and validity: A meta-analysis. *Personnel Psychology, 60,* 63–91.

McDaniel, M. A., Morgeson, F. P., Finnegan, E. B., & Campion, M. A. (2001). Use of situational judgment tests to predict job performance: A clarification of the literature. *Journal of Applied Psychology, 86*(4), 730–740.

McDaniel, M., & Nguyen, N. (2001). Situational judgment tests: A review of practice and constructs assessed. *International Journal of Selection and Assessment, 9*(1/2), 103–113.

McDaniel, M., & Whetzel, D. (2007). Situational judgment tests. In D. Whetzel & G. Wheaton (Eds.), *Applied measurement: Industrial psychology in human resources management* (pp. 235–257). Mahwah, NJ: Lawrence Erlbaum and Associates.

McDaniel, M. A., Whetzel, D. L., Schmidt, F. L., & Maurer, S. D. (1994). The validity of employment interviews: A comprehensive review and meta-analysis. *Journal of Applied Psychology, 79*(4), 599–616.

Motowidlo, S. J., & Beier, M. E. (2010). Differentiating specific job knowledge from implicit trait policies in procedural knowledge measured by a situational judgment test. *The Journal of Applied Psychology, 95*(2), 321–333. https://doi.org/10.1037/a0017975.

Motowidlo, S. J., Crook, A. E., Kell, H., & Naemi, B. (2009). Measuring procedural knowledge more simply with a single-response situational judgment test. *Journal of Business and Psychology, 24*(3), 281–288.

Motowidlo, S. J., Hooper, A. C., & Jackson, H. L. (2006). Implicit policies about relations between personality traits and behavioral effectiveness in situational judgment items. *Journal of Applied Psychology, 91*(4), 749–761. https://doi.org/10.1037/0021-9010.91.4.749.

Mussel, P., Gatzka, T., Hewig, J., Mussel, P., Gatzka, T., & Hewig, J. (2016). Situational judgment tests as an alternative measure for personality assessment. *European Journal of Psychological Assessment,* 1–9. https://doi.org/10.1027/1015-5759/a000346.

O'Connell, M. S., Hartman, N. S., McDaniel, M. A., Grubb, W. L., & Lawrence, A. (2007). Incremental validity of situational judgment tests for task and contextual job performance. *International Journal of Selection and Assessment, 15*(1), 19–29. https://doi.org/10.1111/j.1468-2389.2007.00364.x.

O'Neill, L., Vonsild, M., Wallstedt, B., & Dornan, T. (2013). Admission criteria and diversity in medical school. *Medical Education, 47*(6), 557–561.

Oswald, F., Schmitt, N., Kim, B., Ramsay, L. J., & Gillespie, M. A. (2004). Developing a biodata measure and situational judgment inventory as predictors of college student performance. *Journal of Applied Psychology, 89*(2), 187–207. https://doi.org/10.1037/0021-9010.89.2.187.

Pangallo, A., Zibarras, L., & Patterson, F. (2016). Measuring resilience in palliative care workers using the situational judgement test methodology. *Medical Education, 50,* 1131–1142. https://doi.org/10.1111/medu.13072.

Patterson, F., Aitkenhead, A., Edwards, H., Flaxman, C., Shaw, R., & Rosselli, A. (2015). *Analysis of the situational judgement test for selection to the foundation programme 2015: Technical Report.*

Patterson, F., Ashworth, V., Kerrin, M., & O'Neill, P. (2013). Situational judgement tests represent a measurement method and can be designed to minimise coaching effects situational judgement tests represent a measurement method and can be designed to minimise coaching effects. *Medical Education* (February). https://doi.org/10.1111/medu.12100.

Patterson, F., Ashworth, V., Mehra, S., & Falcon, H. (2012). Could situational judgement tests be used for selection into dental foundation training? *British Dental Journal, 213*(1), 23–26.

Patterson, F., Ashworth, V., Zibarras, L., Coan, P., Kerrin, M., & Neill, P. O. (2012). Evaluations of situational judgement tests to assess non-academic attributes in selection. *Medical Education, 46*(9), 850–868. https://doi.org/10.1111/j.1365-2923.2012.04336.x.

Patterson, F., Baron, H., Carr, V., Plint, S., & Lane, P. (2009). Evaluation of three short-listing methodologies for selection into postgraduate training in general practice. *Medical Education, 43*(1), 50–57.

Patterson, F., Carr, V., Zibarras, L., Burr, B., Berkin, L., Plint, S., … Gregory, S. (2009). New machine-marked tests for selection into core medical training: Evidence from two validation studies. *Clinical Medicine, 9*(5), 417–420.

Patterson, F., Knight, A., Dowell, J., Nicholson, S., Cousans, F., & Cleland, J. (2016). How effective are selection methods in medical education? A systematic review. *Medical Education, 50,* 36–60. https://doi.org/10.1111/medu.12817.

Patterson, F., Knight, A., Mcknight, L., & Booth, T. C. (2016). Evaluation of two selection tests for recruitment into radiology specialty training. *BMC Medical Education, 16*(170), 1–10. https://doi.org/10.1186/s12909-016-0687-0.

Patterson, F., Lievens, F., Kerrin, M., Munro, N., & Irish, B. (2013). The predictive validity of selection for entry into postgraduate training in general practice: Evidence from three longitudinal studies. *British Journal of General Practice, 63*(616), 734–741. https://doi.org/10.3399/bjgp13X674413.

Patterson, F., Lievens, F., Kerrin, M., Zibarras, L., & Carette, B. (2012). Designing selection systems for medicine: The importance of balancing predictive and political validity in high-stakes selection contexts. *International Journal of Selection and Assessment, 20*(4), 486–496. https://doi.org/10.1111/ijsa.12011.

Patterson, F., Lopes, A. S., Harding, B. S., Vaux, C. E., E, D. L. B., & F, D. B. (2017). *The predictive validity of a situational judgement test, a clinical problem solving test and the core medical training selection methods for performance in specialty training (February)*. https://doi.org/10.7861/clinmedicine.17-1-13.

Patterson, F., Prescott-Clements, L., Zibarras, L., Edwards, H., Kerrin, M., & Cousans, F. (2015). Recruiting for values in healthcare: A preliminary review of the evidence. *Advances in Health Sciences Education, 21*(4), 859–881. https://doi.org/10.1007/s10459-014-9579-4.

Patterson, F., Rowett, E., Hale, R., Grant, M., Roberts, C., Cousans, F., et al. (2016). The predictive validity of a situational judgement test and multiple-mini interview for entry into postgraduate training in Australia. *BMC Medical Education, 16*(1), 87. https://doi.org/10.1186/s12909-016-0606-4.

Patterson, F., Zibarras, L., & Ashworth, V. (2015). Situational judgement tests in medical education and training: Research, theory and practice: AMEE Guide No. 100. *Medical Teacher, 0*(0), 1–15. https://doi.org/10.3109/0142159X.2015.1072619.

Ployhart, R., & Ehrhart, M. G. (2003). Be careful what you ask for: Effects of response instructions on the construct validity and reliability of situational judgment tests. *International Journal of Selection and Assessment, 11*(1), 1–16. https://doi.org/10.1111/1468-2389.00222.

Ployhart, R., & Weekley, J. (2006). Situational judgment tests: A research synthesis and directions for future research. In J. Weekley & R. E. Ployhart (Eds.), *Situational judgment tests* (pp. 345–350). Mahwah, NJ: Lawrence Earlbaum.

Ployhart, R. E., Weekley, J. A., Holtz, B. C., & Kemp, C. (2003). Web-based and paper-and-pencil testing of applicants in a proctored setting: Are personality, biodata, and situational judgment tests comparable? *Personnel Psychology, 56*, 733–752.

Powis, D. (2014). Selecting medical students: An unresolved challenge*. *Medical Teacher* (April), 252–260. https://doi.org/10.3109/0142159X.2014.993600.

Rust, J., & Golombok, S. (1999). *Modern psychometrics: The science of psychological assessment*. London: Routledge.

Schmidt, F. (1994). The future of personnel selection in the U.S. Army. In J. Weekley & R. Ployhart (Eds.), *Personnel selection and classification* (pp. 333–350). Hillsdale, NJ: Lawrence Erlbaum Associates.

Simon, E., Walsh, K., Paterson-Brown, F., & Cahill, D. (2015). Does a high ranking mean success in the Situational Judgement Test? *The Clinical Teacher, 12*(1), 42–45.

Stemig, M. S., Sackett, P. R., & Lievens, F. (2015). Effects of organizationally endorsed coaching on performance and validity of situational judgment tests. *International Journal of Selection and Assessment, 23*(2), 174–181.

Stemler, S., Aggarwal, V., & Nithyanand, S. (2016). Knowing what not to do is a critical job skill: Evidence from 10 different scoring methods. *International Journal of Selection and Assessment, 24*(3), 229–245.

Wakeford, R., Denney, M.-L., Ludka-Stempien, K., Dacre, J., & McManus, I. (2015). Cross-comparison of MRCGP & MRCP (UK) in a database linkage study of 2,284 candidates taking both examinations: Assessment of validity and differential performance by ethnicity. *BMC Medical Education, 15*(1), 1–12.

Weekley, J. A., & Jones, C. (1999). Further studies of situational tests. *Personnel Psychology, 52*(3), 679–700.

Wernimot, P., & Campbell, J. (2009). Situational judgment tests: An overview of current research. *Human Resource Management Review, 3,* 188–202.

Whetzel, D. L., & McDaniel, M. A. (2009). Situational judgment tests: An overview of current research. *Human Resource Management Review, 19*(3), 188–202. https://doi.org/10.1016/j.hrmr.2009.03.007.

Whetzel, D. L., McDaniel, M. A., & Nguyen, N. T. (2008). Subgroup differences in situational judgment test performance: A meta-analysis. *Human Performance, 21*(3), 291–309. https://doi.org/10.1080/08959280802137820.

Whetzel, D. L., & Reeder, M. C. (2016). Why some situational judgment tests fail to predict job performance (and others succeed). *Human Resources Research Organization, 9*(1), 71–77.

Woolf, K., Potts, H., & McManus, I. (2011). Ethnicity and academic performance in UK trained doctors and medical students: Systematic review and meta-analysis. *BMJ, 342,* d901.

5

Interviews, Multiple Mini-Interviews, and Selection Centers

Mirjana Knorr, Johanna Hissbach and Wolfgang Hampe

Overview

This chapter focuses on interviews, multiple mini-interviews (MMI), and selection centers (SC). In the first two sections of this chapter, we describe each method, point to conceptual overlaps and present current theoretical frameworks. Next, we give an overview of the current state of research within the healthcare context. This research section mainly focuses on MMIs, which have dominated the recent literature, and it includes a case study about the dimensionality of the Hamburg MMI as well as directions for future research. We will then provide a short

M. Knorr (✉) · J. Hissbach · W. Hampe
University Medical Center Hamburg-Eppendorf, Hamburg, Germany
e-mail: m.knorr@uke.de

J. Hissbach
e-mail: j.hissbach@uke.uni-hamburg.de

W. Hampe
e-mail: hampe@uke.de

F. Patterson and L. Zibarras (eds.), *Selection and Recruitment in the Healthcare Professions*, https://doi.org/10.1007/978-3-319-94971-0_5

outlook on technological advances. Finally, we will conclude this chapter with a list of practice points.

By the end of this chapter, you should:

- understand the differences and commonalities between traditional interviews, MMIs, and SCs
- know how candidate, situation, and assessors contribute to the interpretation of a score and consider Trait-Activation Theory (TAT) as a starting point for a theoretical framework
- be familiar with key research findings revolving MMIs and be aware of the gaps in the literature especially regarding construct validation
- have an idea how video-interviewing and computerized simulations might contribute to the delivery of these selection methods in the future.

Definitions and Examples

Interviews for employment or admission have a long tradition. The vast majority (up to 99%) of medical schools in the United States and Canada used interviews in their admission process and a similar high percentage was reported for physiotherapy education as well as occupational therapy (Morris, 1999; Salvatori, 2001). Selection interviews can be roughly divided into individual interviews, panel or board interviews, and serial interviews (Dixon, Wang, Calvin, Dineen, & Tomlinson, 2002). Moreover, interviews can be structured, semi-structured, and unstructured. Structured interviews should ideally be developed based on a job analysis, use standardized questions and a standardized rating procedure (Edwards, Johnson, & Molidor, 1990). The most popular types of interview questions are behavioral questions and situational questions (Levashina, Hartwell, Morgeson, & Campion, 2014). A behavioral question asks candidates to recount their actual past behavior relevant for the target job or position, whereas situational questions present a hypothetical scenario and candidates are asked to indicate how they would respond (Huffcutt, Weekley, Wiesner, Degroot, & Jones, 2001). Other types of questions include questions on background, knowledge, opinions, values, attitudes, goals, aspirations, self-descriptions, or self-evaluations (Campion, Palmer, & Campion, 1997; see Table 5.1 for examples).

Within these categorizations, an MMI can be considered to be a highly structured serial interview which consists of a circuit of several short stations with different interviewers at each station (Eva, Rosenfeld, Reiter, & Norman, 2004). The first MMI was introduced by McMaster University for the selection of medical students in 2002. The McMaster MMI targets non-academic dimensions such as communication or collaboration with a focus on ethical decision making (Eva et al., 2009). It comprises ten to twelve stations that last eight minutes with a two minute break between stations. At each station, candidates either interact with the interviewer or a simulated patient. Their performance is then evaluated by one assessor on a seven-point Likert scale. MMIs have found widespread application at other institutions, mainly in the healthcare sector ranging from selection into medical, dental, pharmacy, or veterinary school to selection into specialty training or for specific programs or positions. They differ markedly in their design with regard to station number, station duration, number of assessors, and rating schemes. Finally, MMIs are not limited to interview questions but they can also include simulations such as role plays, group discussions, and

Table 5.1 Examples of interview questions

Question type	Example
Behavioral	Give an example of a challenge that you faced as a medical student and handled effectively
Situational	Suppose you notice your supervisor has given out a wrong prescription to a patient. What would you do?
Background	What previous experience do you have in the healthcare sector?
Knowledge	How would you conduct a [specific medical procedure]?
Opinions and attitudes	What is your opinion on homeopathic treatment?
Goals and aspirations	Where do you see yourself in 5 years?
Self-descriptions and self-evaluations	How do you handle pressure?

presentations (Knorr & Hissbach, 2014). With the possibility of including simulations, MMIs come close to the concept of SCs.

SCs are assessment centers (AC) used for selection purposes. According to the International Taskforce on Assessment Centre Guidelines a SC "consists of multiple components, which include behavioral simulation exercises, within which multiple trained assessors observe and record behaviors, classify them according to the behavioral constructs of interest, and (either individually or collectively) rate (either individual or pooled) behaviors" (Rupp et al., 2015, p. 1248). The guidelines further describe ten essential elements of SCs:

1. systematic analysis of job-relevant behavioral constructs,
2. behavioral classification,
3. multiple SC components (e.g., simulations, psychometric tests, structured interviews, situational judgment tests, questionnaires),
4. linkages between behavioral constructs and assessment center components,
5. simulation exercises,
6. multiple assessors,
7. assessor training,
8. recording and scoring of behaviors,
9. data integration,
10. and standardization (Rupp et al., 2015).

Within healthcare, a well-established SC is used for the selection into postgraduate training in general practice (GP) in the United Kingdom (UK) (Lievens & Patterson, 2011). This SC aims to assess five dimensions (empathy, communication, problem solving, professional integrity, and coping with pressure) via three simulations, including an interaction with a simulated patient, a group discussion of a work-related issue, and a written prioritizing task, each lasting 20–40 minutes. Candidates are evaluated on a four-point Likert scale for each dimension by one assessor per exercise (Lievens & Patterson, 2011).

In practice, each of these selection methods can be designed and applied in numerous ways. Due to this great variability, there is also a considerable overlap between interviews, MMIs, and SCs. A structured

Table 5.2 Design aspects of the selection method, their possible variations, and typical applications in one-to-one or panel interviews, multiple mini-interviews, and selection centers

	One-to-one or panel interviews	Multiple mini-interviews	Selection centers
Components include different types of questions (behavioral, situational, etc.), simulations (role play, group discussion, in-box-exercise, etc.), written tests or questionnaires	Focus on questions	Focus on behavioral and situational questions as well as role plays	Focus on simulations (must include at least one), can be combined with any other component (i.e., interview questions, written tests or questionnaires)
Each component can be **structured**, **semi-structured,** or **unstructured**	Unstructured to highly structured	Semi-structured to highly structured	Usually highly structured
A candidate may have a **single or multiple encounters** with assessors	Single	Multiple	Multiple
One **encounter** can be of short (1–10 min), medium (10–60 min), or long (>1 hour) **duration**	Medium to long	Short, usually all components have the same length	Short to medium
Candidates may be evaluated by **one or more than one assessors** at each encounter	Single interviewer or panel	One or two per station	Multiple assessors for each component
Multiple assessors can be **dependent** (consensus rating) or **independent**	Usually consensus	Usually independent	Both, guidelines advise independent

serial interview might as well be called an MMI, an MMI that includes simulations might be considered as an SC, and an SC can be designed to include an interview or an MMI (Gafni, Moshinsky, Eisenberg, Zeigler, & Ziv, 2012; Roberts et al., 2014; Ziv et al., 2008). While a clear distinction is not possible, there are typical approaches to the design for each of the methods. Table 5.2 gives an overview of design aspects and how they are usually varied in practice for each method.

Theoretical Background

A principle that has guided traditional interviews is the assumption that past behavior predicts future behavior (Wernimont & Campbell, 1968). Behavioral questions provide an indicator for the candidates' past behavior in job-relevant situations and they should therefore predict future behavior in comparable situations. Another principle is that goals and intentions predict future behavior (Locke & Latham, 2002). Situational questions that ask how candidates would behave in hypothetical situations are considered as indicators of goals and intentions and should therefore predict future behavior (Campion et al., 1997). While it could be demonstrated that structured interviews and SCs do in fact predict future performance (Schmidt & Hunter, 1998), another question remains controversial: What exactly do they measure?

In interviews, MMIs, and SCs, assessors make inferences based on observations of a candidate's statements and behavior. The final result is an evaluation of the candidate which is usually expressed in an overall score. Recent theoretical developments provide more insight into which variables and processes determine the generation of the final score. We will consider three aspects: the candidate, the situation, and the assessor.

The Candidate

Based on a review of the employment interview construct literature, Huffcutt (2011) developed a model of all constructs that lie within a candidate and have an effect on interview ratings. The model distinguishes three major sources of influence. The first source encompasses general traits (i.e., mental ability, personality, interest, goals, and values), experiential factors (i.e., experience, education, and training), and core job elements (i.e., declarative knowledge, procedural skills and abilities, and motivation) that are all directly related to the requirements of the job/position. The second source is related to the way an interviewee performs in the interview. Interviewees' social effectiveness skills (i.e., social influences behaviors, interpersonal presentation) and other personal/contextual factors such as interview training and experience, interview self-efficacy, and interview motivation play a role in this context. Finally, there are personal and demographic characteristics such as attractiveness, race and gender, background, and attitudinal similarity, as well as cultural background, and/or setting. Although ideally interviewer ratings should not be influenced by this set of characteristics, they do play a role in the way interviewers perceive the candidate (Huffcutt, 2011).

The Situation

With the development of the MMI, Eva, Rosenfeld, et al. (2004) put an emphasis on the importance of situational influences for a candidate's performance. The context specificity of human behavior refers to the observation that the performance in one particular situation only weakly predicts the performance in a different situation (Eva, 2003). Therefore, the MMI provides a set of different situations in order to achieve more reliable inferences. Scores do not only represent stable dispositions (traits) that lie within the candidate but also depend on the situation (Eva et al., 2009). Likewise, recent theoretical developments in the SC literature consider the person-situation interaction for the explanation of a candidate's behavior in an SC exercise. Lievens, De Koster, and Schollaert (2008) proposed a model that applies Trait Activation Theory (TAT) (Tett & Burnett, 2003) to the SC context. TAT has two key assumptions that explain whether and how a candidate's underlying traits will be expressed in behavior (Lievens et al., 2008). The first assumption posits that trait-relevant cues need to be present in the situation (i.e., SC exercise) in order to elicit trait-expressive behavior (situation trait relevance). Therefore, if we aim to see a candidate's level of conscientiousness, we need to present the candidate with a situation that demands conscientious behavior. Second, it is assumed that it depends on the strength of a situation whether differences in trait levels will be expressed and observed in a situation (situation strength). Situations that present very clear instructions and situations (strong situations) will more likely result in uniform candidate behavior irrespective of trait differences. Conversely, situations that are ambiguous (weak situations) will more likely lead to variability in candidate behavior. The clarity of instructions and situations does not only depend on the way they are formulated but also on the candidate's knowledge about the situation due to prior experience or coaching.

The Interviewer/Assessor

So far, the theoretical considerations described how candidate variables, situational influences, and their interaction determine a candidate's behavior in an interview or simulation. The final missing component that determines a candidate's score is the assessor. Lievens, Schollaert, and Keen (2015) combined TAT with a model that explains evaluation processes: the realistic accuracy model (RAM) (Funder, 2012). It describes four process stages that lead from the observation of a behavior to its evaluation. The candidate has to demonstrate behavior that is relevant for the trait (relevance) and it has to be available for the assessor, meaning that it has to be demonstrated in a high enough quantity (accessibility). Next, assessors have to be able to detect trait-relevant behavior. Therefore, the assessor's cognitive load should not be too high (detection). Finally, the behavioral information has to be utilized and classified into the right dimensional category (utilization). While TAT describes the processes by which trait-relevant behavior is elicited, RAM describes how the trait-relevant behavior is picked up and processed by the assessor. All four process stages have to be completed successfully in order for assessors to make accurate judgments

(Lievens et al., 2015). It should be noted that in this model assessors are mainly perceived as trainable, but differences in ratings between assessors can also be considered as meaningful assessment information and reflect differences in expertise (Gingerich, Kogan, Yeates, Govaerts, & Holmboe, 2014). Thus, assessor characteristics such as expertise and personality, as well as assessor's sociodemographic variables and their interaction with candidate variables, also have to be considered for the interpretation of scores.

What do scores in interviews, MMIs, and SCs represent? The described theoretical frames reveal that a score is a complex measure which is influenced by different sources: the candidate, the situation, the assessor and the interaction between these three. Each of the three sources has its own stream of research history and needs to be considered for the development of tasks and rating forms, the selection and training of assessors, and the interpretation of scores. For these reasons, a score cannot be seen as a simple representation of an underlying stable trait and any approach of construct validation has to consider the interplay between these influential factors.

Key Findings from Recent Research Relating to Interviews, MMIs, and SCs in a Healthcare Context

Following the criticism of traditional interviews (Eva, Rosenfeld, et al., 2004; Morris, 1999), research on selection interviews in healthcare settings over the past 15 years was dominated by studies on MMIs as many institutions switched from a traditional interview to an MMI format. Research on SCs in a healthcare context is published to a smaller extent and mainly focuses on the selection into specialty training. Therefore, we summarize key findings from research on the acceptability and feasibility, sociodemographic and personality factors, reliability, and validity of MMIs and complement this account with relevant findings from the SC and traditional interview literature.

Acceptability and Feasibility

The MMI and SC method typically finds approval by candidates and assessors (Gale et al., 2010; Oosterveld & ten Cate, 2004; Rees et al., 2016). Although there are concerns that the MMI method is more stressful for candidates, MMIs and more structured interviews seem to be preferred over less structured or traditional interviews (Patterson, Knight, et al., 2016; Rees et al., 2016). A major drawback of these selection methods is that they are more resource-intensive than other methods such as multiple-choice tests (Patterson, Knight, et al., 2016). Compared to traditional interviews, the MMI requires more resources for development and logistics but it is more efficient in terms of interview hours (Rosenfeld, Reiter, Trinh, & Eva, 2008). Two of the highest cost factors for MMIs are assessor time and station development (Hissbach, Sehner, Harendza, & Hampe, 2014). Suggestions to reduce these costs include the use of active assessors (i.e., interviewers or role players also assess the performance) (Hofmeister, Lockyer, & Crutcher, 2009; Roberts, Gale, Sice, & Anderson, 2013), the inclusion of written exercises or questionnaires (Raghavan, Burnett, et al., 2013; Ziv et al., 2008), and reusing stations (Hissbach et al., 2014). So far, there are no indications that stations become easier or less differentiating if they are used repeat times (Dowell, Lynch, Till, Kumwenda, & Husbands, 2012; Moshinsky, Ziegler, & Gafni, 2017) and there was no significant difference in performance for candidates who knew MMI station instructions in advance (Reiter, Salvatori, Rosenfeld, Trinh, & Eva, 2006). Candidates who repeated the MMI showed an improvement in the average score. However, regression to the mean effects have to be kept in mind (Griffin, Harding, Wilson, & Yeomans, 2008; Moshinsky et al., 2017). Finally, prior interview or coaching experience does not seem to provide an advantage (Griffin et al., 2008; Moshinsky et al., 2017).

Sociodemographic and Personality Factors

Lumb, Homer, and Miller (2010) found that gender, ethnic background, socioeconomic group, and type of school of both candidates and assessors had no influence on interview scores. This is also the case for many MMIs with regard to gender, age, socioeconomic status (SES), or ethnicity. Significant gender differences are mostly in favor of women (Griffin & Hu, 2015; Ross et al., 2017). In some cases, older candidates tend to achieve higher scores (Jerant et al., 2015; Reiter, Lockyer, Ziola, Courneya, & Eva, 2012). There have also been rare reports of lower scores for applicants with a rural background (Raghavan, Martin, et al., 2013), lower SES (Jerant et al., 2015), or a foreign nationality and language (Kelly et al., 2014; Leduc, Rioux, Gagnon, Bourdy, & Dennis, 2017). The reasons for these heterogeneous findings most likely lie within the different MMI approaches but they have yet to be explored systematically.

The most consistent finding regarding candidates' personality factors is a small to moderate positive correlation between extraversion and MMI scores (Griffin & Wilson, 2012; Jerant et al., 2012; Oliver, Hecker, Hausdorf, & Conlon, 2014). Another construct that has drawn attention in recent research is a candidate's ability to identify rating criteria (ATIC) which has been found to be positively related to interview, SC, and MMI performance (Griffin, 2014; König, Melchers, Kleinmann, Richter, & Klehe, 2007). Perceiving selection center stations as a challenge rather than a threat had a weak positive effect on SC performance (Roberts, Gale, McGrath, & Wilson, 2016).

Reliability

The reliability of traditional interviews in the healthcare context has been criticized for a long time (Patterson, Knight, et al., 2016). For example, a study by Kreiter, Yin, Solow, and Brennan (2004) reported Generalizability coefficients (*G*) lower than 0.40, and Harasym, Woloschuk, Mandin, and Brundin-Mather (1996) reported that 56% of the variance in ratings was attributable to assessors. A *G*-study estimates the percentage of the overall variance in scores that is explained by candidate differences (variance component of interest) and that is explained by other sources (assessors, stations, items, interactions between variance sources, and error). The biggest advantage of the MMI method over traditional interviews is an increase in reliability which is usually above 0.50 (Knorr & Hissbach, 2014) with the highest percentage of systematic assessor variance reported for an MMI of 25% (Griffin & Wilson, 2010). Likewise, *G* values higher than 0.70 (Gafni et al., 2012; Oosterveld & ten Cate, 2004) have been reported for SCs in healthcare.

Several factors have a positive impact on reliability. A higher level of structure in interviews is usually associated with higher reliability (Levashina et al., 2014). Raising the number of MMI stations and/or the number of assessors per station both improves reliability, but it has been consistently demonstrated that increasing the number of stations has a larger impact on reliability (Axelson & Kreiter, 2009). Studies showed that station durations of five or six minutes yield acceptable reliability values (Cameron & MacKeigan, 2012; Dodson et al., 2009). Removing stations that do not differentiate between candidates can also lead to better reliability (Uijtdehaage, Doyle, & Parker, 2011). However, whether certain types of stations, such as behavioral or situational questions, are more reliable than the other cannot be concluded based on current research (Eva & Macala, 2014; Yamada et al., 2017). To reduce unwanted variance that is attributable to assessor differences, skills-based or frame-of-reference trainings have been advocated in the MMI and SC literature (Griffin & Wilson, 2010; Schleicher, Day, Mayes, & Riggio, 2002). Another possibility to deal with differences in assessors' levels of leniency is to statistically adjust scores for these effects (Roberts, Rothnie, Zoanetti, & Crossley, 2010).

Validity Evidence

Dimensionality

Dimensionality refers to the underlying assumptions about how items and components in a test are interrelated. Although dimensionality highly depends on the construction of the test, some tendencies emerged from the accumulated research. Items within MMI stations are typically highly correlated (Eva, Reiter, Rosenfeld, & Norman, 2004) and exploratory factor analyses with these items find that each station forms a factor (Cox, McLaughlin, Singer, Lewis, & Dinkins, 2015;

Lemay, Lockyer, Collin, & Brownell, 2007). This phenomenon is also known in the SC literature, where exercises rather than dimensions form factors (Lance, 2008). Multifaceted Rasch modeling suggests that items fit within a broad unidimensional construct (Roberts, Zoanetti, & Rothnie, 2009; Sebok, Luu, & Klinger, 2014). If the focus is on overall station or exercise scores, correlations between stations are mostly small to medium which is explained by context specificity (Dowell et al., 2012; Eva, Rosenfeld, et al., 2004; Jerant et al., 2012). Studies that provide a clear theoretical rational for the assumed internal structure of the MMI are rare (Oliver et al., 2014).

Convergent and Discriminant Validity Evidence

In direct comparison, traditional interviews and MMIs demonstrated non-significant to large correlations (Eva, Rosenfeld, et al., 2004; Pau, Chen, Lee, Sow, & De Alwis, 2016). MMIs and Situational Judgement Tests (SJTs), which both aim to assess non-academic competencies, show small to medium correlations (Patterson, Rowett, et al., 2016; see Case Study 5.1). MMI performance is typically unrelated to prior academic attainment (Cameron & MacKeigan, 2012; Kim, Nam, & Kwon, 2017; Reiter et al., 2012). If positive correlations are found with aptitude tests, they mostly relate to specific parts of the aptitude test such as the "verbal reasoning" part of the MCAT (Jerant et al., 2012) and the "social understanding" part of the UMAT (Griffin, 2014).

Case Study 5.1: Relationship of MMI Components with a Situational Judgement Test (SJT) in the Context of Undergraduate Medical School Selection

Summary

Our research group was interested in the factorial structure of our selection MMI for undergraduate medical students. A principal components analysis (PCA) of our 2016 MMI data revealed a two factorial structure. We found that the simulation component of our MMI was significantly related to the SJT, while the interview component was not related to the SJT.

Objective
The aim of this work was to examine the structure of our MMI and to relate the observed structure to our SJT in order to see which components could be represented in the SJT. We report the correlation with the overall score as well as the correlation with the factor scores of the two principal components of the MMI.

Our Approach
Our research group uses MMIs for undergraduate student selection since 2009. The 2016 MMI comprised three simulated patient tasks, one video task, and two group discussions. We performed PCA of MMI station overall scores. In the same year we piloted an SJT for psychosocial competencies and correlated the results with our MMI total score and the factor scores. Test results of 177 candidates were analyzed (93% of all test takers).

Results and Outcome
The PCA revealed two components. The first component, which comprised the simulation, video, and group stations, approximately explained 25% of the variance and the second component, the interview stations, explained 17% of the variance. The MMI total score was significantly related to the SJT score ($r = 0.20$, $p = 0.007$). However, looking at the separate components, we found that this correlation was based on the simulation component ($r=0.25$, $p=0.001$), while the second, analytical component was not related to the SJT score ($r=-0.03$; $p=0.666$).

Even though this relationship is weak, the simulation-based tasks seem to be more strongly reflected by the SJT scores. More cognitively loaded tasks, e.g. the characterization of a person, showed no relation to the SJT scores.

Continuing Work
The issue of dimensionality is unresolved as MMIs show diverse factorial structures. We did not replicate these 2016 results with the following 2017 cohort which rather suggested a unidimensional structure (with no relation to the SJT).

Predictive Validity Evidence

A meta-analysis found that performance in selection interviews into health-related professions very weakly predicts academic success but shows a modest positive correlation with performance in a clinical setting (Goho & Blackman, 2006). Similarly, the relationship between MMIs and academic achievements in written tests is small to non-significant (Lee et al., 2016). MMIs demonstrated correlations of small to medium size with objective structured clinical examinations (OSCE) which have a very similar multi-station approach (Husbands & Dowell, 2013; Kelly et al., 2014; Reiter, Eva, Rosenfeld, & Norman, 2007). MMIs and SCs could also predict supervisor ratings (Bindal, Wall, & Goodyear, 2007; Cameron, MacKeigan, Mitsakakis, & Pugsley, 2017; Patterson, Lievens, Kerrin, Munro, & Irish, 2013; Reiter et al., 2007), peer evaluations (Hadad et al., 2016), and other indicators of progress during practical training (Gale et al., 2010; Pashayan et al., 2016). Finally, three MMIs and one SC were predictive of end-of-training and licensing examinations with the strongest prediction for the OSCE part of the exams (Cameron et al., 2017; Eva et al., 2012; Patterson et al., 2013; Patterson, Rowett, et al., 2016).

Directions for Future Research

Generally, more evidence is needed regarding selection centers. While acceptability and reliability of MMIs have been studied to a large extent (Rees et al., 2016), future studies should focus on the following main directions:

1. **Sociodemographic background**: Differences in performance depending on candidate's sociodemographic variables are found in some studies, but not in others. It should be systematically analyzed under which conditions or types of tasks these differences occur.
2. **Construct validity evidence**: Studies that published findings on the dimensionality have been mostly exploratory. TAT can serve as a framework that could be applied to MMI and SC research in order to derive more theory-driven assumptions on the dimensionality.
3. **Predictive validity evidence**: Further evidence of the predictive validity, preferably in a practical context, is needed. Ideally, this would be analyzed in large-scale multi-site studies that compare different interview, MMI, and SC methods and use the same standardized outcome measures. Outcome measures should be relevant for the dimensions that the selection method aims to assess (Rees et al., 2016).

Technological Advances

Various technological advances have emerged that provide possibilities to save costs and resources, facilitate the selection process, and create more realistic simulations. Interviews no longer require a face-to-face interaction as they can be conducted via telephone or internet-based video telephony (Levashina et al., 2014). Thereby, the interaction does not necessarily have to be synchronous (i.e., interviewee and interviewer participate at the same time) (Levashina et al., 2014). Asynchronous video interviewing is a new screening method in which candidates are asked to record their answers to pre-defined questions at home, and assessors evaluate the answers at a later time point (Brenner, Ortner, & Fay, 2016). Further advances include the automated scoring of interview recordings on the basis of voice patterns and micro-expressions as well as facial features and habitual expression to read emotions and generate personality profiles (Chamorro-Premuzic, Winsborough, Sherman, & Hogan, 2016). In the healthcare field, synchronous video-interviewing has been mainly discussed for the selection into specialty training (Hariton, Bortoletto, & Ayogu, 2016). Furthermore, Tiller et al. (2013) introduced video-interviews in an MMI format ("iMMI") for international applicants to medical and dental school. Both candidates and institutions have lower expenses when using video interviews compared to in-person interviews (Edje, Miller, Kiefer, & Oram, 2013; Tiller et al., 2013). Asynchronous video interviewing gives candidates and assessors more flexibility but it does not allow them to ask clarifying questions (Torres & Mejia, 2017). In general, video interviewing is perceived as a screening tool or an optional alternative rather than a replacement of in-person interviews (Shah et al., 2012; Tiller et al., 2013). While it is already widely used in the corporate sector, research on the validity of video-interviewing and automated scoring is lagging behind in healthcare (Chamorro-Premuzic et al., 2016; Levashina et al., 2014).

An early technological development in the context of SCs was the use of computer-based rating systems instead of paper forms which facilitates data integration and scoring (Guidry, Rupp, & Lanik, 2013). Other examples include computerized in-basket exercises

(Guidry et al., 2013) and virtual reality (VR) applications, a "collection of technologies that allow people to interact efficiently with 3D computerized databases in real time using their natural senses and skills" (McCloy & Stone, 2001, p. 912). VR already finds wide application in the healthcare field from education and training (Issenberg, McGaghie, Petrusa, Lee Gordon, & Scalese, 2005) to treatment and rehabilitation (Schultheis & Rizzo, 2001). It is not limited to the assessment of technical skills but can also simulate personal interactions (Letterie, 2002). The benefit of simulation technology in the educational context is "a controlled, safe and forgiving environment" (Issenberg et al., 2005) to acquire skills without risks to real patients. However, reports on the application of VR in selection procedures are difficult to find (Panait et al., 2011). A major drawback are high costs for acquisition. Similar to video-interviewing, validity evidence for technology-enhanced simulations as assessment tools for health professions, including VR, is sparse (Cook, Brydges, Zendejas, Hamstra, & Hatala, 2013).

Overall, the major potential of video-interviewing is its cost- and time-efficiency and virtual reality applications provide possibilities to create controlled simulations that would otherwise be impossible to conduct. However, more research is needed before these tools can be recommended for high-stakes selection procedures.

Conclusion

Interviews, MMIs, and SCs share common characteristics and, therefore, some of the theoretical assumptions and research findings for one method can also be applied to the other method. Research has demonstrated that these methods can be designed to be reliable. Most importantly, they predict relevant outcome measures such as licensing examination scores which justifies their use. Interactionist theories, such as TAT in the context of SC research, provide a fruitful basis for future research. Regarding the implementation of interviews, MMIs, and SCs, some practice points can be derived from the literature and are summarized below.

Practice Points

1. The development process of interviews, MMIs, and SCs should start with a thorough analysis of the required competencies. They should be defined clearly and provided with behavioral descriptors (Rupp et al., 2015; also see Chapter 6).
2. Define appropriate outcome criteria that you wish to predict in the design process.
3. As to the overall process, highly structured approaches to interviews have been demonstrated to be more reliable and more valid.
4. In order to increase reliability, increase the number of components/stations (i.e., questions, simulations, written tests, or questionnaires).
5. It is advisable to create a systematic database of components/stations ("item bank") including information on psychometric properties (Roberts et al., 2009). The components/stations can be reused or adjusted in order to save future development costs.
6. Assessor training should focus on the skills underlying the application of the rating criteria. The major goal of the training is a common understanding of the criteria and frame of reference.

Explore Further

http://www.assessmentcenters.org/	This webpage about the past and future International Congress on Assessment Center Methods provides a free PDF of the Assessment Center Guidelines developed by international experts
Duncan J. R. Jackson, Charles E. Lance, and Brian J. Hoffman (Eds.). The Psychology of Assessment Centers. New York, NY: Routledge, 2012	The book provides a recent overview of different views on the theory about assessment centers
Morris (1999) Rees et al. (2016)	The most recent systematic reviews on traditional interviews and MMIs in student selection

References

Axelson, R. D., & Kreiter, C. D. (2009). Rater and occasion impacts on the reliability of pre-admission assessments. *Medical Education, 43*(12), 1198–1202.

Bindal, T., Wall, D., & Goodyear, H. M. (2007). Performance of paediatric Senior House Officers following changes in recruitment. *Medical Teacher, 29*(5), 501–503.

Brenner, F. S., Ortner, T. M., & Fay, D. (2016). Asynchronous video interviewing as a new technology in personnel selection: The applicant's point of view. *Frontiers in Psychology, 7,* 863.

Cameron, A. J., & MacKeigan, L. D. (2012). Development and pilot testing of a multiple mini-interview for admission to a pharmacy degree program. *American Journal of Pharmaceutical Education, 76*(1), 9.

Cameron, A. J., MacKeigan, L. D., Mitsakakis, N., & Pugsley, J. A. (2017). Multiple mini-interview predictive validity for performance on a pharmacy licensing examination. *Medical Education, 51*(4), 379–389.

Campion, M. A., Palmer, D. K., & Campion, J. E. (1997). A review of structure in the selection interview. *Personnel Psychology, 50*(3), 655–702.

Chamorro-Premuzic, T., Winsborough, D., Sherman, R. A., & Hogan, R. (2016). New talent signals: Shiny new objects or a brave new world? *Industrial and Organizational Psychology, 9*(3), 621–640.

Cook, D. A., Brydges, R., Zendejas, B., Hamstra, S. J., & Hatala, R. (2013). Technology-enhanced simulation to assess health professionals: A systematic review of validity evidence, research methods, and reporting quality. *Academic Medicine, 88*(6), 872–883.

Cox, W. C., McLaughlin, J. E., Singer, D., Lewis, M., & Dinkins, M. M. (2015). Development and assessment of the multiple mini-interview in a school of pharmacy admissions model. *American Journal of Pharmaceutical Education, 79*(4), 9.

Dixon, M., Wang, S., Calvin, J., Dineen, B., & Tomlinson, E. (2002). The panel interview: A review of empirical research and guidelines for practice. *Public Personnel Management, 31*(3), 397–428.

Dodson, M., Crotty, B., Prideaux, D., Carne, R., Ward, A., & de Leeuw, E. (2009). The multiple mini-interview: How long is long enough? *Medical Education, 43*(2), 168–174.

Dowell, J., Lynch, B., Till, H., Kumwenda, B., & Husbands, A. (2012). The multiple mini-interview in the UK context: 3 years of experience at Dundee. *Medical Teacher, 34*(4), 297–304.

Edje, L., Miller, C., Kiefer, J., & Oram, D. (2013). Using skype as an alternative for residency selection interviews. *Journal of Graduate Medical Education, 5*(3), 503–505.

Edwards, J. C., Johnson, E. K., & Molidor, J. B. (1990). The interview in the admission process. *Academic Medicine, 65*(3), 167–177.

Eva, K. W. (2003). On the generality of specificity. *Medical Education, 37*(7), 587–588.

Eva, K. W., & Macala, C. (2014). Multiple mini-interview test characteristics: 'Tis better to ask candidates to recall than to imagine. *Medical Education, 48*(6), 604–613.

Eva, K. W., Reiter, H. I., Rosenfeld, J., & Norman, G. R. (2004). The relationship between interviewers' characteristics and ratings assigned during a multiple mini-interview. *Academic Medicine, 79*(6), 602–609.

Eva, K. W., Reiter, H. I., Rosenfeld, J., Trinh, K., Wood, T. J., & Norman, G. R. (2012). Association between a medical school admission process using the multiple mini-interview and national licensing examination scores. *JAMA, 308*(21), 2233–2240.

Eva, K. W., Reiter, H. I., Trinh, K., Wasi, P., Rosenfeld, J., & Norman, G. R. (2009). Predictive validity of the multiple mini-interview for selecting medical trainees. *Medical Education, 43*(8), 767–775.

Eva, K. W., Rosenfeld, J., Reiter, H. I., & Norman, G. R. (2004). An admissions OSCE: The multiple mini-interview. *Medical Education, 38*(3), 314–326.

Funder, D. C. (2012). Accurate personality judgment. *Current Directions in Psychological Science, 21*(3), 177–182.

Gafni, N., Moshinsky, A., Eisenberg, O., Zeigler, D., & Ziv, A. (2012). Reliability estimates: Behavioural stations and questionnaires in medical school admissions. *Medical Education, 46*(3), 277–288.

Gale, T. C. E., Roberts, M. J., Sice, P. J., Langton, J. A., Patterson, F. C., Carr, A. S., …, Davies, P. R. F. (2010). Predictive validity of a selection centre testing non-technical skills for recruitment to training in anaesthesia. *British Journal of Anaesthesia, 105*(5), 603–609.

Gingerich, A., Kogan, J., Yeates, P., Govaerts, M., & Holmboe, E. (2014). Seeing the 'black box' differently: Assessor cognition from three research perspectives. *Medical Education, 48*(11), 1055–1068.

Goho, J., & Blackman, A. (2006). The effectiveness of academic admission interviews: An exploratory meta-analysis. *Medical Teacher, 28*(4), 335–340.

Griffin, B. (2014). The ability to identify criteria: Its relationship with social understanding, preparation, and impression management in affecting predictor performance in a high-stakes selection context. *Human Performance, 27*(2), 147–164.

Griffin, B., Harding, D. W., Wilson, I. G., & Yeomans, N. D. (2008). Does practice make perfect? The effect of coaching and retesting on selection tests used for admission to an Australian medical school. *Medical Journal of Australia, 189*(5), 270–273.

Griffin, B., & Hu, W. (2015). The interaction of socio-economic status and gender in widening participation in medicine. *Medical Education, 49*(1), 103–113.

Griffin, B., & Wilson, I. (2012). Associations between the big five personality factors and multiple mini-interviews. *Advances in Health Sciences Education, 17*(3), 377–388.

Griffin, B. N., & Wilson, I. G. (2010). Interviewer bias in medical student selection. *Medical Journal of Australia, 193*(6), 343–346.

Guidry, B. W., Rupp, D. E., & Lanik, M. (2013). *Tracing cognition with assessment center simulations: Using technology to see in the dark*. New York: Springer.

Hadad, A., Gafni, N., Moshinsky, A., Turvall, E., Ziv, A., & Israeli, A. (2016). The multiple mini-interviews as a predictor of peer evaluations during clinical training in medical school. *Medical Teacher, 38*(11), 1172–1179.

Harasym, P. H., Woloschuk, W., Mandin, H., & Brundin-Mather, R. (1996). Reliability and validity of interviewers' judgments of medical school candidates. *Academic Medicine, 71*(Suppl. 1), S40–S42.

Hariton, E., Bortoletto, P., & Ayogu, N. (2016). Residency interviews in the 21st century. *Journal of Graduate Medical Education, 8*(3), 322–324.

Hissbach, J. C., Sehner, S., Harendza, S., & Hampe, W. (2014). Cutting costs of multiple mini-interviews—Changes in reliability and efficiency of the Hamburg medical school admission test between two applications. *BMC Medical Education, 14,* 20.

Hofmeister, M., Lockyer, J., & Crutcher, R. (2009). The multiple mini-interview for selection of international medical graduates into family medicine residency education. *Medical Education, 43*(6), 573–579.

Huffcutt, A. I. (2011). An empirical review of the employment interview construct literature. *International Journal of Selection and Assessment, 19*(1), 62–81.

Huffcutt, A. I., Weekley, J. A., Wiesner, W. H., Degroot, T. G., & Jones, C. (2001). Comparison of situational and behavior description interview questions for higher-level positions. *Personnel Psychology, 54*(3), 619–644.

Husbands, A., & Dowell, J. (2013). Predictive validity of the Dundee multiple mini-interview. *Medical Education, 47*(7), 717–725.

Issenberg, S. B., McGaghie, W. C., Petrusa, E. R., Lee Gordon, D., & Scalese, R. J. (2005). Features and uses of high-fidelity medical simulations that lead to effective learning: A BEME systematic review. *Medical Teacher, 27*(1), 10–28.

Jerant, A., Fancher, T., Fenton, J. J., Fiscella, K., Sousa, F., Franks, P., & Henderson, M. (2015). How medical school applicant race, ethnicity, and socioeconomic status relate to multiple mini-interview-based admissions outcomes: Findings from one medical school. *Academic Medicine, 90*(12), 1667–1674.

Jerant, A., Griffin, E., Rainwater, J., Henderson, M., Sousa, F., Bertakis, K. D., …, Franks, P. (2012). Does applicant personality influence multiple mini-interview performance and medical school acceptance offers? *Academic Medicine, 87*(9), 1250–1259.

Kelly, M. E., Dowell, J., Husbands, A., Newell, J., O'Flynn, S., Kropmans, T., …, Murphy, A. W. (2014). The fairness, predictive validity and acceptability of multiple mini interview in an internationally diverse student population—A mixed methods study. *BMC Medical Education, 14*, 13.

Kim, K.-J., Nam, K.-S., & Kwon, B. S. (2017). The utility of multiple mini-interviews: Experience of a medical school. *Korean Journal of Medical Education, 29*(1), 7–14.

Knorr, M., & Hissbach, J. (2014). Multiple mini-interviews: Same concept, different approaches. *Medical Education, 48*(12), 1157–1175.

König, C. J., Melchers, K. G., Kleinmann, M., Richter, G. M., & Klehe, U.-C. (2007). Candidates' ability to identify criteria in nontransparent selection procedures: Evidence from an assessment center and a structured interview. *International Journal of Selection and Assessment, 15*(3), 283–292.

Kreiter, C. D., Yin, P., Solow, C., & Brennan, R. L. (2004). Investigating the reliability of the medical school admissions interview. *Advances in Health Sciences Education, 9*(2), 147–159.

Lance, C. E. (2008). Why assessment centers do not work the way they are supposed to. *Industrial and Organizational Psychology, 1*(1), 84–97.

Leduc, J.-M., Rioux, R., Gagnon, R., Bourdy, C., & Dennis, A. (2017). Impact of sociodemographic characteristics of applicants in multiple mini-interviews. *Medical Teacher, 39*(3), 285–294.

Lee, H. J., Park, S. B., Park, S. C., Park, W. S., Ryu, S.-W., Yang, J. H., ..., Chae, G. B. (2016). Multiple mini-interviews as a predictor of academic achievements during the first 2 years of medical school. *BMC Research Notes, 9*, 93.

Lemay, J. F., Lockyer, J. M., Collin, V. T., & Brownell, A. K. W. (2007). Assessment of non-cognitive traits through the admissions multiple mini-interview. *Medical Education, 41*(6), 573–579.

Letterie, G. S. (2002). How virtual reality may enhance training in obstetrics and gynecology. *American Journal of Obstetrics and Gynecology, 187*(Suppl. 3), S37–S40.

Levashina, J., Hartwell, C. J., Morgeson, F. P., & Campion, M. A. (2014). The structured employment interview: Narrative and quantitative review of the research literature. *Personnel Psychology, 67*(1), 241–293.

Lievens, F., De Koster, L., & Schollaert, E. (2008). Current theory and practice of assessment centers: The importance of trait activation. In S. Cartwright & C. L. Cooper (Eds.), *The Oxford Handbook of Personnel Psychology* (pp. 215–233). Oxford: Oxford University Press.

Lievens, F., & Patterson, F. (2011). The validity and incremental validity of knowledge tests, low-fidelity simulations, and high-fidelity simulations for predicting job performance in advanced-level high-stakes selection. *Journal of Applied Psychology, 96*(5), 927–940.

Lievens, F., Schollaert, E., & Keen, G. (2015). The interplay of elicitation and evaluation of trait-expressive behavior: Evidence in assessment center exercises. *Journal of Applied Psychology, 100*(4), 1169–1188.

Locke, E. A., & Latham, G. P. (2002). Building a practically useful theory of goal setting and task motivation. A 35-year odyssey. *American Psychologist, 57*(9), 705–717.

Lumb, A. B., Homer, M., & Miller, A. (2010). Equity in interviews: Do personal characteristics impact on admission interview scores? *Medical Education, 44*(11), 1077–1083.

McCloy, R., & Stone, R. (2001). Virtual reality in surgery. *BMJ: British Medical Journal, 323*(7318), 912–915.

Morris, J. G. (1999). The value and role of the interview in the student admissions process: A review. *Medical Teacher, 21*(5), 473–481.

Moshinsky, A., Ziegler, D., & Gafni, N. (2017). Multiple mini-interviews in the age of the internet: Does preparation help applicants to medical school? *International Journal of Testing, 17*(3), 253–268.

Oliver, T., Hecker, K., Hausdorf, P. A., & Conlon, P. (2014). Validating MMI scores: Are we measuring multiple attributes? *Advances in Health Sciences Education, 19*(3), 379–392.

Oosterveld, P., & ten Cate, O. (2004). Generalizability of a study sample assessment procedure for entrance selection for medical school. *Medical Teacher, 26*(7), 635–639.

Panait, L., Larios, J. M., Brenes, R. A., Fancher, T. T., Ajemian, M. S., Dudrick, S. J., & Sanchez, J. A. (2011). Surgical skills assessment of applicants to general surgery residency. *Journal of Surgical Research, 170*(2), 189–194.

Pashayan, N., Gray, S., Duff, C., Parkes, J., Williams, D., Patterson, F., …, Mason, B. W. (2016). Evaluation of recruitment and selection for specialty training in public health: Interim results of a prospective cohort study to measure the predictive validity of the selection process. *Journal of Public Health, 38*(2), E194–E200.

Patterson, F., Knight, A., Dowell, J., Nicholson, S., Cousans, F., & Cleland, J. (2016). How effective are selection methods in medical education? A systematic review. *Medical Education, 50*(1), 36–60.

Patterson, F., Lievens, F., Kerrin, M., Munro, N., & Irish, B. (2013). The predictive validity of selection for entry into postgraduate training in general practice: Evidence from three longitudinal studies. *The British Journal of General Practice, 63*(616), E734–E741.

Patterson, F., Rowett, E., Hale, R., Grant, M., Roberts, C., Cousans, F., & Martin, S. (2016). The predictive validity of a situational judgement test and multiple-mini interview for entry into postgraduate training in Australia. *BMC Medical Education, 16,* 8.

Pau, A., Chen, Y. S., Lee, V. K. M., Sow, C. F., & De Alwis, R. (2016). What does the multiple mini interview have to offer over the panel interview? *Medical Education Online, 21,* 7.

Raghavan, M., Burnett, M., Martin, B. D., Christensen, H., Young, D. G., MacKalski, B., & Aoki, F. (2013). Utility of a writing station in the multiple mini-interview. *Journal of Veterinary Medical Education, 40*(2), 177–183.

Raghavan, M., Martin, B. D., Burnett, M., Aoki, F., Christensen, H., MacKalski, F., …, Ripstein, I. (2013). Multiple mini-interview scores of medical school applicants with and without rural attributes. *Rural and Remote Health, 13*(2), 9.

Rees, E. L., Hawarden, A. W., Dent, G., Hays, R., Bates, J., & Hassell, A. B. (2016). Evidence regarding the utility of multiple mini-interview (MMI) for selection to undergraduate health programs: A BEME systematic review: BEME Guide No. 37. *Medical Teacher, 38*(5), 443–455.

Reiter, H. I., Eva, K. W., Rosenfeld, J., & Norman, G. R. (2007). Multiple mini-interviews predict clerkship and licensing examination performance. *Medical Education, 41*(4), 378–384.

Reiter, H. I., Lockyer, J., Ziola, B., Courneya, C. A., & Eva, K. (2012). Should efforts in favor of medical student diversity be focused during admissions or farther upstream? *Academic Medicine, 87*(4), 443–448.

Reiter, H. I., Salvatori, P., Rosenfeld, J., Trinh, K., & Eva, K. W. (2006). The effect of defined violations of test security on admissions outcomes using multiple mini-interviews. *Medical Education, 40*(1), 36–42.

Roberts, C., Clark, T., Burgess, A., Frommer, M., Grant, M., & Mossman, K. (2014). The validity of a behavioural multiple-mini-interview within an assessment centre for selection into specialty training. *BMC Medical Education, 14,* 11.

Roberts, C., Rothnie, I., Zoanetti, N., & Crossley, J. (2010). Should candidate scores be adjusted for interviewer stringency or leniency in the multiple mini-interview? *Medical Education, 44*(7), 690–698.

Roberts, C., Zoanetti, N., & Rothnie, I. (2009). Validating a multiple mini-interview question bank assessing entry-level reasoning skills in candidates for graduate-entry medicine and dentistry programmes. *Medical Education, 43*(4), 350–359.

Roberts, M. J., Gale, T. C. E., McGrath, J. S., & Wilson, M. R. (2016). Rising to the challenge: Acute stress appraisals and selection centre performance in applicants to postgraduate specialty training in anaesthesia. *Advances in Health Sciences Education, 21*(2), 323–339.

Roberts, M. J., Gale, T. C. E., Sice, P. J. A., & Anderson, I. R. (2013). The relative reliability of actively participating and passively observing raters in a simulation-based assessment for selection to specialty training in anaesthesia. *Anaesthesia, 68*(6), 591–599.

Rosenfeld, J. M., Reiter, H. I., Trinh, K., & Eva, K. W. (2008). A cost efficiency comparison between the multiple mini-interview and traditional admissions interviews. *Advances in Health Sciences Education, 13*(1), 43–58.

Ross, M., Walker, I., Cooke, L., Raman, M., Ravani, P., Coderre, S., & McLaughlin, K. (2017). Are female applicants rated higher than males on the multiple mini-interview? Findings from the University of Calgary. *Academic Medicine, 92*(6), 841–846.

Rupp, D. E., Hoffman, B. J., Bischof, D., Byham, W., Collins, L., Gibbons, A., …, Thornton, G. (2015). Guidelines and ethical considerations for assessment center operations. *Journal of Management, 41*(4), 1244–1273.

Salvatori, P. (2001). Reliability and validity of admissions tools used to select students for the health professions. *Advances in Health Sciences Education, 6*(2), 159–175.

Schleicher, D. J., Day, D. V., Mayes, B. T., & Riggio, R. E. (2002). A new frame for frame-of-reference training: Enhancing the construct validity of assessment centers. *Journal of Applied Psychology, 87*(4), 735–746.

Schmidt, F. L., & Hunter, J. E. (1998). The validity and utility of selection methods in personnel psychology: Practical and theoretical implications of 85 years of research findings. *Psychological Bulletin, 124*(2), 262–274.

Schultheis, M. T., & Rizzo, A. A. (2001). The application of virtual reality technology in rehabilitation. *Rehabilitation Psychology, 46*(3), 296–311.

Sebok, S. S., Luu, K., & Klinger, D. A. (2014). Psychometric properties of the multiple mini-interview used for medical admissions: Findings from generalizability and Rasch analyses. *Advances in Health Sciences Education, 19*(1), 71–84.

Shah, S. K., Arora, S., Skipper, B., Kalishman, S., Timm, T. C., & Smith, A. Y. (2012). Randomized evaluation of a web based interview process for urology resident selection. *The Journal of Urology, 187*(4), 1380–1384.

Tett, R. P., & Burnett, D. D. (2003). A personality trait-based interactionist model of job performance. *Journal of Applied Psychology, 88*(3), 500–517.

Tiller, D., O'Mara, D., Rothnie, I., Dunn, S., Lee, L., & Roberts, C. (2013). Internet-based multiple mini-interviews for candidate selection for graduate entry programmes. *Medical Education, 47*, 801–810.

Torres, E. N., & Mejia, C. (2017). Asynchronous video interviews in the hospitality industry: Considerations for virtual employee selection. *International Journal of Hospitality Management, 61*(Suppl. C), 4–13.

Uijtdehaage, S., Doyle, L. H., & Parker, N. (2011). Enhancing the reliability of the multiple mini-interview for selecting prospective health care leaders. *Academic Medicine, 86*(8), 1032–1039.

Wernimont, P. F., & Campbell, J. P. (1968). Signs, samples, and criteria. *Journal of Applied Psychology, 52*(5), 372–376.

Yamada, T., Sato, J., Yoshimura, H., Okubo, T., Hiraoka, E., Shiga, T., …, Ban, N. (2017). Reliability and acceptability of six station multiple mini-interviews: Past-behavioural versus situational questions in postgraduate medical admission. *BMC Medical Education, 17*, 7.

Ziv, A., Rubin, O., Moshinsky, A., Gafni, N., Kotler, M., Dagan, Y., …, Mittelman, M. (2008). MOR: A simulation-based assessment centre for evaluating the personal and interpersonal qualities of medical school candidates. *Medical Education, 42*(10), 991–998.

6

Role Analysis: The Foundation for Selection Systems

Máire Kerrin, Liz Mossop, Emma Morley, Gail Fleming and Charlotte Flaxman

Overview

Selection into healthcare professions internationally is often competitive, with high stakes for the individual, organization, and public (Patterson et al., 2016). This is the case at every stage of the career pathway, from admissions to undergraduate courses, through to the various transition stages during postgraduate training. Ensuring that selection processes are valid, reliable, and fair to all applicants is, therefore, crucial across healthcare professions. Research has consistently shown that the cornerstone of effective selection is identifying selection criteria through role analysis studies; a fundamental first step in selection design

M. Kerrin (✉) · E. Morley · C. Flaxman
Work Psychology Group, Derby, UK
e-mail: m.kerrin@workpsychologygroup.com

E. Morley
e-mail: e.morley@workpsychologygroup.com

C. Flaxman
e-mail: c.flaxman@workpsychologygroup.com

F. Patterson and L. Zibarras (eds.), *Selection and Recruitment in the Healthcare Professions*, https://doi.org/10.1007/978-3-319-94971-0_6

(Ash, 1998; Patterson, Ferguson, & Knight, 2013). Through role analysis, the knowledge, skills, abilities, and other characteristics (KSAOs) associated with competent performance in a role can be identified and used to inform the selection process (Arnold et al., 2016; Brannick, Cadle, & Levine, 2012; Breaugh, 2017).

This chapter draws upon the latest role analysis research, while providing practical case material on the application of role analyses and their outputs, within a range of healthcare professions. By the end of this chapter, you should:

- understand role analyses methodologies and their application in the healthcare professions,
- understand how the outputs of role analyses can be used to develop role-specific selection criteria and inform the choice and design of selection methods,
- have an awareness of the benefits of conducting specific role analyses for individual healthcare professions,
- understand the use of role analyses outputs to enhance the validity of selection methods/processes,
- have insight into potential challenges and practical implications associated with role analyses,
- and have insight into the future of role analysis and how we can ensure outputs remain current.

Throughout the chapter, we will draw upon three case studies as illustrative examples to explore the points set out above in more depth. These include Veterinary Undergraduate Admissions, Pre-registration

L. Mossop
Vice Chancellor's Office, University of Lincoln, Lincoln, UK
e-mail: LMossop@lincoln.ac.uk

G. Fleming
Health Education England, London, UK
e-mail: Gail.Fleming@hee.nhs.uk

Pharmacy, and General Practice (family physicians), which represent three different healthcare professions across various stages of the career pathway. We draw upon the international research literature, in particular, relating to role analysis used for General Practice selection (Patterson, Howe, Tavabie, & Watson, 2013; Patterson, Tavabie, et al., 2013; Patterson et al., 2000), in addition to the broader literature (Brannick et al., 2012; Nikolaou & Oostrom, 2017).

Introduction

The terms "role analysis," "job analysis," and "work analysis" are often used interchangeably to refer to processes that inform the development of selection criteria, job descriptions, role and team design, recruitment and selection of personnel, workforce development, performance management and compensation (Morgeson & Dierdorff, 2011). "Practice analysis" is also a term used in healthcare to unpick the core components of a job by soliciting information from professionals in the field about the elements that underpin effective delivery of a role (McKenzie et al., 2016). For ease, we use the term "role analysis" throughout this chapter, which is applicable to undergraduate, postgraduate, and senior-level selection settings.

In the context of selection, role analysis is a systematic process for collecting and analyzing job-relevant information; outputs of which provide a framework of the important KSAOs required for both selection into training and subsequent performance in clinical practice, and can be used to identify, and prioritize, role-specific selection criteria (Arnold et al., 2016).

Research consistently demonstrates that an important first phase when designing effective selection processes is identifying selection criteria through role analyses (Ash, 1998; Brannick et al., 2012; Patterson, Ferguson, & Thomas, 2008; Pearn & Kandola, 1993; Sanchez & Levine, 2012a). However, in practice, role analysis is often overlooked, due to selection design being driven by a preference for or acceptability of a particular selection method. While the choice of selection method is important, the validity of each method depends on accurately

Table 6.1 Role analysis case studies for three UK healthcare professions

Healthcare profession	Case study description
Veterinary (undergraduate)	Selection into undergraduate veterinary education in the UK is extremely competitive. The traditional approach of reviewing application forms and scoring based on academic achievement alone was seen as insufficient to select upon for one Veterinary school in the UK. In order to understand better what criteria should be included in the selection process, a role analysis was necessary to identify the broader KSAOs required
Pharmacy (postgraduate pre-registration)	Within the UK, as the role of pharmacy is evolving, the skills required of pharmacists to provide high-quality service and engagement with patients are also changing. Due to these changes and a new national recruitment process in the UK, it was determined that a role analysis was necessary to identify KSAOs to inform the selection criteria for the national recruitment process
General Practice (specialty training)	Selection criteria for entry into General Practitioner training in the UK was established over 18 years ago (Patterson et al., 2000) and reviewed in 2005. However, due to the broadening of the General Practitioner role in 2010 (Department of Health, 2010), it was determined that a role analysis was required to evaluate whether the current selection criteria was still suitable

assessing relevant criteria important to the role. By identifying and specifying content and construct valid selection criteria, more accurate blueprinting of a selection system and method is possible.

This chapter addresses several key issues, including the *value* of conducting a role analysis; best practice *methods* of conducting role analyses in healthcare; the use of role analysis *outputs* to improve the validity and reliability of selection procedures; potential challenges and the *future* of role analysis studies. Throughout, for illustration purposes, we draw upon evidence relating to role analyses conducted in three different healthcare professions in the UK; Veterinary, Pharmacy, and General Practice. The three case studies were selected to show a range of roles (veterinary, pharmacy, and medical) across different stages within the career pathway (undergraduate, postgraduate, and specialty training). The three examples also enable us to draw upon the similarities and differences in role analysis process, outputs, and subsequent uses. Table 6.1 provides an overview of each case study.

What is the Value of Role Analysis?

Investment in a multi-source, multi-method role analysis study can result in many benefits that influence the full lifecycle of selection system design. One benefit of conducting a role analysis is the greater knowledge of selection criteria that distinguish high performing professionals; which in turn allows for the development of evidence-based job specifications, the formulation of person specifications, evidence-based (and appropriately blueprinted) selection methods, and the attraction and recruitment of suitable candidates for the role. Role analysis outputs can inform many elements of the selection methodology including, for example, interview question design, development of interview stations and simulations, and informing the specification of any tests used in selection [(e.g., situational judgment tests (SJTs)]. The wide range of value adding components are depicted in Fig. 6.1.

A role analysis study can also have the potential to reduce extended training costs by more accurately identifying those who are at more risk of falling into difficulty during training (Naidoo, Lopes, Patterson, Mead, & Macleod, 2016). For example, a recent review of medical admissions research found that well-designed selection processes, that include an accurate assessment of job-relevant criteria, are more predictive of subsequent job performance (Kreiter & Axelson, 2013).

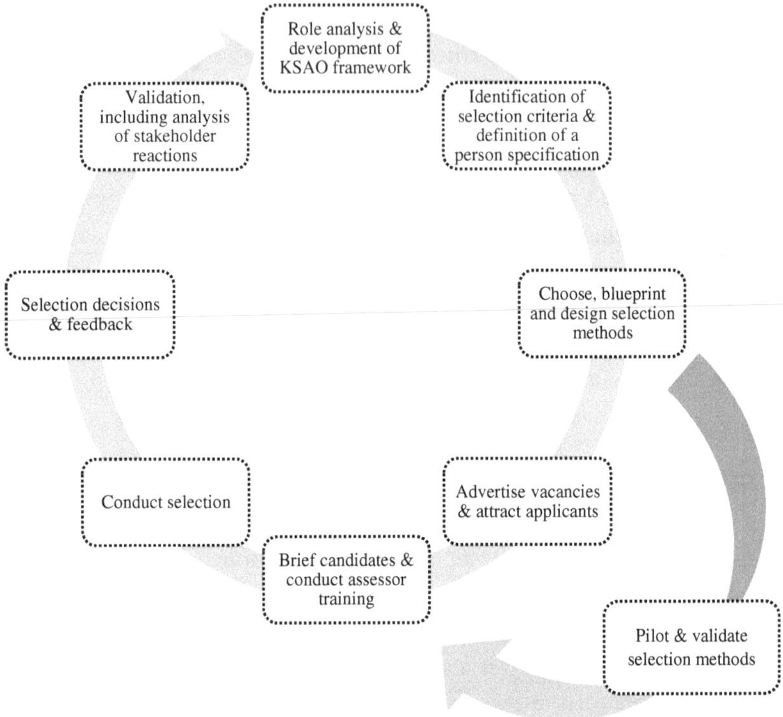

Fig. 6.1 Role analysis contribution to best practice selection process design

In addition, role analyses can play a valuable part in widening access to the healthcare professions. Some medical schools are broadening the mapping of job KSAOs and designing selection systems to be more inclusive of groups that might have traditionally had barriers to entering medical training programs. This includes applicants from lower socio-economic groups and diverse cultural backgrounds. As a result, there is a growing appreciation of applicants' non-academic attributes that might be desirable in healthcare service delivery, such as skills in intercultural awareness, which can be defined as part of role analysis studies.

Role analysis studies are often particularly valuable at transitional points in the career pathway; this is where individuals progress into different roles, and therefore, as the role changes, a different set of KSAOs required are likely to be. Using the General Practitioner case study as an example, in the UK, this is the transition in the medical career pathway between the Foundation Programme and General Practitioner Specialty Training. Therefore, when selecting into roles at these transition points, it is even more important that a role analysis is conducted to ensure that the appropriate KSAOs are being selected for at that stage. Over time, a range of external factors, such as changes in legislation, patient demand, or advances in technology can mean that the job requirements and important KSAOs can change (Singh, 2008). Therefore, it is recommended that role analyses are future oriented, to ensure that the KSAOs required to be successful in the future (as for example, the discipline of medicine changes rapidly), is specified in the selection criteria (Arnold et al., 2016; Singh, 2008).

Role Analysis Methodologies and their Application in Healthcare Professions

Role analysis studies, used to inform selection into healthcare training programs and job roles, play a critical role in determining whether professionals, trainees, and students have the relevant KSAOs suited for delivery of competent clinical practice. A role analysis study can help validate "good practice" and capitalize on emerging patterns of effective practice. These benefits may, however, be dependent on the methodology employed.

An influential framework that defines key competencies for the medical profession is the Canadian Medical Education Directives for Specialists, known as the CanMEDS initiative. CanMEDS was originally developed in the 1990s and revised in 2015 by the Royal College of Physicians and Surgeons of Canada to better prepare trainee physicians for a rapidly changing healthcare environment. Developed using a role analysis methodology, CanMEDS defined the key competencies required by physicians to adapt to a changing landscape of healthcare delivery. The role analysis process was underpinned by the key question, "How can we best prepare physicians to deliver high quality healthcare to meet the needs of patients?"

There is no one best way to conduct a role analysis; different methods have their relative advantages and disadvantages and thereby, best practice is the use of multi-source, multi-method approaches to triangulate different sources of information. Good quality role analysis most often includes a bespoke solution designed for a role that gathers information from different sources using multiple means. There are a range of data collection methods available to assist in analyzing the suite of KSAOs that underpin healthcare practice. A number of methods are outlined in Table 6.2 describing how they might be administered and indicating the appropriateness of each method. Each of these methods described are suitable to use for both existing and newly created job roles, such as the recently created Physician Associate (British Medical Association, 2017) and Nurse Associate (Nursing and Midwifery Council, 2017) roles in the UK.

A multi-source, multi-method approach to conducting a role analysis (e.g., through combining the use of a number of methods outlined in Table 6.2) is recommended, because it allows the identification of aspects of a role that are unlikely to be accessible through a single methodology (Gutman, 2000; Koch et al., 2012; Patterson et al., 2000; Robertson & Smith, 2001). The validity and reliability of a role analysis study is improved when data are gathered from multiple perspectives (Dierdorff & Wilson, 2003; Patterson et al., 2000). For example, gathering data from experienced practitioners, as well as patients receiving services from those practitioners, supervisors overseeing practice, or medical educators delivering programs to trainees. These multiple sources of data enable triangulation of results, making role analyses more comprehensive (Campion et al., 2011).

Each of the case studies in this chapter used multi-source, multi-method approaches to analyze the KSAOs required to perform effectively within the role. The specific methodology used in the role analyses was designed according to the organizational context and resource availability. Each role analysis study uses a combination of literature or desk reviews, interviews, stakeholder consultations, and behavioral observations (Arnold et al., 2016). The methodology

Table 6.2 Role analysis methods suitable for healthcare

Method	Administration	Appropriateness
Questionnaire/survey	• Online, mail or face-to-face • Structured and/or open questions • Bespoke solution for a specific context	Useful for gathering data from a large sample in different contexts and locations; often used for incumbents, validation of role analysis outputs arising from the collection of other data
Interviews/focus groups	• Face-to-face, via phone or teleconference • Structured and/or semi structured interviews • Individual or group interviews • Focus groups	Conducted with subject matter experts (such as role incumbents, supervisors, members of the multi-disciplinary team, patients). Often combined with other objective data
Observation methods	• Direct and indirect observation of a role, e.g., the work environment, tools and equipment used, interrelationships with other workers, handling of critical incidents • Data collected can include both quantitative (proportion of time spent) and qualitative (demands of different tasks) • Job shadowing	Often healthcare roles are complex, involving diverse behavioral responses, novel situations, creative problem solving, multi-disciplinary team work and use of technology. Therefore, direct observation can be very helpful in unpicking some of the required KSAOs
Task analysis	• Breaking down the detailed components of how a task is performed including various elements such as; duration, frequency, complexity, cognitive requirements, manual handling, environmental conditions, role of team members, necessary equipment, safety requirements and any other unique factors	Due to the complexity of job roles, breaking the task down into smaller components can be very helpful in defining the KSAOs required

(continued)

Table 6.2 (continued)

Method	Administration	Appropriateness
Analysis of existing policy documentation	• Organizational charts • Strategic plans • Task inventories • Competency frameworks • Graduate selection material • Application forms • Job descriptions • Professional body requirements and standards • Documentation for other relevant professions	This is a key foundational activity, often appropriate when conducting role analysis. A mapping exercise may be helpful once a new competency framework has been defined, to ensure that no behavioral indicators have been overlooked
Work records	• Healthcare administration data • Human resource records and statistics • Staff engagement and culture survey data • Workplace health and safety data • Job applicant test scores correlated against job performance	Particularly useful when looking to understand the organizational factors (e.g., culture, staff engagement, turn over, safety) that impact on a job role. Supports the understanding of the job factors required within a particular context, such as public health versus private health setting
Delphi technique	• Involves experts responding to a series of questions • Qualitative analysis is conducted on the expert opinions gathered in an attempt to identify common themes • Identified themes are then delivered to a group of experts who are required to rate the importance of them. At this stage, consensus is achieved among experts concerning the most important themes	This is a useful method for generating accurate knowledge and identifying KSAOs through group consensus of technical experts (Keeney, Hasson, & McKenna, 2011; Rowe & Wright, 1999; Steurer, 2011)

used for the General Practitioner role analysis is outlined in Fig. 6.2. Critical Incident Technique (CIT; Flanagan, 1954) was used in the stakeholder interviews and consultations to identify specific incidents of behaviors that were particularly effective or ineffective. Behavioral observations in General Practices were undertaken. Data collected were then triangulated, in order to collate the information into an initial KSAO framework presented for feedback which was validated through a large scale validation survey, before the KSAOs were finalized.

Once validated through a survey that was completed by stakeholders, outputs from the role analysis were used to improve the selection process, for example, by acting as a basis to shape specific selection tools.

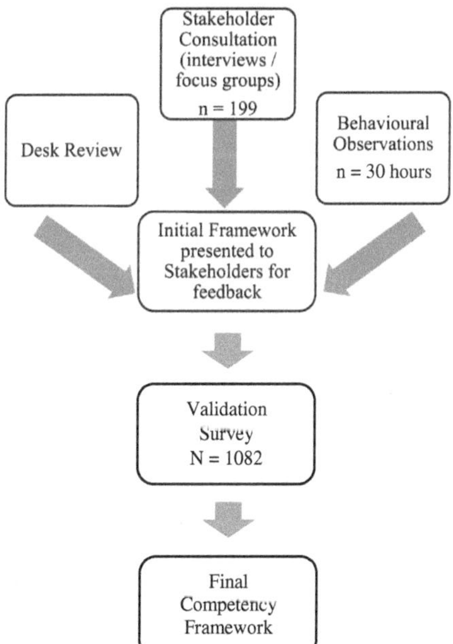

Fig. 6.2 Role analysis methodology utilized for general practitioners (Patterson, Tavabie, et al. 2013)

Role Analysis Outputs

Following completion of a role analysis, the output is a role-specific framework which includes the final KSAOs relevant to the role, and for each, further information detailing how each KSAO may manifest itself in that role (which are often referred to as positive and negative behavioral indicators or behavioral descriptors). An overview of the KSAOs that emerged from each of the three role analyses are outlined in Table 6.3.

While it is sometimes argued that these high level KSAOs domains could be identified relatively quickly and without the need for a full analysis of the role, the value of a thorough role analysis is evident in the level of detail provided by the positive and negative behavioral indicators or descriptors that are generated for each domain. Such indicators can be used as assessment markers when operationalizing the role analysis outputs as a blueprint for selection criteria. Research by Patterson et al. (2008) offers an example of this, whereby three independent role analysis studies were conducted across three medical specialties (Obstetrics & Gynecology, Pediatrics, and Anesthesia). While a model was developed comprising 14 domain areas common across the

Table 6.3 Overview of KSAOs, for three healthcare professions

Veterinary	Pharmacy	General practice
• Business awareness • Communication skills • Empathy & building client relationships • Professional integrity & trust • Resilience • Team work • Technical knowledge/skills & continuous learning • Work standards & time management	• Communication & consultation skills • Multi-professional working & leadership • Person-centred care • Pharmacy in practice • Problem-solving, clinical analysis & decision making • Professional integrity & ethics • Quality management & organisation • Resilience & adaptability • Self-directed learning & motivation	• Clinical knowledge & expertise • Communication skills • Conceptual thinking & problem solving • Coping with pressure • Effective team working • Empathy & perspective taking • Leading for continuing improvement • Learning & development of self & others • Organization & management of resources • Professional integrity • Respect for diversity & the law

three specialties, significant differences in relation to the definitions and behavioral descriptors of each domain were evident (reflecting the context of the target roles) along with differences in the perceived importance of each domain across the three specialties.

To further illustrate this, behavioral indicators for "teamwork" are provided in Table 6.4. Each behavioral indicator was generated through validating the description of the behavior from various sources and demonstrates the richness of the data that emerges through using thorough role analysis techniques.

Using the example of teamwork as a common domain, here we examine the differences and commonalities in the teamwork behavioral descriptors, to explore the extent to which behavioral descriptors are specific to different roles and levels. Figure 6.3 shows areas of commonality and difference across the three health professional roles. At the point of intersection, the three healthcare professions share the requirement to work collaboratively in teams and draw on others for support and learning. Within pre-registration pharmacy and General Practitioner, there is a focus on the ability to respect different people's roles and expertise in a multi-disciplinary team and motivating colleagues. In contrast, the veterinary descriptors (undergraduate trainee level) focus more on working in partnership to achieve team goals and building on the ideas of others, which is more appropriate given the expectations of an individual at that level.

Pre-registration pharmacy also shares similarities with veterinary descriptors around building effective relationships both within the immediate team and more broadly. The greater overlap that the pharmacy indicators have with the other two roles is unsurprising given that this role sits in the middle of the other two in relation to career progression. Pre-registration pharmacy behavioral descriptors also specify facilitation of learning in others, delegation of tasks based on availability across the team, and providing constructive feedback. Although there are overlaps in behavioral indicators between these three professions, it is also important to note that subtle but important variations still remain within the wording, thus suggesting small role-specific differences. For example, for veterinary students, "collaboration" is purely about working in partnership, while for pre-registration pharmacists,

Table 6.4 Behavioral indicators for team work, for three healthcare professions

Profession	Teamwork Indicators
Veterinary	• Actively participating as a member of a team to move the team toward the completion of goals • Demonstrates a collaborative style, seeks to work in partnership with others • Supports others and builds on their ideas • Builds effective working relationships with people from many backgrounds and professions
Preregistration pharmacist[a]	• Understands, values and respects all roles within the immediate and wider team • Willing and able to facilitate others' learning through sharing own knowledge/experience and/or supporting others when learning • Builds and maintains meaningful and trusting relationships with team members and other health and social care professionals outside of the immediate team • Demonstrates an awareness of other team members' workloads and pressures and adapts their interactions accordingly • Works collaboratively, provides assistance, support and guidance to other members of the team for the benefit of the person receiving care • Provides constructive feedback for individual development • Motivates and leads others, acts as a role model • Demonstrates willingness and ability to actively learn from others • Demonstrates an awareness of the available resources within the team and makes use of these through delegation to achieve person-centred outcomes
General practice	• Able to effectively influence and negotiate with others; promotes an inclusive approach; motivates others to achieve goals • Supportive of colleagues; offers advice and assistance as required; understands and respects others' roles within the wider multi-professional team • Is open to sharing information; collaborative with other professionals; acknowledges and appreciates others' expertise; willing to learn from others

[a]In this role analysis, teamwork was described in the context of multi professional working and leadership as for this role teamwork was one element of a broader domain

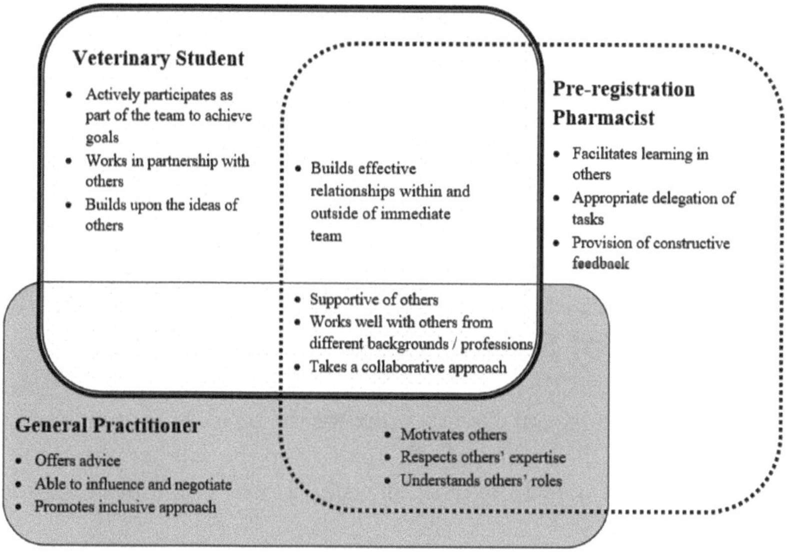

Fig. 6.3 Behavioral descriptors for team work, for three healthcare professions

"collaboration" extends to providing support and assistance to colleagues and the importance of doing this to benefit the patient.

Role analysis outputs, or identified KSAOs, are used to inform selection methods in a number of ways. Firstly, by informing which KSAOs are prioritized as selection criteria and which selection method best assess these (e.g., interview, role play, group exercise). Not all of the identified KSAOs and behavioral indicators will be assessed during a selection process, for several reasons. For example, the KSAOs may not all be deemed appropriate to assess at point of selection as they may not be required on entry into the role but will rather be developed during the education and training/curriculum (e.g., legal and technical aspects). Practically, there are time limits for assessing a single candidate, particularly within large scale selection. Therefore, the KSAOs most often need to be prioritized.

A second way that the outputs contribute to the selection methods is in the design of the selection methods. For example, for the General Practitioner selection center, role analysis outputs were used to guide the design of simulation exercise to assess empathy and sensitivity, a key output from the role analysis. A final way in which the outputs can be used is in the design of the assessment and scoring guidance. Again, for the General Practitioner simulation exercise, behavioral descriptors helped to guide assessor scoring contributing to a more reliable assessment of the criteria.

The Use of Role Analysis Outputs to Enhance the Validity of Selection Systems

Role analysis outputs can directly enhance the validity of selection systems. In assessing the impact of role analysis on the validity of selection, evidence in relation to four types of validity are commonly examined (Arnold et al., 2016).

Content Validity
Content validity refers to the content of a selection method and its relevance to the role. To establish the content validity of selection criteria, a validation questionnaire can be used as part of role analysis to validate KSAOs and behavioral indicators by gaining wider feedback from stakeholders. Evidence from the validation surveys conducted for each of the case examples discussed within this chapter demonstrated support for each of the KSAOs, and the behavioral indicators contained within; as all KSAOs and behavioral indicators were rated on average as "important," by stakeholders.

Face Validity
Face validity refers to whether a selection method looks appropriate or relevant for the role, which has a positive impact on user acceptability. It can be evaluated through stakeholder reactions (applicants, recruiters) to a given selection criterion or method. Evidence suggests that a majority of stakeholders agree that the content of the selection methods that have been designed using outputs of role analyses, are appropriate for, and relevant to, the target roles, as well as being fair and at an appropriate level of difficulty (Koczwara et al., 2012;

Patterson, Zibarras, Carr, Irish, & Gregory, 2011; Plint & Patterson, 2010; Roberts et al., 2014). This provides support for the face validity of these methods in their respective healthcare selection processes. We would argue that this directly relates to the way in which the selection methods have been designed, specific to each role and based on thorough role analysis.

Predictive Validity

Predictive validity broadly refers to the extent to which selection scores correlate with subsequent performance in the role (Arnold et al., 2016). Evidence from three longitudinal studies has demonstrated that the General Practitioner selection process, designed based on the outputs of a role analysis, has good evidence of predictive validity. Results show that the best predictor of end-of-training licensing examinations outcomes is the combination of a clinical problem-solving test, an SJT, and a selection center (Patterson, Lievens, Kerrin, Munro, & Irish, 2013) whereby each selection method was significantly correlated with examinations (corrected r ranging from 0.41 to 0.85, $p < 0.01$).

Construct Validity

Construct validity refers to the extent to which selection methods accurately measure what they are designed to measure. This can be evaluated by comparing how the measurement of constructs in newly developed selection methods compare with the same constructs measured by alternative, more established methods. For construct validity to exist, there needs to be strong correlations between the two methods. Construct validity is not established through one analysis, instead it becomes apparent over time through the use of the selection method and further analyses.

Role analysis can add to the validity of a selection system, particularly in content, face, and predictive validity. However, there are still challenges that need to be addressed for both research and practice in understanding the future of role analysis in selection which we now explore.

The Challenges and the Future of Role Analysis

A key challenge with staying up to date with contemporary practice is that role analysis methodologies tend to analyze the KSAOs required of a healthcare professional at one point in time. One way to ensure the output remains relevant for as long as possible is to consider the *future direction* of the role when conducting the role analysis, therefore, not only seeking to understand the KSAOs important for success in the role now but also what skills may be necessary for the role in the future. This has resulted in recommendations for role analyses to focus on future needs of professions, and gather current and future perspectives of roles (Koch et al., 2012; Singh, 2008). Focusing on the current and future perspectives of required KSAOs was the approach used in the pre-registration pharmacist case study, as the role had already begun to evolve.

However, for some roles where change has not yet been anticipated, this approach may not be possible. This presents a challenge when the pace of change is rapid, such as how digital technology reconfigures what knowledge and skills are required for a role within a short time period. A review of the outputs of a role analysis may be required when there has been an update in the way equipment is used in the delivery of healthcare; significant changes in interdependencies between roles (e.g., nurses' role in medication prescription); critical incidents or events that have shaped new work processes (e.g., triage of emergency patients away from hospitals to out of hours services); or legal changes have opened up new processes (e.g., medically monitored illicit substance injecting rooms).

Whether change is being instigated by a triggering factor, innovation, or the lapsing of time (Bennett, Alliger, Wilson, & Gibson, 2013), the move to renew role analysis information is an important part of the quality audit process that should underpin competitive selection processes, and a common theme in the role analysis literature is when, or how often, role analyses should take place and the importance of ensuring a future focus on the analysis, particularly given the changing nature of the workplace (Sanchez & Levine, 2012b; Singh, 2008). For example, the outputs of UK General Practitioner role analysis were reviewed 12 years following the original role analysis study was conducted, due to significant changes in the role. A revised model of the KSAOs included a new competency domain and the results signified that the role had significantly increased in breadth since the original KSAOs were identified (Patterson, Tavabie, et al., 2013).

A second challenge is that role analysis strives toward a clear demarcation of tasks and responsibilities, and yet healthcare professionals are increasingly working in more complex and multi-professional *team-based environments* (Singh, 2008). Some authors have argued the sharp differentiation of responsibilities in a role analysis process limits the adoption of innovation (Drucker, 1987; Olian & Rynes, 1991; Sanchez & Levine, 1999). The nature of health systems and healthcare roles increasingly require more flexible and adaptive work competencies and role analysis methodologies need to accommodate these changes. This requires role analysis assessments to be able to ascertain diverse yet complimentary KSAOs that might not only be specific to an individual role and health discipline, but also need to accommodate working across multi-disciplinary teams. Similarly, a role analysis might need to pick up KSAOs required at a specific level of training as well as those that are applicable across various stages in the career trajectory. Better role analysis methodologies to assist with assessing the cross-role transferability of skills (Lance, Kavanagh, & Brink, 2002) will grow in importance as the trend increases toward the high rates of role changes within a career and longer working lives due to older retirement age in many parts of the globe (especially in healthcare).

Health professions need to identify the KSAOs that prepare people to confidently meet the future emerging trends and the changing nature of job roles (Burke & Ng, 2006; Schabracq & Cooper, 2000). To remain viable, role analysis needs to be able to encompass the strategic challenges that healthcare professionals collectively face, including the growing interdependencies across traditional role boundaries. The boundary spanning orientation of health professionals needs to be combined with a focus on foundational KSAOs specific to each role and areas of specialization.

It is likely that an emphasis on social, interpersonal, and communications skills in addition to technical skills will continue in the future. Non-academic attributes (personality, attitudes, values, emotional intelligence) will continue to grow in importance in the selection of healthcare professions and role analysis methods will need to continue to forge reliable and valid means to measure these attributes in role analysis studies (Farr & Tippins, 2013).

Future research should focus on a broader diversity of health professional roles, locations, and context with adequate sample sizes to ensure sufficient evidence to make meaningful inferences from the findings. Role analysis techniques need to meet the various healthcare professions' current and emerging challenges. In a rapidly changing environment, practice changes can be proactively monitored by conducting longitudinal trend analysis from various data sources (role analysis, health administration data, research findings, recruitment, training, and job performance data). The future seems likely to hold a greater emphasis in exploring the impact of macro dimensions, such as organizational strategy, structure, and culture on the KSAOs required of a job during the selection process and in the actual work tasks performed. This will require increasingly drawing upon diverse types of macro organization data in the role analysis process (demographics trends, measures of desired organizational culture, business, and strategy plans); looking at work practice innovations from across different industries; engaging diverse subject matter experts and including more macro units of analysis.

Implications for Practice

Despite the clear importance of conducting a thorough role analysis as an initial stage in developing selection processes, a role analysis is not always straightforward to implement. There may be a resistance within professions to tackle the issue of selection and stakeholders may feel that they "know" the requirements they are looking for without conducting a thorough role analysis. Managing some of these challenges in conducting and implementing role analyses have been documented elsewhere; in particular, the social pressures to agree with a perceived view of the job role (Morgeson & Dierdorff, 2011).

Role analyses can be time consuming, and there is a practical and research need, to be able to demonstrate the added value to selection.

Measures of added value often need to be at multiple levels; for the individual applicants or trainees, the organization (e.g., medical college, hospital, or clinic), and government in relation to its investment in health services. Throughout the career pathway, from undergraduate admissions to selection into postgraduate training and employment, reducing the time spent dealing with challenges resulting from poor selection decisions has a strong economic and legal argument. The sound identification of selection criteria through robust role analysis can support the defensibility of a selection system and the individual decisions selection panels make (Plint & Patterson, 2010). While role analysis has been discussed here in the context of selection, there are also significant benefits to related areas of development, performance strategy, and even organizational culture. Using robust methodologies to identify and accurately articulate the key KSAOs required in a role now and in the future can provide an important platform for education and development interventions at the individual, team, and organizational level.

Conclusions

This chapter has outlined the use of role analyses and implications for selection, at different stages of professional healthcare training using three case examples. The three case examples cover relatively diverse roles in healthcare, and the use of role analyses have proved critical in defining KSAOs required for success in these healthcare roles. While conducting a role analysis can be a relatively time-consuming process, this chapter has identified the return of investment that is possible by using the information to develop valid and effective selection processes tailored to a specific role. There are both economic and professional implications of not conducting adequate role analysis to identify selection criteria, as good quality role analysis ensures the selection methods are assessing the most appropriate and relevant criteria for the role, and is powerful in enhancing performance in training (Kreiter & Axelson, 2013) and on the job.

While the three role analyses presented in this chapter are from different healthcare professions, and different stages of training, the resulting headline KSAO domains can be similar (i.e., all three analyses included elements of team work). However, at the behavioral indicator level, the focus of the KSAOs can look very different, with important nuances depending on the role. This detailed information can support the design of the selection methods, and inform developments required in these KSAOs at important transitional stages. For example, which elements of team work become more important when transitioning into postgraduate training? Subtle but important developments may be required, and what has worked well previously in team work at an undergraduate level, may not be effective in postgraduate training. In addition, in an increasingly multi-professional healthcare context, understanding the commonalities and differences across roles and levels could help to inform targeted training and development.

The evidence presented in this chapter illustrates the importance of conducting a role analysis for each transitional stage of training. It is important to recognize the need to return to role analyses on a regular basis and ensure changes in KSAOs required for professions at each selection stage are reflected in the selection processes employed. Outputs have the potential to evolve as the job role changes as reflected in the General Practitioner role analysis (Patterson, Tavabie, et al., 2013). Integrating these new and evolving KSAOs into existing selection processes is often an under-reported part of the role analysis process, and continues to be an important element in ultimately improving selection practices in healthcare.

Practice Points

- There is no single best way to conduct a role analysis, but multi-source, multi-method role analysis approaches allow for a range of perspectives to be gathered.
- Role analysis outputs are central to shaping selection blueprints, methods, and scoring.
- By gathering information relating to relevant KSAOs, role analysis can improve the validity and reliability of selection procedures.

- When conducting a role analysis, there should be an element of future focus so that identified KSAOs remain relevant over time.
- Anticipate change in health systems and roles so that identified KSAOs remain relevant in the future.
- Adapt role analysis studies to consider technology and the increasingly team based and multi-disciplinary nature of healthcare roles, where demarcation of tasks are potentially less clear.

Explore Further

Full details for all references are given in the list of references at the end of this chapter.

1. To gain a broader understanding of role analysis, consult a comprehensive text on the topic, such as book chapters by Breaugh (2017) *The Contribution of Job Analysis to Recruitment* or Morgeson and Dierdorff's (2011) *Work Analysis: From technique to theory.*
2. Comprehensive recruitment and selection texts are also useful for obtaining a broader understanding of role analysis, in-depth discussions are presented in Goldstein and Passmore's (2017) book *The Wiley Blackwell Handbook of the Psychology of Recruitment, Selection, and Employee Retention* and Nikolaou and Oostrom's (2017) *Employee Recruitment, Selection, and Assessment.*
3. Further detailed information concerning best practice in role analysis can be seen in the text by Arnold et al. (2016) *Work Psychology: Understanding human behaviour in the workplace* and the article by Campion et al. (2011) *Doing competencies well: Best practices in competency modelling.*
4. Text highlighting the value of role analysis in healthcare, in terms of improving assessment, and selection include the book chapter by Patterson, Ferguson, et al. (2013) *Selection for medical education and training*; as well as articles by McGuire, Rankin, Mathews, Cerinus, and Zaveri (2016) *Improving the quality of the NHS workforce through values and competency-based selection.*

References

Arnold, J., Randall, R., Patterson, F., Silvester, J., Robertson, I., Cooper, C., … Den Hartog, D. (2016). *Work psychology: Understanding human behaviour in the workplace* (6th ed.). Essex: Pearson Education Limited.

Ash, R. A. (1998). Job analysis in the world of work. In S. Gael (Ed.), *The Job analysis handbook* (pp. 3–13). New York: Wiley.

Bennett, W., Jr., Alliger, G. M., Wilson, M. A., & Gibson, S. G. (2013). Concluding thoughts: Challenges and opportunities in work analysis. In M. A. Wilson, W. Bennett, Jr., S. G. Gibson, & G. M. Alliger (Eds.). *The handbook of work analysis: Methods, systems, applications and science of work measurement in organizations* (pp. 741–747). New York: Routledge Academic.

Brannick, M. T., Cadle, A., & Levine, E. L. (2012). Job analysis for KSAOs, predictor measures, and performance outcomes. In N. Schmitt (Ed.), *The Oxford handbook of personnel assessment and selection* (pp. 119–146). New York: Oxford University Press.

Breaugh, J. A. (2017). The contribution of job analysis to recruitment. In H. Goldstein & J. Passmore (Eds.), *The Wiley Blackwell handbook of the psychology of recruitment, selection and employee retention* (pp. 12–28). Chichester, UK: Wiley-Blackwell.

British Medical Association. (2017). *Physician associates in the UK*. London: British Medical Association.

Burke, R. J., & Ng, E. (2006). The changing nature of work and organizations: Implications for human resource management. *Human Resource Management Review, 16*(2), 86–94.

Campion, M., Fink, A., Ruggeberg, B., Carr, L., Phillips, G., & Odman, R. (2011). Doing competencies well: Best practices in competency modelling. *Personnel Psychology, 64*, 225–262.

Department of Health. (2010). *Equity and excellence: Liberating the NHS*. London: DoH.

Dierdorff, E. C., & Wilson, M. A. (2003). A meta-analysis of job analysis reliability. *Journal of Applied Psychology, 88*(4), 635–646.

Drucker, P. F. (1987, August 2). Workers hands bound by tradition. *Wall Street Journal*, 18.

Farr, J. L., & Tippins, N. T. (2013). *Handbook of employee selection*. New York: Routledge.

Flanagan, J. C. (1954). The critical incident technique. *The Psychological Bulletin, 51*, 327–358.

Goldstein, H., & Passmore, J. (2017). *The Wiley Blackwell handbook of the psychology of recruitment, selection, and employee retention*. Chichester, UK: Wiley Blackwell.

Gutman, A. (2000). *EEO law and personnel practices* (2nd ed.). Thousand Oaks, CA: Sage.

Keeney, S., Hasson, F., & McKenna, H. (2011). *The Delphi technique in nursing and health research*. Chichester, UK: Wiley-Blackwell.

Koch, A., Strobel, A., Miller, R., Garten, A., Cimander, C., & Westhoff, K. (2012). Never use one when two will do: The effects of a multi-perspective approach on the outcome of job analyses using the critical incident technique. *Journal of Personnel Psychology, 11*, 95–102.

Koczwara, A., Patterson, F., Zibarras, L., Kerrin, M., Irish, B., & Wilkinson, M. (2012). Evaluating cognitive ability, knowledge tests and situational judgement tests for postgraduate selection. *Medical Education, 46*, 399–408.

Kreiter, C. D., & Axelson, R. D. (2013). A perspective on medical school admission research and practice over the last 25 years. *Teaching and Learning in Medicine, 25*, 50–56.

Lance, C. E., Kavanagh, M. J., & Brink, K. E. (2002). Retraining climate as a predictor of retraining success and as a moderator of the relationship between cross-job retraining time estimates and time to proficiency in the new job. *Group and Organization Management, 27*(2), 294–317.

McGuire, C., Rankin, J., Matthews, L., Cerinus, M., & Zaveri, S. (2016). Improving the quality of the NHS workforce through values and competency-based selection. *Nursing Management, 23*(4), 26–33.

McKenzie, J. F., Dennis, D., Auld, M. E., Lysoby, L., Doyle, E., Muenzen, P. M., …, Kusorgbor-Narh, C. S. (2016). Health education specialist practice analysis 2015 (HESPA 2015) process and outcomes. *Health Education & Behavior, 43*(3), 286–295.

Morgeson, F. P., & Dierdorff, E. C. (2011). Work analysis: From technique to theory. In S. Zedeck (Ed.), *APA handbook of industrial and organizational psychology* (Vol. 2, pp. 3–41). Washington, DC: American Psychological Association.

Naidoo, S., Lopes, S., Patterson, F., Mead, H. M., & Macleod, S. (2016). Can colleagues', patients' and supervisors' assessments predict successful completion of postgraduate medical training? *Medical Education, 51*(4), 423–431.

Nikolaou, I., & Oostrom, J. K. (2017). *Employee recruitment, selection, and assessment*. Howe, UK: Psychology Press.

Nursing and Midwifery Council. (2017, October 16). Retrieved from https://www.nmc.org.uk/standards/nursing-associates/.

Olian, J. D., & Rynes, S. L. (1991). Making total quality work: Aligning organizational processes, performance measures, and stakeholders. *Human Resource Management, 30*(3), 303–333.

Patterson, F., Ferguson, E., & Knight, A. (2013). Selection for medical education and training. In T. Swanwick (Ed.), *Understanding medical education: Evidence, theory and practice* (2nd ed., pp. 352–365). Chichester: Wiley-Blackwell.

Patterson, F., Ferguson, E., Lane, P., Farrell, K., Martlew, J., & Wells, A. (2000). A competency model for general practice: Implications for selection and development. *British Journal of General Practice, 50,* 188–193.

Patterson, F., Ferguson, E., & Thomas, S. (2008). Using job analyses to identify core and specific competencies for three secondary care specialties: Implications for selection and recruitment. *Medical Education, 42,* 1195–1204.

Patterson, F., Howe, A., Tavabie, A., & Watson, M. (2013). Is UK general practice education and training now fit for purpose? *British Journal of General Practice, 63,* 567–568.

Patterson, F., Knight, A., Dowell, J., Nicholson, S., Cousans, F., & Cleland, J. (2016). How effective are selection methods in medical education and training? Evidence from a systematic review. *Medical Education, 50*(1), 36–60.

Patterson, F., Lievens, F., Kerrin, M., Munro, N., & Irish, B. (2013). The predictive validity of selection for entry into postgraduate training in general practice: Evidence from three longitudinal studies. *British Journal of General Practice, 63*(616), 734–741.

Patterson, F., Tavabie, A., Denney, M., Kerrin, M., Ashworth, V., & Koczwara, A. (2013). A new competency model for general practice: Implications for selection, training and careers. *British Journal of General Practice, 63*(610), 331–338.

Patterson, F., Zibarras, L., Carr, V., Irish, B., & Gregory, S. (2011). Evaluating candidate reactions to selection practices using organisational justice theory. *Medical Education, 45,* 289–297.

Pearn, M., & Kandola, B. (1993). *Job analysis: A practical guide for managers.* London: Institute of Personnel Managers.

Plint, S., & Patterson, F. (2010). Identifying critical success factors for designing selection processes into postgraduate specialty training: The case of UK general practice. *Postgraduate Medicine, 86,* 323–327.

Roberts, C., Clark, T., Burgess, A., Frommer, M., Grant, M., & Mossman, K. (2014). The validity of a behavioural multiple-mini-interview within an assessment centre for selection into specialty training. *BMC Medical Education, 14*(1), 1–11.

Robertson, I., & Smith, M. (2001). Personnel selection. *Journal of Occupational and Organizational Psychology, 74*, 441–472.

Rowe, G., & Wright, G. (1999). The Delphi technique as a forecasting tool: Issues and analysis. *International Journal of Forecasting, 15*, 353–375.

Sanchez, J., & Levine, E. (1999). Is job analysis dead, misunderstood, or both? New forms of work analysis and design. In A. I. Kraut & A. K. Korman (Eds.), *Evolving practices in human resource management* (pp. 43–68). San Francisco: Jossey-Bass.

Sanchez, J., & Levine, E. (2012a). The rise and fall of job analysis and the future of work analysis. *Annual Review of Psychology, 63*, 397–425.

Sanchez, J., & Levine, L. (2012b). Evaluating work analysis in the 21st century. In M. Wilson, W. Bennett, Jr., S. Gibson, & G. Alliger (Eds.). *The handbook of work analysis: Methods, systems, applications and science of work measurement in organizations* (pp. 127–138). New York: Routledge.

Schabracq, M. J., & Cooper, C. L. (2000). The changing nature of work and stress. *Journal of Managerial Psychology, 15*(3), 227–241.

Singh, P. (2008). Job analysis for a changing workplace. *Human Resource Management Review, 18*, 87–99.

Steurer, J. (2011). The Delphi method: An efficient procedure to generate knowledge. *Skeletal Radiology, 40*(8), 959–961.

7

New Approaches to Selection System Design in Healthcare: The Practical and Theoretical Relevance of a Modular Approach

Filip Lievens and Jan Corstjens

Introduction

Traditionally, healthcare selection practices and research can be characterized by a "holistic" view on selection procedures. For example, prior reviews on the various selection procedures that can be used as part of healthcare selection (Patterson et al., 2016; Roberts et al., 2017) focus on ability tests, aptitude tests, references, interviews, personality inventories, situational judgement tests, etc. Clearly, such a holistic focus is relevant because this is how the selection procedures are typically used in practice.

F. Lievens (✉)
Lee Kong Chian School of Business, Singapore Management University, Singapore, Singapore
e-mail: filiplievens@smu.edu.sg

J. Corstjens
Department of Personnel Management,
Work and Organizational Psychology, Ghent University, Ghent, Belgium
e-mail: jan.corstjens@ugent.be

F. Patterson and L. Zibarras (eds.), *Selection and Recruitment in the Healthcare Professions*, https://doi.org/10.1007/978-3-319-94971-0_7

Recently, Lievens and Sackett (2017) introduced a new approach to conceptualizing and examining selection systems, methods, and processes. Specifically, they argued in favor of a modular approach to personnel selection. In a modular approach, a selection procedure is broken down into smaller components (aka "building blocks"). This means that a selection procedure is seen as an assemblage of such loosely-coupled and relatively independent building blocks. Examples of such building blocks are stimulus format (e.g., video-based vs. text-based item presentation) or instruction format (e.g., loose or more direct directions to take the test). These components can then be flexibly recombined to construct a wide variety of new "hybrid" selection procedures. Whereas Lievens and Sackett (2017) applied such a modular approach to the broader personnel selection field, the aim of this chapter is to present and apply a modular approach to the healthcare selection field.

The structure of this chapter is as follows. First, we introduce the essential characteristics of a modular approach and delineate its conceptual and practical merits. Next, we review research in healthcare selection that has already adopted a modular approach. At the same time, we propose avenues for future research to promote modular thinking in healthcare selection practices. Finally, we present case studies that apply such a modular approach in a specific practical setting.

By the end of this chapter, you should have some understanding of and be able to explore further:

- the essentials of a modular approach to selection system design;
- the seven building blocks of a modular approach to selection;
- the conceptual and practical merits of a modular approach;
- how to apply a modular approach in healthcare selection research;
- and how to use a modular approach to healthcare selection in practice.

What is a Modular Approach to Selection?

The term "modular" originated in the product design literature. In that literature, two schools are often distinguished: integrated architectures in which systems are seen as holistic "all-in-one" packages versus a modular perspective that breaks down systems into key loosely coupled components (aka "building blocks"). So far, the holistic "all-in-one" perspective has dominated the selection field.

Lievens and Sackett (2017) conducted an in-depth literature review and identified seven such key building blocks (aka the "Super Seven"). First, the stimulus format refers to the modality by which the test stimuli (e.g., information, questions, and prompts) are presented to test-takers. For example, stimuli might be presented in a written (e.g., written verbal reasoning items), pictorial (e.g., facial pictures in an emotional intelligence task), or auditory (e.g., telephone interview questions) format; other options are dynamic audio-visual stimuli (e.g., video scenes or 3D animated scenes), videoconference (remote, online) interactions, and live face-to-face interactions.

Second, contextualization is defined as the extent to which test stimuli are embedded in a detailed and realistic context. In selection, some tests are decontextualized because no context is provided to test-takers. Examples are the classic cognitive ability tests. In low levels of contextualization, a situational keyword (i.e. tag) is added. An example is adding an "at work" tag to existing personality items. A medium level of contextualization means that the context is described in terms of "who", "when", "where", and "why" (Johns, 2006). Examples are situational interviews and situational judgement tests (SJTs). Conversely, in high levels of contextualization, more detailed information is given about each of these aspects (e.g., a one-page description of the main characters). Examples include serious games or selection center exercises.

Third, stimulus presentation consistency refers to the level of standardization that interviewers/assessors/test administrators adopt in presenting test stimuli to test-takers. In other words, this factor refers to the degree to which procedural variations in presenting test stimuli across test takers are reduced. Lievens and Sackett (2017) made a distinction between three subcategories. In the first subcategory, little standardization is undertaken regarding the stimuli to be presented ("free stimuli"). Examples are interviews or role plays without question standardization. In the second subcategory ("adaptive stimuli"), there exist predetermined and standardized guidelines about the key stimuli to be presented but the administration of sub-stimuli depends on test-takers' responses to the previous stimuli. Examples are branched/nonlinear/nested SJTs or computer adaptive cognitive ability tests. The highest level of stimulus presentation consistency is exemplified by fixed stimuli: all test-takers are presented the same or comparable stimuli in the same order (no matter how they respond to the stimuli) and progress in the same way (e.g., paper-and-pencil ability tests or structured interviews).

Fourth, the response format denotes the modality by which test-takers are required to respond to test stimuli. Closed-ended response formats (multiple-choice or forced-choice response formats) in which possible response options are predetermined and prompts are frequently used. Candidates choose, rank, or rate the predetermined response options. The closed-ended response options might be text-based, pictorial, auditory, or video-based. Apart from closed-ended formats, open-ended (i.e. constructed) response formats have also been used. The same subcategories (textual, pictorial, audio, audio-visual, videoconference, and face-to-face) apply here as the ones discussed for stimulus format. For example, in recent times candidates have submitted video resumes (Waung, Hymes, & Beatty, 2014), have answered test items via webcam (Lievens, De Corte, & Westerveld, 2015), or have engaged in videoconference (remote) or live interactions with interviewers.

Fifth, response evaluation consistency refers to the level of standardization that evaluators adopt to evaluate test-takers' responses. Again, different subcategories can be distinguished. In unconstrained judgment, candidates are evaluated without having pre-established answers or a scoring key. Conversely, calibrated judgment signifies that evaluators are trained to use pre-established answers and/or evaluative standards when evaluating candidates, as is often the case in scoring interview answers, essays, and role-plays. Automated scoring represents the category highest in terms of response evaluation standardization.

Sixth, information source refers to the individuals responding to the test stimuli. The typical distinction here is between the focal person and reports by other informants. These persons should be well acquainted with the focal person and motivated to share job-related information about him/her. Examples of such others are co-workers, supervisors, or direct subordinates. The effects of using different judges to evaluate candidate performance also fall under this component.

Finally, instructions denote the extent to which directions are made explicit to test-takers about which perspective to take to respond to test stimuli. A distinction can be made between general (weaker e.g., "rate

Table 7.1 Predictor method factors, their definitions, and categories (see Lievens & Sackett, 2017)

Predictor method factor	Definition	Predictor method factor category/choice
Stimulus format	Modality by which test stimuli (information, questions, prompts) are presented to test-takers	– Textual stimuli – Pictorial stimuli – Auditory stimuli – Dynamic audio-visual stimuli – Videoconference/remote interactive stimuli – Face-to-face interactive stimuli
Contextualization	The extent to which a detailed context is provided to test-takers	– Decontextualized – Low contextualization – Medium contextualization – High contextualization
Stimulus presentation consistency	Level of standardization adopted in presenting test stimuli to test-takers	– Free stimuli – Adaptive stimuli – Fixed stimuli
Response format	Modality by which test-takers are required to respond to test stimuli	– Close-ended – Textual constructed – Pictorial constructed – Audio constructed – Audio-visual constructed – Videoconference/remote interaction – Face-to-face interaction
Response evaluation consistency	Level of standardization adopted in terms of evaluating test-takers' responses	– Unconstrained judgment – Calibrated judgment – Automated scoring
Information source	Individual responding to the test stimuli	– Behavior exhibited (or choices made) by the candidate in the assessment context – Self-reports by the candidate about events beyond the assessment context – Reports by others about events outside the assessment context
Instructions	The extent to which directions are made explicit to test-takers about which perspective they should take to respond to the test stimuli	– General instructions – Specific instructions

yourself on the following statements") and specific (stronger) instructions (e.g., with clearer directions on how to solve the item/task). Table 7.1 summarizes these seven building blocks, their definitions, and subcategories (see also Lievens & Sackett, 2017).

What are the Benefits of a Modular Approach to Selection?

A modular approach has a lot of merit for healthcare selection. Generally, Lievens and Sackett (2017) argued that a modular approach has various conceptual and practical benefits. Two conceptual benefits of a modular approach are of most importance. First, a modular approach leads to greater insight into the workings of each of the separate components because the isolated impact of these components is examined on key selection outcomes. For example, when one focuses on a holistic selection procedure such as a selection center, it is difficult to determine why it leads to valid predictions of future performance. It might be because the assessors are well trained, the exercises are contextualized, or because the response format is open-ended. Conversely, if one examines the effect of one component such as response format (while keeping all the others factors constant), one might determine whether an open-ended (as compared to a closed-ended) response format leads to better predictions.

Second, a modular approach creates more integration and cross-fertilization across different selection procedures because these components cut across various selection procedures. Returning to the selection center example above, suppose one finds that an open-ended response format leads to better predictions and thus higher validity, such insights might inform not only selection center design but also a variety of other selection procedures such as work samples, simulations, etc. Other examples are that there exist different literatures per selection procedure. Think, for example, about the panel interview literature and the selection center literature. By focusing on building blocks (e.g., response scoring consistency) that underlie both selection procedures, one generates insights for both literatures and accordingly fosters integration and theoretical connectivity among them.

As a key practical benefit, a modular perspective permits developing a myriad of new selection procedures by "mixing and matching" different building blocks. That is, one might design a new selection procedure by changing one or more building blocks of an existing one. For example, one might invest in higher levels of response scoring consistency or more contextualization when designing an interview. Similarly, one might increase the level of contextualization of a personality inventory. Such changes might be made to improve reliability, validity, applicant perceptions, or reduce costs and gender, ethnic, or socioeconomic differences in test scores, thereby widening access to healthcare education for minority groups. This ability to change building blocks leads to increased agility in (re)designing selection procedures, which serves as a catalyst for innovation and change.

Review of Healthcare Selection Research using a Modular Approach

Two types of studies can typically provide data on the effects of how each of these building blocks affect key selection criteria such as reliability, validity, minority group test score differences, or applicant reactions. First, there are primary studies that conduct a comparative evaluation of predictor method factor choices. In a prototypical primary study, one building block (e.g., stimulus format, Chan & Schmitt, 1997) might be manipulated, with other aspects (i.e., test content, other method factors) being held constant. Second, moderator studies in meta-analyses can shed light onto the effects of building blocks. Such meta-analytic evidence has the advantage of being more cumulative. Yet, this also comes with a price because other potentially important factors are often not controlled for.

As compared to the personnel selection field in general (e.g., Christian, Edwards, & Bradley, 2010), we are not aware of such meta-analyses in the healthcare selection domain. However, so far, various primary studies in healthcare selection have already adopted a (partially) modular approach. Below, for each building block, we present some examples of these studies when available, without having the intention to be comprehensive in our coverage. In addition, we outline various avenues for future research per building block.

Effect of the Stimulus Format

The choice of modality by which test stimuli (information, questions, prompts) are presented to test-takers might affect important selection outcomes. For example, varying stimulus format might change the selection method's construct saturation (i.e., the strength of the relation with constructs such as cognitive ability or personality), criterion-related validity, minority group differences in test scores, and applicant reactions. Evidence from the broader selection field attested to this for selection interviews (videoconference vs. face-to-face interviews, Van Iddekinge, Raymark, & Roth, 2005) and situational judgement tests (SJT, Lievens & Sackett, 2006).

In the healthcare selection domain, an example of a primary study varying the stimulus format is one conducted by Lievens and Sackett (2006) in the context of the healthcare admissions exam in Flanders. This exam includes an SJT to measure students' knowledge of interpersonal and communication skills. In one cohort of candidates, the SJT was presented in a video-based format, while in a subsequent albeit similar cohort, the stimulus format was changed to a textual one. All other components of the SJT were held constant. This allowed the researchers to study how these different stimulus formats affected important outcomes while the rest of the procedure was held exactly the same. Results revealed that the SJT with the video-based stimulus format evidenced a significantly lower correlation with cognitive measures, as well as significantly higher validity for predicting performance on interpersonally oriented courses later on. Moreover, the SJT with the video-based stimulus format showed significant incremental validity over other selection tests in the healthcare admission exam (i.e., a cognitive ability and a work sample test), whereas the textual version did not. Lastly, applicant perceptions were also more positive for the video-based format compared to the written SJT.

Dore, Reiter, Kreuger, and Norman (2017a, 2017b) adopted a similar approach as the Lievens and Sackett study, although they administered two different stimulus formats in one and the same cohort of medical school applicants. The SJT contained items with either a written or a video-based stimulus format. Predictive validity showed a similar pattern as in the Lievens and Sackett study: the video-based format was significantly predictive for interpersonally oriented criteria gathered during a national licensure exam, whereas the written component was not. Other studies where stimulus format is varied could potentially adopt the same approach. For example, Husbands et al. (2015) examined the reliability and construct-related validity of an integrity-based SJT by combining scores of three different stimulus formats (written format, video-based format, and a written verbatim transcript of the video-based format). While the combined SJT evidenced satisfactory reliability and construct-related validity with integrity measures, applying the modular approach could have addressed whether these metrics would differ for each stimulus format.

In the future, technological advancements that enable including novel stimulus formats could also be used and studied in a healthcare selection context. For instance, 3D or avatar-based multimedia environments have advanced to a point that they can represent high fidelity social interactions. Use of such high-fidelity technology might further increase favorable applicant reactions and criterion-related validity and reduce minority group differences in test scores (Weekley, Hawkes, Guenole, & Ployhart, 2015). Translating this research to healthcare selection has the advantage of identifying a stimulus format or a range of stimulus formats that a healthcare school, for example, finds most beneficial in fulfilling its objectives (e.g., in terms of validity improvement, ensuring favorable applicant perceptions, widening access to minority populations).

Effect of Contextualization

In healthcare selection, methods such as selection centers or situational judgement tests often frame stimuli such as questions, information, or cues in a context that closely resembles practice (e.g., a physician's practice). Simulations with standardized patients are a prime example of such a contextualized selection procedure. Standardized patients are commonly trained role-players that have been instructed to play the role of a patient and present various disease symptoms to the student trainee during a simulation (Barrows, 1993; Cleland, Abe, & Rethans, 2009). In the healthcare selection literature and the selection literature more broadly though, studies that focus on contextualization as a distinct component of a selection method are sparse.

Future research could therefore focus on identifying and manipulating different levels of contextualization which allows us to study the effects of these differences on test scores and selection outcomes. Along these lines, Johns (2006) differentiated between omnibus (who, where, when, why) and discrete descriptions (specific details about social, task, and physical aspects of the context) as important levels of context. Besides varying the amount of contextualization provided, test stimuli could also be embedded in different types of contexts. For example, an entry-level student selection system could embed items in either a familiar context such as a classroom team project setting or opt to frame items in unfamiliar situations such as a future physician's daily patient encounters (see also Case Study 7.2). Clearly, investigating contextualization as a selection method component might have important implications for practice. For example, if scores on test items that strip away context show similar validity coefficients compared to their more highly contextualized counterparts, investments in such items may be more efficient.

Effect of Stimulus Presentation Consistency

Selection test developers often have to deal with making trade-offs between presenting stimuli to test takers in a highly fixed (and arguably more artificial) manner versus presentation of stimuli in a more open-ended or adaptive format. The former increases test standardization, whereas the latter ensures a higher amount of real-world likeness and, therefore, more realistic presentations of a practicing physician's daily encounters. To maximize the selection method's potential to predict a physician's career success, developers attempt to create simulations that mimic these actual situations encountered in medical practice as closely as possible. Returning to the standardized patient example outlined before, the psychometric disappointments that arose when presenting stimuli only in a fixed format in patient management problems and the fact that real-life patient–physician interactions are a free inquiry process, led to the development of patient–physician simulations with standardized patients (Vu & Barrows, 1994).

Although we were not able to identify primary examples in the healthcare selection literature that directly compared different stimulus presentation consistency formats within the same selection method, we believe such comparisons might shed further light on important selection outcomes (criterion-related and construct validity, gender/ethnicity differences) and might inform schools where in the healthcare education pathway each format would be most suited to maximize the potential of selecting the best candidates (e.g., entry-level selection versus selection for specialty training). Future studies examining the effects of stimulus presentation consistency can also vary the signals or cues that are presented by simulated patients to be able to differentiate between students' swiftness in their ability to pick up on important disease signals. For example, a simulated patient can first present symptoms of the flu in a subtle nonverbal way (e.g., sniff), and when this is not picked up by the student the patient can move on to expressing a more obvious prompt (e.g., cough) and finally a verbally clear prompt (e.g., complain about a sore throat and runny nose).[1]

Effect of the Response Format

"Life is not about multiple choice" is an often-heard critique on selection methods with closed-ended response formats. Returning to the example outlined above, written patient management problems provide students with a written patient description and a list of options to choose from related to eliciting medical information about the patient. Although such cued and closed-ended simulations are cost-effective to administer to large groups, they do not simulate the critical patient–doctor free-inquiry process (Vu & Barrows, 1994). Patient–physician simulations with standardized patients have an open-ended constructed response format and, therefore, can be thought to more closely resemble a physician's actual practice.

In one of the studies in healthcare selection that directly compared different response formats, Norman and Feightner (1981) comparatively evaluated medical students' performance on closed-ended patient management problems versus open-ended patient–physician simulations with simulated patients. Clerkship students had to partake in periodical evaluations that presented them with either written patient management problems (close-ended format) or simulated patient encounters (open-ended format). The patient management problems were structured around a case (a patient with an illness) that was followed by a list of options the student could select to cue the patient for more information which then ideally should result in the ability to correctly diagnose the patient and solving of the case. When comparing performance of the clerkship students on these written patient management problems with their performance on simulated patient cases, the students selected many more options to elicit information from the patient in the close-ended format than they would ask the simulated patient questions in the open-ended free-inquiry process. The authors concluded that the test format with fixed stimuli introduced error variance resulting from the test format and that the higher levels of standardization thus came at a cost in comparison to the less standardized free inquiry process with simulated patient formats. It should be noted, though, that in this study (apart from the response format) stimulus format was also manipulated (written case vs. actual interactions), which makes it difficult to draw strong conclusions about the response format effects.

Research in the broader personnel selection literature further evaluated whether open-ended response formats (that are arguably more life-like than closed-ended formats) also translated into higher predictive validity. For interpersonal skill measurement, it seems the constructed response format improves criterion-related validity over closed-ended formats for predicting interpersonal criteria (Lievens, De Corte, & Westerveld, 2015, see also Case Study 7.1). Importantly, other benefits of the open-ended constructed response format seem to be a reduction of cognitive load, lower ethnicity differences in test scores, and more favorable applicant perceptions (for a review, see Lievens & Sackett, 2017).

Future research in healthcare selection might attempt to echo these investigations from the broader personnel selection literature and seek to comparatively evaluate validity of different forms of response formats while keeping the remaining test content constant. For example, computerized assessments of clinical and interpersonal skills can record respondents' constructed answers with a webcam and compare them with answers provided in multiple-choice formats.

Effect of Response Evaluation Consistency

The validity of many selection methods is likely influenced by the level of standardization adopted in the scoring method. Examples in the domain of objective structured clinical examinations (OSCEs, Harden, Stevenson, Downie, & Wilson, 1975) illustrate how this component has already been investigated in healthcare selection utilizing a modular approach. Examinations of response evaluation consistency within OSCE stations showed that interrater agreement was higher when checklists were used than when rating scales were used. It was argued that this could be due to checklists being more concrete and objective definitions of potential behaviors to be demonstrated by candidates (van der Vleuten & Swanson, 1990). Conversely, interstation reliability was higher for more global and arguably more subjective rating scales, suggesting that across situations global judgments seem to provide more reliable estimates of candidates' abilities than specific ones (Swanson & van der Vleuten, 2013).

Another example of a recent study that can serve as an example here deals with an investigation of the effects of situational judgement test scoring method on internal reliability estimates and ethnic differences in test scores (De Leng et al., 2017). In this study conducted in the context of medical selection in the Netherlands, an extensive set of scoring methods were compared. The authors compared the psychometric properties of scoring methods that used raw consensus scoring (scores are awarded when test takers' ratings resemble the ratings provided by a reference group), versus standardizing techniques (applying the same comparison technique as raw consensus scoring after applying a within-person standardization of the scores to a scale with mean 0 and *SD* 1), and dichotomizing scores (awarding scores when test takers' ratings are on the same end of the scale as those of the reference group). By varying these response evaluation consistency components, the authors showed that ethnic differences in test scores could be influenced by the choice of the scoring method. Raw consensus scoring appeared the most suited technique to maximize test score reliability and simultaneously minimize differences in test scores resulting from ethnic descent.

A modular approach might be especially beneficial for future research in further improving interview reliability and validity in healthcare selection. Different scoring rubrics can be experimented with. In healthcare selection (and the broader domain of personnel selection), the admission interview has been plagued by mixed findings regarding its predictive validity (see Patterson et al., 2016). This seems to be in part related not only to the level of standardization adopted in presenting stimuli (high vs. low levels of question standardization), but also to the level of standardization taken when evaluating responses (scoring). For example, scoring the performance of healthcare students can be conducted in an absolute (criterion-referenced) or a relative fashion (norm-referenced). Uijtdehaage, Doyle, and Parker (2011) compared these two scoring schemes in multiple mini interview (MMI) stations and found that norm-referenced scoring removed the ceiling effect that was apparent in the criterion-referenced scoring system, thereby enabling assessors to differentiate between the most highly competent students.

Effect of Information Source

Apart from the distinction between methods that require different information sources to provide information about the candidate (e.g., self-reports vs. other-reports), one can also study the effects of various rating sources who evaluate a candidate's performance within one selection method. For example, in order to reduce costs and time investments from experienced practicing physicians, several studies in the context of OSCEs comparatively evaluated different rating sources to examine whether rating source affects the reliability of the scores. The typical comparison has been between experienced physicians and non-faculty experts or standardized patients. Although experienced physicians would appear to be the most qualified group to rate and evaluate the performance of candidates, when given sufficient training the ratings provided by non-faculty experts or standardized patients were found to be equally reliable and accurate (Swanson & van der Vleuten, 2013; Vu & Barrows, 1994). In addition, the number of assessors seems to matter: optimal reliability of performance ratings is achieved when the number of assessors in OSCE-style assessments is kept limited within stations (1–2 raters) in favor of increasing the number of stations (Eva, Rosenfeld, Reiter, & Norman, 2004; Knorr & Hissbach, 2014).

Future research on the effect of different information sources can turn its attention towards other selection methods such as letters of recommendation or reference letters. These methods are often used in healthcare selection and calls have been made to improve their reliability and validity (DeZee et al., 2014; Kuncel, Kochevar, & Ones, 2014). Again, a modular approach can be fruitfully used. For example, one might experiment with the type of information source (peers, professors, internship supervisors), the number of referees, or the length of acquaintance with the target person. One could also vary the format of the letters (in the context of varying response evaluation consistency) such as using unstructured, narrative letters vs. letters that require ratings on dimensions that were deemed relevant.

Effect of Instructions

Instructions are a last building block with key theoretical and practical importance in the design of selection procedures. As with the other building blocks, choices made with this component might affect a selection method's construct saturation, criterion-related validity, or ethnic/gender differences. For example, one can change the amount of specificity or level of detail provided by the response instructions (i.e., instructing participants about what perspective they should take when responding to test items), or switch from knowledge-based instructions to behavioral-tendency instructions (i.e., "What should you do?" vs. "What would you do?").

In another study conducted in the Flemish healthcare admission exam, Lievens, Sackett, and Buyse (2009) showed that altering the response instructions of an SJT from knowledge based to behavioral tendency instructions had no effect on the scores obtained on the test and did not affect the validity of the SJT for predicting student performance on interpersonally oriented courses after their first year of healthcare school. They further showed that different response instructions affected the SJT's cognitive loading (i.e., the processing difficulty) only slightly (the relation with cognitive ability test scores was stronger when the response format was knowledge-based). These results led the authors to conclude that in a high stakes context, test takers do not respond differently when response instructions were changed from one format to the other and that the knowledge-based response format is the preferred choice to minimize "faking good" on the test on the part of the candidates.

Clearly, we need more research on response instructions. An example is the question how much specificity of instructions should be chosen in scenario-based assessment in healthcare selection. Indeed, a dilemma often mentioned is whether one should use general instructions (e.g., How do/did you solve this issue?) vs. more specific instructions (e.g., How do/did you use your interpersonal skills to solve this issue?). With a general instruction, one might get insight in how people spontaneously express their trait(s). Situations with little available cues about what to do might also more accurately depict real-life complex decision-making situations. Yet, this low level of instruction specificity might come at a price for the ability to measure constructs of interest since people might fail to give the desired response not because they do not know what to do but because the situation becomes too ambiguous. This in turn could lead to unreliability in the selection method resulting from its inability to differentiate between people that simply did not know what was expected of them versus people who really did not know the correct answer. Conversely, with more specific instructions it becomes easier to measure constructs of interest but at the same time these instructions could increase the risk of not being able to detect whether people would respond similarly in real life where specific information is also often lacking. At worst, instructions might become so transparent that they give away the correct answer completely, thereby also affecting the ability of a selection method to assess important skills and predict criteria (Ingold, Kleinmann, König, & Melchers, 2016).

Case Studies: Putting the Modular Approach to Selection into Action

In this section, we present two Case Studies (7.1 and 7.2). Although the first case study is not situated in healthcare selection, it is a good example of the utility of a modular approach in selection.

Case Study 7.1: Building New Selection Procedures in Police Officer Selection

In this case, we worked with an organization that had always used a holistic ("all-in-one") approach. The organization had stopped using classic selection center exercises (because of their less standardized nature and limited coverage of job situations) in favor of a more standardized SJT approach. However, the organization also perceived shortcomings in this SJT approach because actual candidate behavior was no longer assessed.

This is the point where we decided to adopt a modular approach and move the selection system into the twenty-first century. In line with the basic axiom of a modular approach, the first thing we did was break down these two classic selection procedures (selection centers and SJTs) into their basic building blocks. Presentation format and response format emerged as the two pivotal building blocks. This led to a two-dimensional map as visualized in Fig. 7.1. We then placed the two assessment procedures into this map (see the crosses): Selection centers require responding with actual behavior to the behavioral (role-player) stimuli presented to them, whereas SJTs typically present the situations in a written format and ask people to respond in a written format. As a critical implication, this visualization shows that those two selection procedures that organizations have been using for decades take extreme positions (they are situated at the outskirts of the map). In addition, it becomes clear that there are many empty cells on the map, which might all serve as potential unexplored hybrids between these two extremes. We then decided to create two such "hybrids," namely (a) an online multimedia simulation

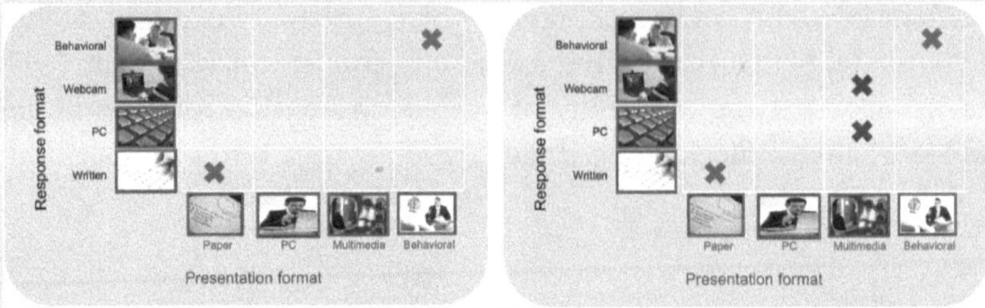

Fig. 7.1 Predictor method map showing response format and stimulus format

with a webcam response format and (b) an online multimedia simulation in which people had to respond by typing their answer in a text balloon.

Using an evidence-based approach, we then set up a field experiment to examine the effects of these two new selection procedures (whose results had no bearing on the selection decision). Results in terms of validity, precision of measurement, and applicant experience favored the webcam hybrid. The organization then considered using the modular approach to further adjust this webcam hybrid by modifying another building block, namely, response scoring consistency. That is, they chose to score transcribed webcam responses (that had the advantage of not revealing the gender of the candidates) instead of the actual webcam responses.

Case Study 7.2: Examining Type of Contextualization in Healthcare Student Admission

In this case study, we worked together with an organization that was involved in designing the SJT of a healthcare student admission procedure. The SJT aimed to assess interpersonal skills. The SJT was regarded as an ideal tool for screening high volumes of candidates to broaden skill coverage (besides cognitively-oriented tests) and increase diversity.

Contextualization is assumed to increase the predictive validity of SJT scores. This assumption is based on the notion that better predictions can be made when there is a point-to-point correspondence between the domain to be predicted (criterion) and the predictor (selection procedures). That is, when SJTs present situations to candidates that closely mirror job-related situations, one can expect that the responses of candidates will be indicative of how they will respond on the job. However, this does not tell us whether the type of contextualization should be framed in "prior familiar realistic situations" vs. "future unfamiliar realistic situations". A dilemma came up when designing the SJT. One option consisted of embedding the SJT items in a realistic student/educational context. Examples of such a student/educational context are course work, library, or cafeteria student interactions. The other option was to frame the items in a realistic healthcare context. In this case, example situations included an ongoing interaction between a physician and a patient. At a practical level, this dilemma invokes questions about the potential costs and gains of investing in contextualization in SJTs. In case the decision was made to embed the items in a healthcare context, it was clear that (more expensive) subject matter experts would be required for developing (elaborate) situational descriptions, response options, and the scoring key. This is less of an issue if it had been decided to embed items in a student educational context.

We framed this dilemma in a modular approach in which we focused on contextualization as one of the key components of selection procedures. We made a distinction between the level of contextualization (low, medium, and high) and the type of contextualization (educational vs. work). This visualization created six cells. In the next step, we decided together with the organization to examine two of these cells. That is, we aimed to compare an SJT with items in an educational, student context to an SJT with items in a work (healthcare) context. The level of contextualization of both of these SJTs was medium. We set up a within-subjects design for examining the effects of type of contextualization. That is, the SJT used in this admissions process consisted of both contextualized items about realistic future healthcare situations (interpersonal physician–patient situations) and contextualized items about realistic past educational situations (interpersonal student-student situations). The effects of this comparison were cast in terms of mean scores (difficulty level), cognitive saturation (correlation with cognitive ability), applicant perceptions, and validity (prediction of future interpersonal course grades). We also scrutinized the potential moderating impact of candidate background (i.e., whether one of the parents had already been working as a health professional) because this might also affect (e.g., potentially bias) the SJT scores.

This examination is currently underway. Results are expected to shed light on which type of contextualization might work best for healthcare admission exams. At a practical level, it might also suggest considerable resource savings in SJT development. So far, lack of understanding of the effects of contextualization leaves practitioners in the dark when choosing between different types and levels of contextualization.

Conclusion

In summary, this chapter presents a modular approach to healthcare selection system design that emphasizes a closer look at the components of selection procedures to complement the traditional holistic view of selection procedures. Our framework identified seven key design components of selection procedures and provided examples of studies in the healthcare selection literature that varied and compared the effect of these components on key selection outcomes. A modular approach has merit in that it allows researchers to gain and provide insights into how the different components underlying selection procedures differentially affect important selection outcomes. Furthermore, such an approach allows drawing conceptual similarities between components of different selection procedures. Lastly, it creates opportunities for experimentation by varying these components and then studying their differential effects on outcomes. Practically, a modular approach permits developing a myriad of new selection procedures by "mixing and matching" different building blocks.

Future research in healthcare selection should apply the modular approach and move beyond typical studies of selection procedures as a whole. Accordingly, such healthcare selection studies should adopt designs where single components are being varied while holding the rest of the selection procedure constant. Although tightly controlled laboratory-style experimental designs with full randomization of participants to conditions are typically viewed as the gold standard for isolating and studying the effects of a variable on important outcomes, the primary and case studies presented in this chapter show that it is also possible to apply the modular approach in quasi-experimental designs with pre-existing samples in field studies. Some shortcomings notwithstanding, such quasi-experimental designs can provide a good starting point to adopt a modular approach and move the healthcare selection field forward.

Practice Points

- This chapter introduces a modular approach to conceptualizing and examining healthcare selection procedures. This approach departs from viewing selection methods as holistic entities and instead takes a closer look at the "building blocks" or components of selection methods.

- Selection tests can be broken down into seven distinct components. These "Super Seven" are the stimulus format, contextualization, stimulus presentation consistency, the response format, response evaluation consistency, information source, and instructions.
- Each of these building blocks can be isolated and then varied to study their effects (while keeping the rest of the selection method constant) on important selection outcomes.
- (Quasi-)experimental lab and field studies can be set up to conduct research using a modular angle.
- Examining components in isolation reveals their potentially differential effects on important selection outcomes, thereby progressing theoretical and practical understandings of how these components work.
- Drawing conceptual similarities between components across different selection methods also opens up new possibilities to mix and match these components and design new types of "hybrid" selection methods that best suit the clients' goals and needs.

Explore Further

Below there is a list of useful articles/books related to a modular approach to selection procedures and a modular approach in general:

Lievens, F., & Sackett, P. R. (2017). The effects of predictor method factors on selection outcomes: A modular approach to personnel selection procedures. *Journal of Applied Psychology, 102*, 43–66. http://doi.org/10.1037/apl0000160.

Lievens, F., De Corte, W., & Westerveld, L. (2015). Understanding the building blocks of selection procedures: Effects of response fidelity on performance and validity. *Journal of Management, 41*, 1604–1627. http://doi.org/10.1177/0149206312463941.

Arthur, W. J., & Villado, A. J. (2008). The importance of distinguishing between constructs and methods when comparing predictors in personnel selection research and practice. *The Journal of Applied Psychology, 93*, 435–442. http://doi.org/10.1037/0021-9010.93.2.435.

Gershenson, J. K., Prasad, G. J., & Zhang, Y. (2003). Product modularity: Definitions and benefits. *Journal of Engineering Design, 14*, 295–331. http://doi.org/10.1080/0954482031000091068.
Baldwin, C. Y., & Clark, K. B. (2000). *Design Rules: Vol. 1. The Power of Modularity*. Cambridge, MA: MIT Press.

Note

1. Note that these examples can also be regarded as a manipulation of the instruction strength (more specific instructions versus more vague global ones).

References

Barrows, H. S. (1993). An overview of the uses of standardized patients for teaching and evaluating clinical skills. *Academic Medicine, 68*, 443–451. https://doi.org/10.1097/00001888-199306000-00002.
Chan, D., & Schmitt, N. (1997). Video-based versus paper-and-pencil method of assessment in situational judgment tests: Subgroup differences in test performance and face validity perceptions. *Journal of Applied Psychology, 82*, 143–159. https://doi.org/10.1037/0021-9010.82.1.143.
Christian, M. S., Edwards, B. D., & Bradley, J. C. (2010). Situational judgment tests: Constructs assessed and a meta-analysis of their criterion-related validities. *Personnel Psychology, 63*, 83–117. https://doi.org/10.1111/j.1744-6570.2009.01163.x.
Cleland, J., Abe, K., & Rethans, J. (2009). The use of simulated patients in medical education: AMEE Guide No. 42. *Medical Teacher, 31*, 477–486. https://doi.org/10.1080/01421590903002821.
De Leng, W. E., Stegers-Jager, K. M., Husbands, A., Dowell, J. S., Born, M. P., & Themmen, A. P. N. (2017). Scoring method of a situational judgment test: Influence on internal consistency reliability, adverse impact and correlation with personality. *Advances in Health Sciences Education, 22*, 243–265. https://doi.org/10.1007/s10459-016-9720-7.
DeZee, K. J., Magee, C. D., Rickards, G., Artino, A. R., Gilliland, W. R., Dong, T., …, Durning, S. J. (2014). What aspects of letters of

recommendation predict performance in medical school? Findings from one institution. *Academic Medicine, 89*, 1408–1415. http://doi.org/10.1097/ACM.0000000000000425.

Dore, K. L., Reiter, H. I., Kreuger, S., & Norman, G. R. (2017a). CASPer, an online pre-interview screen for personal/professional characteristics: Prediction of national licensure scores. *Advances in Health Sciences Education, 22*, 327–336. https://doi.org/10.1007/s10459-016-9739-9.

Dore, K. L., Reiter, H. I., Kreuger, S., & Norman, G. R. (2017b). Correction to: CASPer, an online pre-interview screen for personal/professional characteristics: Prediction of national licensure scores. *Advances in Health Sciences Education, 22*, 1321–1322. https://doi.org/10.1007/s10459-017-9798-6.

Eva, K. W., Rosenfeld, J., Reiter, H. I., & Norman, G. R. (2004). An admissions OSCE: The multiple mini-interview. *Medical Education, 38*, 314–326. https://doi.org/10.1046/j.1365-2923.2004.01776.x.

Harden, R. M., Stevenson, M., Downie, W. W., & Wilson, G. M. (1975). Assessment of clinical competence using objective structured examination. *British Medical Journal, 1*(5955), 447–451. https://doi.org/10.1136/bmj.1.5955.447.

Husbands, A., Rodgerson, M. J., Dowell, J., Patterson, F., Eva, K., Reiter, H., … Nevo, B. (2015). Evaluating the validity of an integrity-based situational judgement test for medical school admissions. *BMC Medical Education, 15*, 1–9. http://doi.org/10.1186/s12909-015-0424-0.

Ingold, P. V., Kleinmann, M., König, C. J., & Melchers, K. G. (2016). Transparency of assessment centers: Lower criterion-related validity but greater opportunity to perform. *Personnel Psychology, 69*, 467–497. https://doi.org/10.1111/peps.12105.

Johns, G. (2006). The essential impact of context on organizational behavior. *Academy of Management Review, 31*, 386–408. https://doi.org/10.5465/AMR.2006.20208687.

Knorr, M., & Hissbach, J. (2014). Multiple mini-interviews: Same concept, different approaches. *Medical Education, 48*, 1157–1175. https://doi.org/10.1111/medu.12535.

Kuncel, N. R., Kochevar, R. J., & Ones, D. S. (2014). A meta-analysis of letters of recommendation in college and graduate admissions: Reasons for hope. *International Journal of Selection and Assessment, 22*, 101–107. https://doi.org/10.1111/ijsa.12060.

Lievens, F., De Corte, W., & Westerveld, L. (2015). Understanding the building blocks of selection procedures: Effects of response fidelity on

performance and validity. *Journal of Management, 41,* 1604–1627. https://doi.org/10.1177/0149206312463941.
Lievens, F., & Sackett, P. R. (2006). Video-based versus written situational judgment tests: A comparison in terms of predictive validity. *Journal of Applied Psychology, 91,* 1181–1188. http://doi.org/10.1037/0021-9010.91.5.1181.
Lievens, F., & Sackett, P. R. (2017). The effects of predictor method factors on selection outcomes: A modular approach to personnel selection procedures. *Journal of Applied Psychology, 102,* 43–66. https://doi.org/10.1037/apl0000160.
Lievens, F., Sackett, P. R., & Buyse, T. (2009). The effects of response instructions on situational judgment test performance and validity in a high-stakes context. *The Journal of Applied Psychology, 94,* 1095–1101. https://doi.org/10.1037/a0014628.
Norman, G. R., & Feightner, J. W. (1981). A comparison of behaviour on simulated patients and patient management problems. *Medical Education, 15,* 26–32. https://doi.org/10.1111/j.1365-2923.1981.tb02311.x.
Patterson, F., Knight, A., Dowell, J., Nicholson, S., Cousans, F., & Cleland, J. (2016). How effective are selection methods in medical education and training? Evidence from a systematic review. *Medical Education, 50,* 36–60. https://doi.org/10.1111/medu.12817.
Roberts, C., Khanna, P., Rigby, L., Bartle, E., Llewellyn, A., Gustavs, J., … Lynam, J. (2017). Utility of selection methods for specialist medical training: A BEME (best evidence medical education) systematic review: BEME Guide No. 45. *Medical Teacher,* 1–17. http://doi.org/10.1080/0142159X.2017.1367375.
Swanson, D. B., & van der Vleuten, C. P. M. (2013). Assessment of clinical skills with standardized patients: State of the art revisited. *Teaching and Learning in Medicine, 25,* S17–S25. https://doi.org/10.1080/10401334.2013.842916.
Uijtdehaage, S., Doyle, L. H., & Parker, N. (2011). Enhancing the reliability of the multiple mini-interview for selecting prospective healthcare leaders. *Academic Medicine, 86,* 1032–1039. https://doi.org/10.1097/ACM.0b013e3182223ab7.
van der Vleuten, C. P. M., & D. Swanson, D. (1990). Assessment of clinical skills with standardized patients: State of the art. *Teaching and Learning in Medicine, 2,* 58–76. http://doi.org/10.1080/10401334.2013.842916.
Van Iddekinge, C. H., Raymark, P. H., & Roth, P. L. (2005). Assessing personality with a structured employment interview: Construct-related validity

and susceptibility to response inflation. *Journal of Applied Psychology, 90,* 536–552. https://doi.org/10.1037/0021-9010.90.3.536.

Vu, N. V., & Barrows, H. S. (1994). Use of standardized patients in clinical assessments: Recent developments and measurement findings. *Educational Researcher, 23,* 23–30. https://doi.org/10.3102/0013189X023003023.

Waung, M., Hymes, R. W., & Beatty, J. E. (2014). The effects of video and paper resumes on assessments of personality, applied social skills, mental capability, and resume outcomes. *Basic and Applied Social Psychology, 36,* 238–251. https://doi.org/10.1080/01973533.2014.894477.

Weekley, J. A., Hawkes, B., Guenole, N., & Ployhart, R. E. (2015). Low-fidelity simulations. *Annual Review of Organizational Psychology and Organizational Behavior, 2,* 295–322. https://doi.org/10.1146/annurev-orgpsych-032414-111304.

8

Applicant Perceptions and Reactions to Selection

Lara Zibarras

Overview

This chapter explores the theory, research, and evidence relating to the applicant's perspective of selection processes within the healthcare context. First, an overview of the theoretical underpinning of applicant reactions is presented, along with key research findings from both the wider organizational context, and within healthcare. Two case studies are presented from the General Practitioner and Public Health specialty (postgraduate) selection processes in the UK. Finally, some future directions for research and practice are considered.

By the end of this chapter, you should:

- understand the importance of exploring the applicants' perspective during selection and recruitment processes
- recognize why applicant reactions are important in a healthcare context

L. Zibarras (✉)
Department of Psychology, City, University of London, London, UK
e-mail: Lara.Zibarras.1@city.ac.uk

F. Patterson and L. Zibarras (eds.), *Selection and Recruitment in the Healthcare Professions*, https://doi.org/10.1007/978-3-319-94971-0_8

- understand the key factors that influence the extent to which applicants perceive a selection process to be fair
- appreciate what organizations can do to ensure that candidates leave selection processes feeling positive about the process and/or organization
- consider some of the key topics for a future research agenda.

Why Consider Applicant Perceptions?

The research evidence focusing on applicant perceptions stems from a broad range of occupational settings, however, the last decade has seen an increasing amount of research focused in the healthcare context (Patterson et al., 2012; Patterson, Zibarras, Carr, Irish, & Gregory, 2011; Zibarras & Patterson, 2015). Within healthcare professions, there may be several entry points to careers, for example, initial entry into University, entry into postgraduate education or training, and then into specialty posts. It is not only important to ensure that selection is valid and reliable for each career stage, but it is also important to consider perceptions of fairness of the applicants going through these processes.

Fair selection methods can be seen from two perspectives. First, in many countries, selection methods must meet equal opportunities legislation requirements so must be valid and reliable. Second, the concept of *political validity*—coined by Patterson and her colleagues (Patterson et al., 2012; Patterson & Zibarras, 2011)—is considered important. This is the acceptance of selection by a range of stakeholders, including the perceptions of recruiters, regulatory bodies, government, and the general public. Indeed, selection into healthcare is a high-profile topic that attracts both public and media interest, and there is a high level of scrutiny and public accountability (Kelly, Gallagher, Dunne, & Murphy, 2014). In addition, the applicants' perspective must be considered since they experience the selection methods (Harris, 2000). Indeed, in a 2001 review, Anderson highlights the role of selection methods starting a pre-entry socialization process where the methods unavoidably influence candidates' reactions, expectations, and attitudes. It is, therefore, thought that applicant perceptions are important in healthcare for several reasons:

1. negative reactions can result in the loss of good applicants from the selection process (Kelly, Gallagher, Dunne, & Murphy, 2014; McLarty & Whitman, 2016), having a detrimental effect on its utility (Murphy, 1986);
2. perceptions of unfairness may result in legal challenges of the process which is not only costly (Schmitt & Chan, 1999), but would also have a knock-on effect of negative publicity; and
3. if applicants perceive the process is unfair or feel mistreated, they may not re-apply and/or actively dissuade other applicants, reducing the total number or quality of the applicant pool (Anderson, 2011; McCarthy, Hrabluik, & Jelley, 2009; McLarty & Whitman, 2016; Patterson et al., 2011).

Considering the applicants' perspective can ensure that the best applicants are recruited. In high-stakes selection settings, applicants must have confidence in the selection process (Humphrey, Dowson, Wall, Diwakar, & Goodyear, 2008) to maximize the size and quality of the applicant pool (McCarthy et al., 2009).

Background and Introduction to Applicant Reactions

Historically, selection was viewed as assessing an individual's suitability for a job using selection methods intended to predict future job or in-training performance; however, there was little acknowledgement of the applicant's part in the process. Candidates are not passive within selection processes, instead evidence shows they actively present themselves in a favorable way (Burgess, Roberts, Clark, & Mossman, 2014). As such, the last three decades has seen a more applicant-focused research agenda with a growing body of literature (Anderson, Salgado, & Hülsheger 2010; Gilliland, 1994; Zibarras & Patterson, 2015) examining the attitudes, affect, and cognitions applicants may have about a selection process. The fundamental premise is that applicants' reactions to selection will influence personal and organizational outcomes including applicant decision-making, organization attractiveness, and potential litigation (Gilliland, 1993).

Organizational Justice Theory

Within the wider selection literature, the dominant model for research on applicant reactions is presented by Gilliland (1993, 1995) who proposes organizational justice theory (Greenberg, 1987) as a framework to consider applicant reactions. As with organizational justice theory, Gilliland makes a distinction between *procedural* and *distributive justice*. In a selection context, procedural justice refers to the fairness of the selection process itself, while distributive justice refers to the fairness of the selection outcome. The model displayed in Fig. 8.1 proposes that the extent to which applicants believe selection processes satisfy or violate certain procedural and distributive justice rules leads to overall fairness perceptions (Gilliland, 1993). This, in turn, leads to individual and organizational outcomes (Gilliland, 1993, 1995; Schinkel, van Vianen, & Marie Ryan, 2016; Schinkel, van Vianen, & van Dierendonck, 2013).

Gilliland (1993) proposed 10 procedural justice rules of selection. These encompass three domains that influence perceptions of overall fairness: formal characteristics, interpersonal treatment, and explanation. The formal characteristics incorporate job relatedness, opportunity to perform, opportunity for reconsideration, and consistency of administration. Interpersonal treatment relates to interpersonal effectiveness, two-way communication, and propriety of questions. Explanation relates to feedback, selection information, and honesty in treatment.

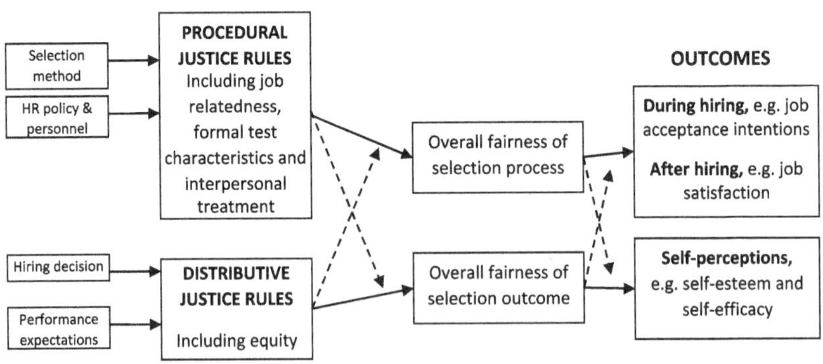

Fig. 8.1 Organizational justice model of applicants' perceptions to selection processes

These 10 procedural justice rules are outlined in Table 8.1. The formal test characteristics and interpersonal treatment domains refer to the test-taking process itself, while explanation relates to the final stage of the selection process when feedback is received. The "selection fairness" model put forward by Gilliland (1993, 1994) has been the most widely cited framework in applicant perceptions research and has influenced much of the current debate on this topic.

The main approach to unify and organize the research findings relating to applicant perceptions has been to focus on the determinants and outcomes of applicant perceptions (e.g., Hausknecht, Day, & Thomas, 2004). The following sections briefly summarize this research, drawn predominantly from contexts outside of healthcare, since there is less research in a healthcare context.

Table 8.1 Procedural justice rules underlying reactions to selection processes

Rule	Description
1. Job relatedness	The extent to which selection methods appear to measure content that is relevant to the job role or appears to be valid
2. Opportunity to perform	The extent to which candidates can demonstrate their knowledge, skills and abilities
3. Reconsideration opportunity	The opportunity to review test results or challenge scores, or to be able to re-test
4. Administration consistency	The degree to which selection processes are consistent or standardized across people and over time
5 Feedback	Provision of feedback that is timely and informative regarding test results and selection decision
6. Selection information	Information on, and justification for, the use of selection methods and decisions made
7. Honesty	The extent to which communication with candidates is candid
8. Interpersonal effectiveness	The extent to which candidates are treated with respect during the selection process
9. Two-way communication	The opportunity for candidates to ask questions during interpersonal interaction throughout the selection process
10. Propriety of questions	The degree to which the questions asked of candidates during the selection process are appropriate

Determinants of Applicant Perceptions

Selection Methods

Variability has been found in the perceived fairness of different selection methods where several studies have compared cross-national perceptions of process fairness for 10 common selection methods (interviews, CVs, work samples, biodata, ability tests, references, personality questionnaires, honesty tests, personal contacts and graphology; Anderson & Witvliet, 2008; Hoang, Erdogan, Truxillo, & Bauer, 2011; Moscoso & Salgado, 2004; Nikolaou & Judge, 2007; Phillips & Gully, 2002; Steiner & Gilliland, 1996). Findings indicate a relatively stable pattern of results with few cross-national differences in process fairness perceptions of these methods. Generally, interviews, CVs, and work samples are rated most favorably, while personal contacts, graphology, and honesty tests are rated least favorably with very few differences found between countries. Authors (Anderson & Witvliet, 2008; Anderson et al., 2010) conclude that similarities in applicant perceptions are more prevalent than differences, suggesting that findings may generalize internationally. Although these results provide a compelling case supporting which selection methods are perceived as fair, this work has been largely dependent on student-based samples (Bauer, Maertz, Dolen, & Campion, 1998; Carless, 2006; Hausknecht, Halpert, Di Paolo, & Moriarty Gerrard, 2007), which may not generalize to operational settings (Landy & Conte, 2009). Nevertheless, field-based studies to some extent replicate previous lab-based findings (e.g., Carless, 2006; Rosse, Miller, & Stecher, 1994).

It is notable that the list of 10 common selection methods outlined above includes neither SJTs or multiple mini interviews (MMIs), both of which are commonly used selection methods in the healthcare context (Patterson, Knight, et al., 2016; Patterson, Rowett, et al., 2016). Nevertheless, some research has explored perceptions of MMIs, for example, Humphrey and colleagues (2008) examined applicant and interviewer perceptions of newly implemented MMIs for selection to a UK regional pediatric program and found that both parties perceived this selection method to be fair and reliable. Similarly, in a study focused on medical students' perceptions of MMIs, Kelly and colleagues (2014) found several themes emerged during focus groups: MMI authenticity, relevance to clinical practice, and cultural awareness (which was sometimes positive, e.g., the ability to witness wider cultural issues during the selection process; and sometimes negative, e.g., potential discrimination). Some drawbacks of MMIs were that they over emphasized communication skills and that the candidate's experience depended on the skill and friendliness of the interviewer. Thomas and colleagues (2015) found occupational therapy MSc candidates perceived an MMI to be fair, enjoyable, and appeared to measure professional attributes. Finally, in an admissions process for otolaryngology residency, Campagna-Vaillancourt, Manoukian, Razack, and Nguyen (2014) found that the MMI gave them the opportunity to display their strengths, evaluated the relevant competencies and was considered fair.

Selection Procedural Justice Rules

Other determinants of fairness perceptions include the perceived selection procedural justice rules identified by Gilliland (1993, 1994), and outlined in Table 8.1, such as job relatedness, opportunity to perform, and two-way communication (Bauer et al., 1998; Van Vianen, Taris, Scholten, & Schinkel, 2004). The most frequently examined justice concern is job relatedness, considered by Gilliland (1993) to have greatest impact on fairness compared to other characteristics of a selection process. Much of the early research in this area (e.g., Rynes, 1993; Smither, Reilly, Millsap, Pearlman, & Stoffey, 1993) found job-related selection methods received the most favorable ratings, such as simulation-based interviews, business-related tests, and selection centers. However, rating descriptions of the methods or sample cognitive ability items limits the generalizability to general applicant samples. Other studies have shown that different aspects of selection methods are perceived as differentially fair. For example, in a field-based study using police applicants, Truxillo, Bauer, and Sanchez (2001) found a video-based oral test was perceived as more *job related* than the written multiple-choice test; but the multiple-choice test was perceived to have more *consistent administration* than the video-based test.

Within healthcare, a study using applicants to GP specialty training (Koczwara et al., 2012) found a clinical problem-solving test was rated more favorably than a situational judgement test; while two "off-the-shelf" cognitive ability tests were rated least favorably (low job relevance and insufficient opportunity to demonstrate competence). The use of generic cognitive ability tests was not positively received for postgraduate recruitment due to lack of job-relevance and rejection via cognitive ability test results potentially conflicting with the high academic success that enabled selection into medical school in the first place.

In a qualitative study focusing on nurses and their experience during recruitment, Kanerva, Lammintakanen, and Kivinen (2010) found procedural aspects of the selection process resulted in fairness perceptions, including: opportunity to demonstrate skills; adequate information provided; a well-organized process; and two-way interaction. On the other hand, feelings of unfairness were felt by: a poorly organized process; lack of information especially feedback; no opportunity to demonstrate skills; and one-way interaction. These authors also pointed out the negative experiences felt by internal applicants which posed problems in retaining staff. In qualitative research by Kelly and her colleagues (2014), the concept of *job relatedness* was a key theme that emerged in exploring doctors' perceptions of the Health Professions Admissions Test.

Research based in Australia focusing on GP selection into training examined candidate perceptions of multiple mini interviews (Burgess et al., 2014). The national assessment center was perceived as fair and transparent, with relevant information given about the job and GP career. There were mixed findings relating to the MMI itself where candidates felt it allowed the portrayal of personal and professional attributes, however, candidates who were unable to gain relevant work experience in Australia felt that some of the experienced-based questions were less fair.

Similarly, Kumar, Roberts, Rothnie, du Fresne, and Walton (2009) examined applicant and interviewer perceptions of MMIs for graduate entry medical school admission in Australia. Qualitative data showed that MMIs were positively received by applicants and interviewers alike; specifically, that applicants liked the one-to-one format and the multiple assessment opportunities which they felt enhanced their opportunity to demonstrate skills. However, neither study used a theoretical framework within which to explore their findings.

One study that has used a theoretical framework to explore findings was Patterson and colleauges' (2011) study using Gilliland's (1993) model of organizational justice theory to examine applicant perceptions to the UK General Practice selection process over three consecutive years. Findings indicated positive perceptions of the process overall and significant positive increases (over time) in job relevance perceptions for a situational judgement test, group, and written exercise. Examining perceptions in this context helped to understand what interventions were needed regarding information about the types of selection method and reasons for their use.

Psychological and Behavioral Outcomes of Applicant Perceptions

Three types of outcomes of applicant perceptions relating to selection processes are reviewed: psychological outcomes, including: (a) *attitudes*; (b) behavioral *intentions* and behavioral outcomes; and (c) *behaviors*. These are outlined below.

Attitudes

The most commonly-examined attitude is *organizational attractiveness* (that is, the appeal of an organization). Studies have typically shown positive relationships between applicant perceptions and organizational attractiveness (Anseel & Lievens, 2009; Bauer et al., 2001; Judge, Van Vianen, & De Pater, 2004; Schinkel et al., 2013). In a study by Bauer and colleagues (1998), procedural justice perceptions were positively related to perceptions of organizational attractiveness even after controlling for pre-test perceptions. However, those who passed the test evaluated the organization more positively than those who failed; suggesting that passing or failing is more important in determining organizational attractiveness than procedural perceptions, although procedural justice still has incremental value. Anseel and Lievens (2009) showed in an experimental study with students, that perceptions of organizational attractiveness were mediated by perceptions of feedback accuracy on a personality questionnaire.

By contrast, field-based studies have found mixed relationships. Truxillo, Bauer, Campion, and Paronto (2002) found no relationship between selection fairness information and perceptions of organizational attractiveness. However, sample characteristics may have influenced this: in the context of police recruitment, applicants are likely to have already considered the relative advantages and disadvantages of the job role and organization and so perceptions of fairness were relatively unimportant in this context. Similarly, Carless (2003) found no relationship between perceptions of an interview and psychometric test and organizational attractiveness in a telecommunications company. Instead, the author found that other variables, such as type of work, organizational reputation, pay, and job security, were significant predictors of organizational attractiveness. Conversely, in research conducted in a publishing company, Schinkel et al. (2013) found selection outcome and procedural fairness interacted to influence organizational attractiveness such that applicants who were hired reported more organizational attractiveness when they perceived a fair *outcome*; while applicants who were rejected reported higher organizational attractiveness when they perceived a fair *process*. In later research, Schinkel and her colleagues (2016) concluded that applicants with more optimistic attributional styles reacted more strongly to (un)fairness than less optimistic people. When the outcome was seen as fair, optimistically attributing applicants reported more positive perceptions of the organization than less optimistic applicants; by contrast, when the outcome was perceived to be unfair, optimistic applicants reported lower organizational attractiveness than less optimistic applicants.

Overall, these mixed findings suggest that procedural justice perceptions may be related to organizational attractiveness to a degree, but that other perceived job role and organizational variables are also important. Since attitudes develop over time, attitudinal responses may develop over the course of a recruitment process as an individual interacts with organizational representatives and selection methods (Carless, 2003; Harold & Ployhart, 2008). Therefore, the attitudinal response to an initial selection method may be somewhat different to attitudes at a later date in the entire recruitment process. This may explain the somewhat diverse findings relating to attitudinal outcomes.

Behavioral Intentions

Applicant reactions are also related to several behavioral intentions. These include *job acceptance intentions* (Bauer, Paronto, & Campion, 2004; Carless, 2003; Ployhart & Ryan, 1998; Truxillo et al., 2002); *recommendation intentions* (Anseel & Lievens, 2009; Gilliland et al., 2001; McCarthy et al., 2009); *re-application intentions* (Bauer et al., 1998, 2001), and *litigation intentions* (Bauer et al., 2001; Seymour, 1988).

Bauer et al. (2004) found the only positive predictor of job acceptance intentions was passing the selection process, while Carless (2003) found the positive predictors were pre-selection job acceptance intentions and number of alternative job offers. Conversely, Ployhart and Ryan (1998) found that job acceptance intentions were high regardless of participants' perceptions of administration consistency; however, when the process was perceived as unfair, the least favorable recommendation intentions were reported even if selected for the job. This shows that even if a person is hired, negative reactions can occur.

In further research, Bauer et al. (1998) found that procedural justice characteristics positively predicted recommendation and re-application intentions; while Anseel and Lievens (2009) found that the effect of passing/failing the selection process on recommendation intentions was fully mediated by perceived feedback accuracy on a personality questionnaire. Finally, Bauer et al. (2001) found a negative relationship between legal intentions and communication and interpersonal treatment during the selection process. Overall, there seems to be a positive relationship between procedural characteristics and various behavioral intentions, the extent of which changes depending on sample and contextual characteristics.

Behavioral Outcomes

Gilliland (1993) suggested that fairness perceptions influence behavioral outcomes such as job acceptance, legal challenges, and subsequent job performance and satisfaction. However, research evidence for the link between applicant perceptions and behavioral outcomes remains unclear because intentions rather than actual behavior have been measured (Schmitt & Chan, 1999). Selection fairness perceptions *have* been positively linked to work performance (Gilliland, 1994); subsequent re-application among rejected candidates (Gilliland et al., 2001) and later performance on an alternate test (Anseel & Lievens, 2009). Gilliland (1994) showed that those selected by an unfair selection process had poorer job performance and work attitudes than those who believed the process to be fair. However, the sample was undergraduate students and the "job" was a four-hour journal-coding task; with limited ecological validity since the artificial setting and "job" were not representative of what real applicants may encounter. Gilliland et al. (2001) found that when applicants received rejection letters implying that the selection decision was beyond the company's control, they were more than twice as likely to re-apply for a position as applicants who received a letter with no such explanation. Finally, Anseel and Lievens (2009) found that participants who reported higher feedback accuracy on an in-basket exercise were more likely to perform better on a subsequent alternate form of the exercise.

By contrast, research evidence is inconsistent in explaining behaviors such as applicant withdrawal (Schmit & Ryan, 1997; Truxillo et al., 2002) and turnover among those who were subsequently hired (Truxillo et al., 2002). Bauer et al. (2001) found a negative relationship between "process factors" and legal intentions (the link to actual behavior remains unknown). Although outside a selection context, Goldman (2001) found that perceptions of procedural and distributive justice positively predicted self-reported behavior of filing a discrimination claim. Findings may be similar in a selection context, which is important because legal challenges would be costly (for all concerned), and have a negative impact on an organization's image (Schmitt & Chan, 1999).

Finally, intentions and behavior were moderately related in one study examining the relationship between job acceptance intentions and actual acceptance (Carless, 2003), though there was no relationship between fairness perceptions and job acceptance behavior. Further research may support the claim that applicant perceptions and behavioral intentions are related to subsequent behaviors since the intention-behavior link has been found in other areas of psychology (Ajzen, 1991).

The inconsistent findings may be because these behavioral outcomes measured were proximal (e.g., Anseel & Lievens, 2009) and others were distal (e.g., Truxillo et al., 2002). Linking fairness perceptions to distal behavioral outcomes may be harder because other moderator variables (job market, organizational culture) may reduce the potency of these relationships (Schmitt & Chan, 1999).

Following this literature review, the subsequent sections present two case studies outlining applicant reactions in two different healthcare contexts (see Case Studies 8.1 and 8.2). The General Practitioner and Public Health selection processes differ somewhat from one another because the applicant numbers and posts available are very different. For the 2016 recruitment round, in UK General Practice, there were 4863 applications received for 3802 available posts, a competition ratio of 1.28 applicants for each post; by contrast, Public Health had 738 applications for 70 posts, a competition ratio of 10.54 applicants for every post (https://specialtytraining.hee.nhs.uk/Competition-Ratios). So, although competition ratios are higher for Public Health, many more applicants are rejected from the GP selection process. Another key difference is that Public Health attracts two distinct types of applicants: both doctors who have completed medical school and foundation training and people from other professional backgrounds, such as psychologists and nursing.

Case Study 8.1: Candidate Perceptions of the General Practitioner Selection Process (Zibarras & Patterson, 2015)

The general practitioner (GP) selection process (outlined in Fig. 8.2) included:

- Stage 1 eligibility checks, with an electronic application process.
- Stage 2 shortlisting—a Job Knowledge Test (JKT; candidates apply clinical knowledge to solve problems); and a Situational Judgement Test (SJT), where candidates respond to written work-related scenarios and

choose a response from a list of alternatives (Patterson, Carr, et al., 2009; Patterson, Baron, Carr, Plint, & Lane, 2009).

- Stage 3 selection center with three selection methods, a group exercise (GE) involving a group discussion of a work-related issue; a simulated patient consultation (SPC) where candidates play the role of the doctor and an actor plays the patient; and a written exercise (WE) where candidates prioritize work-related issues and justify their choices (Patterson, Ferguson, Norfolk, & Lane, 2005).

The first sample of applicants were from Stage 2 shortlisting, while the second sample came from Stage 3 selection center. Job relatedness perceptions of the selection methods were measured immediately after testing, along with self-efficacy. Then following outcome feedback (i.e., pass/fail about one month later), fairness perceptions were measured along with self-efficacy. For Stage 2, outcome feedback was whether the candidate was accepted for further consideration in the selection process; while outcome feedback at Stage 3 was whether the candidate had been accepted for a GP post.

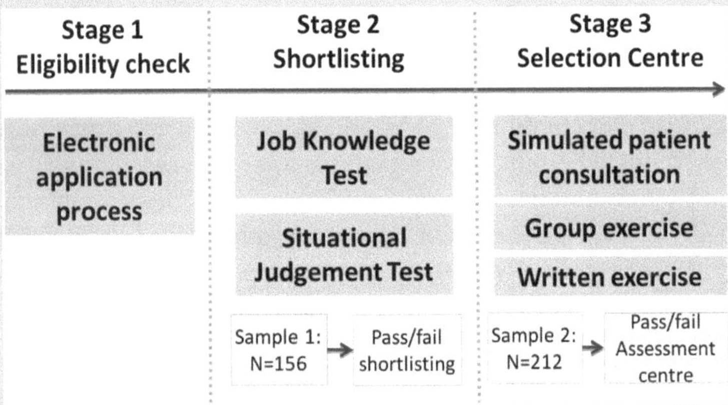

Fig. 8.2 General practice selection process, and associated samples

Results
There were three important findings:

1. For both samples, job relatedness perceptions measured at the time of testing predicted overall fairness perceptions measured following outcome (pass/fail) feedback (even after controlling for whether candidates had passed or failed).

2. The selection process stage (shortlisting versus selection center) was important in determining whether job relatedness perceptions predicted overall fairness. At shortlisting, job relatedness perceptions significantly predicted fairness perceptions but pass/fail did not; conversely, for the selection center, the outcome (pass/fail) rather than procedural factors better predicted fairness perceptions. Failing the process at the final stage of the selection process had a greater influence on fairness perceptions; possibly because candidates have invested more into the process so failing has a significant negative impact on future careers (Kelly et al., 2014; Patterson & Ferguson, 2010; Truxillo et al., 2002).
3. Finally, findings suggested that self-efficacy was a predictor (rather than an outcome variable) in applicant fairness perceptions in this high-stakes setting. Applicants who report higher self-efficacy are more likely to perceive selection processes as procedurally fair and are less impacted by the outcome results.

Case Study 8.2: Candidate Perceptions of the Public Health Selection Process

This case study focused on candidates applying for Public Health (PH) specialty posts in the UK National Health Service. The PH selection process comprised three stages:

- Stage 1 eligibility checks and an online application form;
- Stage 2 shortlisting via two tests, a Numerical Reasoning (NR) test, which assessed the extent to which respondents could understand and analyze numerical data, and a Critical Thinking (CT) test, which assessed the ability to identify, analyze and evaluate information to reach appropriate conclusions.
- Stage 3 selection center involved a series of three panel interviews; and a group exercise where four candidates solved a work-based issue (Pashayan, Duff, & Mason, 2007). Applicants were tracked through the selection process from shortlisting (stage 2) to selection center (stage 3) and completed the selection procedural justice scale (Bauer et al., 1998) questions immediately after testing at both time points, but before they were aware of their outcome results (see Fig. 8.3).

The following procedural justice dimensions were explored: *job relatedness* of selection methods; *chance to perform*, the opportunity for candidates to demonstrate their knowledge, skills and abilities; *consistency of administration*, selection process being consistent across people and over time; *information known*, information and explanation prior to selection assessment; *treatment*, the extent to which candidates are treated respectfully, and *communication*, the opportunity for candidates to have their views considered during the selection process (Bauer et al., 2001).

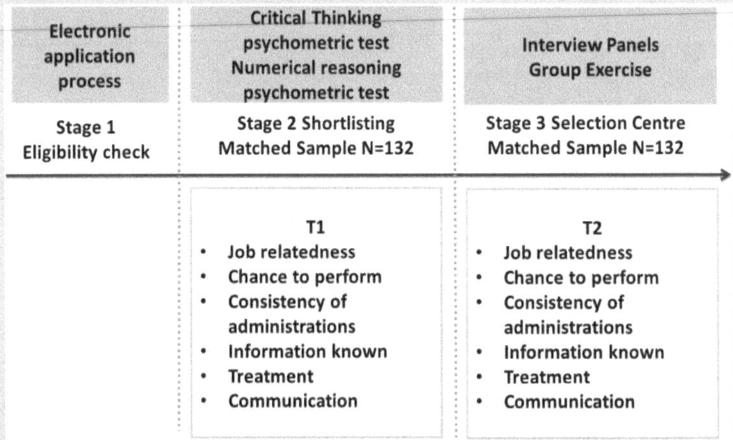

Fig. 8.3 Public health selection process matched sample and selection process

Results
There were three important findings:

1. Applicants distinguished between the job relatedness of several different selection methods, including differentiating between content and predictive validity.
2. Findings indicated a 'justice dilemma' because the methods with the highest criterion-related validity (i.e., the psychometric tests) were perceived as least job relevant.
3. Contrary to hypotheses, not all the procedural justice perceptions in this study were determinants of fairness perceptions. It is possible that this is because the measure of procedural justice did not include issues that were salient to these applicants.

Implications for Healthcare

Overall, there are several implications for recruitment and selection into healthcare. First, research suggests that to enhance positive applicants' perceptions, organizations should strive to ensure that their selection methods appear job related as this has important consequences for recruitment. This should include information regarding a method's relevance to the role (job content-relevance and ability to predict future performance); and with less familiar methods, information regarding their format. This can improve applicant perceptions, reduce potential anxiety, and is a cost-effective way to improve perceptions (Truxillo, Steiner, & Gilliland, 2004; Truxillo, Bodner, Bertolino, Bauer, & Yonce, 2009).

Second, the necessary point of selection involves discriminating between candidates to select the best candidate for the job, leaving some candidates who are disappointed with the outcome (Roberts et al., 2014). In most cases, more candidates will be rejected than accepted, making selection a "weapon of mass rejection." Since failing a selection process has a significant negative influence on perceptions of process fairness (e.g., Case Study 8.1), many applicants may leave with negative perceptions despite the organizations' best efforts. Organizations will have to "work hard" to overcome the disappointment that comes from being rejected from a highly desirable job.

Third, targeted interventions may be used to reduce potential anxiety by giving candidates as much pre-selection information as possible. These interventions may provide information such as explanations for the use of a specific selection method, its format, and its relation to the job role; and may also be aimed at improving interpersonal experiences of the candidates (Hausknecht et al., 2004).

Fourth, practically, selection must be examined from the applicants' perspective. Some healthcare selection processes already conduct evaluation from the point of view of the organization (e.g., predictive validation studies; Patterson, Carr, et al., 2009), but selection should also involve the applicants' perspective (McCarthy et al., 2009; Patterson et al., 2012; Zibarras & Patterson, 2015). Regular monitoring of applicant perceptions can alert organizations about the potential shifts in perceptions of the quality of the process, in terms of selection method content, job relevance, or administration (McCarthy et al., 2009).

Fifth, fairness perceptions are important for continued applicant attraction and research suggests that applicants are more attracted to organizations with better reputations (Turban & Cable, 2003). A fair selection process may positively influence an organization's continued ability to attract the best applicants and recruit effectively within a given job market.

Applicant Perceptions of Technology and Web-Based Selection

Over the last two decades, the Internet has emerged as an important medium for recruitment and selection, spanning pre-selection, online applications, completing web- or mobile-based psychometric tests, through to complex and interactive work sample tasks (Konradt, Warszta, & Ellwart, 2013). It is noteworthy that at the time of publication of this book (2018), there is still relatively little in the academic literature examining applicant perceptions of technology or web-based selection in healthcare or otherwise, despite its proliferation in practice.

As highlighted by Konradt and colleagues (2013), the use of technology or web-based selection might influence candidate reactions in several ways:

- Direct personal contact with organizational representatives may be established later in the selection process.
- Web-based technologies may speed up the application and selection process, resulting in expectations of reduced response and feedback times, which may not be realistic for hiring organizations.
- Web-based selection requires that applicants use their own equipment, which will have differences in speed of access to the Internet, screen size, and usability.
- Lack of supervision in web-based selection may result in some applicants cheating, leading to a sense of unfairness.

- Transmission of personal data may also raise concerns around privacy or confidentiality, which may negatively influence candidate reactions.

There are many challenges with using web-based selection and recruitment methods, yet little research has been conducted to explore the applicants' perspective. We now turn to a review of the directions for future research.

Directions for Future Research

Outlined below are five key areas around which future research could focus.

Applicant Perceptions and Recruitment

It is worth noting that the vast majority of the literature on applicant perceptions is focused on the selection process (once the candidate has applied for the post), rather than the pre-application stage. Further research is necessary to explore the extent to which job adverts or information sought during the recruitment stage (e.g., website, "a day in the life of…" videos, job specification) can influence potential applicants' attitudes towards the job and/or organization. Currently, the literature is sparse, though some research (Walker, Feild, Giles, & Bernerth, 2008) indicates that job adverts and peripheral clues (such as people shown in recruitment material) do indeed impact organizational attractiveness perceptions.

Longitudinal Research

Longitudinal research is important to explore how applicant perceptions change and develop across various stages in the selection process (Hausknecht et al., 2004). Applicant reactions may be different depending on what stage in the selection process data were collected (e.g., Case Study 8.1). Using longitudinal research will ensure that longer-term impact and outcomes of exposure to different selection methods can be examined (Anderson & Goltsi, 2006; Sackett & Lievens, 2008), and those who withdraw from the selection process. Since most applicants will be rejected, examining the rejected applicant group may reveal certain behavioral outcomes such as re-application (e.g., Gilliland et al., 2001), propensity to initiate legal proceedings (Anderson, 2011), or outcomes such as stress and well-being (Hülsheger & Anderson, 2009). Research including rejected applicants may indicate that some justice rules are more important than others; therefore, steps could be taken to mitigate the negative perceptions that candidates may have about failing a selection process.

Fair versus Unfair Selection Processes

One limitation of applicant reaction research is that selection processes perceived as *fair* are most likely to be examined. However, researchers may also explore issues and selection processes perceived as *unfair*. Research is needed to clearly differentiate between justice and injustice; this includes their conceptualization, measurement, and what influence these constructs might have on applicant perceptions (Chan & Schmitt, 2004). It is likely that justice and injustice will be associated with different outcomes, for example, litigious behavior is potentially only likely in instances of extreme injustice (Anderson et al., 2010).

Further Qualitative Research

In much of the applicant reaction research, a questionnaire-based approach is used. However, using pre-defined variables may omit salient aspects of a selection process. Indeed, the very nature of the phenomenon under investigation may challenge the utility of pre-defined variables, since quantitative research methods may only partially explain why fairness occurs. Gilliland's framework was proposed 25 years ago, with significant changes in the workplace since that time including the Internet revolution. It is clearly plausible that other aspects of a selection process may be salient to today's applicant: qualitative research methodologies could explore whether this is the case.

Impact of Social Media use in Selection

In 2016, a US-based survey found that *60% of employers use social networking sites to research job candidates* and that this number was up from 52% the previous year (CareerBuilder, 2016). Although this survey is US-based only, selection via social networking is increasingly the norm. Yet, there is little research on the impact this might have on applicant reactions, especially since some searches lead to disqualifying applicants based on content found (Berger & Zickar, 2016; Zeidner, 2007). The use of social networking for selection may be seen as an invasion of privacy, with concerns by applicants around how information is collected and obtained. Organizations using social networking sites as a selection tool may be perceived as less fair than those who do not (Madera, 2012); however, more research is needed in this area.

Conclusion

In summary, this chapter has explored why the applicant's perspective during selection and recruitment is important, particularly in healthcare settings. It has also outlined some of the key factors that influence whether or not an applicant will perceive the process to be fair, which should subsequently lead to better understanding of the effects of fairness on various outcomes in future research. There are also ethical reasons for examining applicant fairness perceptions in selection, since promoting fairness in selection systems is considered important simply because it is the right thing to do. As pointed out by Hülsheger and Anderson (2009), we must continue our study of the impact of selection processes on applicants for the sake of the applicants' well-being; the so-called negative psychological effects of selection (Anderson, 2004). Therefore, despite inconsistent and sometimes contradictory findings, it is important to consider fairness and more broadly, applicant perceptions because there are ethical obligations to do so.

Practice Points

1. Organizations should strive to ensure that selection methods appear job related to applicants—job analysis can ensure good content validity (see Chapter 6).
2. Giving as much pre-selection information as possible to candidates is important to help reduce potential anxiety; including explanations for the use of a specific selection method, its format, and its relation to the job role.
3. It is important to evaluate and monitor the quality of any selection process, including from the applicants' perspective. Regular monitoring can alert organizations to potential shifts in perceptions of quality.
4. Perceptions of a fair selection process can influence an organization's ability to attract the best applicants and recruit effectively within a given job market.
5. The impact on applicant perceptions when using technology in recruitment/selection is relatively under-explored.
6. Future research should be conducted in operational selection processes, longitudinal, and explore issues like social media and technology.

Explore Further

- Reference from Case Study 8.1: Zibarras, L. D., & Patterson, F. (2015). The role of job relatedness and self-efficacy in applicant perceptions of fairness in a high-stakes selection setting. *International Journal of Selection and Assessment, 23*(4), 332–344.
- http://users.ugent.be/~flievens/Site/Key/Key.html—Research from Filip Lievens

References

Ajzen, I. (1991). The theory of planned behavior. *Organizational Behavior and Human Decision Processes, 50*(2), 179–211.

Anderson, N. (2004). Editorial – The dark side of the Moon: Applicant perspectives, Negative Psychological Effects (NPEs), and candidate decision making in selection. *International Journal of Selection and Assessment, 12*(1–2), 1–8.

Anderson, N., & Goltsi, V. (2006). Negative psychological effects of selection methods: Construct formulation and an empirical investigation into an assessment center. *International Journal of Selection and Assessment, 14*(3), 236–255.

Anderson, N. R. (2011). Perceived job discrimination (PJD): Toward a model of applicant propensity to case initiation in selection. *International Journal of Selection and Assessment, 19*(3), 229–244.

Anderson, N. R., Salgado, J. F., & Hülsheger, U. R. (2010). Applicant reactions in selection: Comprehensive meta-analysis into reaction generalization versus situational specificity. *International Journal of Selection and Assessment, 18*(3), 291–304.

Anderson, N. R., & Witvliet, C. (2008). Fairness reactions to personnel selection methods: An international comparison between the Netherlands, the United States, France, Spain, Portugal, and Singapore. *International Journal of Selection and Assessment, 16*(1), 1–13.

Anseel, F., & Lievens, F. (2009). The mediating role of feedback acceptance in the relationship between feedback and attitudinal and performance outcomes. *International Journal of Selection and Assessment, 17*(4), 362–376.

Bauer, T. N., Maertz, C. P., Dolen, M. R., & Campion, M. A. (1998). Longitudinal assessment of applicant reactions to employment testing and test outcome feedback. *Journal of Applied Psychology, 83,* 892–903.

Bauer, T. N., Paronto, M. E., & Campion, M. A. (2004). Applicant reactions to different selection technology: Face-to-face, interactive voice response, and computer-assisted telephone screening interviews. *International Journal of Selection and Assessment, 12*(1–2), 135–148.

Bauer, T. N., Truxillo, D. M., Sanchez, R. J., Craig, J. M., Ferrara, P., & Campion, M. A. (2001). Applicant reactions to selection: Development of the selection procedural justice scale (SPJS). *Personnel Psychology, 54*(2), 387–419.

Berger, J. L., & Zickar, M. J. (2016). Theoretical propositions about cybervetting: A common antecedents model. In *Social media in employee selection and recruitment* (pp. 43–57). Cham: Springer.

Burgess, A., Roberts, C., Clark, T., & Mossman, K. (2014). The social validity of a national assessment centre for selection into general practice training. *BMC Medical Education, 14,* 261.

Campagna-Vaillancourt, M., Manoukian, J., Razack, S., & Nguyen, L. H. P. (2014). Acceptability and reliability of multiple mini interviews for admission to otolaryngology residency. *Laryngoscope, 124*(1), 91–96.

CareerBuilder. (2016, May 23). Number of employers using social media to screen candidates has increased 500 percent over the last decade.

Carless, S. A. (2003). A longitudinal study of applicant reactions to multiple selection procedures and job and organizational characteristics. *International Journal of Selection and Assessment, 11*(4), 345–351.

Carless, S. A. (2006). Applicant reactions to multiple selection procedures for the police force. *Applied Psychology, 55*(2), 145–167.

Chan, D., & Schmitt, N. (2004). An agenda for future research on applicant reactions to selection procedures: A construct-oriented approach. *International Journal of Selection and Assessment, 12*(1–2), 9–23.

Gilliland, S. W. (1993). The perceived fairness of selection systems: An organizational justice perspective. *The Academy of Management Review, 18*(4), 694–734.

Gilliland, S. W. (1994). Effects of procedural and distributive justice on reactions to a selection system. *Journal of Applied Psychology, 79*(5), 691–701.

Gilliland, S. W. (1995). Fairness from the applicant's perspective: Reactions to employee selection procedures. *International Journal of Selection and Assessment, 3*(1), 11–18.

Gilliland, S. W., Groth, M., Baker, R. C., Dew, A. F., Polly, L. M., & Langdon, J. C. (2001). Improving applicants' reactions to rejection letters: An application of fairness theory. *Personnel Psychology, 54*(3), 669–704.

Goldman, B. M. (2001). Toward an understanding of employment discrimination claiming: An integration of organizational justice and social information processing theories. *Personnel Psychology, 54*(2), 361–386.

Greenberg, J. (1987). A taxonomy of organizational justice theories. *The Academy of Management Review, 12*(1), 9–22.

Harold, C. M., & Ployhart, R. (2008). What do applicants want? Examining changes in attribute judgments over time. *Journal of Occupational and Organizational Psychology, 81*(2), 191–218.

Harris, L. (2000). Procedural justice and perceptions of fairness in selection practice. *International Journal of Selection and Assessment, 8*(3), 148–157.
Hausknecht, J., Day, D. V., & Thomas, S. C. (2004). Applicant reactions to selection procedures: An updated model and meta-analysis. *Personnel Psychology, 57*(3), 639–683.
Hausknecht, J., Halpert, J., Di Paolo, N., & Moriarty Gerrard, M. (2007). Retesting in selection: A meta-analysis of coaching and practice effects for tests of cognitive ability. *Journal of Applied Psychology, 92*, 373–385.
Hoang, T. G., Erdogan, B., Truxillo, D. M., & Bauer, T. N. (2011). Cross-cultural applicant reactions to selection methods: Vietnam and United States. *International Journal of Selection and Assessment, 20*(2), 209–219.
Hülsheger, U. R., & Anderson, N. (2009). Applicant perspectives in selection: Going beyond preference reactions. *International Journal of Selection and Assessment, 17*(4), 335–345.
Humphrey, S., Dowson, S., Wall, D., Diwakar, V., & Goodyear, H. M. (2008). Multiple mini-interviews: Opinions of candidates and interviewers. *Medical Education, 42*(2), 207–213.
Judge, T. A., Van Vianen, A. E. M., & De Pater, I. E. (2004). Emotional stability, core self-evaluations, and job outcomes: A review of the evidence and an agenda for future research. *Human Performance, 17*(3), 325.
Kanerva, A., Lammintakanen, J., & Kivinen, T. (2010). Experiences of the fairness of recruitment from unsuccessful applicants in the field of nursing. *Journal of Nursing Management, 18*(3), 293–301.
Kelly, M. E., Dowell, J., Husbands, A., Newell, J., O'Flynn, S., Kropmans, T., … Murphy, A. W. (2014). The fairness, predictive validity and acceptability of multiple mini interview in an internationally diverse student population—A mixed methods study. *BMC Medical Education, 14*(1), 267.
Kelly, M. E., Gallagher, N., Dunne, F. P., & Murphy, A. (2014). Views of doctors of varying disciplines on HPAT-Ireland as a selection tool for medicine. *Medical Teacher, 36*(9), 775–782.
Koczwara, A., Patterson, F., Zibarras, L. L., Kerrin, M., Irish, B., & Wilkinson, M. (2012). Evaluating cognitive ability, knowledge tests and situational judgement tests for postgraduate selection. *Medical Education, 46*(4), 399–408.
Konradt, U., Warszta, T., & Ellwart, T. (2013). Fairness perceptions in web-based selection: Impact on applicants' pursuit intentions, recommendation intentions, and intentions to reapply. *International Journal of Selection and Assessment, 21*(2), 155–169.

Kumar, K., Roberts, C., Rothnie, I., du Fresne, C., & Walton, M. (2009). Experiences of the multiple mini-interview: A qualitative analysis. *Medical Education, 43,* 360–367.

Landy, F. J., & Conte, J. M. (2009). *Work in the 21st century: An introduction to industrial and organizational psychology* (3rd ed.). Hoboken, NJ: Wiley-Blackwell.

Madera, J. M. (2012). Using social networking websites as a selection tool: The role of selection process fairness and job pursuit intentions. *International Journal of Hospitality Management, 31*(4), 1276–1282.

McCarthy, J., Hrabluik, C., & Jelley, B. (2009). Progression through the ranks: Assessing employee reactions to high-stakes employment testing. *Personnel Psychology, 62*(4), 793–832.

McLarty, B. D., & Whitman, D. S. (2016). A dispositional approach to applicant reactions: Examining core self-evaluations, behavioral intentions, and fairness perceptions. *Journal of Business and Psychology, 31*(1), 141–153.

Moscoso, S., & Salgado, J. F. (2004). Fairness reactions to personnel selection techniques in Spain and Portugal. *International Journal of Selection and Assessment, 12*(1–2), 187–196.

Murphy, K. R. (1986). When your top choice turns you down: Effect of rejected offers on the utility of selection tests. *Psychological Bulletin, 99*(1), 133–138.

Nikolaou, I., & Judge, T. A. (2007). Fairness reactions to personnel selection techniques in Greece: The role of core self-evaluations. *International Journal of Selection and Assessment, 15*(2), 206–219.

Pashayan, N., Duff, C., & Mason, B. W. (2007). Selection into specialty training in public health: Performance of the Medical Training Application Service shortlisting. *Journal of Public Health, 29*(4), 331–337.

Patterson, F., Baron, H., Carr, V., Plint, S., & Lane, P. (2009). Evaluation of three short-listing methodologies for selection into postgraduate training in general practice. *Medical Education, 43*(1), 50–57.

Patterson, F., Carr, V., Zibarras, L., Burr, B., Berkin, L., Plint, S., … Gregory, S. (2009). New machine-marked tests for selection into core medical training: evidence from two validation studies. *Clinical Medicine, 9*(5), 417–420.

Patterson, F., & Ferguson, E. (2010). Selection for medical education and training. In T. Swanwick (Ed.), *Understanding Medical Education: Evidence, Theory and Practice* (pp. 352–365). Wiley-Blackwell.

Patterson, F., Ferguson, E., Norfolk, T., & Lane, P. (2005). A new selection system to recruit general practice registrars: Preliminary findings from a validation study. *British Medical Journal, 330*(7493), 711–714.

Patterson, F., Knight, A., Dowell, J., Nicholson, S., Cousans, F., & Cleland, J. (2016). How effective are selection methods in medical eduction and training? Evidence from a systematic review. *Medical Education, 50*(1), 36–60.

Patterson, F., Lievens, F., Kerrin, M., Zibarras, L. L., Koczwara, A., & Carette, B. (2012). Designing selection systems for medicine: The importance of balancing predictive and political validity in high-stakes selection contexts. *International Journal of Selection and Assessment, 20*(4), 486–496.

Patterson, F., Rowett, E., Hale, R., Grant, M., Roberts, C., Cousans, F., et al. (2016). The predictive validity of a situational judgement test and multiple-mini interview for entry into postgraduate training in Australia. *BMC Medical Education, 16*(1), 87.

Patterson, F., & Zibarras, L. D. (2011). Exploring the construct of perceived job discrimination in selection. *International Journal of Selection and Assessment, 19*(3), 251–257.

Patterson, F., Zibarras, L., Carr, V., Irish, B., & Gregory, S. (2011). Evaluating candidate reactions to selection practices using organisational justice theory. *Medical Education, 45*(3), 289–297.

Phillips, J. M., & Gully, S. M. (2002). Fairness reactions to personnel selection techniques in Singapore and the United States. *The International Journal of Human Resource Management, 13*(8), 1186–1205.

Ployhart, R., & Ryan, A. M. (1998). Applicants' reactions to the fairness of selection procedures: The effects of positive rule violations and time of measurement. *Journal of Applied Psychology; 12th Annual Meeting of the Society-for-Industrial-and-Organizational-Psychology, 83*(1), 3–16.

Roberts, C., Clark, T., Burgess, A., Frommer, M., Grant, M., & Mossman, K. (2014). The validity of a behavioural multiple-mini-interview within an assessment centre for selection into specialty training. *BMC Medical Education, 14*(1), 169.

Rosse, J. G., Miller, J. L., & Stecher, M. D. (1994). A field study of job applicants' reactions to personality and cognitive ability testing. *Journal of Applied Psychology, 79*(6), 987–991.

Rynes, S. (1993). Who's selecting whom? Effects of selection practices on applicant attitudes and behaviours. In N. Schmitt & W. Borman (Eds.), *Personnel selection in organisations* (pp. 240–274). San Francisco, CA: Jossey-Bass.

Sackett, P., & Lievens, F. (2008). Personnel selection. *Annual Review of Psychology, 59,* 419–450.

Schinkel, S., van Vianen, A. E. M., & Marie Ryan, A. (2016). Applicant reactions to selection events: Four studies into the role of attributional style and fairness perceptions. *International Journal of Selection and Assessment, 24*(2), 107–118.

Schinkel, S., van Vianen, A., & van Dierendonck, D. (2013). Selection fairness and outcomes: A field study of interactive effects on applicant reactions. *International Journal of Selection and Assessment, 21*(1), 22–31.

Schmit, M. J., & Ryan, A. M. (1997). Applicant withdrawal: The role of test-taking attitudes and racial differences. *Personnel Psychology, 50*(4), 855–876.

Schmitt, N., & Chan, D. (1999). The status of research on applicant reactions to selection tests and its implications for managers. *International Journal of Management Reviews, 1*(1), 45–62.

Seymour, R. T. (1988). Why plaintiffs' counsel challenge tests, and how they can successfully challenge the theory of 'validity generalization'. *Journal of Vocational Behavior, 33,* 331–364.

Smither, J. W., Reilly, R. R., Millsap, R. E., Pearlman, K., & Stoffey, R. W. (1993). Applicant reactions to selection procedures. *Personnel Psychology, 46,* 49–76.

Steiner, D. D., & Gilliland, S. W. (1996). Fairness reactions to personnel selection techniques in France and the United States. *Journal of Applied Psychology, 81*(2), 134–141.

Thomas, A., Young, M. E., Mazer, B. L., Lubarsky, S. E., & Razack, S. I. (2015). Candidates' and interviewers' perceptions of multiple-mini interviews for admission to an occupational therapy professional program. *Occupational Therapy in Health Care, 29*(2), 186–200.

Truxillo, D. M., Bauer, T. N., Campion, M. A., & Paronto, M. E. (2002). Selection fairness information and applicant reactions: A longitudinal field study. *Journal of Applied Psychology, 87*(6), 1020–1031.

Truxillo, D. M., Bauer, T. N., & Sanchez, R. J. (2001). Multiple dimensions of procedural justice: Longitudinal effects on selection system fairness and test-taking self-efficacy. *International Journal of Selection and Assessment, 9*(4), 336–349.

Truxillo, D. M., Bodner, T. E., Bertolino, M., Bauer, T. N., & Yonce, C. A. (2009). Effects of explanations on applicant reactions: A meta-analytic review. *International Journal of Selection and Assessment, 17*(4), 346–361.

Truxillo, D. M., Steiner, D. D., & Gilliland, S. W. (2004). The importance of organizational justice in personnel selection: Defining when selection fairness really matters. *International Journal of Selection and Assessment, 12*(1–2), 39–53.

Turban, D. B., & Cable, D. M. (2003). Firm reputation and applicant pool characteristics. *Journal of Organizational Behavior, 24*(6), 733–751.

Van Vianen, A. E. M., Taris, R., Scholten, E., & Schinkel, S. (2004). Perceived fairness in personnel selection: Determinants and outcomes in different stages of the assessment procedure. *International Journal of Selection and Assessment, 12*(1–2), 149–159.

Walker, H. J., Feild, H. S., Giles, W. F., & Bernerth, J. B. (2008). The interactive effects of job advertisement characteristics and applicant experience on reactions to recruitment messages. *Journal of Occupational and Organizational Psychology, 81*(4), 619–638. https://doi.org/10.1348/096317907X252487.

Zeidner, R. (2007). How deep can you probe? *HR Magazine, 52*(10), 57–60.

Zibarras, L. D., & Patterson, F. (2015). The role of job relatedness and self-efficacy in applicant perceptions of fairness in a high-stakes selection setting. *International Journal of Selection and Assessment, 23*(4), 332–344.

9

Coaching Issues

Barbara Griffin

Overview

The use of commercial coaching services to gain a competitive advantage has become an issue across industries and countries, particularly in the high-stakes contexts of employment selection and admission into sought-after university degrees including law, business and medicine. Indeed, it appears so pervasive that by 2004 McGagie, Downing, and Kulilius (p. 203) were claiming that commercial test preparation had become "*part of the fabric of U.S. medical education*".

This chapter begins with a definition of the term "coaching" and a brief description of its development within educational settings, including information on the prevalence of the use of commercial coaching. A discussion of the potential impact of coaching, both positive and negative, follows. Empirical evidence is then examined, considered in the light of methodological limitations of the extant literature. The chapter

B. Griffin (✉)
Macquarie University, Sydney, Australia
e-mail: barbara.griffin@mq.edu.au

F. Patterson and L. Zibarras (eds.), *Selection and Recruitment in the Healthcare Professions*, https://doi.org/10.1007/978-3-319-94971-0_9

concludes with a summary of the practical implications, illustrated by a case study of how one university adjusted its process to limit the effect of coaching on selection decisions. Given the limited research available in the broader healthcare professions, most of the statistics presented here relate to medicine and the selection of medical students.

By the end of this chapter you should:

- understand how and why commercial coaching has developed into a significant industry
- be able to evaluate the potential benefits and risks of coaching for selection of healthcare professionals
- have some evidence for developing processes designed to limit any unwanted effects of coaching on selection decisions.

Definition, Description and Prevalence

There is a broad range of education and training activities encompassed under the umbrella term of "coaching". For example, athletes can be coached to improve their underlying skill and in educational settings students can seek external support in developing skills such as understanding mathematics, improving essay-writing skill, or revising resuscitation techniques. However, the coaching discussed in this chapter concerns commercial training in test-taking strategies. This form of coaching focuses on a specific test (usually used for selection purposes) with the aim of improving test scores, regardless of whether or not the underlying skill or ability measured by the test is improved.

Lievens, Buyse, Sackett, & Connelly (2012, p. 273) define this sort of coaching as "*a formal intervention of a coaching firm to teach candidates test-related content and test-taking strategies (i.e., test familiarization, drill and practice with feedback, training in strategies for specific item formats and for general test taking).*" The focus is typically on test content and drill rather than skill development and is largely instructor-driven. Commercial coaching implies that applicants must pay to attend such a program. Within the education literature, commercial coaching falls under the rubric of what is classed as "shadow education", being activities that fall outside of formal schooling (Buchman, Condron, & Roscigno, 2010). Researchers typically distinguish the commercial coaching industry from the large array of informal or freely available preparation activities. Some describe the latter as "test familiarization," which is driven by the applicant and likely to reduce individual differences in test familiarity (Arendasy, Sommer, Gutierrez-Lobos, & Punter, 2016).

The first recorded commercial coaching company was founded by Stanley Kaplan in 1938. His focus was on increasing clients' scores on the Scholastic Aptitude Test (SAT), used for selection into tertiary education in the United States of America. With successful marketing, it was not long before the coaching industry was flourishing. It remains a significant force today, with substantial revenue. In 2016, Kaplan Inc's test preparation division alone earned US$287 million (Graham Holdings, 2016), with one of its Medical College Admission Test (MCAT) courses advertised for US$9499 per person. A basic coaching program for the Undergraduate Medical and Health Sciences Test (UMAT), used in Australia and New Zealand for admission into health-related training programs, can cost up to AUS$1970 (MedEntry, 2017). In Britain, expensive coaching courses for the UK Clinical Aptitude Test (UKCAT) are not only offered locally, but also in many countries across Asia.

The coaching industry appears to respond quite rapidly to trends in selection, seen in the development of manuals and courses designed to specifically address the growing use of situational judgement tests for selection (Lievens et al., 2012) and multiple mini interviews (e.g., To, 2013). The companies, which generally exist outside national education accreditation regulations, undertake quite aggressive marketing, arguably capitalizing on the anxiety and vulnerability of applicants who face significant hurdles in becoming one of the small proportion to actually be offered a place in a medical or other health science degrees (Tompkins, 2011). For example, one company (MedEntry, 2017) not only asserts on its website that that 90% of their "students" have been offered places in one or more medical schools but makes the somewhat grandiose claim that "*our training is geared towards making you a better person, with better reasoning and problem-solving skills, and emotional intelligence.*"

But just how prevalent is the uptake of commercial coaching? Despite anecdotal accounts of its ubiquitous use in high stakes selection contexts, there are limited data available (Stemig, Sackett, & Lievens, 2015), and figures may be downwardly biased if applicants believe they may somehow be disadvantaged by admitting to having been coached. In relation to applicants to medical schools, Stemig et al. (2015) report that while 69% of those applying in Belgium completed freely available practice exercises, just 26% paid for coaching. In a study of those sitting the UKCAT (Lambe, Waters, & Bristow, 2012), only 9% of respondents admitted to attending a commercial coaching course, although significantly more made use of commercially available resources. This contrasts with the figures from New Zealand (Wilkinson & Wilkinson, 2013), where 60% of applicants to healthcare programs said they were coached by a commercial company. In Australia, reported prevalence ranges from 36% (Laurence, Zajac, Lorimer, Turnbull, & Sumner, 2013) to 56.2% (Griffin, Carless, & Wilson, 2013a), while one study in Israel indicated 20–25% of applicants attended commercial coaching (Moshinsky, Ziegler, & Gafni, 2017). Similarly, an early study of MCAT test takers in North America (Jones, 1986), estimated 25% used commercial coaching. However, this figure is unlikely to reflect current prevalence given increasing competition for places and evidence that the number of MCAT practice tests sold increased by over 20,000 in the two years from 2007 to 2009 (Matthew, 2010).

Potential Impact of Coaching

This section outlines the four major areas that raise concerns in terms of the impact of coaching on the use of selection tests, namely the implications for widening participation of disadvantaged applicants, the possible impact on the construct validity and predictive validity of the test, and how applicant well-being might be affected.

Widening Participation

Given the potential for higher education to improve social mobility (Brown, Reay, & Vincent, 2013), governments have enacted policies that encourage and enable those from disadvantaged groups to enroll in university degrees. Initially the focus was on gender and ethnicity where there has been some success in widening participation (Cleland, Nicholson, Kelly, & Moffat, 2015), but more recently attention has turned to the lack of diversity with regard to socioeconomic status (SES). This is highlighted within healthcare training programs, particularly medicine, psychology, and dentistry. Griffin and Hu (2015), for example, showed how there are not only fewer low SES background applicants for medical degrees, but that the cognitive ability testing used in making selection decisions has a further adverse impact on these applicants, disproportionally reducing their success rate. The high cost of commercial coaching (see above) may be one factor that accounts for these findings (see Chapter 10 for a review).

As discussed later, many applicants have quite an entrenched view on the efficacy of commercial coaching (Moshinsky et al., 2017; Wilkinson & Wilkinson, 2013). Low SES individuals, with a lack of financial resources to access coaching, may not even bother applying if they believe that their chance of success is minimal without it. Alternatively, if one of few aspirants in a low SES high school environment, they may not even be aware of opportunities for coaching regarding university entrance tests (Arendasy, Sommer, Gutierrez-Lobos, & Punter, 2016).

If such coaching does actually increase test scores, then lack of access to coaching (either because one can't afford it or lives remote from the urban training centers) creates an issue of measurement fairness in the use of testing. Not only ethically unfair that they don't have the opportunity to increase performance, but psychometrically biased because, as outlined in the next section, the selection test could measure different latent constructs for uncoached compared to coached applicants, invalidating any rank ordering (Arendasy et al., 2016). So seriously is this viewed that some have argued that shadow education activities, such as coaching, could well magnify inequality and undermine efforts to provide education fairly across all sectors of a country (Arendasy et al., 2016).

Construct Validity

Coaching may alter the construct validity (what is being measured) of a test, in either a positive or negative manner.

First, if coaching familiarizes people with test format, reduces their anxiety, and increases their self-confidence about being able to perform on the test, then it can actually remove error variance from the test scores thereby enhancing construct validity. In other words, the test score has the noise, or construct-irrelevant variance, taken out of it and is therefore more likely to reflect whatever it is supposed to measure (Ryan, Ployhart, Greguras, & Schmit, 1998).

Second, coaching may have the opposite effect by *increasing* construct-irrelevant variance, thus undermining measurement by artificially inflating scores. This outcome has been attributed to coached applicants having increased "test-wiseness", defined as understanding rules or procedures for how to take a test (Chung-Herrera, Ehrhart, Solamon, & Kilian, 2009). When coaching focuses on drill and teaching specific strategies for answering test items, it can result in higher

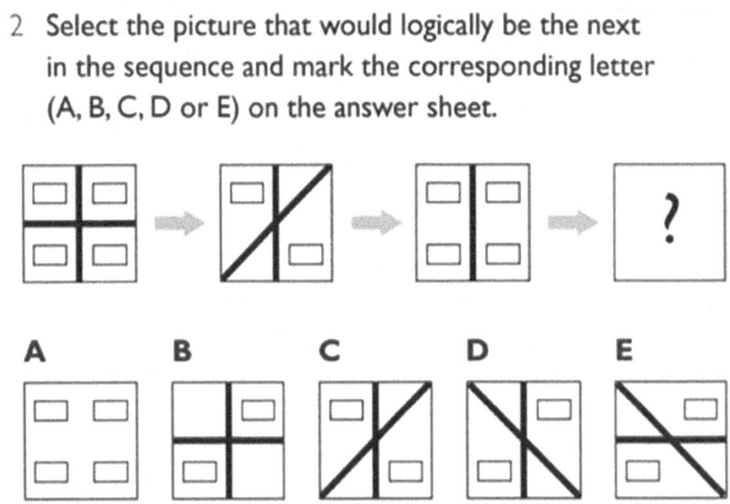

Fig. 9.1 Example item of the UMAT Section 3 (used with permission UMAT Candidate Information Booklet (ACER, 2017)

scores without actually altering the test-taker's true level of the construct (e.g., cognitive ability) that the test was designed to measure (Millman, Bishop, & Ebel, 1965).

Arendasy et al. (2016) describe a third alternative (other than coaching having no effect on construct validity), whereby coaching might increase the very specific ability assessed in the test but the improved ability will only be for those types of test items. The ability to generalize knowledge or ability beyond that domain will be significantly compromised. For example, a test such as the UMAT Section 3 assesses abstract reasoning via items that require non-verbal pattern recognition, such as identifying the next picture in a series of pictures (see Fig. 9.1 for an example). Coaching to assist in answering these types of items might well improve performance on similar items but will not generalize to improving overall abstract reasoning.

Predictive Validity

It follows that if the construct validity of a test is not altered then there should be no changes to its predictive validity. However, if coaching removes construct-irrelevant variance (e.g., anxiety, slowness due to unfamiliarity) then predictive validity may well be improved. If, on the other hand, the test is a less pure assessment of the quality/construct it was designed to measure due to the effect of coaching, we might expect that the predictive validity of the test will be degraded. In this case, scores of coached applicants should over-predict their later performance—they will not, for instance, achieve as good a GPA once enrolled in a degree as their selection test result might indicate. Evidence of measurement bias such as altered predictive validity, could increase the risk of litigation for any institution using the test.

Applicant Well-Being

Much of the attention in research on coaching has been from the perspective of the educational/employing institution, with far less focus on the applicant's reaction to coaching. And yet, if we have a duty of care to applicants and future students, then the potential effect of coaching on their well-being is worth considering.

Selection into one's preferred training program can be the fulfilment of long-held career aspirations. When high levels of uncertainty are attached to this outcome due to the extremely competitive nature of the admissions process, it is bound to engender stress and anxiety in the applicant. It appears that many applicants are of the firm belief that coaching will improve their chances of selection (Bardes, Best, Kremer, & Dienstag, 2009; Wilkinson & Wilkinson, 2013), and so it is not surprising that there is a relatively high uptake of commercial coaching. There is little research to show if coaching does reduce this test-related anxiety. However, anecdotally, it seems that the coaching industry, by means of aggressive marketing, capitalizes on this selection anxiety and may even make it worse in their effort to secure more clients.

Also, not generally considered is the ongoing effect on coached applicants who end up being selected. If their test scores over-predict performance, we would expect students who were coached on admission tests who fall into the category of "false positive" (should not have been selected due to inadequate true ability) to be under-performing academically; possibly at risk of failure. By decaying the validity of a selection decision, coaching might have a long-term effect of creating greater stress in students who struggle to maintain satisfactory performance.

In the next sections, the empirical evidence regarding the four issues identified above is presented.

Empirical Evidence of the Effect of Coaching

There are decades of research in educational settings on the effect of test preparation, including several large meta-analyses. Much of this has been concentrated on the Scholastic Aptitude Test (SAT), used for selection into college in North America. More recently, researchers have turned from general college admission to the more high-stakes context of medical student selection. Before examining these findings, it is important to understand the methodological issues that can influence studies of coaching, to the extent that the design might result in an under- or over-estimation of any effects. The next section reviews four factors that potentially impact study results: type of participant, type of test, type of coaching, and study design.

Methodological Challenges to Studying Coaching Effects

First is the problem of generalizability of findings across *participant groups*. There is likely to be, for example, a greater range of ability among those undertaking the SAT exam (bulk of research studies) than those who are applying for medicine or another high-stakes, high ability-requirement degree. Not only are there restriction of range issues in the latter, but studies have shown that pre-existing ability influences the extent that an individual will benefit from coaching (Griffin, Carless & Wilson, 2013a). Therefore, when there is a broader range of ability among a coached group the effect of coaching might be diminished.

Second is the problem of generalizability of findings *across tests*. It appears that some tests and some test items (e.g., the UMAT Section 3 items compared to the UMAT Section 2 items) are more easily coachable than others (Domingue & Briggs, 2009; Griffin et al., 2013a) and therefore omnibus conclusions about the effectiveness of coaching may not be warranted.

Third is the problem of generalizability of findings across *types of coaching*. As indicated above, coaching activities can range from simple test familiarization to paid one-on-one tutoring by commercial companies. Studies (e.g., Lievens et al., 2012) that compare these typically find differential effects, which can also depend on the length of time spent in the coaching "intervention" (Ryan et al., 1998).

Perhaps more importantly is the actual *study design*. Apart from the fact that the majority, if not all, field studies rely on self-reports of coaching behavior, a significant proportion of the empirical work on the effectiveness of coaching has been criticized for its lack of rigorous control and potential bias through the unavoidable self-selection that occurs into coaching programs (McGaghie et al., 2004). For example, applicants who seek coaching are found to have high motivation and higher test anxiety than those who choose not to be coached, and they are more likely to be male, from a non-minority culture, and of higher SES (Domingue & Briggs, 2009; Ryan et al., 1998; Stemig et al., 2015). It may well be these differences that influence test scores rather than the coaching itself. Indeed, Powers (1993) reports that researchers who do not control for self-selection find effects four to five times greater than the more rigorously designed studies.

Although laboratory studies allow random assignment into coached and uncoached groups, the fidelity of these is questionable as the typical research participant is unlikely to have the same motivation as a real-world applicant. However, because of the high-stakes nature of many of the selection contexts, it would not really be ethical to conduct prospective randomized trials on real-world applicants. More recently, propensity score matching has been used to overcome some of the self-selection bias effects (see Domingue & Briggs, 2009; Lievens et al., 2012). Propensity scoring involves identifying a set of covariates likely to influence outcomes, then estimating the probability each participant has of being in the coached group based on these. This enables comparisons between coached and uncoached groups by matching individuals with equal probabilities of having been coached.

Research Findings on Coaching Effects

As mentioned, the majority of early studies examined the effect of coaching on performance in the SAT, followed by studies of general cognitive ability or IQ tests. These have been summarized in a number of meta-analyses (e.g., Hausknecht, Halpert, Di Paolo, & Moriarty Gerrard, 2007; Kulik, Bangert-Drowns, & Kulik, 1984; te Nijenhuis, van Vianen, & Flier, 2007), which will be referred to briefly below. However, most of the cited studies in this section have been chosen for their relevance to healthcare (albeit predominantly in the selection of medical students).

Relationship of Socioeconomic Status (SES) to Coaching

Although limited, findings indicate that those from low SES backgrounds are less likely to engage in commercial coaching for college entry tests such as the SATs (Buchmann et al., 2010). With regard to applicants to medical school, Griffin (2016) reported that those from lower SES areas had a lower rate of coaching than those from high SES areas, and longer time spent living in an area of inequality predicted lower likelihood of engaging in coaching. However, it seems that this difference may not be due solely to financial reasons as Stemig et al. (2015) showed that low SES background applicants for medical school were also less likely to attend freely available information sessions.

Effect of Coaching on Selection Test Performance

The following section reflects the fact that there is quite an extensive literature on the effectiveness of coaching on tests of cognitive ability (such as the SAT, IQ tests, MCAT, and UMAT), with far fewer studies on other types of tests (such as interviews or personality tests).

1. Tests of cognitive ability

Meta-analytic evidence of tests used on wider populations, including the SAT (Kulik et al., 1984) and cognitive ability tests used in employee selection (Hausknecht et al., 2007), suggest that coaching has a significant positive effect on performance, although the incremental variance of commercial coaching over mere test familiarization is relatively small at approximately 0.25 SD.

The picture is less clear when it comes to tests used in medical student selection such as the MCAT, UKCAT, and UMAT. Jones (1986) and McGaghie et al. (2004) found small to minimal positive effects respectively in studies on the effects of commercial coaching on the MCAT. Lambe et al. (2012) reported that coaching per se did not impact performance on the UKCAT, but time spent practicing or being coached did have a small positive relationship with scores. In contrast, the four recent studies that investigated the effects of coaching on the UMAT (Griffin et al., 2008; Griffin, Carless & Wilson, 2013a; Laurence et al., 2013; Wilkinson & Wilkinson, 2013) showed a small benefit of coaching when overall score was examined. However, this benefit was driven by just one of the three sections of the test.

The UMAT's three sub-sections are problem-solving, which relates primarily to verbal reasoning; understanding people, which relates to verbal and emotional intelligence; and non-verbal reasoning, which relates most strongly to numerical reasoning (Griffin, Carless & Wilson, 2013b). Griffin and colleagues (2008, 2013a) and Wilkinson and Wilkinson (2013) showed that commercial coaching had no ability to increase scores for the items assessing problem-solving or understanding people but did increase the non-verbal reasoning score. The non-verbal section is similar to tests like the Raven's progressive matrices (Raven, Raven, & Court, 1998), which consists of geometric designs with a missing piece that the test-taker must identify from a number of possible choices. Such tests require rapid pattern recognition, but apparently, the solutions depend on a limited number of rules, which are likely to be implicitly learnt with regular practice (Carpenter, Just, & Shell, 1990; Verguts & de Boeck, 2002). Interestingly, this differential effect of coaching is found in the non-medical domain, where verbal tests appear to have limited coachability, while numerical tests seem somewhat more sensitivity to coaching interventions (Domingue & Briggs, 2009; Hausknecht et al., 2007; Ryan et al., 1998). Furthermore, there is consistent evidence (e.g., Griffin et al., 2008; Kulik et al., 1984; Ryan et al., 1998) that, contrary to expectations, the only applicants who benefit from coaching are those of high ability, who would probably do well regardless.

These studies of cognitive ability tests highlight an important feature of the effect of coaching on the construct validity of a test. Briefly, there is evidence supporting the hierarchical structure of cognitive ability (see Carroll, 1993), whereby narrow abilities (e.g., verbal, quantitative, and abstract reasoning) are sub-facets of a general cognitive ability factor, widely referred to as "*g*". The variance in a cognitive ability test score is comprised of variance due to the narrow ability that is targeted by the test plus variance due to *g*. It is the *g* component of each test that is generalizable across domains and drives predictive validity for later performance (te Nijenhuis et al., 2007). There is ample evidence that a test's *g* saturation is reduced by coaching (Estrada, Ferrer, Abad, Román, & Colom, 2015; Hayes, Petrov, & Sederberg, 2015; te Nijenhuis, Voskuijl, & Schijve, 2001; te Nijenhuis et al., 2007). In other words, coaching does not increase *g* or the applicant's general intelligence, only (if anything) the very narrow ability assessed by the test. This principle was underscored in a major recent review of so-called "brain training" exercises (Simons et al., 2016), which demonstrated how practice and coaching on cognitive exercises may improve performance on closely related tasks but has no effect in improving everyday cognitive performance. Similarly, a study by Arendasy et al. (2016) of applicants to the Medical University of Vienna found that test preparation (including commercial coaching) did not lead to increases in *g*, and that gains in test-specific factors only exhibited minimal transfer to general science knowledge. These authors argue that coaching does not compromise the fair use of cognitive ability tests for selection.

In summary, applicants who engage in coaching may sometimes achieve higher cognitive ability test scores, but these scores reflect a different construct than those achieved by uncoached applicants, although it may not be sufficient to alter predictive validity. Nevertheless, there is little research on how much coaching gains in cognitive ability tests, which are generally small in medical selection contexts, actually result in an improved chance of selection.

2. Situational judgment tests

In recent years, there has been quite a rapid uptake of the use of situational judgment tests (SJTs) for high-stakes selection, including in medical contexts. Perhaps unsurprisingly, this has been accompanied by a growth in coaching firms targeting SJTs in their courses and material (Lievens et al., 2012).

Lievens et al. (2012) estimated the positive effects of coaching for SJT performance to be as large as 0.5 SDs. In a subsequent study (Stemig et al., 2015), a positive effect was also found for other test familiarization activities (attending an information session, completing practice exercises, etc.) although private tutoring actually had a negative effect on performance. Furthermore, the authors showed that higher SJT scores (as a result of preparation) did not necessarily improve interpersonal skills.

As with any selection method, as its use increases in popularity, so too does demand for commercial coaching programs, designed to teach candidates strategies for improving their SJT scores, so that they might increase their chance of success in the selection process (Lievens et al., 2008). Given that SJTs are a measurement *method*, factors relating to coachability and coaching effects will vary between individual SJTs. As such, the potential risks and impacts of coaching should be assessed for each SJT used in selection (Patterson, Ashworth, Kerrin, & Neill, 2013).

Although research on the "coachability" of SJTs is limited and merits further exploration, some studies have addressed this issue and contribute valuable points to consider to reduce the risk of coaching effects. Evidence from research suggests elements of best practice SJT development and design can also serve as precautionary measures to mitigate risk of an SJT of being "coachable". First, SJTs designed for a specific target role should contain content that is highly contextualized for that role.

Second, tailoring response instructions and formats to the test specification is also advisable (Patterson et al., 2013). Response formats that involve a greater cognitive load, such as ranking formats and "choose three"/multiple choice formats are less susceptible to coaching effects than less cognitively loaded formats (i.e., "choose one best response from four"). Additionally, research supports the use of cognitively oriented response instructions (e.g., "what should you do?") over behaviorally oriented instructions (i.e., "what would you do?") as the latter are more susceptible to self-deception and impression management and thus coaching effects (Patterson et al., 2013).

3. Personality inventories

Although there is widespread use of personality questionnaires for selection in corporate settings, its use for selection into healthcare professions or training programs is less common. There are also few studies on the effect of coaching on personality test scores—most of the research focus has been on applicants faking good (even without the assistance of coaching). For example, medical school applicants showed clear evidence of faking good on a personality test battery at the time of selection (using their answers after acceptance as a comparison) despite the fact that they were told the test would not be used to make selection decisions (Griffin & Wilson, 2012).

It is therefore not surprising that coached applicants (for the police force) achieved higher scores than uncoached applicants on a test of conscientiousness (Miller & Barrett, 2008). Interestingly though, this study also found that coached applicants were able to fake the test more effectively than those who just faked good without having training on how to do so.

4. Interviews

Interviews, which are ubiquitous in corporate selection contexts, are also utilized to make selection decisions by a growing number of medical schools and medical specialty training programs, and increasingly, for entry into other health-related training programs such as psychology and physiotherapy. Nevertheless, there are few studies on the effects of coaching on selection interview performance despite the fact that an internet search will reveal hundreds, if not thousands, of sites offering training designed to improve interview performance.

Using police and fire department employees applying for promotion, Maurer, Solamon, Andrews, and Troxtel (2001) found that those who attended an interview coaching session had higher ratings on a situational interview than those who didn't attend. In contrast to this result (which replicated Maurer and colleagues' earlier study in 1998), two studies on the effect of coaching on multiple mini interviews (Griffin et al., 2008; Moshinsky et al., 2017) found that coaching had no influence on station ratings. Indeed, at one station in the Griffin et al. study, coached students had significantly lower scores. It may be that coached students are quicker to assume what they think is being assessed at a particular station, so may be less aware of subtle cues and therefore provide the wrong information (Griffin, 2014) or that interviewers have been trained to identify "coached" responses.

Predictive Validity

As previously explained, when construct validity is altered there is a risk that the predictive validity of the test also suffers. Predictive validity studies investigate whether the relationship between selection test scores and later performance (on the job or in an educational program) is different for those who have been coached compared to those who haven't. Such studies are rare because the data are not easily obtainable.

In terms of cognitive ability tests used in general selection contexts (where the range of ability is typically less restricted than in medical selection), te Nijenhuis et al. (2001) argue that a session of short coaching is unlikely to have a substantial impact on predictive validity. However, this type of coaching is quite different to the intensive coaching courses and associated practice material that are marketed today for applicants to many health professions. For example, in the course of research on this topic, I have had applicants to medical school confess that they spent half an hour a day answering practice items for six months prior to the UMAT test.

Lievens, Reeve, and Heggestad (2007) studied medical school applicants who were retested on selection tests (cognitive ability) and found that scores gained on the second occasion had significantly poorer predictive ability, which was due to a reduction in *g*-loading caused by retesting. Even though coaching may or may not have occurred during the period between the first and second testing, both coaching and retesting have the similar effect of reducing the *g*-loading of test scores. We might therefore expect a similar reduction in validity for coached scores. However, there are no direct predictive validity studies of cognitive ability tests used for selection in the healthcare professions.

Nevertheless, Griffin, Yeomans, and Wilson (2013) have shown that when applicants coached for the UMAT test in Australia were accepted into a medical degree, they went on to achieve a significantly lower GPA than those who had not been coached. A later analysis (Griffin, Bayl-Smith, & Hu, under review) found that, even after controlling for selection test scores, having been coached significantly increased the odds that a student would be among those who consistently achieved below-average results across the whole degree. These findings could imply that coached scores did not represent true ability or that those who rely on coaching cope less well with the rigors of medical study.

In contrast, when Stemig et al. (2015) compared the ability of SJT scores of coached and uncoached applicants (for Belgium medical schools) to predict interpersonal skill (measured after enrolling), there was only a small, but non-significant, decrement in validity for the coached scores. Coaching may therefore not be hugely problematic for SJT prediction. There is too little available evidence to indicate whether this is due to the stability of SJT constructs in the face of coaching.

Coaching and Applicant Well-Being

It seems clear that those with poor stress tolerance are more likely to engage in a coaching intervention when faced with the demands of a selection process (Ryan et al., 1998). However, while coaching is not very effective in reducing this anxiety (Ryan et al., 1998), coached applicants are convinced that they will perform better as a result of being coached, even though this confidence has been shown to be misplaced (Wilkinson & Wilkinson, 2013). A letter from two senior medical students highlights this concern when they state that those applying for medicine "now opt to undertake coaching for fear of 'missing out' on what may potentially be an edge obtained by other prospective students. It is the psychological comfort provided to students that they have done some preparation that marketers of coaching courses have been exploiting" (Wong & Roberts-Thomson, 2009).

Given the initial evidence described above that medical students who were coached on admissions tests underperform compared to their uncoached peers, there may be a lasting negative effect of coaching. Students may even suspect that they would not be enrolled without external assistance to boost their selection scores, setting up potential issues about fear of ongoing failure or lack of ability. This is an area for future research.

Finally, applicant attitudes and reactions to selection tests have important implications for both their performance on the test, their attraction to the hiring organization, their behavior and attitudes after being hired, their well-being, and their propensity to initiate legal proceedings regarding unfairness (Ryan & Ployhart, 2000; Truxillo, Bauer, & McCarthy, 2015; see also Chapter 8 for a review). The perceived coachability of tests such as the UMAT and UKCAT are strong factors in creating negative attitudes to these tests among applicants (Brown & Griffin, 2014; Cleland et al., 2011).

Future Research

The above review of the empirical research on coaching has identified some areas for ongoing research. Primarily, we need predictive validity studies to provide evidence of the accuracy of current selection decision-making. Related information is needed on the extent to which any score improvements that exist as a result of coaching actually result in "false positive" selection decisions or cause "false negative" choices regarding potentially more deserving applicants.

Clearly, more work is needed on non-academic assessment tests to determine if they are more or less amenable to coaching. Lievens et al. (2012) add that there may be some types of items (for example in an SJT) that are more resilient to coaching efforts and therefore greater understanding on what determines coachability is an important avenue for future research. In addition, while there have been a few studies on the type of coaching and familiarization programs that are most effective, more information on this and whether there are individual differences in who benefits from what type of intervention will also assist in identifying any negative impact (te Nijenhuis et al., 2007).

In the face of applicant perceptions regarding unfairness related to coaching, one institution made the decision to make all the MMI station content from one year's testing freely available on the internet the following year (Moshinsky et al., 2017). One presumes that this then requires new station content to be developed each year. Not only is this resource-intensive, but may threaten the reliability of items when there is little chance of pilot testing, etc. It would be useful to have more evidence of the effects of this practice, which is not uncommon for some of the larger cognitive ability selection tests.

Implications for Practice

While nearly 30 years ago, it appears that Bond's (1989, p. 442) observation remains true that "*the coaching debate will probably continue unabated for some time to come. One reason for this of course is that so long as tests are used in college admission decisions, employment, and professional certification, people will continue to seek a competitive advantage.*" Knowing how or whether to implement policies or procedural changes to selection processes in light of the above evidence is a complex issue, in particular because it is not generally known at the time of selection who has or hasn't undertaken commercial coaching, which after all, is not an illegal activity.

A number of test providers make public comment that coaching is of no value for performance on their test [see for example, the UMAT (Australian Council for Educational Research, 2017)]. However, it seems that applicants are impervious to or actively disbelieve such statements (McGaghie et al., 2004; Moshinsky et al., 2017; Wilkinson & Wilkinson, 2013). In response, one strategy is to make training and training materials freely available to counteract any fairness issues (Arendasy et al., 2016). However, as Stemig et al. (2015) caution, this will not ensure, in and of itself, that all applicants, especially those from low SES backgrounds whose parents do not have tertiary education, will access such material. Institutions therefore need to develop processes that will promote wide access.

Another focus for dealing with the effect of coaching is to develop strategies for managing potentially biased scores. For example, McDaniel, Psotka, Legree, Yost, and Weekley (2011) offer a suggestion for eliminating certain response styles on SJT items. As described in the Case Study 9.1, one Australian university also changed the way they utilized scores of the most coachable section of the UMAT test in an effort to eliminate from the shortlisting pool those who have benefited overly from coaching.

Case Study 9.1: Minimizing the Effect of Coaching on Selection Success

Griffin and Hu (2015b) report on efforts to reduce any impact of coaching on selection decisions. This action was motivation by three research findings (described above). First, evidence that one of the three components of the UMAT test, which was used to shortlist applicants for interview, was amenable to coaching. Second, scores on this subtest had a negative correlation with GPAs obtained in medical school. Third, those who were coached at the point of selection appeared to be consistently underperforming throughout their medical degree, suggesting that they cope less well in a high-pressure training program, either for academic or psychological reasons, than students who did not attend coaching.

In the first few cohorts of this new medical school, based in an area of disadvantage, just over 50% of selected applicants had undertaken commercial coaching. The metric used for combining scores of the UMAT's three components was altered in 2014. This action resulted in a significant drop in the number of interviewees who had attended coaching to 35.5%. Furthermore, there were now no differences in either UMAT scores or MMI scores when comparing coached and uncoached applicants. This change in policy appears to have significantly reduced the likelihood of coached applicants gaining a place in medical school, making the competition more even.

Conclusion

The global rise of shadow education activities including commercial coaching has not gone unnoticed by major bodies such as the United Nations Educational, Scientific and Cultural Organization (UNESCO). A UNESCO report (Bray, 2007) suggests that private tutoring and commercial coaching have the potential to negatively impact national education systems in terms of both equity and quality. In this chapter, the existing evidence has been reviewed, which indicates that coaching may well produce small improvements in test scores (depending on the test), but whether these are large enough to make a difference to selection decisions is not yet clear. They are however, not as large as the coaching companies would assert. Nonetheless, they may contribute to the problem of widening participation of low SES applicants.

Among others, applicants to healthcare professional jobs and training programs appear willing to invest in large sums of money to gain a competitive advantage. Given the impact on them as individuals and the potential for poor selection decisions into what are safety-critical and demanding roles, it is important for researchers to continue to investigate the effects of commercial coaching programs and for practitioners who have influence on selection policy and procedure to consider this evidence.

Practice Points

1. Large numbers of applicants will undertake commercial coaching to gain a competitive advantage when large-scale testing is used to make selection decisions.
2. Coaching could potentially improve scores on some tests of cognitive ability without improving the test-taker's actual level of cognitive ability. However, this may not necessarily impact on the predictive validity on the test or an improved chance of selection.
3. Coaching potentially poses a risk to accurate selection decisions.
4. Tests should be designed to minimize coaching effects, particularly in high-stakes selection.

Explore Further

Key references to provide a background to coaching effects include:

Arendasy, M. E., Sommer, M., Gutierrez-Lobos, K., & Punter, J. F. (2016). Do individual differences in test preparation compromise the measurement fairness of admission tests? *Intelligence, 55*, 44–56.

Buchman, C., Condron, D. J., & Roscigno, V. J. (2010). Shadow education, American style: Test preparation, the SAT and college enrollment. *Social Forces, 89*(2), 435–461.

Hausknecht, J. P., Halpert, J. A., Di Paolo, N. T., & Moriarty Gerrard, M. O. (2007). Retesting in selection: A meta-analysis of coaching and practice effects for tests of cognitive ability. *Journal of Applied Psychology, 92*, 373–385.

References

Arendasy, M.E., Sommer, M., Gutierrez-Lobos, K., & Punter, J. F. (2016). Do individual differences in test preparation compromise the measurement fairness of admission tests? *Intelligence, 55,* 44–56.

Australian Council for Educational Research. (2017). https://umat.acer.edu.au/. Website Accessed 8 December.

Bardes, C. L., Best, P. C., Kremer, S. J., & Dienstag, J. L. (2009). Perspective: Medical school admissions and noncognitive testing: Some open questions. *Academic Medicine, 84*(10), 1360–1363.

Bond, L. (1989). The effects of special preparation on measures of scholastic ability. In R. Linn (Ed.), *Educational measurement* (3rd ed., pp. 429–444). Washington, DC: National Council on Education and American Council on Education.

Bray, M. (2007). *The shadow education system: Private tutoring and its implications for planners* (2nd ed.). Paris: UNESCO, International Institute for Educational Planning.

Brown, J., & Griffin, B. (2014). *Stakeholder perceptions of selection in a high-stakes context.* Poster presented at the 29th Annual conference of the society for industrial and organizational psychology, Honolulu, Hawaii.

Brown, P., Reay, D., & Vincent, C. (2013). Education and social mobility. *British Journal of Sociology of Education, 34*(5–6), 637–643.

Buchman, C., Condron, D. J., & Roscigno, V. J. (2010). Shadow education, American style: Test preparation, the SAT and college enrollment. *Social Forces, 89*(2), 435–461.

Carpenter, P. A., Just, M. A., & Shell, P. (1990). What one intelligence test measures: A theoretical account of the processing in the Raven Progressive Matrices Test. *Psychological Review, 97*(3), 404–431.

Carroll, J. B. (1993). *Human cognitive abilities: A survey of factor analytic studies.* New York: Cambridge University Press.

Chung-Herrera, B. G., Ehrhart, K. H., Ehrhart, M. G., Solamon, J., & Kilian, B. (2009). Can test preparation help to reduce the black—White test performance gap? *Journal of Management, 35*(5), 1207–1227.

Cleland, J. A., French, F. H., Johnston, P. W., & Scottish Medical Careers Cohort Study Group. (2011). A mixed-methods study identifying and exploring medical students' views of the UKCAT. *Medical Teacher, 33*(3), 244–249.

Cleland, J. A., Nicholson, S., Kelly, N., & Moffat, M. (2015). Taking context seriously: Explaining widening access policy enactments in UK medical schools. *Medical Education, 49*(1), 25–35.

Domingue, B., & Briggs, D. C. (2009). Using linear regression and propensity score matching to estimate the effect of coaching on the SAT. *Multiple Linear Regression Viewpoints, 35*(1), 12–29.

Estrada, E., Ferrer, E., Abad, F. J., Román, F. J., & Colom, R. (2015). A general factor of intelligence fails to account for changes in tests' scores after cognitive practice: A longitudinal multi-group latent-variable study. *Intelligence, 50,* 93–99.

Graham Holdings. (2016). *2016 Annual Report*. Arlington, VA: Graham Holdings.

Griffin, B. (2014). The ability to identify criteria: its relationship with social understanding, preparation, and impression management in affecting predictor performance in a high stakes selection context. *Human Performance, 27*(2), 147–164.

Griffin, B. (2016). Coaching: Much ado about nothing? Keynote address InRESH conference, Perth, Australia.

Griffin, B., Carless, S., & Wilson, I. (2013a). The effect of commercial coaching on selection test performance. *Medical Teacher, 35*(4), 295–300.

Griffin, B., Carless, S., & Wilson, I. (2013b). The undergraduate medical and health sciences admissions test: What is it measuring? *Medical Teacher, 35*(9), 727–730.

Griffin, B., Harding, D. W., Wilson, I. G., & Yeomans, N. D. (2008). Does practice make perfect? The effect of coaching and retesting on selection tests used for admission to an Australian medical school. *The Medical Journal of Australia, 189*(5), 270–273.

Griffin, B., & Hu, W. (2015a). The interaction of socio-economic status and gender in widening participation in medicine. *Medical Education, 49*(1), 103–113.

Griffin, B., & Hu, W. (2015b). Reducing the impact of coaching on selection into medicine. *Medical Journal of Australia, 203*(9), 363.

Griffin, B., & Wilson, I. G. (2012). Faking good: Self-enhancement in medical school applicants. *Medical Education, 46*(5), 485–490.

Griffin, B., Yeomans, N. D., & Wilson, I. G. (2013). Students coached for an admission test perform less well throughout a medical course. *Internal Medicine Journal, 43*(8), 927–932.

Hausknecht, J. P., Halpert, J. A., Di Paolo, N. T., & Moriarty Gerrard, M. O. (2007). Retesting in selection: A meta-analysis of coaching and practice effects for tests of cognitive ability. *Journal of Applied Psychology, 92,* 373–385.

Hayes, T. R., Petrov, A. A., & Sederberg, P. B. (2015). Do we really become smarter when our fluid-intelligence test scores improve? *Intelligence, 48*, 1–14.

Jones, R. F. (1986). The effect of commercial coaching courses on performance on the MCAT. *Academic Medicine, 61*(4), 273–284.

Kulik, J. A., Bangert-Drowns, R. L., & Kulik, C. L. C. (1984). Effectiveness of coaching for aptitude tests. *Psychological Bulletin, 95*(2), 179–188.

Lambe, P., Waters, C., & Bristow, D. (2012). The UK clinical aptitude test: Is it a fair test for selecting medical students? *Medical Teacher, 34*(8), 557–565.

Laurence, C. O., Zajac, I. T., Lorimer, M., Turnbull, D. A., & Sumner, K. E. (2013). The impact of preparatory activities on medical school selection outcomes: A cross-sectional survey of applicants to the university of Adelaide medical school in 2007. *BMC Medical Education, 13*(1), 159.

Lievens, F., Buyse, T., Sackett, P. R., & Connelly, B. S. (2012). The effects of coaching on situational judgment tests in high-stakes selection. *International Journal of Selection and Assessment, 20*(3), 272–282.

Lievens, F., Peeters, H., & Schollaert, E. (2008). Situational judgment tests: A review of recent research. *Personnel Review, 37*(4), 426–441.

Lievens, F., Reeve, C. L., & Heggestad, E. D. (2007). An examination of psychometric bias due to retesting on cognitive ability tests in selection settings. *Journal of Applied Psychology, 92*(6), 1672–1682.

Matthew, D. (2010). Evolving behaviors of MCAT examinees who apply to U.S. medical schools. *Academic Medicine, 85*(6), 1100.

Maurer, T., Solamon, J., & Troxtel, D. (1998). Relationship of coaching with performance in situational employment interviews. *Journal of Applied Psychology, 83*(1), 128–136.

Maurer, T. J., Solamon, J. M., Andrews, K. D., & Troxtel, D. D. (2001). Interviewee coaching, preparation strategies, and response strategies in relation to performance in situational employment interviews: An extension of Maurer, Solamon, and Troxtel (1998). *Journal of Applied Psychology, 86*(4), 709–711.

McDaniel, M. A., Psotka, J., Legree, P. J., Yost, A. P., & Weekley, J. A. (2011). Toward an understanding of situational judgment item validity and group differences. *Journal of Applied Psychology, 96*(2), 327–336.

McGaghie, W. C., Downing, S. M., & Kubilius, R. (2004). What is the impact of commercial test preparation courses on medical examination performance? *Teaching and Learning in Medicine, 16*(2), 202–211.

MedEntry UMAT Products. (2017). https://www.medentry.edu.au/courses/umat-courses. Accessed July 5.

Miller, C. E., & Barrett, G. V. (2008). The coachability and fakability of personality-based selection tests used for police selection. *Public Personnel Management, 37*(3), 339–351.

Millman, J., Bishop, C. H., & Ebel, B. (1965). An analysis of test-wiseness. *Educational and Psychological Measurement, 18,* 787–790.

Moshinsky, A., Ziegler, D., & Gafni, N. (2017). Multiple mini-interviews in the age of the internet: Does preparation help applicants to medical school. *International Journal of Testing*. https://doi.org/10.1080/15305058.2016.1263638.

Patterson, F., Ashworth, V., Kerrin, M., & O'Neill, P. (2013). Situational judgement tests represent a measurement method and can be designed to minimize coaching effects. *Medical Education, 47*(2), 220–221.

Powers, D. E. (1993). Coaching for the SAT: A summary of the summaries and an update. *Educational Measurement: Issues and Practice, 12,* 24–30.

Raven, J., Raven, J. C., & Court, J. H. (1998). *Manual for Raven's progressive matrices and vocabulary scales*. Oxford: Information Press.

Ryan, A., Ployhart, R. E., Greguras, G. J., & Schmit, M. J. (1998). Test preparation programs in selection contexts: Self-selection and program effectiveness. *Personnel Psychology, 51*(3), 599–621.

Ryan, A. M., & Ployhart, R. E. (2000). Applicants' perceptions of selection procedures and decisions: A critical review and agenda for the future. *Journal of Management, 26*(3), 565–606.

Simons, D. J., Boot, W. R., Charness, N., Gathercole, S. E., Chabris, C. F., Hambrick, D. Z., & Stine-Morrow, E. A. (2016). Do "brain-training" programs work? *Psychological Science in the Public Interest, 17*(3), 103–186.

Stemig, M. S., Sackett, P. R., & Lievens, F. (2015). Effects of organizationally endorsed coaching on performance and validity of situational judgment tests. *International Journal of Selection and Assessment, 23*(2), 174–181.

te Nijenhuis, J., van Vianen, A. E., & van der Flier, H. (2007). Score gains on g-loaded tests: No g. *Intelligence, 35*(3), 283–300.

te Nijenhuis, J., Voskuijl, O. F., & Schijve, N. B. (2001). Practice and coaching on IQ tests: Quite a lot of g. *International Journal of Selection and Assessment, 9*(4), 302–308.

To, K. (2013). *Multiple Mini Interview (MMI) for the mind*. Advisor Prep Education: United States.

Tompkins, J. (2011). Money for nothing? The problem of the board-exam coaching industry. *The New England Journal of Medicine, 365*(2), 104–105.
Truxillo, D. M., Bauer, T. N., & McCarthy, J. M. (2015). Applicant fairness reactions to the selection process. In R. Cropanzano & M. Ambrose (Eds.), *The Oxford handbook of justice in work organizations* (pp. 621–640). Oxford: Oxford University Press.
Verguts, T., & de Boeck, P. (2002). The induction of solution rules in Raven's Progressive Matrices Test. *European Journal of Cognitive Psychology, 14*(4), 521–547.
Wilkinson, T. M., & Wilkinson, T. J. (2013). Preparation courses for a medical admissions test: Effectiveness contrasts with opinion. *Medical Education, 47,* 417–424.
Wong, C. X. J., & Roberts-Thomson, R. L. (2009). Does practice make perfect? The effect of coaching and retesting on selection tests used for admission to an Australian medical school [letter]. *Medical Journal of Australia, 190*(2), 101–102.

10

Widening Access: Achieving Equity in Medical Education

Jennifer Cleland, Kirsty Alexander and Sandra Nicholson

Introduction

Globally, medicine and other elite subjects and institutions struggle to get in people from lower socio-economic groups. The opposite is true for other healthcare professions. Across the world, young people with the academic and personal attributes to successfully study medicine and become doctors face disadvantages associated with demographic factors

J. Cleland (✉) · K. Alexander
Centre for Healthcare Education Research and Innovation (CHERI),
School of Medicine, Dentistry and Nutrition,
University of Aberdeen, Aberdeen, Scotland, UK
e-mail: jen.cleland@abdn.ac.uk

K. Alexander
e-mail: kirsty.alexander@abdn.ac.uk

S. Nicholson
Centre for Medical Education, Barts and The London School of Medicine,
Queen Mary University of London, London, UK
e-mail: s.nicholson@qmul.ac.uk

F. Patterson and L. Zibarras (eds.), *Selection and Recruitment in the Healthcare Professions*, https://doi.org/10.1007/978-3-319-94971-0_10

Table 10.1 Widening participation (WP) versus widening access (WA)

Widening participation (WP) refers to the policy that people such as those coming from disadvantaged backgrounds, mature students, students from ethnic and cultural groups and disabled students should be encouraged to take part, and be represented proportionately, within higher education (HE)
Widening access (WA) refers to the policy that people from groups which are under-represented in Higher Education, should be encouraged and supported in applying for higher education. This may refer to specific selection policies that increase the matriculation of certain unrepresented groups

such as ethnicity, minority group membership and/or low income. It is important to understand, and address, the educational disadvantages and the inequalities experienced by certain medical school applicants in order to bring about change in terms of increasing medical student diversity globally. In this topic, the terms widening participation and widening access are often used interchangeably. We present some definitions first in Table 10.1, to aid clarity.

The focus of this chapter is WA. The movement to "widen access" (WA) to those who have not traditionally participated in Higher Education is a global issue but the focus of WA is driven by each country's historical and current social issues. For example, USA WA initiatives may particularly aim to attract students from under-represented minority (URM) ethnicity and racial groups (Castillo-Page, 2012; Lakhan, 2003), whilst in Canada and Australia medical schools also aim to recruit those from rural or Indigenous communities (Behrendt, Larkin, Griew, & Kelly, 2012; Dhalla et al., 2002; Hay et al., 2017; Puddey, Mercer, Playford, Pougnault, & Riley, 2014). In the UK, the focus for WA is widening the profession's socio-economic diversity. Statistics have constantly shown that around 9% of the medical student population comes from the lowest socio-economic groups, compared to around 26% of the general population (Cleland, Dowell, McLachlan, Nicholson, & Patterson, 2012; Steven, Dowell, Jackson, & Guthrie, 2016).

Given this, we first explore the myriad of social, individual and structural reasons why the resources invested in WA activities have not significantly increased the representation of applicants from lower socio-economic groups within UK medical schools. Second, and shifting focus more to admissions processes, we examine the synergies and tensions between WA and maintaining quality, the gap between political directives and policy enactment within high schools and medical schools, how selection methods and the proposed use of "contextual admissions" fit with common discourses of WA in our context.

Finally, as a case study example, we explore the experiences of those from WA backgrounds who entered medicine to explore their experiences of the application process and medical school. We review the key evidence for variation in performance across different groups of students and will look at how enculturation into medicine may serve to maintain the status quo.

We conclude by summarizing the current state of play in terms of the issues facing integration and the promotion of social diversity in medicine, then commenting on areas for future research, policy and practice internationally.

The Complexity of Addressing Widening Access to Medicine

For WA to be successful, it is first important to understand how multiple factors may contribute to an applicant's disadvantage.

Disadvantage is initially evident when examining the inequalities between applicants' pre-university educational experiences (Chowdry, Crawford, Dearden, Goodman, & Vignoles, 2013; Nicholson & Cleland, 2015). Worldwide, high academic achievement is a key requirement of all competitive medical courses, yet worldwide, students in higher socio-economic groups significantly outperform students in lower groups in school exit examinations (Bowes, Thomas, Peck, & Nathwani, 2013; Chowdry et al., 2013; Gorard et al., 2006). As a result, a selection process centered strongly around academic attainment is likely to be biased in favor of those in higher socio-economic classes, who generally have access to higher achieving and better resourced schools (Cleland et al., 2012; Southgate, Kelly, & Symonds, 2015). Moreover, students who are able and motivated to apply for medicine may lack important knowledge about the admissions procedures or requirements because of the level of preparation and support offered by their school (Kamali, Nicholson, & Wood, 2005; Nicholson & Cleland, 2017; Robb, Dunkley, Boynton, & Greenhalgh, 2007).

Research consistently shows that a (high) school's culture regarding academic attainment, work ethic and aspiration to certain careers also plays a major role in students' choices (Archer & Leathwood, 2003; DFES, 2003; Gorard et al., 2006; Reay, Davies, David, & Ball, 2001; Slack, 2003). Students may be discouraged from considering or applying to medicine by factors such as school culture and teachers' expectations (McHarg, Mattick, & Knight, 2007; Medical Schools Council, 2014a; Robb et al., 2007; Southgate et al., 2015).

These inequalities are obvious when looking at schools' application rates to highly selective universities and to competitive subjects such as medicine (Hemsley-Brown, 2015; Medical Schools Council, 2014b). Applications to medicine are highly differentiated by school: 80% of UK applicants come from only 20% of UK schools, and half the schools in the UK have sent no applicants to medicine in recent years (Medical Schools Council, 2014b). However, schools are just one piece of the jigsaw: larger societal influences, peer and familial expectations, as well as a student's beliefs about their ability, also strongly influence students' educational and career choices (Bridges, 2006; DCSF, 2008; Hill et al., 2004; Miller & Cummings, 2009; Robb et al., 2007). Financial concerns about the cost of tuition fees and living costs whilst a student may also deter capable applicants, and particularly those from poorer backgrounds who may be more likely to be worried by debt (Callender & Jackson, 2008; Minty, 2015).

Overall, the choice to attend university generally, and medicine particularly, may be seen as presenting more risk for a student from a non-traditional background (Archer & Hutchings, 2000; Archer & Leathwood, 2003). Sadly, this perception of risk, or negativity, about medicine as a career choice may be justified as studies suggest medical school is not always welcoming to diverse students (Beagan, 2005; Greenhalgh, Seyan, & Boynton, 2004; Orom, Semalulu, & Underwood, 2013), nor do systems provide them with enough support to concentrate on their studies (BMA Medical Student Committee, 2015). As a result, there are still potential applicants who feel that medicine is not "for the likes of them" (Greenhalgh et al., 2004; Mathers & Parry, 2009).

These issues are typically addressed at two levels: national and local. At the national level, many countries have put in place change initiatives to safeguard and monitor fair access to HE generally (OFFA, 2008); affirmative action legislation (Rosenbaum, Teitelbaum, & Scott, 2013) or the use of compensatory approaches at the point of application to medicine (Gale & Parker, 2013). At a local level, medical schools interpret such policy and political drivers to decide how they will support WA. This may be by amending their systems or structures, for example, by offering extended medical programs for students from certain backgrounds (Garlick & Brown, 2008) or accrediting specific Foundation to Medicine programs (Mathers, Sitch, Marsh, & Parry, 2011). There is some evidence of effectiveness from this type of intervention (Kumwenda, Cleland, Greatrix, MacKenzie, & Prescott, 2017; Mathers et al., 2011). Most medical schools also offer in-reach (e.g., information, advice and guidance (IAG), open days) and/or out-reach activities (e.g., visiting schools).

Unfortunately, while there is a lot of activity in terms of pre-entry activities, there is little evidence of their effectiveness, at least in part because of weak (observational) research designs (Nicholson & Cleland, 2015). For example, very few places collected "hard" outcomes data (e.g., number of participants who then applied to medical school and/or received an offer), instead focusing on assessing student satisfaction or motivation to apply for medicine. There is a pressing need to identify consistencies, variability and generalizability across studies of local WA interventions to gain cumulative knowledge and gather evidence of effectiveness (Eva, 2009).

Widening Access at the Point of Selection

Here, we consider how current selection systems may support WA, or not. Whilst there are differences between countries in terms of which selection tools are favored, there is now clearer consensus on the relative accuracy and validity of different selection methods, and increasing commonality in the aims and processes of selection into medicine (Cleland et al., 2012; Patterson et al., 2016).

Selection Methods

In recent years, UK medical schools have made changes to their admissions procedures with the stated goals of reducing bias and increasing fairness in selection (Medical Schools Council, 2014b; Schwartz, 2004). The most obvious change has been a move away from an over-reliance on prior academic achievement as the primary, or only, selection method and towards using a variety of tools to judge potential and ability to become a practicing clinician (see MacKenzie, Cleland, Ayansina, & Nicholson (2016) for a good overview of medical selection processes, and (Patterson et al., 2016) for a review of the effectiveness of various methods). Attaining the required grades remains the first hurdle in medical admissions, and failure to do so is the most common cause of rejection. Yet—as discussed earlier—the link between potential and prior achievement requires more than just looking at academic attainment given the association between systemic and social factors, and academic attainment (Williamson, 2004).

In part to address this dilemma, aptitude tests were introduced into UK medical selection in the mid-2000s, with the UKCAT (UK Clinical Aptitude Test: introduced in 2006) being the most commonly used aptitude test currently (UKCAT, 2017). Aptitude tests are now used globally for selection to medicine—for example in: Ireland (HPAT, 2017); Australia (UMAT, 2017); Canada and the USA (AAMC, 2017). Aptitude tests were thought to be a useful tool to assist WA to medicine, as outcomes were thought to be influenced less by the socio-economic and educational background of applicants and tests could not be "coached" for to the same extent as traditional school exams (Cleland et al., 2012).

However, although initial, smaller scale studies indicated this might be the case, emerging research is conflicting. For example, Tiffin et al. found that certain ways of using the UKCAT were associated with a higher proportion of students from under-represented groups being admitted to UK medical schools (Tiffin, Dowell, & McLachlan, 2012; Tiffin, McLachlan, Webster, & Nicholson, 2014). Conversely, Mathers and colleagues failed to identify any consistent effect of different usages of the UKCAT on equity in selection processes (Mathers, Sitch, & Parry, 2016). In another context (Denmark) O'Neill, Vonsild, Wallstedt, and Dornan (2013) showed that selection strategy (grade-based or attribute-based) had no effect on the social diversity of their medical student population.

Why is this the case? The majority of UK medical schools use a selection sequence of prior academic attainment, aptitude test then local assessment (e.g., interview, MMI). How aptitude tests and other selection tools are used varies widely. Typically, however, prior academic attainment is the first hurdle and/or the most heavily weighted component in medical selection. This may limit the impact of any of the subsequent tools used in selection as most applicants are rejected on the basis of prior academic attainment.

Moreover, selection research has typically focused on the qualities of one particular tool or method in its own right, rather than whether or not various tools can be combined effectively. Where studies have looked at combining tools, the focus has typically been on examining the psychometric properties of doing so (i.e., incremental validity; e.g., McManus, Dewberry, Nicholson, & Dowell, 2013; Patterson et al., 2016; Tiffin et al., 2014). The few studies which have considered the impact of combining tools suggest that different weighting (e.g., 50% for prior academic attainment, 30% aptitude test, and 20% local assessment) may lead to different outcomes in terms of who is selected (e.g., Fernando, Cleland, Greaves, & McKenzie, 2009; Tiffin et al., 2012). Certain combinations of selection tools put some groups at less of a disadvantage (e.g., lower socio-economic groups), but biases remain towards other groups (e.g., certain ethnic groups) (e.g., Lievens, Patterson, Corstjens, Martin, & Nicholson, 2016; Wright & Bradley, 2010).

Whether or not there is a way to combine the "best" medical school selection methods to give both selection validity (i.e., identifying those who will not only excel academically but also possess personal attributes befitting a career in medicine) and achieving desired diversity outcomes remains to be seen (e.g., De Corte, Lievens, & Sackett, 2006, 2007). Evidence-based guidance on how to design robust and fair selection processes which impact positively on WA is urgently required.

Contextual Admissions (CA)

One way of addressing the inherent bias of using prior academic attainment as the first hurdle in medical selection (see earlier) is the use of contextual admissions, or CA (Medical Schools Council, 2014b; Panel on Fair Access to the Professions, 2009). Using CA has been proposed as a means to acknowledge that the link between potential and prior academic achievement requires more than just looking at A Levels/Highers given the association between systemic and social factors, and attainment (Williamson, 2004).

Various different types of CA have been proposed for use by UK universities. These include individual-focused markers (e.g., first in family to attend university), school-focused markers (e.g., attending a school which sends a lower than average proportion of pupils to HE), area-focused (e.g., living in a socio-economically deprived area/postcode zone) and out-reach focused markers (e.g., having attended a WA pre-entry program: see Boliver, Gorard, & Siddiqui, 2015; Moore et al., 2013 for further detail). But evidence is lacking as to which of these CA markers are "best" (i.e., objective, valid, reliable). Nor is it known how CA markers can be used fairly, transparently, and in an evidence-based way within the selection process (e.g., Chetwynd, 2014; Skyrme, 2014). The latter is not straightforward, particularly in the variably-weighted multi-step process of application and selection into medical school (Bridger, Shaw, & Moore, 2012; Cleland et al., 2012).

The uncertainties and preferences alluded to above have led to a situation where universities may be supportive (or not, see below), in principle, of WA via the use of CA, but how it is used varies significantly by institution (Thomas et al., 2009). This state of affairs is not helped by a lack of research on this topic: our recent review of the CA literature identified a few studies which focused on the use of CA in higher education (including medicine) generally, but none which looked directly at the use of CA markers in admissions (Cleland, Nicholson, Patterson, & Cousans, under revision).

Case Study 10.1: How Do Medical Schools Use Contextual Admissions?

Given the above questions, we were recently commissioned to explore how medical schools access, verify and use different CA measures. As part of this program of work, we carried out individual interviews with UK medical Admissions Deans from approximately two-thirds of all UK medical schools, to elicit their views, experiences, and concerns relating to the use of CA in medical admissions. We found that most of the medical schools interviewed used CA but they had concerns over reliability of markers and which markers to use.

> *"So, the issue that we had was in terms of the [geodemographic] data, looking at the locality; because you could technically have a student who is from a wealthier background who lives in that area"* . (Interview 19)

There was also a more practical, internal tension related to resource as checking data is time-consuming and difficult.

> *"...we won't actually count them as [having been in] care until they've completed an additional form and we've managed to verify that with their assigned social worker"* . (Interview 8)

The (unacknowledged) potential value of applicants selected via CA is overshadowed by a focus on the worry of opening doors to students who have achieved slightly less well in terms of prior attainment, an anecdotally perceived "lowering of standards", and the potential negative impact this may have on school performance in University league tables (Cleland, Nicholson, Kelly, & Moffat, 2015). There is a tension between the political drivers to WA and the (equally politically driven) competitive nature of neoliberal university education in the UK. This puts increasing pressure on universities and medical schools to promote a reputation of excellence, high quality experience and standards (see for example, Fairclough, 1993; Molesworth, Scullion, & Nixon, 2011). Yet, concurrently UK devolved governments are also putting increasing pressure on universities to widen access (DBIS, 2016; Scottish Government, 2016). WA, with its aims of broader inclusivity and participation, can thus be seen at odds with the market pressure to convey more mainstream forms of excellence and of exclusivity and selectiveness in admissions. The implication is that medical schools "can't win", in a system that does not sufficiently compensate for, or reward, WA efforts which may pose both cost and risk to the institution (Cleland et al., 2015).

In conclusion, while in theory at least, the use of CA heralds a significant step toward seeking to select on ability rather than purely attainment and has considerable potential to reduce bias towards those in lower socio-economic groups. However, in practice "ability" is much harder to identify than "attainment" is to assess (Boliver et al., 2015; Cleland, Patterson, Dowell, & Nicholson, 2014; Nicholson & Cleland, 2015) and numerous questions about the reliability of the markers and the use of CA remain unanswered.

"Getting On" in Medicine as a Non-traditional Student

This chapter has so far highlighted the issues applicants from disadvantaged backgrounds face, and how WA policies and activities seek to raise aspirations, and present increased opportunities for these students to consider, and then apply for entry to medical degree programs. A small proportion of applicants from less advantaged backgrounds do manage to successfully negotiate the complex processes of application and selection into medicine. We are also interested in their experiences, and to explore these usefully requires considering the philosophies of education and how selection intersects with other educational structures.

Philosophies of Education

In the UK, there are two main arguments to justify WA to medicine. The first is to increase social mobility; the second is to improve healthcare provision by recruiting a diversity of staff to deliver care. These drivers mirror those in many other countries which also face similar challenges regarding a lack of diversity in the medical profession. In relation to the first, the UK has long-standing and increasing levels of inequality in income (Eurofound, 2015), health (RCPCH, 2017), and education (Jerrim & Shure, 2016), coupled with limited social mobility so disadvantage is perpetuated from generation to generation (Nicholson & Cleland, 2015). The concept of social mobility is closely tied to ideas of meritocracy, where people achieve or are selected on the basis of their merits or abilities rather than because of their money or social position (Jost, Pelham, Sheldon, & Ni-Sullivan, 2003; Young, 1961).

Meritocratic systems are strongly cherished for their perceived fairness, productivity and for opportunities they offer individuals within all social strata. However, although the meritocratic approach is the preferred philosophy of education in the UK (Sheeran, Brown, & Baker, 2007), there are limits to its effectiveness. As discussed earlier, the level of educational, social, cultural and financial resources and opportunities an applicant possesses, or is able to access, before they apply to medicine may set them at a considerable disadvantage in a competitive application system. This is evidenced by the fact that the proportion of medical students from lower socio-economic groups has remained static over many years (Milburn, 2012). In other words, the meritocratic approach is not working.

The second reason to "widen access" to the medical profession addresses the need to build a healthcare workforce that reflects and understands the needs of patients from diverse cultures and in diverse locations. There is increasing recognition that a more diverse student cohort may benefit the medical school learning environment. Amongst other strengths, diverse students are understood to contribute a better understanding of diverse populations (Guiton, Chang, & Wilkerson, 2007; Morrison & Grbic, 2015; Saha, Guiton, Wimmers, & Wilkerson, 2008; Whitla et al., 2003), multilingualism (Flores, 2000), as well as resilience and persistence with overcoming barriers (Cleland & Medhi, 2015; Jardine, 2012). Diversity in the workplace may not only improve the competence of staff, but also provide the workforce with more practitioners who choose to work in underprivileged communities, locations and specialties (Bailey & Willies-Jacobo, 2012; Cooter et al., 2004; Dowell, Norbury, Steven, & Guthrie, 2015; Komaromy et al., 1996; Puddey et al., 2014; Walker, Moreno, & Grumbach, 2012).

Exactly how the social justice and workforce management motivations for WA are currently combined within the context of UK medical schools is unclear. Cleland et al. (2015) study of UK medical school Admissions Deans found various, and often conflicting, interpretations and translations of WA policy. Many schools found reconciling the political goals of WA with their own aims, interests and resources problematic, especially with regard to a firmly held belief in "selecting for excellence" through academic meritocracy. Interestingly, when we looked at the Admissions Deans' use of language (Fahey Palma & Cleland, 2017), we found this served to reinforce pre-existing stereotypes and a significant "us" and "them" rhetoric existed. WA students were represented as having specific traits and characteristics that at times served to position them in position of academic and social inferiority. There was no indication in the data set that having a diverse student body may bring value to the medical school and ultimately patient care. A discourse analysis of UK medical school WA webpages identified similar tensions (Alexander, Fahey Palma, Nicholson, & Cleland, 2017).

Little is known about the influence that these differing values and attitudes to WA may have on aiding WA or reproducing processes of exclusion in the UK (see Razack and colleagues' work for how this plays out in another context, that of Canada Razack, Hodges, Steinert, & Maguire, 2015). However, the data does suggest an inherent desire to maintain the existing social hierarchy (Jost & Hunyady, 2005) and this has implications not just for applicants but also for those under-represented students who do negotiate the complex territory of medical admissions successfully. Under the meritocratic model, there is the assumption that once these students have access to the facilities and teaching (in this case, at medical school), previous disadvantage evaporates and the desired "level playing field" is created (Sheeran et al., 2007). Is this the case?

The Experience and Outcomes of Non-traditional Students

Although there is a paucity of good quality research examining the experience and outcomes of non-traditional students once enrolled onto medical degrees, what is emerging is of interest. Recent large-scale (national) quantitative studies demonstrate that although students from independent and state schools enter with similar pre-entry grades, once in medical school, students from state-funded schools are likely to outperform students from independent schools (Kumwenda, Cleland, Walker, Lee, & Greatrix, 2017). This reflects a pattern seen in the wider HE literature (HEFCE, 2014). Moreover, Kumwenda and colleagues found other indicators of socio-economic class (such as coming from neighborhoods of low participation in higher education, and individual markers such as being first in family to university) were not significant independent predictors of performance at medical school. While this is encouraging, and tentatively suggests that less advantaged students gain more from medical school, other studies suggest that disadvantage may continue. For example, MacKenzie et al. (2016) found that medical students from higher socio-economic backgrounds performed better on the selection process for the next stage of medical training in the UK, the Foundation Programme, than those from lower social groups (see also Stegers-Jager, Steyerberg, Lucieer, & Themmen, 2015).

The possible, subtle nature of this disadvantage is illustrated in qualitative studies. For example, our own research indicates medical students from lower socio-economic backgrounds may fail to recognize the need for, "upwards" networking and expanding their social circles during medical school (Nicholson & Cleland, 2017). This reflected sharply with their more advantaged peers, who appear to instinctively understand and value the benefits of increasing their social capital [or social networks; (Bourdieu, 1986)]. This can be understood from the following quotation excerpt from an UK clinical medical student from higher socio-economic group commenting on his observations of his peers from lower socio-economic groups (Nicholson & Cleland, 2017):

Interviewer : On day to day interaction with staff on the wards, do you think generally speaking things are equal?

Participant : No, it's not equal. I think probably interaction is better with people like traditional *medical students and not as good for the non-traditional medical students*

Interviewer : But why?
Participant : I always go back to the way people speak but it's important because that's the first thing, that's one of the first things you notice about people the way they speak, so, I think the way people speak and the kind of discussions they have with people, and obviously the doctors, they're more likely to be from a traditional background as well (Nicholson and Cleland, 2017, p. 484).

It appears then that disadvantage in accessing resources is primarily through a lack of contacts resulting from varying social capital, but this is compounded by financial constraints, and persists for some students from under-represented groups. For some students, socializing and networking opportunities have to take a lower priority than paid work, family time and religious practices (Stuart, Lido, Morgan, Solomon, & May, 2011). Brosnan et al. (2016) found similar issues with students from one Australian medical school who were first in their family to attend university, additionally noting that the value of an individual student's diversity and what this may bring to medicine was unacknowledged.

How Selection Intersects with other Educational Structures

Increasing the diversity of medical students brings with it concerns about whether entrants to medicine are appropriately equipped for the rigor of academic work. On the other hand, questions can be asked about the readiness of contemporary curricula to create learning environments in which patients' needs come first and all students have the potential to thrive. This raises questions about institutional systems and assumptions, and staff beliefs, about student support. For example, is perceived underperformance of students from lower socio-economic groups within a meritocratic system an artefact which assumes that only certain types of knowledge are legitimate? Such a stance leads to widely accepted medical models of WA provision that "pathologize" medical students from disadvantaged backgrounds rather than valuing their difference and dismisses the benefits that a diverse student body may actually bring to the medical school and ultimately patient care (Deas et al., 2012; Fuller, Heath, & Johnston, 2011).

Furthermore, medical education research has neglected exploring the sociocultural aspects of learning that seem critically relevant to medical student retention, engaging effectively with learning clinical medicine and their own professional development (Nicholson, 2013). This involves gaining a better understanding of what facilitates the participation of medical students in clinical settings, and hence what may be more challenging for non-traditional students, including developing their own professional identities.

Ways Forward for Research, Policy and Practice

Throughout this chapter we have highlighted areas for future research to explore how the sequence of selection, and by which means, best benefits WA across contexts. We expand on these ideas below and position them globally.

There is an urgent need to:

- Use "routine data" to track the progression of students admitted on the basis of CA, to compare their achievements with those of students who attained traditional entry criteria.
- Given the relatively small numbers of students are who likely to enter using CA, we urge regulators and national bodies to encourage medical schools to work together to record data consistently, and to share data via large data sets. To do so will enable robust, quantitative studies comparing performance across groups (CA entrants and traditionally qualified entrants) to address concerns about CA relating to underperformance.
- In terms of policy, it is critical for each country to establish an agreed definition of WA, support its aims and minimize other conflicting

political drivers. This may mean rewarding medical schools for widening access via league table markers (rather than the current international system which is heavily weighted in favor of high entry qualifications).

- Also, in terms of policy, if governments seriously wish to increase the numbers of students from under-represented groups then sufficient resource is required to appropriately support these students once enrolled.

Conclusion

In summary, WA is a deeply contested area in educational policy and politics. Medical schools and universities are not always clear as to what WA should be "for", how it should be "done" and what the measures of "success" should be. Meritocratic selection on the basis of academic capability remains a cherished cornerstone of medical schools' selection procedures. Such initiatives have failed, however, to significantly change the socio-economic profile of UK medical students. Yet at the time of writing this chapter, UK medical schools, for example, are under increasing pressure to meet new, ambitious governmental targets requiring increased admission to under-represented groups. They need guidance in how best to do this. A first step in achieving this is to seek consensus across all key stakeholders, including but not limited to medical schools, as to what is the desired overall endpoint for WA. Students are stakeholders in any change, so parents and applicants also need to "buy-in" to any repositioning of medical education. There is also a need for change at policy level. Medical schools currently operate in a context where league tables reward schools that admit and graduate the highest academically achieving students. This means the goal of academic excellence will be prioritized. If, however, funding and prestige is available for courses that prioritize selecting and training medical students from under-represented backgrounds, widening access may become more attractive.

References

AAMC. (2017). Taking the MCAT® exam. Retrieved July 26, 2017 from https://students-residents.aamc.org/applying-medical-school/taking-mcat-exam/. Accessed July 4, 2017.

Alexander, K., Fahey Palma, T., Nicholson, S., & Cleland, J. (2017). "Why not you?" Discourses of widening access on UK medical school websites. *Medical Education, 51*(6), 598–611. https://doi.org/10.1111/medu.13264.

Archer, L., & Hutchings, M. (2000). "Bettering yourself"? Discourses of risk, cost and benefit in ethnically diverse, young working-class non-participants' constructions of higher education. *British Journal of Sociology of Education, 21*(4), 555–574. https://doi.org/10.1080/713655373.

Archer, L., & Leathwood, C. (2003). Identities, inequalities and higher education. In L. Archer, M. Hutchings, & A. Ross (Eds.), *Higher education and social class: Issues of exclusion and inclusions* (pp. 175–191). London: Routledge Falmer.

Bailey, J. A., & Willies-Jacobo, L. J. (2012). Are disadvantaged and underrepresented minority applicants more likely to apply to the program in medical education-health equity? *Academic Medicine, 87*(11), 1535–1539. https://doi.org/10.1097/ACM.0b013e31826d6220.

Beagan, B. L. (2005). Everyday classism in medical school: Experiencing marginality and resistance. *Medical Education, 39*(8), 777–784. https://doi.org/10.1111/j.1365-2929.2005.02225.x.

Behrendt, L., Larkin, S., Griew, R., & Kelly, P. (2012). *Review of higher education access and outcomes for aboriginal and Torres Strait Islander people.* https://docs.education.gov.au/system/files/doc/other/heaccessandoutcomesforaboriginalandtorresstraitislanderfinalreport.pdf. Accessed March 5, 2015.

BMA Medical Student Committee. (2015). *Medical student finances and the effect on wider participation.* https://www.bma.org.uk/connecting-doctors/community_focus/m/mediagallery/185. Accessed July 5, 2017.

Boliver, V., Gorard, S., & Siddiqui, N. (2015). Will the use of contextual indicators make UK higher education admissions fairer? *Education Sciences, 5*(4), 306–322. https://doi.org/10.3390/educsci5040306.

Bourdieu, P. (1986). The forms of capital. In J. Richardson (Ed.), *Handbook of theory and research for the sociology of education* (pp. 241–258). New York, NY: Greenwood Press.

Bowes, L., Thomas, L., Peck, L., & Nathwani, T. (2013). *International research on the effectiveness of widening participation.* Retrieved July 7, 2016, from http://www.hefce.ac.uk/pubs/rereports/year/2013/wpeffectiveness/.

Bridges, D. (2006). Ethics and education adaptive preference, justice and identity in the context of widening participation in higher education Adaptive preference, justice and identity in the context of widening participation in higher education. *Ethics and Education, 1*(1), 15–28. https://doi.org/10.1080/17449640600584946.

Brosnan, C., Southgate, E., Outram, S., Lempp, H., Wright, S., Saxby, T., & Kelly, B. (2016). Experiences of medical students who are first in family to attend university. *Medical Education, 50*(8). http://doi.org/10.1111/medu.12995.

Callender, C., & Jackson, J. (2008). Does the fear of debt constrain choice of university and subject of study? *Studies in Higher Education*, 33(4), 405–429. http://doi.org/10.1080/03075070802211802.

Castillo-Page, L. (2012). *Diversity in medical education: Facts and figures.* Washington, DC. https://members.aamc.org/eweb/upload/DiversityinMedicalEducation_FactsandFigures2012.pdf. Accessed August 8, 2015.

Chetwynd, P. (2014). *SPA good practice statement admissions policies.* www.spa.ac.uk. Accessed September 4, 2017.

Chowdry, H., Crawford, C., Dearden, L., Goodman, A., & Vignoles, A. (2013). Widening participation in higher education: Analysis using linked administrative data. *Journal of the Royal Statistical Society: Series A (Statistics in Society), 176*(2), 431–457. http://doi.org/10.1111/j.1467-985X.2012.01043.x.

Cleland, J., Dowell, J., McLachlan, J., Nicholson, S., & Patterson, F. (2012). *Identifying best practice in the selection of medical students: Literature review and interview survey.* London: Medical Schools Council.

Cleland, J., & Medhi, M. (2015). *Optimism and grit: Key to success in the widening access student's journey into medical school.* In Association for Medical Education Europe (AMEE). Research Paper presented at the Association for Medical Education Europe (AMEE) Annual Conference, September 5–9. Glasgow, UK.

Cleland, J., Nicholson, S., Kelly, N., & Moffat, M. (2015). Taking context seriously: Explaining widening access policy enactments in UK medical schools. *Medical Education, 49*(1), 25–35. https://doi.org/10.1111/medu.12502.

Cleland, J., Nicholson, S., Patterson, F., & Cousans, F. The use of contextual data in medical school selection processes: A narrative synthesis. Under revision for *BMJ Open.*

Cleland, J., Patterson, F., Dowell, J., & Nicholson, S. (2014). *How can greater consistency in selection between medical schools be encouraged? A mixed-methods programme of research that examines and develops the evidence base.* London: Medical Schools Council.

Cooter, R., Erdmann, J. B., Gonnella, J. S., Callahan, C. A., Hojat, M., & Xu, G. (2004). Economic diversity in medical education: The relationship between students' family income and academic performance, career choice, and student debt. *Evaluation and the Health Professions, 27*(3), 252–264. https://doi.org/10.1177/0163278704267041.

DBIS. (2016). *Success as a knowledge economy: Teaching excellence, social mobility & student choice.* London. https://www.gov.uk/government/uploads/system/uploads/attachment_data/file/523546/bis-16-265-success-as-a-knowledge-economy-web.pdf. Accessed May 1, 2017.

DCSF. (2008). *The impact of parental involvement on children's education.* Nottingham. https://www.ucy.ac.cy/nursery/documents/ThemaVdomadas/DCSF-Parental_Involvement_1.pdf. Accessed July 17, 2017.

Deas, D., Pisano, E., Mainous, A., Johnson, N., Singleton, M., & Gordon, L. (2012). Improving diversity through strategic planning: A 10-year (2002–2012) experience at the medical University of South Carolina. *Academic Medicine, 87*(11), 1548–1555.

De Corte, W., Lievens, F., & Sackett, P. R. (2006). Predicting adverse impact and mean criterion performance in multistage selection. *Journal of Applied Psychology, 91*(3), 523–537. https://doi.org/10.1037/0021-9010.91.3.523.

De Corte, W., Lievens, F., & Sackett, P. R. (2007). Combining predictors to achieve optimal trade-offs between selection quality and adverse impact. *Journal of Applied Psychology, 92*(5), 1380–1393. https://doi.org/10.1037/0021-9010.92.5.1380.

DFES. (2003). *The future of higher education.* London. http://webarchive.nationalarchives.gov.uk/20040117001247/dfes.gov.uk/highereducation/hestrategy/. Accessed July 17, 2017.

Dhalla, I. A., Kwong, J. C., Streiner, D. L., Baddour, R. E., Waddell, A. E., & Johnson, I. L. (2002). Characteristics of first-year students in Canadian medical schools. *Canadian Medical Association Journal, 166*(8), 1029–1035.

Dowell, J., Norbury, M., Steven, K., & Guthrie, B. (2015). Widening access to medicine may improve general practitioner recruitment in deprived and rural communities: Survey of GP origins and current place of work. *BMC Medical Education, 15*(1), 1–7. https://doi.org/10.1186/s12909-015-0445-8.

Eurofound. (2015). *Recent developments in the distribution of wages in Europe.* https://www.eurofound.europa.eu/sites/default/files/ef_publication/field_ef_document/ef1510en1.pdf. Accessed July 5, 2017.

Eva, K. W. (2009). Broadening the debate about quality in medical education research. *Medical Education, 43*(4), 294–296. https://doi.org/10.1111/j.1365-2923.2009.03342.x.

Fahey Palma, T., & Cleland, J. (2017). "Aspirations of people who come from state education are different": How language reflects social exclusion in medical education. *Advances in Health Sciences Education*. Published online January 24, 2018. https://link.springer.com/content/pdf/10.1007%2Fs10459-018-9809-2.pdf.

Fairclough, N. (1993). Critical discourse analysis and the marketization of public discourse: The universities. *Discourse & Society, 4*(2), 133–168. https://doi.org/10.1177/0957926593004002002.

Fernando, N., Cleland, J., Greaves, K., & McKenzie, H. (2009). Comparing the newly introduced UKCAT with the standardised admission selection process at a Scottish Medical School. *Medical Teacher, 31*, 1018–1023.

Flores, G. (2000). Culture and the patient–physician relationship: Achieving cultural competency in health care. *The Journal of Pediatrics, 136*(1), 14–23. https://doi.org/10.1016/S0022-3476(00)90043-X.

Fuller, A., Heath, S., & Johnston, B. (2011). In A. Fuller, S. Heath, & B. Johnston (Eds), *Rethinking widening participation in higher education: The role of social networks*. London and New York: Routledge.

Gale, T., & Parker, S. (2013, October). Widening participation in Australian higher education: Report submitted to HEFCE and OFFA (October 2013). http://www.ncsehe.edu.au/wp-content/uploads/2013/10/2013_WPeffectivenessAus.pdf. Accessed September 4, 2017.

Garlick, P. B., & Brown, G. (2008). Widening participation in medicine. *BMJ, 336*(7653), 1111–1113. https://doi.org/10.1136/bmj.39508.606157.BE.

Gorard, S., Smith, E., May, H., Thomas, L., Adnett, N., & Slack, K. (2006). *Review of widening participation research: Addressing barriers to participation in higher education*. http://dera.ioe.ac.uk/6204/1/barriers.pdf. Accessed June 16, 2015.

Greenhalgh, T., Seyan, K., & Boynton, P. (2004). "Not a university type": Focus group study of social class, ethnic, and sex differences in school pupils' perceptions about medical school. *British Medical Journal, 328*(7455), 1541–1544. https://doi.org/10.1136/bmj.328.7455.1541.

Guiton, G., Chang, M. J., & Wilkerson, L. (2007). Student body diversity: Relationship to medical students' experiences and attitudes. *Academic Medicine, 82*(10), S85–S88. https://doi.org/10.1097/ACM.0b013e31813ffe1e.

Hay, M., Mercer, A. M., Lichtwark, I., Tran, S., Hodgson, W. C., Aretz, H. T., et al. (2017). Selecting for a sustainable workforce to meet the future healthcare needs of rural communities in Australia. *Advances in Health Sciences Education, 22*(533–551), 1–19. https://doi.org/10.1007/s10459-016-9727-0.

HEFCE. (2014). *Differences in degree outcomes: Key findings* (March), 1–62. http://www.hefce.ac.uk/pubs/year/2014/201403/. Accessed July 5, 2017.

Hemsley-Brown, J. (2015). Getting into a Russell Group university: High scores and private schooling. *British Educational Research Journal, 41*(3), 398–422. https://doi.org/10.1002/berj.3152.

Hill, N. E., Castellino, D. R., Lansford, J. E., Nowlin, P., Dodge, K. A., Bates, J. E., et al. (2004). Parent academic involvement as related to school behavior, achievement, and aspirations: Demographic variations across adolescence. *Child Development, 75*(5), 1491 1509. https://doi.org/10.1111/j.1467-8624.2004.00753.x.

HPAT. (2017). *Home | HPAT Ireland.* https://hpat-ireland.acer.org/. Accessed July 16, 2017.

Jardine, A. (2012). *Indicators of persistence and their influence on the first year experience of university students from low socio-economic backgrounds.* Doctoral thesis, University of Melbourne.

Jerrim, J., & Shure, N. (2016). *Achievement of 15-year-olds in England: PISA 2015 national report.* London. http://dera.ioe.ac.uk/27761/1/PISA-2015_England_Report.pdf. Accessed July 5, 2017.

Jost, J., & Hunyady, O. (2005). Antecedents and consequences of system-justifying ideologies. *Current Directions in Psychological Science, 14,* 260–265. https://doi.org/10.1111/j.0963-7214.2005.00377.x.

Jost, J., Pelham, B., Sheldon, O., & Ni-Sullivan, B. (2003). Social inequality and the reduction of ideological dissonance on behalf of the system: Evidence of enhanced system justification among the disadvantaged. *European Journal of Social Psychology, 33,* 13–36. https://doi.org/10.1002/ejsp.127.

Kamali, A. W., Nicholson, S., & Wood, D. F. (2005). A model for widening access into medicine and dentistry: The SAMDA-BL project. *Medical Education, 39*(9), 918–925. https://doi.org/10.1111/j.1365-2929.2005.02227.x.

Bridger, K., Shaw, J., & Moore, J. (2012). *Fair admissions to higher education research to describe the use of contextual data in admissions at a sample of universities and colleges in the UK.* Supporting Professionalism in Admissions (SPA). https://www.spa.ac.uk/sites/default/files/Research-CA-Report-2012-full.pdf. Accessed September 4, 2017.

Komaromy, M., Grumbach, K., Drake, M., Vranizan, K., Lurie, N., Keane, D., et al. (1996). The role of black and Hispanic physicians in providing health care for underserved populations. *New England Journal of Medicine, 334*(20), 1305–1310. https://doi.org/10.1056/NEJM199605163342006.

Kumwenda, B., Cleland, J., Greatrix, R., MacKenzie, R., & Prescott, G. (2017). *Do graduates increase diversity of the UK medical student body? A national cohort study* (submitted for publication).

Kumwenda, B., Cleland, J. A., Walker, K., Lee, A. J., & Greatrix, R. (2017). The relationship between school type and academic performance at medical school: A national, multi-cohort study. *British Medical Journal Open, 7*(8), e016291. https://doi.org/10.1136/bmjopen-2017-016291.

Lakhan, S. E. (2003). Diversification of U.S. medical schools via affirmative action implementation. *BMC Medical Education, 3*(1), 6. https://doi.org/10.1186/1472-6920-3-6.

Lievens, F., Patterson, F., Corstjens, J., Martin, S., & Nicholson, S. (2016). Widening access in selection using situational judgement tests: Evidence from the UKCAT. *Medical Education, 50*(6). http://doi.org/10.1111/medu.13060.

MacKenzie, R., Cleland, J., Ayansina, D., & Nicholson, S. (2016). Does the UKCAT predict performance on exit from medical school? A national cohort study. *British Medical Journal Open, 6*, e1011313. http://doi.org/10.1136/bmjopen-2016-011313.

Mathers, J., & Parry, J. (2009). Why are there so few working-class applicants to medical schools? Learning from the success stories. *Medical Education, 43*(3), 219–228. https://doi.org/10.1111/j.1365-2923.2008.03274.x.

Mathers, J., Sitch, A., Marsh, J. L., & Parry, J. (2011). Widening access to medical education for under-represented socioeconomic groups: Population based cross sectional analysis of UK data, 2002–6. *British Medical Journal (Clinical Research Ed.), 342,* d918. https://doi.org/10.1136/bmj.d918.

Mathers, J., Sitch, A., & Parry, J. (2016). Longitudinal assessment of the impact of the use of the UK clinical aptitude test for medical student selection. *Medical Education, 50*(10), 1033–1044. https://doi.org/10.1111/medu.13082.

McHarg, J., Mattick, K., & Knight, L. V. (2007). Why people apply to medical school: Implications for widening participation activities. *Medical Education, 41*(8), 815–821. https://doi.org/10.1111/j.1365-2923.2007.02798.x.

McManus, I., Dewberry, C., Nicholson, S., & Dowell, J. (2013). The UKCAT-12 study: Educational attainment, aptitude test performance, demographic and socio-economic contextual factors as predictors of first year outcome in a cross-sectional collaborative study of 12 UK medical schools. *BMC Medical,* 11. http://doi.org/10.1186/1741-7015-11-244.

Medical Schools Council. (2014a). *A journey to medicine: Outreach guidance.* London. http://www.medschools.ac.uk/SiteCollectionDocuments/MSC-A-Journey-to-Medicine-Outreach-Guidance.pdf. Accessed March 3, 2015.

Medical Schools Council. (2014b). *Selecting for excellence* (Final Report). London. http://www.medschools.ac.uk/SiteCollectionDocuments/Selecting-for-Excellence-Final-Report.pdf. Accessed March 3, 2015.

Milburn, A. (2012). *Fair access to professional careers*. London. https://www.gov.uk/government/uploads/system/uploads/attachment_data/file/61090/IR_FairAccess_acc2.pdf. Accessed December 2, 2015.

Miller, K., & Cummings, G. (2009). Gifted and talented students' career aspirations and influences: A systematic review of the literature. *International Journal of Nursing Education Scholarship, 6*(1), 1–26. http://doi.org/10.2202/1548-923X.1667.

Minty, S. (2015). Young people's attitudes towards student debt in Scotland and England. In S. Riddell, E. Weedon, & S. Minty (Eds.), *Higher education in Scotland and the UK: Diverging or converging systems?* (pp. 56–70). Croydon: Edinburgh University Press.

Molesworth, M., Scullion, R., & Nixon, E. (2011). *The marketisation of higher education and the student as consumer*. Oxon: Routledge.

Moore, J., Mountford-Zimdars, A., Wiggans, J., Gittoes, M., McArdle, S., Johnson School, D., & McCarthy, K. (2013). *Contextualised admissions: Examining the evidence* (Report to SPA). The Supporting Professionalism in Admissions Programme. www.spa.ac.uk/sites/default/files/Research-CA-Report-2013-full.pdf. Accessed July 26, 2017.

Morrison, E., & Grbic, D. (2015). Dimensions of diversity and perception of having learned from individuals from different backgrounds: The particular importance of racial diversity. *Academic Medicine, 90*(7), 937–945. https://doi.org/10.1097/ACM.0000000000000675.

Nicholson, S. (2013). *Exploring the academic experience of medical students coming from a non-traditional socio-economic background. A study of their models of learning and professionalization within an undergraduate medical curriculum*. Doctoral thesis, University of London.

Nicholson, S., & Cleland, J. (2015). Reframing research on Widening participation in medical education. In J. Cleland & S. Durning (Eds.), *Researching medical education* (pp. 231–242). Oxford: Wiley-Blackwell.

Nicholson, S., & Cleland, J. (2017). "It's making contacts": Notions of social capital and implications for widening access to medical education. *Advances in Health Sciences Education, 22*(2), 477–490. https://doi.org/10.1007/s10459-016-9735-0.

OFFA. (2008). *Access agreement monitoring*. Office of Fair Access. https://www.offa.org.uk/wp-content/uploads/2008/01/embargoeduntil0001_24108_fullreport_monitoringoutcomesfor2006.pdf. Accessed September 4, 2017.

O'Neill, L., Vonsild, M. C., Wallstedt, B., & Dornan, T. (2013). Admission criteria and diversity in medical school. *Medical Education, 47*(6), 557–561. https://doi.org/10.1111/medu.12140.

Orom, H., Semalulu, T., & Underwood, W. (2013). The social and learning environments experienced by underrepresented minority medical students. *Academic Medicine, 88*(11), 1765–1777. https://doi.org/10.1097/ACM.0b013e3182a7a3af.

Panel on Fair Access to the Professions. (2009). *Unleashing aspiration: The final report of the panel on fair access to the professions.* London. http://dera.ioe.ac.uk/5284/1/finalreport.pdf. Accessed July 26, 2017.

Patterson, F., Knight, A., Dowell, J., Nicholson, S., Cousans, F., & Cleland, J. (2016). How effective are selection methods in medical education? A systematic review. *Medical Education, 50*(1), 36–60. https://doi.org/10.1111/medu.12817.

Puddey, I. B., Mercer, A., Playford, D. E., Pougnault, S., & Riley, G. J. (2014). Medical student selection criteria as predictors of intended rural practice following graduation. *BMC Medical Education, 14*(218). http://doi.org/10.1186/1472-6920-14-218.

Razack, S., Hodges, B., Steinert, Y., & Maguire, M. (2015). Seeking inclusion in an exclusive process: Discourses of medical school student selection. *Medical Education, 49*(1), 36–47. https://doi.org/10.1111/medu.12547.

Royal College for Paediatric and Child Health (RCPCH). (2017). State of Child Health Report 2017. https://www.rcpch.ac.uk/resources/state-child-health-report-2017. Accessed July 1, 2018.

Reay, D., Davies, J., David, M., & Ball, S. J. (2001). Choices of degree or degrees of choice? Class, 'race' and the higher education choice process. *Sociology, 35*(4), 855–874. https://doi.org/10.1177/0038038501035004004.

Robb, N., Dunkley, L., Boynton, P., & Greenhalgh, T. (2007). Looking for a better future: Identity construction in socio-economically deprived 16-year olds considering a career in medicine. *Social Science and Medicine, 65*(4), 738–754. https://doi.org/10.1016/j.socscimed.2007.03.011.

Rosenbaum, S., Teitelbaum, J., & Scott, J. (2013). Raising the bar on achieving racial diversity in higher education. *Academic Medicine, 88*(12), 1792–1794. https://doi.org/10.1097/ACM.0000000000000022.

Saha, S., Guiton, G., Wimmers, P. F., & Wilkerson, L. (2008). Student body racial and ethnic composition and diversity-related outcomes in US medical schools. *Journal of the American Medical Association, 300*(10), 1135–1145. https://doi.org/10.1001/jama.300.10.1135.

Schwartz, S. (2004). *Fair admissions to higher education: Recommendations for good practice.* Department for Education and Skills. http://dera.ioe.ac.uk/5284/1/finalreport.pdf. Accessed September 4, 2017.

Scottish Government. (2016). *The final report of the commission for widening access: A blueprint for fairness.* Edinburgh. http://www.gov.scot/Resource/0049/00496535.pdf. Accessed May 1, 2017.

Sheeran, Y., Brown, B. J., & Baker, S. (2007). Conflicting philosophies of inclusion: The contestation of knowledge in widening participation. *London Review of Education, 5*(3), 249–263. https://doi.org/10.1080/14748460701661302.

Skyrme, J. (2014). *Contextual admissions and social justice in selective english higher education institutions.* Doctoral thesis, University of Manchester.

Slack, K. (2003). Whose aspirations are they anyway? *International Journal of Inclusive Education, 7*(4), 325–335. https://doi.org/10.1080/1360311032000110016.

Southgate, E., Kelly, B. J., & Symonds, I. M. (2015). Disadvantage and the "capacity to aspire" to medical school. *Medical Education, 49*(1), 73–83. https://doi.org/10.1111/medu.12540.

Stegers-Jager, K. M., Steyerberg, E. W., Lucieer, S. M., & Themmen, A. P. N. (2015). Ethnic and social disparities in performance on medical school selection criteria. *Medical Education, 49*(1), 124–133. https://doi.org/10.1111/medu.12536.

Steven, K., Dowell, J., Jackson, C., & Guthrie, B. (2016). Fair access to medicine? Retrospective analysis of UK medical schools application data 2009–2012 using three measures of socioeconomic status. *BMC Medical Education, 16*(1), 11–21. https://doi.org/10.1186/s12909-016-0536-1.

Stuart, M., Lido, C., Morgan, J., Solomon, L., & May, S. (2011). The impact of engagement with extracurricular activities on the student experience and graduate outcomes for widening participation populations. *Active Learning in Higher Education, 12,* 203–215.

Thomas, L., Storan, J., Wylie, V., Berzins, K., Harley, P., Linley, R., & Rawson, A. (2009). *Review of widening participation strategic assessments 2009.* Omskirk.

Tiffin, P. A., Dowell, J. S., & McLachlan, J. C. (2012). Widening access to UK medical education for under-represented socioeconomic groups: Modelling the impact of the UKCAT in the 2009 cohort. *British Medical Journal, 344,* e1805. https://doi.org/10.1136/bmj.e1805.

Tiffin, P. A., McLachlan, J. C., Webster, L., & Nicholson, S. (2014). Comparison of the sensitivity of the UKCAT and a levels to sociodemographic characteristics: A national study. *BMC Medical Education, 14,* 7. https://doi.org/10.1186/1472-6920-14-7.

UKCAT. (2017). *About us.* https://www.ukcat.ac.uk/about-us/. Accessed July 16, 2017.

UMAT. (2017). *Home | UMAT.* https://umat.acer.edu.au/. Accessed July 16, 2017.

Walker, K. O., Moreno, G., & Grumbach, K. (2012). The association among specialty, race, ethnicity, and practice location among California physicians in diverse specialties. *Journal of the National Medical Association, 104*(1–2), 46–52.

Whitla, D. K., Orfield, G., Silen, W., Teperow, C., Howard, C., & Reede, J. (2003). Educational benefits of diversity in medical school: A survey of students. *Academic Medicine, 78*(5), 460–466.

Williamson, H. (2004). *The Milltown boys revisited.* London: Berg.

Wright, S. R., & Bradley, P. M. (2010). Has the UK clinical aptitude test improved medical student selection? *Medical Education, 44*(11), 1069–1076. https://doi.org/10.1111/j.1365-2923.2010.03792.x.

Young, M. (1961). *The rise of the meritocracy, 1870–2033: An essay on education and equality.* Baltimore, MD: Penguin Books.

11

Values-Based Recruitment

Helena Edwards, Tom Kinirons and Fiona Patterson

Overview

This chapter explores the conceptualization of the term 'values' and how they relate to personality, motivation, and behavior. Values-based recruitment (VBR) is then discussed in the context of healthcare selection with a number of case studies drawn upon. Practical considerations for implementing VBR are discussed while presenting an evidence-base to support the use of specific assessment methods as methods for selecting suitable individuals into healthcare roles.

H. Edwards · T. Kinirons · F. Patterson (✉)
Work Psychology Group, Derby, UK
e-mail: f.patterson@workpsychologygroup.com

H. Edwards
e-mail: h.edwards@workpsychologygroup.com

T. Kinirons
e-mail: t.kinirons@workpsychologygroup.com

F. Patterson and L. Zibarras (eds.), *Selection and Recruitment in the Healthcare Professions*, https://doi.org/10.1007/978-3-319-94971-0_11

By the end of this chapter, you should:

- understand the role of values in motivation and behavior
- understand the different ways in which we can implement VBR
- have an insight into some of the practical considerations when implementing VBR
- appreciate the process involved in developing a selection system for VBR.

Introduction

Few would dispute that to be an effective healthcare professional one should hold and display values such as integrity, empathy, and resilience, in addition to possessing the skills and knowledge necessary to carry out the role safely and appropriately. It therefore follows that assessing such attributes should form part of the selection processes used for healthcare roles and research shows that a range of attributes which relate to values are important for the implementation of high-quality care (Patterson et al., 2000; Patterson, Ferguson, & Thomas, 2008). However, assessing an individual's values is more complex than assessing their level of knowledge since values can be difficult to define and can only be inferred through an interpretation of an individual's behavior or words. This becomes particularly challenging when attempting to measure such attributes on a large scale during high volume recruitment campaigns (Cleland, Dowell, McLachlan, Nicholson, & Patterson, 2012).

This complexity is likely to be one of the reasons why many selection practices for healthcare professionals have tended to focus almost exclusively on assessing academic ability or clinical capabilities, with less attention given to an individual's values (Ferguson, James, & Madeley, 2002). This is despite evidence which demonstrates that academic performance is a good, but not perfect, predictor of performance, for example accounting for approximately 23% of the variance in performance in undergraduate medical training and 6% in postgraduate performance (Trost, Nauels, & Klieme, 1998). It is therefore argued that academic ability alone is a necessary but not sufficient condition for future clinical performance, and that there is a need to increase the focus on the non-academic attributes important for success in clinical practice (Patterson & Ferguson, 2010; Patterson et al., 2016a).

A key challenge for healthcare recruiters therefore is how best to assess such non-academic attributes, including desired values, reliably yet in a cost-efficient manner. This challenge takes on an even greater importance in the context of recent high-profile cases and government enquiries in the UK, where the standards of care received by patients has been criticized, in part, due to the lack of compassion, benevolence or empathy displayed by incumbent healthcare professionals. For example, the Mid-Staffordshire Foundation Trust Public Inquiry (Francis, 2013) into a failing UK NHS hospital uncovered a lack of compassion and care that resulted in significant patient suffering. The inquiry highlighted the critical role played by the workforce in ensuring the provision of high quality and safe healthcare services. Similarly, an independent review into healthcare assistants and support workers in the UK NHS and social care settings (Cavendish, 2013) focused heavily on the importance of making sure healthcare workers have core values in place that ensure the safety of patients. It highlighted the importance of supporting employers in testing for values, attitudes, and aptitude for caring at the recruitment stage. These reports, although UK-based, highlight the critical role that the workplace places in ensuring the provision of high quality and safe healthcare services and, in particular, the significance of staff values and behaviors on the quality of patient care and patient outcomes.

What are Values?

One of the first challenges in implementing a VBR system relates to defining what a 'value' is. Research shows that values are defined as a set of enduring beliefs which a person holds about what is good or desirable in life (Schwartz, 2012), which can be thought of as 'preferences' or 'principles' (Ravlin & Meglino, 1987). Values as preferences (also known as work values) are attitudes that indicate the preferences individuals have for various environments. Values as principles (or personal values) are guiding principles regarding how individuals feel they ought to behave. Work values predict vocational choice and job satisfaction whilst personal values are predictive of a broad range of behaviors throughout life (Locke, 1997; Schwartz, 1992). In the context of designing a selection system to include values, it is likely that personal values are just as important to consider as work values.

Research suggests that values develop through social interactions with role models such as parents. As values are learned, values tend to appear in similar patterns within cultures and are shared and passed from generation to generation (Meglino & Ravlin, 1998; Oishi, Schimmack, Diener, & Suh, 1998). Kapes and Strickler (1975) posit that values are generally shaped during adolescence and remain relatively stable in adulthood. However, as values are shaped through social interactions, they are susceptible to change through exposure to new social environments.

Personality, known as the combination of characteristics or qualities that form an individual's distinctive character, has been shown to relate to performance, motivation, job satisfaction, leadership and other work outcomes (Judge, Heller, & Mount, 2002; Motowidlo, Borman, & Schmidt, 1997; Schmidt & Hunter, 1983; see also Chapter 3 for a review). Both values and personality describe components within individuals and are both believed to impact on behavior, decision-making, motivation, attitudes, and interpersonal relations. However, there are also some important differences. Roccas, Sagiv, Shwartz, and Knafo (2002) refer to personality as enduring dispositions, and to values as enduring goals. Whilst personality relates to what we naturally tend to do, values relate to what we believe we ought to do and so have an additional evaluative component. Personality traits do not conflict with one another (i.e., one can simultaneously express the personality traits of Extraversion and Conscientiousness), yet values can conflict since some are pursued at the expense of others (Schwartz, 1996).

Separating out behavior that is caused by personality as opposed to values can be difficult in practice. However, recent research has explored how these constructs are distinct and how they relate to motivation and behavior. Parks and Guay (2009) propose that values and personality have different influences on different motivational processes whereby values primarily influence the goals that individuals choose to pursue, while personality traits primarily influence the amount of effort and

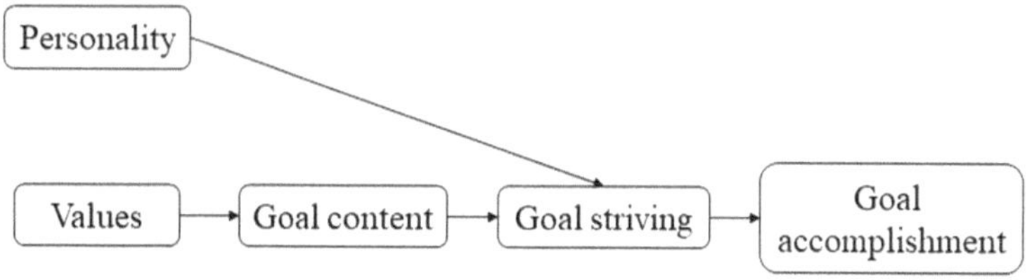

Fig. 11.1 Model of relationship between personality and values on outcomes (Parks & Guay, 2009)

persistence that an individual exhibits in order to meet those goals. Parks and Guay's (2009) model, Fig. 11.1, provides a rationale for values having an incremental contribution to behavior beyond personality. In summary, values can be considered to relate to what we believe we ought to do whilst personality related to what we naturally tend to do (Patterson et al., 2016b).

Assessing Values in Recruitment

Despite the recognized importance of ensuring individual values align with those required within both healthcare education and employment as a healthcare professional, the evidence-base for how to assess such values remains in its infancy and represents a significant gap in the selection and recruitment literature. To date, researchers have focused on evaluating the extent to which existing selection and recruitment methods can be deemed suitable mechanisms for VBR. The purpose of this has been to help identify the methods and techniques considered most appropriate to implement as part of a values-based process at both initial pre-screening or shortlisting stages as well as part of final stage selection. A recent review (Patterson et al., 2016a) summarized the evidence-base for eight popular recruitment methods, focusing on the implications for each method in terms of their effectiveness for VBR (see Table 11.1 for a summary).

At pre-screening and shortlisting stage, commonly used methods include personal statements and references alongside academic performance, however there is little evidence to support the reliability of references, and although the candidate acceptability of personal statements is

Table 11.1 Review of selection methods for values-based recruitment[a]

Selection method	Implications for VBR
Shortlisting methods	
Personal statements	Candidate acceptability is high, but susceptibility to coaching is also high. ***(Ineffective method for VBR)***
References	Use of references remains widespread despite little research supporting validity or reliability. ***(Ineffective method for VBR)***
Situational Judgement Tests (SJTs)	Improved validity over other selection methods (e.g., IQ and personality assessments) and can be mapped to organizational values. Whilst SJTs can be relatively costly to design, they are machine-markable and can be delivered online, producing cost savings especially in high volume selection. ***(Effective method for VBR)***
Personality assessment	There is some evidence for predictive validity, but where there is a high risk of susceptibility to faking and/or coaching, personality assessment may be best used to drive more focused questioning at interview (rather than as a stand-alone instrument without verification). ***(Personality assessment is useful at the attraction phases of selection as part of self-assessment/selection, or to inform later assessment methods such as interviews)***
Final stage selection methods	
Traditional (unstructured) interviews	Across most evaluation criteria, traditional interviews perform poorly. ***(Ineffective for VBR)***
Structured interviews (e.g., behavioral-based and situational)	When interviews are structured and based on a thorough role analysis, with standardized questions with trained interviews, and appropriate scoring they can be reliable and valid. Candidates prefer interviews to other methods although they are relatively resource-intensive. ***(Effective method for VBR)***
Group interviews	Whilst group interviews appear more cost-efficient in terms of assessor time, evidence for reliability, validity and fairness is lacking. ***(Ineffective method for VBR)***
Multiple-mini interviews (MMIs), selection centers (SCs) using work samples (e.g., group exercises, written/in-tray tasks, presentations, interactive exercises)	When designed appropriately, SCs and MMIs are valid predictors of job performance. Candidates are positive towards SCs and MMIs as they have multiple opportunities to perform. However, SCs and MMIs are relatively expensive to design and implement. ***(Effective method for VBR)***

[a]Adapted, with permission, from Patterson et al. (2016a)

high, this approach is susceptible to coaching and may disadvantage those from state schools compared to privately educated peers (Jones, 2016). Consequently, these methods are unlikely to be effective as part of a VBR system. Although there is evidence for the validity and reliability of personality assessments (Salgado, 1997), these self-report methods are also subject to faking and coaching (e.g., Birkeland, Manson, Kisamore, Brannick, & Smith, 2006). Recent research shows that applicants may engage in substantial response distortion in completing personality assessments in medical selection, and that the predictive validity of personality is modest and may be reduced further in selection settings (Anglim, Bozic, Little, & Lievens, 2018). Personality assessments, may therefore be more useful in guiding focused questions during the final stage of selection, rather than being used as a stand-alone screening method (see Chapter 3 for a review).

An assessment method which is becoming increasingly popular in healthcare selection is a Situational Judgement Test (SJT) (see Chapter 4 on SJTs). Research shows that SJTs have improved validity over other selection methods in the healthcare context (Koczwara et al., 2012; Lievens & Patterson, 2011; Patterson et al., 2009) and the attributes typically assessed by such methods can also be mapped against organizational values, or the values can be used as the basis for test specification. Although SJTs can be costly to develop, their scalability is good since they can manage high volumes of applicants (for example, through online delivery or through automated marking of paper-based tests). As such, SJTs are likely to be an effective method for pre-screening applicants as part of a VBR system. Case Study 11.1 describes how an SJT was implemented to assess the values of medical school graduates.

Case Study 11.1: A Situational Judgement Test to Assess the Values of Medical School Graduates in the UK

Context: Every year, nearly 8000 final year medical students apply for junior doctor posts in the two-year Foundation Programme, which is a requirement for all medical graduates wishing to work as doctors in the UK. Competition into the program is intensifying due to the expansion of UK medical schools and an ever-increasing number of international applications.

The Department of Health recommended that an SJT was implemented to assess the professional attributes, judgement, and employability for a

Foundation Programme post and to replace the open-ended white space application questions previously used. The SJT presents applicants with scenarios they are likely to encounter as a Foundation Year 1 (F1) doctor and asks them to make a judgement about the appropriateness of different response options. Their responses are scored against a pre-determined key defined by subject-matter experts (SMEs). The SJT ensures candidates selected have the aptitude and values required of a successful doctor.

Key Issues: In order to understand and define the attributes required to be successful in the role, a role analysis of the F1 doctor was undertaken. A person specification was developed based on this analysis. Each year, educational supervisors, clinical supervisors and other Foundation Programme experts contribute to the development of new test questions based on the person specification. These questions are further reviewed, including input from Foundation doctors to ensure that the hypothetical situations are realistic, relevant and appropriate. From the job analysis, five target domains were identified to be assessed in the SJT, and each item is designed to measure one of these. The five target domains, are outlined in Table 11.2 along with examples of the kinds of scenarios which might be included under each. These domains were then mapped to the values of the NHS Constitution outlined in Table 11.3.

Outcomes: The SJT has been in operational use since 2013, with approximately 8000 UK and international medical school graduates completing the test each year, with results informing their allocation to foundation program places alongside a measure of educational attainment. Each year, the SJT is subject to full psychometric analysis and results consistently show that the SJT is a reliable, valid and appropriate method for foundation selection. Applicant reactions to the test have been largely positive, with the majority of students indicating that the content of the test seems fair, relevant and appropriate. A validation study found evidence to support the predictive validity of the SJT, finding that this method alongside the measure educational attainment were complementary in predicting foundation doctor performance one year into role (Cousans et al., 2017).

Table 11.2 SJT target domains and example SJT scenario types

Commitment to professionalism	Issues of confidentiality such as hearing a colleague talking about a patient outside of work
Coping with pressure	Dealing with confrontation such as an angry relative
Effective communication	Gathering information and communicating intentions to other colleagues
Patient focus	Taking into account a patient's views/concerns
Working effectively as part of a team	Recognizing and valuing the skills and knowledge of colleagues when faced with a disagreement about a patient's care

Table 11.3 UK National Health Service (NHS) constitution values

Value	Description
Working together for patients	Patients come first in everything we do. We fully involve patients, staff, families, carers, communities, and professionals inside and outside the NHS. We put the needs of patients and communities before organizational boundaries. We speak up when things go wrong
Respect and dignity	We value every person—whether patient, their families or carers, or staff—as an individual, respect their aspirations and commitments in life, and seek to understand their priorities, needs, abilities and limits. We take what others have to say seriously. We are honest and open about our point of view and what we can and cannot do
Commitment to quality of care	We earn the trust placed in us by insisting on quality and striving to get the basics of quality of care—safety, effectiveness, and patient experience—right every time. We encourage and welcome feedback from patients, families, carers, staff and the public. We use this to improve the care we provide and build on our successes
Compassion	We ensure that compassion is central to the care we provide and respond with humanity and kindness to each person's pain, distress, anxiety or need. We search for the things we can do, however small, to give comfort and relieve suffering. We find time for patients, their families and carers, as well as those we work alongside. We do not wait to be asked, because we care
Improving lives	We strive to improve health and wellbeing and people's experiences of the NHS. We cherish excellence and professionalism wherever we find it—in the everyday things that make people's lives better as much as in clinical practice, service improvements and innovation. We recognize that all have a part to play in making ourselves, patients and our communities healthier
Everyone counts	We maximize our resources for the benefit of the whole community, and make sure nobody is excluded, discriminated against or left behind. We accept that some people need more help, that difficult decisions have to be taken—and that when we waste resources we waste opportunities for others

Taken from: https://www.gov.uk/government/publications/the-nhs-constitution-for-england/the-nhs-constitution-for-england

At final stage selection, evidence shows that traditional interviews (which are unstructured and have no pre-defined scoring criteria) lack validity and reliability (Klehe, 2004) and are thus ineffective for VBR. Structured interviews, with questions based on role analysis, have better predictive validity (Huffcutt & Arthur, 1994) and can be considered an effective method for VBR if designed and implemented in a robust manner. Case Study 11.2 describes how a structured values-based interview (VBI) has been implemented by a UK healthcare trust to assess the values of staff entering the organization across all levels and roles.

A specific type of interview which is often used, especially by higher education institutions for selection onto healthcare programs, is a group interview. Recruiters may be attracted to the nature of the group interview, which allows for an assessment of how well a candidate manages interaction with others during the interview itself and this approach can appear cost effective due to requiring less interviewer resource than one-to-one or panel interviews. However, evidence for the validity and reliability of group interviews is lacking and there may be an increased likelihood than candidates will perceive these as unfair due to the influence of others, and increased assessor load (Tran & Blackman, 2006). Therefore, group interviews are likely to represent a 'false economy' and be ineffective as a method for VBR.

Selection centers (SCs) (also known as assessment centers) and multiple-mini interviews (MMIs), however, are able to manage large volumes of candidates, who are assessed on an individual basis rather than as part of a group. When designed appropriately, these methods can be a valid predictor of job performance (Patterson, Ferguson, Norfolk, & Lane, 2005) and overcome some of the problems associated with the test-retest reliability of panel interview techniques (Eva, Reiter, Rosenfeld, & Norman, 2004). Recent research in this area has found positive validity for the use of MMIs in VBR (Callwood, Cooke, Bolger, Lemanska, & Allan, 2018). As such both SCs and MMIs are likely to be effective methods for VBR (see Chapter 5 on interviews).

Case Study 11.2: A Values-Based Interview to Select for UK NHS Staff (Joanna Cook, Organizational Psychologist, Northumbria Healthcare NHS Foundation Trust)

Context: Northumbria Healthcare NHS Foundation Trust provides hospital and community services for approximately 500,000 patients, employing around 8500 staff. The Trust has five organizational values which were created through staff consultation: Patients First; Safe and High-Quality Care, Responsibility and Accountability, Everyone's Contribution Counts, and Respect. These are aligned to the NHS Constitution values outlined in Table 11.3. To assess these values at the point individuals enter the organization, the Trust developed a VBR process, starting with the design and implementation of a values-based interview (VBI), which aims to evaluate to what extent a candidate's values align with the organization's values.

Key Issues: The aim was to create a VBI to be used for all roles within the Trust, both for new recruits and promotions, for some roles this is complemented with a selection center and psychometric assessments. Following role analysis, a structured, behavioral interview was devised and a bank of VBI questions were created. Question content was developed using output from the role analysis which gathered information about 'aligned' and 'non-aligned' behaviors, which are behaviors expected (and not expected) to be demonstrated by effective staff members operating in the relevant role. VBI questions were designed to elicit such behaviors (see Fig. 11.2 for an example question and scoring criteria). Guidance for managers is supplied to ensure objective and standardized interview processes, and all interviews are conducted by a panel.

When have you made a patient / their family / a colleague feel valued?						
How did you know how to approach them? Why did you approach them? How did you know you'd made them feel valued? What did you learn from the experience?						
Aligned Behaviors	**Excellent**	**Very Good**	**Good**	**Just Acceptable**	**Unacceptable**	**Non-Aligned Behaviors**
Can provide a relevant example						Cannot provide a relevant example
Seeks to understand others' needs						Makes assumptions about the person and their needs
Tailors their approach and style to meet the patient/their family/a colleague's needs						Focuses on what they need from the relationship, does not adapt their approach
Reflect on the impact of their behavior						Lacks awareness of the impact of their behavior
Average score across the value:						
Excellent	**Very Good**		**Good**		**Just Acceptable**	**Unacceptable**

Fig. 11.2 Example values-based interview question and scoring criteria

Outcomes: Following a series of pilots, a full organization wide roll out was implemented that involved changing all recruitment materials, processes and training 500+recruiting managers through a two-hour interactive skill-based session. A 'trained user' register was created, and guidance was issued which stated at least one panel member must be a trained user. The values have also been incorporated into the appraisal process, probationary period and job descriptions. An evaluation was conducted to measure the impact of VBR within the organization with results suggesting that, in general, staff experience had improved since VBR was introduced. In addition, the Trust received a rating of 'Outstanding' in a Care Quality Commission Inspection remarking that 'Staff consistently communicated with patients in a kind and compassionate way' and 'staff went above and beyond in the ways they cared for patients'.

Practical Considerations for Implementing VBR

Whilst the evidence demonstrates that there are certain selection methods which are more likely to be effective for VBR (e.g., SJTs, structured interviews, MMIs, and SCs) and others that are less likely to be effective (e.g., personal statements, references, traditional interviews, and group interviews), implementing VBR is likely to be faced with the challenge of balancing best-practice and the evidence-base against practical considerations such as scarcity of resources and budget pressures. Therefore, recruiters are likely to have to make a judgement about which type of selection method will achieve the best outcomes, whilst be deliverable within the constraints of the organization within which they are operating. Some evaluation criteria with which to judge the effectiveness of various selection methods and their sustainability for VBR include:

1. accuracy and effectiveness (such as evidence of reliability, validity, and fairness across groups);
2. costs and efficiencies (such as scalability for high volume recruitment);
3. practicalities and implementation (such as ease of administration and interpretation); and,
4. stakeholder acceptance and feedback (such as positive candidate perceptions and positive assessor/interviewer feedback).

However, these criteria are not mutually exclusive and it is possible for some to be at odds with each other. For example, a highly reliable and valid selection method may also be very expensive. Similarly, a highly valid method may not be acceptable to key stakeholders and may generate negative candidate reactions. As a result, recruiters are challenged with needing to balance consideration of these criteria, and it is likely that some will weigh more heavily in the decision-making process than others depending on the specific organizational context within which the recruiter is operating (see also Chapter 1 for a review).

Once a specific selection method(s) is identified, another key challenge for recruiters lies in the development and design of the method. Importantly, a selection method does not need to be designed to measure values *exclusively* and it is possible that a single method (e.g., a structured interview) can be designed to incorporate a measure of both a candidate's values *and* other important attributes for the role (e.g., clinical knowledge). Indeed, selection methods based on a multi-trait, multi-method approach (such as MMIs or SCs) lend themselves very well to this approach of incorporating a measure of values alongside other attributes. For example, an MMI could be designed to incorporate a variety of different stations, some of which focus on specifically on values and others which focus on assessing clinical skills (see Chapter 5 on interviews and MMIs). In developing selection system to be used for VBR, there are a number of important considerations for recruiters to take into account to ensure alignment with best-practice-principles. These are outlined in the form of a checklist in Fig. 11.3.

The development of any selection system begins with a thorough role analysis (see Chapter 6) to define the attributes required of an effective role holder. In the context of VBR, attention should be paid to defining the specific behavioral characteristics required of the role holder in addition to any previous work experience, technical qualifications or level of ability which are also required. For an organization with a pre-existing values framework (such as the NHS constitution values detailed in Table 11.3), this can

The design of a selection system for VBR should:

- ✓ Be based on a thorough role analysis which includes a definition of organizational values
- ✓ Involve input from subject matter experts
- ✓ Include clear and specific evaluation criteria against which a candidate's performance is assessed
- ✓ Be subject to piloting on a relevant population
- ✓ Be accompanied by clear communications to candidates outlining what is expected of them during the assessment
- ✓ Be conducted by appropriated trained assessors
- ✓ Be subject to ongoing evaluation, including studies of predictive validity
- ✓ Be part of a multi-faceted approach to embedding values throughout the organization

Fig. 11.3 A summary checklist for developing a selection system for VBR

be used as a helpful starting point, however how the generic values apply to the specific role in question should be carefully considered and defined. For example, the way in which a surgeon is expected to display the value of "Compassion", may be different from the way in which a pharmacy technician is expected to display the same value, and the specific behaviors expected of each are likely to differ. Therefore, ideally a separate role analysis should be undertaken for each role being selected for. It is also important that individuals who either have direct experience of undertaking the role in question, or who have a good understanding of the role requirements (e.g., those who manage or supervise the role) are involved in the development of the selection methods. The inclusion of subject matter experts (SMEs) in this way ensures that the content of the selection methods (e.g., the interview questions, the SC exercise, or the SJT item) are relevant, realistic, and appropriate for the role and the level being recruited to. Stakeholder acceptability is also likely to be enhanced when SMEs have been involved. Importantly, in the context of VBR, SMEs are likely to be able to provide specific examples of how values might manifest themselves (both positively and negatively) in different individuals undertaking the same role which can inform the development process. Any method should include a clear set of criteria against which each candidate is evaluated, and this should be consistently applied across all candidates applying for the role. These criteria should be based on the outputs from the role analysis and be clear and straightforward to interpret. This helps to maximize inter-rater reliability and minimize some of the risks of assessor bias.

In the context of VBR, criteria should be directly linked to the values being assessed. For example, it should be clear to an interviewer which organizational value(s) an interview question is designed to assess and how these should be assessed (for example including examples of positive/aligned and negative/non-aligned behaviors which a candidate may demonstrate as illustrated in Case Study 11.2 above). Before a selection method is introduced and used to select or reject candidates, it should first be piloted to help ensure it is fit for purpose. This could include using the new method alongside pre-existing methods for a period to gather data and feedback (but not using it to inform the final selection decision). Alternatively, the method could be trialed with a group of incumbent role holders to check that it is considered relevant and fair and is set at an appropriate level of difficulty (see Chapter 4 on SJTs and Chapter 6 on role analysis). Conducting a pilot in this way is helpful as it allows for any issues or limitations with the design of the method or of the evaluation criteria to be identified prior to implementation. However, even once a pilot has taken place, it is still advisable to gather feedback from candidates and assessors on an ongoing basis so that reactions can continue to be monitored over time.

Once a selection method has been developed and integrated into the recruitment process, it is important that appropriate communications are developed to be sent to candidates in advance. Candidates should be informed of which selection methods they will be expected to complete and at which stages of the recruitment process. They should also ideally be made aware of what attributes or competencies they are to be assessed against. However, clearly this needs to be balanced with not providing too much detail regarding the specific exercises or questions that they will be presented with or the specific scoring criteria. In the case of a psychometric method (such as an SJT) it is advisable to provide candidates with a practice question to complete in advance so that they can familiarize themselves with the format and response mechanisms. As VBR is a relatively new concept, it is even more important that candidates are made aware of how values form part of the assessment process and which values they are to be assessed against. This also provides the opportunity for the organizational values to be explicitly shared with candidates up front, building awareness of the organization's expectations and commitments from the outset. Here, a self-selection method whereby a candidate considers to what extent they are suited to the role in question and to what extent their values align with those of the organization, can be helpful as a mechanism for avoiding highly unsuitable candidates, or those with values at odds with the organization, from applying in the first place (see Chapter 8 on candidate perceptions).

Regardless of how well designed a selection method is, where assessor or interviewer judgement is involved, the reliability and accuracy of the decisions made are ultimately determined by these judgements which are subject to inevitable human error. Research demonstrates the positive impact assessor training and experience has on the quality of performance measurement (Viswesvaran, Schmidt, & Ones, 2005). Therefore, in addition to designing clear and straightforward assessment materials (for example, incorporating clearly defined evaluation criteria as described above), it is also critical that all individuals who are involved in assessing candidates undergo thorough training. Training should focus on ensuring all assessors are familiar with their role (i.e., aware what they will be asked to do and familiar with the timetable of assessment events) as well as clear about how to interpret and score the evaluation criteria. Providing assessors with the opportunity to practice applying the assessment criteria (for example by assessing mock candidates), and receiving feedback on this, is a helpful way to ensure consistency across different assessors, and for individual assessors to identify any specific biases they might hold (for example a tendency to be overly lenient or stringent in their scoring) (Patterson, Zibarras, Kerrin, Lopes, & Price, 2014). Training assessors in this way is likely to be of even greater importance when introducing a VBR system, as assessing values may be something which even experienced assessors are less familiar with. Within healthcare recruitment, it is often considered desirable to include healthcare staff as assessors as these individuals are closest to the role and therefore likely to have a good insight as to what is required. However, a study by Roberts, Gale, Sice, and Anderson (2013) showed that when untrained, healthcare staff provide ratings significantly different to those of trained assessors and failed to achieve adequate levels of inter-rater reliabilities. Therefore, whilst there may be value in including a broad range of healthcare staff as assessors, it is important to ensure they are appropriately trained beforehand.

Once a selection system is in place, it is important to continue to undertake reviews and evaluation on an ongoing basis to ensure it remains fit for purpose. Ideally data should be gathered so that an evaluation of the method's reliability and validity can be conducted. However, assessing the extent to which an assessment method can predict in-role performance (predictive validation) is challenging and recruiters need to think carefully about what performance data is available and appropriate to use (see Chapter 1 for an overview of some of the challenges associated with this type of evaluation). As mentioned above, ongoing reviews should also pay attention to gathering feedback from candidates and assessors.

The final point in the checklist is especially pertinent to VBR. It relates to the importance of ensuring that the selection system itself forms only one part of embedding values within a healthcare organization or educational institution. There is evidence that small changes in individuals' values can occur over a period of time following initial employment (De Cooman et al., 2009; Meglino & Ravlin, 1998). Similarly, 'value internalization' and 'behavioral modelling' are reported as having an impact on an individual's values following employment (De Cooman et al., 2009; Maierhofer, Griffin, & Sheehan, 2000; Ostroff, Shin, & Kinicki, 2005). Value internalization explains the subtle change in an individual's values over time following employment as a result of their experiences, and both managers and work colleagues may have a significant impact on new recruits, being powerful role models (Maierhofer et al., 2000). Furthermore, managers also influence employees' behaviors through their own actions. Therefore, individuals recruited with optimal values can be at risk of not displaying such values if placed in suboptimal teams, or they may choose to leave the role if they feel that there is a lack of congruence between their own values and those of the organization they are working for.

Furthermore, the resources, working conditions, and systems in place within an organization are also likely to affect the extent to which an individual is able to display their values, and in certain cases structures may inadvertently prevent staff from exhibiting their values such as compassion and concern for patients. This point is summed up in a quote from the Berwick review (Berwick, 2013), into patient safety in the NHS which stated: "*Good people can fail to meet patients' needs when their working conditions do not provide them with the conditions for success*". Overall, the evidence clearly points to the need for a multifaceted approach to organizational values beyond recruitment issues alone (Rapping, 2009).

Practice Points

- An assessment of an individual's values should form an important part of a selection process for healthcare roles, alongside other attributes such as knowledge and clinical skills.
- Assessing for values is complex, especially when seeking to implement selection systems for high volume recruitment campaigns, and therefore traditionally selection practices for healthcare professionals have tended to focus on assessing academic ability or clinical capabilities.
- Values can be defined as a series of enduring beliefs which a person holds about what is good or desirable in life. When developing a selection system to include values, both work values (preferences for various environments) and personal values (guiding principles for how individuals feel they ought to behave), are important to include. Importantly, values can be considered distinct from personality.
- The evidence-base demonstrates that certain selection methods are more likely to be effective for VBR, these include: SJTs, structured interviews, MMIs and SCs. Personality assessments may also be useful at the attraction phases of selection or to inform later assessment methods such as interviews.
- In deciding upon methods to implement as part of a VBR system, recruiters should consider the following evaluation criteria: accuracy and effectiveness of the method(s); costs and efficiencies; practicalities and implementation; and, stakeholder acceptance and feedback. It is likely that the weighting of the criteria will vary depending

on the specific organizational context within which the recruiter is operating.

- In developing or designing assessment methods for VBR, recruiters should seek to base decisions on a thorough role analysis, involve input from SMEs, include clear evaluation criteria, undertake piloting, develop appropriate candidate communications, undertake thorough assessor training, and put in place mechanisms for ongoing evaluation.
- It is important to recognize that VBR should form only one part of a multi-faceted approach to embedding values throughout the organization.

Conclusion

In summary, whilst the evidence-base for VBR remains in its infancy, the research provides some clear direction for recruiters in terms of which selection methods are likely to be most appropriate for assessing values and there are specific steps which can be followed to help organizations to implement good quality VBR systems. There is a need for further research in this area to continue to build upon the existing evidence. The design of good quality, longitudinal validation studies using appropriate outcomes measures is challenging, however, will help to identify the methods and techniques which are most likely to reliably predict the in-role behavior of healthcare professionals.

Explore Further

NHS Health Education England—Values-based recruitment framework: https://www.hee.nhs.uk/sites/default/files/documents/VBR_Framework%20March%202016.pdf.

A guide for NHS employers and higher education institutions about how to attract and recruit students, trainees, and employees on the basis that their individual values and behaviors align with the values of the NHS Constitution. Contains a literature review into the evidence-base for VBR and case studies where VBR initiatives have been implemented within a variety of healthcare and academic organizations.

References

Anglim, J., Bozic, S., Little, J., & Lievens, F. (2018). Response distortion on personality tests in applicants: comparing high-stakes to low-stakes medical settings. *Advances in Health Sciences Education, 23*(2), 311–321.

Berwick, D. (2013). *A promise to learn—A commitment to act: Improving the safety of patients in England.* London: Department of Health.

Birkeland, S. A., Manson, T. M., Kisamore, J. L., Brannick, M. T., & Smith, M. A. (2006). A meta-analytic investigation of job applicant faking on personality measures. *International Journal of Selection and Assessment, 14*(4), 317–335. https://doi.org/10.1111/j.1468-2389.2006.00354.x.

Callwood, A., Cooke, D., Bolger, S., Lemanska, A., & Allan, H. (2018). The reliability and validity of multiple mini interviews (MMIs) in values based recruitment to nursing, midwifery and paramedic practice programmes: Findings from an evaluation study. *International Journal of Nursing Studies, 77*, 138–144.

Cavendish, C. (2013). *The Cavendish review: An independent review into healthcare assistants and support workers in the NHS and social care settings.* London: Department of Health.

Cleland, J., Dowell, J., McLachlan, J., Nicholson, S., & Patterson, F. (2012). *Identifying best practice in the selection of medical students.* London: General Medical Council. gmc-uk.org/about/research/14400.asp.

Cousans, F., Patterson, F., Edwards, H., McLaughlan, J., & Good, D. (2017). Evaluating the complementary roles of an SJT and academic assessment for entry into clinical practice. *Advances in Health Sciences and Education.* https://doi.org/10.1007/s10459-017-9755-4.

De Cooman, R., De Gieter, S., Pepermans, R., Hermans, S., Bois, C. Du., Caers, R., & Jegers, M. (2009). Person–organization fit: Testing socialization and attraction–selection–attrition hypotheses. *Journal of Vocational Behavior*, 74(1), 102–107.

Eva, K., Reiter, H., Rosenfeld, J., & Norman, G. (2004). The relationship between interviewers' characteristics and ratings assigned during a multiple mini-interview. *Academic Medicine, 79*, 602–609.

Ferguson, E., James, D., & Madeley, L. (2002). Factors associated with success in medical school: Systematic review of the literature. *British Medical Journal, 324*(7343), 952–957.

Francis, R. (2013). *Report of the Mid Staffordshire NHS Foundation Trust public inquiry: Executive summary* (Vol. 947). The Stationery Office. Retrieved from http://www.midstaffspublicinquiry.com/sites/default/files/report/Executivesummary.pdf.

Huffcutt, A. I., & Arthur, W. (1994). Hunter and hunter (1984) revisited: Interview validity for entry-level jobs. *Journal of Applied Psychology, 79*, 184–190.

Jones, S. (2016). *Making a statement. Research brief for the Sutton Trust edition 10.* Retrieved from https://www.research.manchester.ac.uk/portal/files/34145433/2016_Making_a_Statement_FINAL.pdf.

Judge, T. A., Heller, D., & Mount, M. K. (2002). Five-factor model of personality and job satisfaction: A meta-analysis. *Journal of Applied Psychology, 87*(3), 530.

Kapes, J. T., & Strickler, R. E. (1975). A longitudinal study of change in work values between ninth and twelfth grades as related to high school curriculum. *Journal of Vocational Behavior, 6*(1), 81–93.

Klehe, U.-C. (2004). Choosing how to choose: Institutional pressures affecting the adoption of personnel selection procedures. *International Journal of Selection and Assessment, 12*(4), 327–342.

Koczwara, A., Patterson, F., Zibarras, L., Kerrin, M., Irish, B., & Wilkinson, M. (2012). Evaluating the validity of tests of cognitive ability, applied knowledge and situational judgement for postgraduate selection. *Medical Education, 46*(4), 399–408.

Lievens, F., & Patterson, F. (2011). The validity and incremental validity of knowledge tests, low-fidelity simulations, and high-fidelity simulations for predicting job performance in advanced-level high-stakes selection. *The Journal of Applied Psychology, 96*(5), 927–940.

Locke, E. A. (1997). The motivation to work: What we know. In M. L. Maehr & P. R. Pintrick (Eds.), *Advances in motivation and achievement* (pp. 375–412). Greenwich, CT: JAI Press.

Maierhofer, N. I., Griffin, M. A., & Sheehan, M. (2000). Linking manager values and behavior with employee values and behavior: A study of values and safety in the hairdressing industry. *Journal of Occupational Health Psychology, 5*(4), 417–427.

Meglino, B. M., & Ravlin, E. C. (1998). Individual values in organizations: Concepts, controversies, and research. *Journal of Management, 24*(3), 351–389.

Motowidlo, S. J., Borman, W. C., & Schmidt, M. J. (1997). A theory of individual differences in task and contextual performance. *Human Performance, 10*, 71–83.

Oishi, S., Schimmack, U., Diener, E., & Suh, E. (1998). The measurement of values and individualism—Collectivism. *Personality and Social Psychology Bulletin, 24*, 1177–1189.

Ostroff, C., Shin, Y., & Kinicki, A. J. (2005). Multiple perspectives of congruence: Relationships between value congruence and employee attitudes. *Journal of Organizational Behavior, 26*(6), 591–623.

Parks, L., & Guay, R. P. (2009). Personality, values, and motivation. *Personality and Individual Differences, 47*(7), 675–684.

Patterson, F., Carr, V., Zibarras, L., Burr, B., Berkin, L., Plint, S., …, Gregory, S. (2009). New machine-marked tests for selection into core medical training: Evidence from two validation studies. *Clinical Medicine, 9*(5), 417–420.

Patterson, F., & Ferguson, E. (2010). Selection for medical education and training. In T. Swanwick (Ed.), *Understanding Medical Education: Evidence, Theory and Practice* (pp.352–365). Wiley-Blackwell.

Patterson, F., Ferguson, E., Lane, P., Farrell, K., Martlew, J., & Wells, A. (2000). A competency model for general practice: Implications for selection, training, and development. *The British Journal of General Practice, 50,* 188–193.

Patterson, F., Ferguson, E., Norfolk, T., & Lane, P. (2005). A new selection system to recruit general practice registrars: Preliminary findings from a validation study. *British Medical Journal, 330*(7493), 711–714.

Patterson, F., Ferguson, E., & Thomas, S. (2008). Using job analysis to identify core and specific competencies: Implications for selection and recruitment. *Medical Education, 42,* 1195–1204.

Patterson, F., Knight, A., Dowell, J., Nicholson, S., Cousans, F., & Cleleand, J. (2016a). How effective are selection methods in medical education and training? Evidence from a systematic review. *Medical Education, 50*(1), 36–60.

Patterson, F., Prescott-Clements, L., Zibarras, L., Edwards, H., Kerrin, M., & Cousans, F. (2016b). Recruiting for values in healthcare: A preliminary review of the evidence. *Advances in Health Sciences Education, 21*(4), 859–881.

Patterson, F., Zibarras, L., Kerrin, M., Lopes, S., & Price, R. (2014). Development of competency models for assessors and simulators in high-stakes selection processes. *Medical Teacher, 36*(12), 1082–1085.

Rapping, J. A. (2009). You can't build on shaky ground: Laying the foundation for indigent defense reform through values-based recruitment, training, and mentoring. *Harvard Law & Policy Review,3*(161).

Ravlin, E. C., & Meglino, B. M. (1987). Issues in work values measurement. In L. Preston (Ed.), *Research in corporate social performance and policy* (pp. 153–183). Greenwich: JAI Press.

Roberts, M. J., Gale, T. C., Sice, P. J. A., & Anderson, I. R. (2013). The relative reliability of actively participating and passively observing raters in a simulation-based assessment for selection to specialty training in anaesthesia. *Anaesthesia, 68*(6), 591–599.

Roccas, S., Sagiv, L., Schwartz, S. H., & Knafo, A. (2002). The Big Five personality factors and personal values. *Personality and Social Psychology Bulletin, 28,* 789–801.

Salgado, J. F. (1997). The five factor model of personality and job performance in the European Community. *Journal of Applied Psychology, 82*(1), 30–43.

Schmidt, F. L., & Hunter, J. E. (1983). Individual differences in productivity: An empirical test of estimates derived from studies of selection procedure utility. *Journal of Applied Psychology, 68*(3), 407.

Schwartz, S. (1996). Value priorities and behavior: Applying a theory of integrated value systems. In U. C. Seligman, J. M. Olson, & M. P. Zanna (Eds.), *The Ontario Symposium: The psychology of values* (Vol. 8, pp. 1–24). Hillsdale, NJ: Lawrence Erlbaum.

Schwartz, S. H. (1992). Universals in the content and structure of values: Theoretical advances and empirical tests in 20 countries. In M. Zanna (Ed.), *Advances in experimental social psychology* (pp. 1–65). San Diego, CA: Academic Press.

Schwartz, S. H. (2012). An overview of the Schwartz theory of basic values. *Online Readings in Psychology and Culture, 2*(1), 3–4.

Tran, T., & Blackman, M. C. (2006). The dynamics and validity of the group selection interview. *The Journal of Social Psychology, 146*(2), 183–201.

Trost, G., Nauels, H. U., & Klieme, E. (1998). The relationship between different criteria for admission to medical school and student success. *Assessment in Education: Principles, Policy & Practice, 5*(2), 247–254.

Viswesvaran, C., Schmidt, F. L., & Ones, D. S. (2005). Is there a general factor in ratings of job performance? A meta-analytic framework for disentangling substantive and error influences. *Journal of Applied Psychology, 90,* 108–131.

12

Altruism and Prosociality in Healthcare Selection and Recruitment: Insights from Psychology and Behavioral Economics

Eamonn Ferguson

Overview

This chapter focuses on the concepts of altruism and prosociality and draws upon new research insights from psychology and behavioral economics to show how this might be applied in future selection and recruitment practices in healthcare. Specifically, it may be possible to use concepts and methods from behavioral economics to 'profile' and better characterize the altruistic (prosocial) preferences of applicants to various healthcare roles. In reviewing the issues, it is suggested how these insights can be used to: (1) develop improved recruitment campaigns (especially for specialties where there are workforce shortages) and (2) inform the design of selection methods and approaches to decision-making. While evidence from behavioral economics has been applied to enhancing the provision of healthcare (Hallsworth et al., 2016; Rice, 2013) and markets for organs and kidney exchanges for

E. Ferguson (✉)
School of Psychology, University of Nottingham, Nottingham, UK
e-mail: eamonn.ferguson@nottingham.ac.uk

F. Patterson and L. Zibarras (eds.), *Selection and Recruitment in the Healthcare Professions*, https://doi.org/10.1007/978-3-319-94971-0_12

example (Roth, Sonmer & Unver, 2004), at present there is no research exploring how behavioral economics theory can be applied to help understand the altruistic preferences of a physician, and the related implications for recruitment and selection.

By the end of the chapter, you should:

- Appreciate why altruism is an important concept to consider in healthcare
- Appreciate how behavioral economics can be applied to assess altruism
- Understand how behavioral preferences of applicants might inform recruitment and selection strategies.

Avoiding Recruitment Bias: Altruism and Moving Selection and Recruitment Beyond Prior Academic Attainment

Traditionally, both recruitment (i.e., attracting candidates to the job through adverts and/or providing realistic job simulations) and selection (i.e., identifying the candidate best suited to the role, using appropriately validated measures) in medicine have focused on prior academic attainment (Ferguson, James, & Madely, 2002; Patterson & Ferguson, 2007). At the undergraduate level, this has focused on wider general knowledge with an emphasis on science, and at the postgraduate level, clinical knowledge (McManus et al., 2005). While, undoubtedly, prior academic attainment is crucial to success in medicine, it is not the only predictive parameter (Ferguson et al., 2014). Indeed, academic attainment may only be predictive at early stages of undergraduate training, with the long-term power of academic attainment decreasing and diminishing to zero over time (Ferguson et al., 2014; Ferguson, James, O'Hehir, & Sanders, 2003). It may be argued that academic attainment is a necessary component to be a physician and that it acts to kick-start the learning process that then becomes self-sustaining along an academic backbone of learning and training (McManus, Woolf, Darce, Paice, & Dewberry, 2013). Indeed, medicine requires more skills than just academic attributes (see

Patterson et al., 2000; Patterson, Ferguson, & Thomas, 2008; Patterson, Ferguson, Lane, & Norfolk, 2005 and Chapters 4 and 11).

Focusing on prior academic attainment as the primary selection criteria creates a potential recruitment bias. That is, the general public and applicants will come to feel that medicine is primarily about academic skills, rather than seeing medicine as requiring other attributes. This will have the effect that only those who feel that they can achieve the necessary academic level will apply, which will narrow the applicant field. Those who feel they cannot achieve academically will not apply, with these individuals being more likely to be from deprived areas with poorer schooling (Powis, James, & Ferguson, 2007). Interestingly, it has been shown that simply applying to study medicine mitigates some of the negative effects of lower socioeconomic status (SES) on academic attainment (Ferguson, James, Yates, & Lawrence, 2012). Furthermore, with high competition ratios, a primary focus on prior academic attainment in selection also results in '*grade inflation*', with higher and higher grades required to study medicine (McManus et al., 2005), which further restricts the applicant pool in terms of social and psychological diversity. Thus, while keeping academic performance as a selection criterion, we need to advance the agenda so that other skills are also required, and to explore the best ways to characterize what these are with respect to recruitment. Here, I focus on one aspect that is crucial to staff, patients and the continued delivery of high-quality health care: altruism. Specifically, altruism has been highlighted as a key characteristic of the physician, their role in healthcare provision and as having a crucial role to play with respect to workforce planning (Jones, 2002).

What Is Altruism and How Does It Apply in Healthcare?

Altruism has been variously defined across the social and biological sciences (Batson, 1991; Bshary & Bergmüller, 2008; West, Mouden, & Gardner, 2011) so a brief review is provided. From an evolutionary perspective, altruism has a very specific definition: to increase *Darwinian fitness* (i.e., long-term survival and fecundity) of the recipient at a cost to the donor (usually long-term fitness) (Bshary & Bergmüller, 2008; West et al., 2011). While there is some debate over the precise definition of altruism, in healthcare roles it is argued that *psychological* altruism (motives for action) rather than *biological* altruism (Darwinian fitness; Sober & Wilson, 1998) should be the focus. As such, definitions of altruism from the social sciences (psychology and economics particularly) are more applicable to healthcare roles. Definitions of pure altruism across economics, psychology and philosophy tend to converge on the idea that altruism is either a preference for or an ultimate desire to maximize the welfare (utility) of others, by reducing their suffering, at a personal cost, without personal benefit (Andreoni, 1990; Batson, 1991; Nagal, 1970). This may be directed at another individual, group, organization or society (Ma, Tunney, & Ferguson, 2017). With this definition in mind, it is argued that altruism is central to the delivery of high-quality healthcare provision in the following ways.

First, most healthcare systems could not operate to meet and provide the levels of care and service they currently do without the voluntary actions of millions of people to provide (1) organs for transplantation, (2) blood for transfusion, (3) participants for medical trials and experiments, (4) staff for hospital radio, cafes, advice etc., (5) money and time to support medical charities, (6) patient and relative support groups, (7) herd immunity against the flu and so on (see Steinberg, 2010).

Second, physicians often list altruism (rarely defined) and traits linked to altruism (e.g., honesty, empathy, collegiality) as central to their profession (see Brownell & Côté, 2001; Chestnut, 2017). For example, when asked to rate their own values, physicians rate benevolence (directly linked to altruism) as the highest (Eliason, Guse, & Gottlieb, 2000) and thus altruism is viewed as a key defining quality of who they are and what they do.

Third, many healthcare systems (both private and public) list values linked to altruism as key to their operations. The UK National Health Service, for example, has six core values that reflect altruism as broadly defined by benefiting others, with compassion, equity and fairness. These consist of: (1) '*Working together with patients*' by putting the patient first; (2) '*Respect and Dignity*' based on a culture of humility and honesty with an openness to respect different needs and aspirations; (3)

'*Commitment to Quality Care*' by delivering safe and compassionate care for everyone based on a collective endeavor at all levels in the NHS; (4) '*Compassion*' by treating everyone with sensitivity and kindness; (5) '*Improving Lives*' by helping people and their communities to lead healthier lives and (6) '*Everyone Counts*' by ensuring that NHS resources are distributed fairly to those in need.

Having made the case of the importance of altruism in healthcare in general, what does the theory tell us about the mechanisms of altruism and how it might be best assessed in recruitment practices? From an evolutionary theory perspective, pure altruism is a paradox: how does a costly behavior, that benefits another, survive in the population (Nowak, 2006)? However, altruism is rarely pure (i.e., benefiting the survival of another, at personal cost, for no personal benefit) and a number of mechanisms of altruism (MOA) have been suggested to address the paradox of altruism (see Ferguson, 2015 for a detailed review). Indeed, altruism in healthcare settings will rarely be pure and will include some personal gain or strategic behavior (Jones, 2002). Going the extra mile to help a colleague may reflect an expectancy of direct reciprocity (you help others so they will help you in the future: Nowak, 2006), or helping make the medical professional feel good about themselves (the warm-glow of giving: Andreoni, 1990), or working longer unpaid hours to gain a positive reputation to aid promotion.

In assessing an individual's altruism, previous research has been based solely on self-reports which are open to social desirability bias and thereby problematic in selection and recruitment settings. When asked, no one will say they help others to gain favor, or feel good about themselves. To explore altruism in selection settings, it is argued that more objective measures are required and here we explore a range of economic games that have been specifically designed to assess altruistic behavior. In overview, these economic games examine how people allocate resources (usually money) between themselves and others. The pattern of allocations is used to infer aspects of altruism (which is often referred to as prosociality preferences in the economics literature). Once behavioral data is elicited from these games, then correspondence with specific aspects of self-reported altruism (e.g., guilt, reciprocity, trust, fairness) can also be explored (see Ferguson, 2015 for a review).

Assessing Altruism Behaviorally Using Economic Games

Detailed below are some economic games that could be used to assess altruism/prosociality in recruitment in healthcare. For descriptive purposes, we follow Zhao and Smillie (2015) and distinguish between *bargaining games* (usually involving two players and focusing on a trade-off between personal outcomes and the outcomes of others) and *social dilemmas* (usually involving multiple players and focusing on a trade-off between short-term self-interest and the long-term collective interests). Bargaining games are further differentiated into: (1) *unidirectional bargaining games*, where outcomes depend only on the choices of one individual, the decision maker (i.e., the power resides with the decision maker) (2) *bidirectional bargaining games*, where outcomes depend on a combination of the decisions of all individuals. In bidirectional games where there is a sequence of decisions, the initial decision (the first move) represents proactive prosociality. However, subsequent allocations (cooperation, defection or punishment) in a bidirectional game (second mover responses) represent reactive prosociality.

Unidirectional bargaining games: A classic example here is the *one-shot anonymous dictator game* (DG: Forsythe, Horowitz, Savin, & Sefton, 1994; Kahneman, Knetsch, & Thaler, 1986) (see Fig. 12.1). Here there are two players—a dictator and a recipient. The dictator has a financial endowment and can choose to transfer some, none or all to the recipient, who has nothing. The payoff for each is whatever the dictator decides. While the rational choice is to give nothing, dictators allocate 20–30% on average, and this is generally taken to index altruism and prosocial preferences (Engel, 2011).

Bidirectional bargaining games: A classic example here is the *ultimatum game* (UG; Güth, Schmittberger, & Schwarze, 1982) (Fig. 12.2). In the UG there are two players: a proposer and a recipient. The proposer has an endowment and the recipient, who has nothing, knows the value of that endowment. As in the proposer chooses how much of the endowment can be allocated to the recipient, but here the recipient can choose to accept or reject any offer the proposer makes. If the recipient accepts the offer then the proposer's division stands, but if they

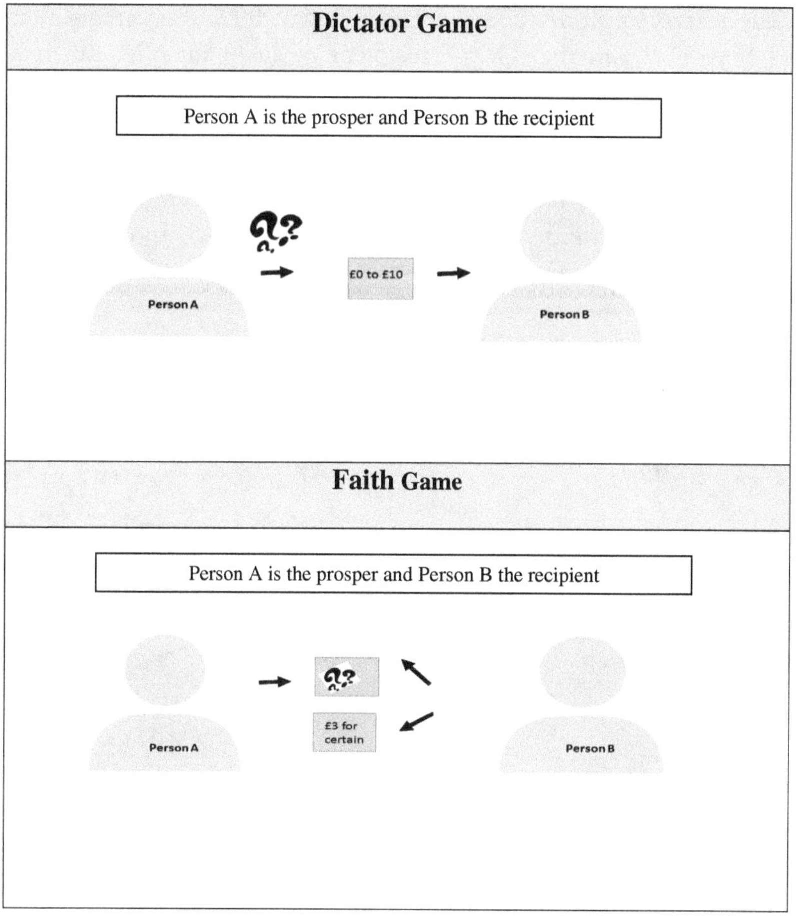

Fig. 12.1 Dictator and faith games

reject the offer both parties get nothing. The recipient should accept all offers as even 10% of any endowment is a better payoff than they started with (which is zero). In fact, recipients are more likely to reject offers as they become increasingly unfair (moving from a 50:50 share to a 90:10 where the first figure reflects the proposer's share and the second, the recipient's). Thus, the UG provides a direct assessment of punishment of unfairness by the recipient (negative reciprocity) or spite. The proposer's behavior indicates altruism and prosocial preferences.

The ***impunity game*** (IG: Yamagishi et al., 2009) is a variant of the UG (Fig. 12.2). In the IG, the recipient of an unfair offer can reject it and receive nothing (as in the standard UG) but this time it has no bearing on what the proposer gets, they still get what they offer. So, if the person offers £2 out of £10 (an unfair offer) and the recipient rejects it in the UG, both get nothing, whereas in the IG the recipient gets nothing and the person making the offer gets £8. Interestingly, in the IG, people still reject unfair offers even when the person making

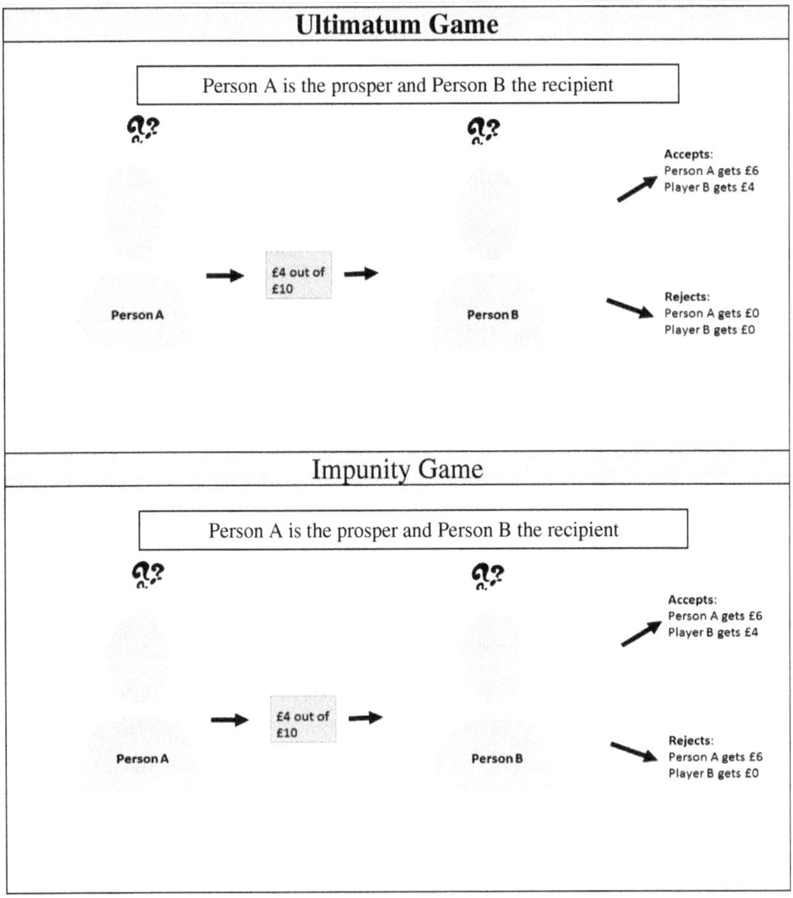

Fig. 12.2 Ultimatum and impunity games

the offer is unaware of whether or not they accept or reject it (this is called the private IG). The private IG reflects not just the emotional response of the recipient to unfairness but also provides some index of their self-image. That is, by rejecting they are signaling to themselves that they are a good person.

Social Dilemma Games. A classic social dilemma game is the *one-shot public goods game* (PGG) (Fig. 12.3), played in groups of four anonymous players. Each has an equivalent endowment (private account) and can contribute some, none, or all to a group (public) account. Whatever is contributed is summed, doubled and paid back equally to all members regardless of their initial contribution. Each person's payoff equals what they keep in their private accounts plus what is returned from the public account. The maximum payoff for the group is when everyone contributes maximally and equally. However, not contributing (free riding) will maximize the individuals' payoff, as long as other group members contribute something. When played over a number of rounds, cooperation levels start high and tend toward free riding. Contributing to the public account indicates cooperation, trust and prosocial preferences.

The prisoner's dilemma and trust games are other examples of social dilemmas. In the *prisoner's dilemma game* (PDG; Flood, 1958;), two players (A and B) simultaneously decide to cooperate (C) to benefit (*b*) the other at some personal cost (*c*) or defect (D) by acting selfishly. If both choose to defect, then neither gains the maximum payoff. If A chooses to cooperate and B chooses defect then B gains, as they have paid no cost, yet make a gain, whereas A has paid a cost. If both choose to cooperate then both gain as long as $b > c$. The PDG can be used to indicate both defection (punishment) and cooperation.

In the *trust game* (TG: Berg, Dickhaut, & McCabe, 1995) (Fig. 12.3), there are two players—an investor and a trustee. The investor has a financial endowment and can choose to invest some, none or all with the trustee, where the amount invested is multiplied (usually by a factor of 3 or 4). The trustee then decides how much (some, none or all) of this multiplied sum to return to the investor. The trustee can 'punish' the investor by returning an unfair or lower than expected amount if they feel the investor has been unfair in their offer. Thus, the investor's behavior is an indicator of trust and the trustee's behavior an indicator of positive (cooperation) or negative (punishment) reciprocity.

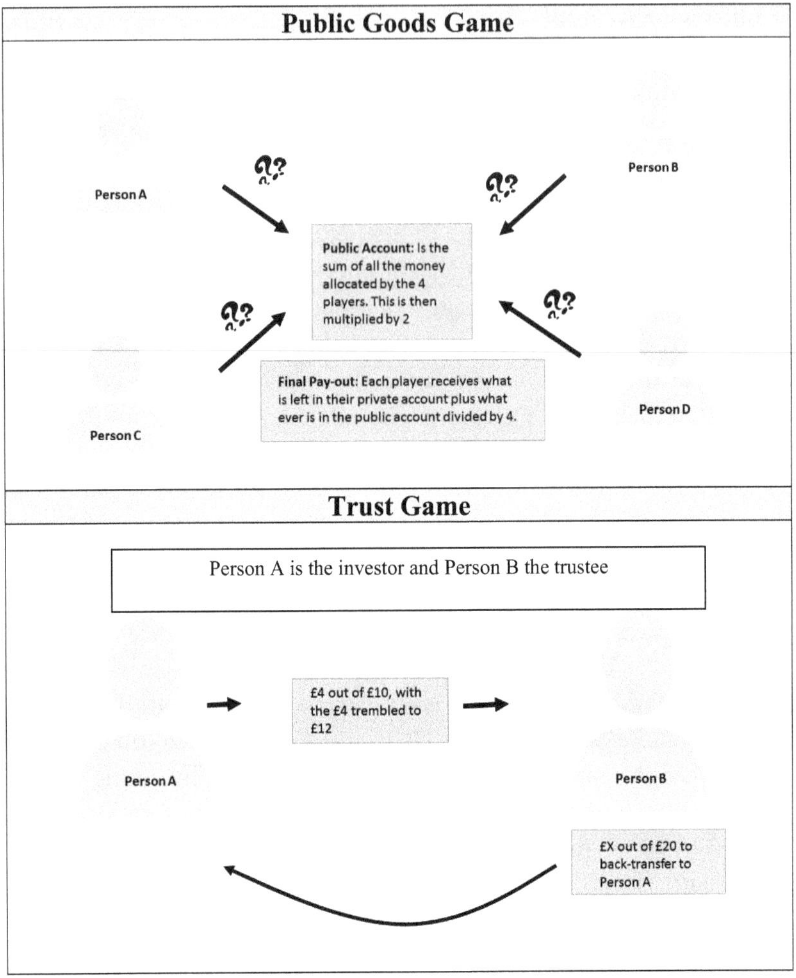

Fig. 12.3 Public goods and trust games

Punishment Effects. The standard one-shot public goods game (described above) can be extended to have multiple rounds where players know each other's identity and/or behavior on previous rounds (see Milinski, Semmann, Bakker, & Krambeck, 2001, for example), and/or include an option to punish free riders (2nd party punishment) at a personal cost (Fehr & Gachter, 2002). This type of punishment is open to 2nd order free riding (non-punishers free riding on others' punishment). Punishment options lead to increased cooperation, but reduced efficiency (less overall resources for the group). It is believed that punishing enforces norms of fairness and is potentially motivated by anger and moral emotions (Fehr & Fischbacher, 2004; Ma et al., 2017; Nelissen & Zeelenberg, 2009).

Punishment can be extended to what is known as 3rd party punishment where a player who is not part of a DG, TG or PGG (i.e., they are a third party) observes the behavior in the game and can punish observed unfairness (Fehr & Fischbacher, 2004) (see Fig. 12.4). For example, in a DG they can choose to pay to punish the dictator at a personal cost, based on the dictator's allocations. People tend to spend their own resources to punish dictators who act unfairly, and this is seen as reflecting people's endorsement of fairness norms, punishment, justice sensitivity, anger and moral outrage (Fehr & Fischbacher, 2004).

This idea can be extended to examine distributive justice choices: should you punish a transgressor or (re)compensate the victim (van Prooijen, 2010) (Fig. 12.4). That is, players who witness an unfair action of a dictator in a DG can either spend some of their money to punish the dictator, as the perpetrator of the unfairness, or to compensate the victim (Leliveld, van Dijk, & van Beest, 2012; Lotz, Okimoto, Schlösser, & Fetchenhauer, 2011). The latter is associated with personality traits reflecting compassion and empathy (Lotz et al., 2011; Zhao et al., 2017a) and justice sensitivity, empathic concern and compassion.

Healthcare Professionals, Altruism and Prosocial Preferences

These games (and other variants not detailed here) can be used to explore basic preferences for altruism, trust, fairness reciprocity and compassion in healthcare professionals. In applying this approach to selection in healthcare, how would healthcare professionals compared to non-healthcare professionals respond to a punishment-(re)compensation game? Would healthcare professionals show more compassion and compensate a victim or punish a transgressor? Would healthcare professionals treated unfairly in an UG be more or less likely to reject offers?

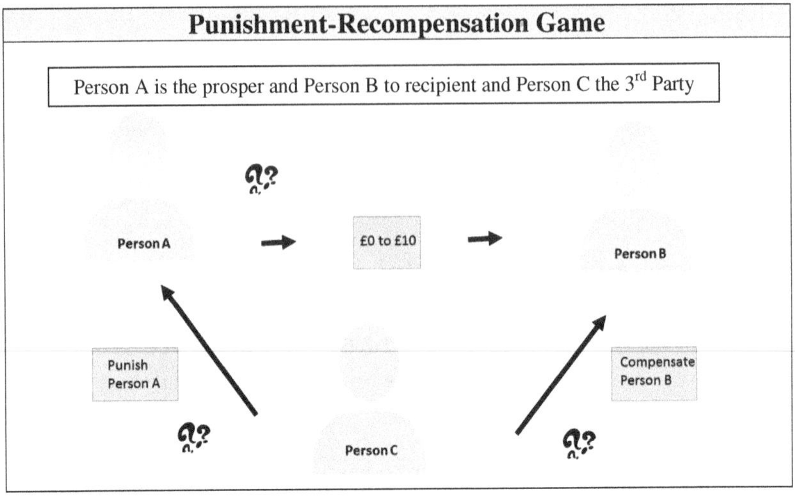

Fig. 12.4 Punishment–recompensation game

That is, are healthcare professionals more or less sensitive to injustice and unfairness? In postgraduate settings in medicine for example, does this vary by specialty (would surgeons and psychiatrists perform differently) and career stage—are early career physicians more tolerant of unfairness, and as they progress, less so? What about PGG games and cooperation? Are physicians who work more often in teams more likely to be cooperative in PGG and those who work more independently less so? By exploring questions such as these, it is possible to build a behavioral profile that characterizes altruism (prosociality) in healthcare professionals and so provide insights that cannot be gained from self-report assessments.

Games can be altered to assess different prosocial preferences. For example, with the DG game the standard DG picks up preferences associated with politeness, but when framed around norms of need and equity, picks up preferences of both politeness and compassion (Zhao et al., 2016, 2017b). This could be used, along with a punishment-(re)compensation game to look for consistency in preferences for compassion in healthcare professionals. The compassionate person will compensate the victim and give more in the framed DG. Empathy can be assessed in the DG by having the person play the role of both a dictator and a recipient and, seeing if their allocations as a dictator are different once they have experienced being a recipient (Andeoni & Rao, 2011). Moral relativism can also be assessed by the DG by including an option to take (List, 2007) as well as give in a variant of the DG (see the case study below for description of the warm-glow dictator game) (Ferguson & Flynn, 2016).

Thus, using behavioral economic games that assess altruism and prosocial preferences could open up new avenues of understanding what characterizes healthcare professionals' preferences for prosocial behavior, which in turn, could be used to develop recruitment campaigns and inform the design of selection tools in future. Below is a case study to illustrate this possibility.

Case Studies Using Behavioral Economics Games to Inform Recruitment Strategies

To illustrate how research from behavioral economics could be applied to research in healthcare selection and recruitment, we introduce two case studies in the context of behaviors that relate to blood and organ donation. Both types of donation have previously been viewed as pure altruistic acts but this assumption is based largely on self-report data which lacks objectivity. In our case material we summarize two research studies using behavioral economic games to explore the extent to which altruism is related to donation behavior. An interpretation of results is offered with a practical demonstration of how the learning can be used to design more effective recruitment campaigns in future. Such approaches are relevant to healthcare recruitment and selection.

The first case study explores blood donation behavior (see Case Study 12.1). Using variants of the charity dictator game, Ferguson, Taylor, Keatley, Flynn, and Lawrence (2012) showed that blood donors are driven to help by 'warm-glow' (defined as the extra emotional utility a person feels from the act of helping others, which may be both anticipated and experienced) and not pure altruism, as is often suggested. This suggests a shift in recruitment campaigns from pure altruism ('donate to save a life') to ones that focus on the actual warm-glow felt by donating blood. This behavioral data corroborates with actual predictors of attendance to donate and results show that warm-glow interventions are significantly more effective for recruiting blood donors (Ferguson, Farrell, & Lawrence, 2008).

Case Study 12.1. Are Blood Donors Altruistic?

Self-reported motivation and theoretical issue	Blood donation and pure altruism vs. warm-glow Traditionally seen by donors, recipients and the general public as an altruistic act. This based on both self-reports by donors and task analysis of blood donation. There is evidence that blood donors may be motivated by war-glow. Use economic games to test pure-altruism vs. warm-glow.
Behavioral economic games and results	**Dictator Games (Ferguson et al.,** 2012**)** Case–control approach: Compared blood donors to non-blood donors two variants of the charity dictator game (CDG). • Standard *st*-CDG: Participants had to decide how much ('some, none or all') of an endowment (£2 in 20p pieces) to donate to a charity of their choice. • Warm-glow *wg*-CDG: Same as the *st*-CDG, however, in this variant the participant is informed that the charity already has £2, by the experimenter, and that any money the participant donates to their chosen charity the experimenter will take the equivalent amount. Thus, the charity will always have £2 no matter how much the participant gives; therefore, the primary motivating has to be warm-glow. **Results** In the *st*-CDG, blood donors gave significantly less than non-donors. A complete reversal, however, was observed in the *wg*-CDG with, blood donors are now more generous than non-donors. **Interpretation** Blood donors are driven to help by warm-glow, and not pure altruism.

Recruitment strategies	Develop recruitment materials that move away from suggesting pure altruism to materials that reflect the personal gain in terms of warm-glow that a donor may get when donating blood. Testing this has shown that warm-glow materials are effective for repeat donors.
	Blood Donors, Fairness Norms and Punishment
Self-reported motivation and theoretical issue	Some evidence to suggest that blood donors may be more sensitive to violations of fairness norms Use the UG to explore if blood donors reject more unfair offers.
Behavioral economic games and results	**Ultimatum Game (Ferguson & Lawrence,** 2018**)** Case–control design: Compared blood donors and non-blood donors' rejection rates on the UG. **Results** Donors exhibited a higher rejections rates of unfair offers than non-donors. **Interpretation** Blood donors more sensitive to violations of fairness norms.
Recruitment strategies	Use recruitment materials that reflect the idea of reciprocal fairness. That we all need blood and if I am ever going to have a transfusion, or others, it is only fair that I also contribute. Again there is some evidence that this can be effective.

Case Study 12.2. Is Signing on the Posthumous Organ Donor Register Altruistic?

	Is signing on the posthumous organ donor register altruistic?
Self-reported motivation and theoretical issue	Traditionally seen as a pure altruistic act However, it may be the case that it is purely altruistic, as signing on the register is costless to the donor both at the time of registering and again when actually donating (they no longer need their organs at that point). We can test this behaviorally using the generosity game which assesses costless generosity.

Behavioral economic games and results	**Generosity and Dictator Games (Ferguson et al., under review)** Case–control design: Compared those on the organ donor register to those not on a standard DG (*st*-DG) and the generosity game (GG). • *st*-DG: Participants had to decide how much ('some, none or all') of an endowment to donate to a stranger. • GG: One player (the proposer) has a fixed amount of money (e.g., £5) to keep, and must decide how much of a given range of money (e.g., £0–£10) to give to another player (Güth et al., 2012) Because the proposer's own windfall is fixed at £5, the cost of allocating to the recipient is zero—the proposer will leave with £5 regardless of what they allocate to the recipient. **Results** Those on the organ donor register gave significantly more on the GG than those not on the register. There was no difference on DG allocations. **Interpretation** Those on the organ donor register show a behavioral preference to costless giving and not costly giving.
Recruitment strategies	Develop campaigns that empathize the generosity of donating organs, but indicate that this helps others tremendously at no cost to the donor.

The second case study (Case Study 12.2) focuses on recruitment of organ donors to the organ donor register. Again, it shows that organ donors are not motivated by pure altruism but more by 'costless generosity' (Ferguson, Zhao, O'Carroll, & Smillie, 2018). This suggests framing future recruitment campaigns around effortless generosity is a more effective strategy.

Behavioral Economics, Psychology, Healthcare Recruitment and Selection

Having explored the use of behavioral economics games to assess altruism and prosociality, what are the implications for recruitment and selection in healthcare?

Recruitment. It is argued that for a successful healthcare system, altruism and prosociality need to be encouraged and selected for in healthcare roles (Jones, 2002). In medicine specifically, altruism should be considered as a selection criterion which can help address a widening access agenda to signal that medicine is not just about academic attainment, but also about being compassionate and willing to cooperate with colleagues and 'go the extra mile' for both colleagues and patients. That said it is surprising to note how little, if anything at all, is really known about the mechanisms of altruism that underlies helping and cooperative behavior in healthcare workers in general. Using behavioral economic games, it would be possible, much like in the work on blood and organ donation described in the case studies above, to identify what mechanisms of altruism and prosociality, if any, are more likely to be expressed by healthcare workers compared to other professions. Furthermore, it is possible that preferences change with experience and status and future research could consider to what extent these preferences predict actual behavior indicative of altruism in the workplace (e.g., discretionary effort including working outside of contracted hours, helping a colleague after a shift etc.).

Future research could explore differences in preferences between medical specialties. For example, imagine a study where surgeons, psychiatrists, anesthetists and pediatricians all completed a 3rd party punishment-recompensation game and an impunity game. As there are sex differences in these types of games, we would want to ensure that we had an equal number of males and females in each and conduct subgroup analyses accordingly. We could look at job analysis data for these roles to make some tentative predictions. For example, we might expect all groups to be more likely to compensate in a 3rd party game (whereby an uninvolved bystander can spend some of their resources to punish a transgressor or compensate a victim) than nonmedical staff, as this would reflect greater compassion in medical staff than the general public. Within medical staff we might expect pediatricians to recompense the most since dealing with children may engender a greater sense of compassion. For the impunity game, we might expect a higher degree of rejection of unfair offers because in this game this reflects a sense of self-worth—I am a good person and even if no one else knows about it, I will still reject unfairness. That is, a medical professional may have a stronger sense of doing the right thing regardless. This type of analysis and finding would then inform future recruitment campaigns to focus on compassion to others, being morally self-consistent and doing the right thing (e.g., 'Are you the sort of person who does the right thing no matter what others might say, and you care about people… then medicine needs you').

A public good game could be used to explore cooperation in healthcare teams. Team work is a key to successful clinical practice and free riding disrupts successful team performance. We could explore whether healthcare professionals cooperate at a greater rate in a PGG than non-healthcare workers, as we might conjecture they would as they understand the importance of team work. We could introduce a 2nd party punishment option and explore whether healthcare workers punish free riders more than non-healthcare staff, again we might expect that they would. From a recruitment perspective, this would suggest that emphasizing the importance of being a team player is a key message to convey.

The above is merely illustrative but shows that applying behavioral economic games focused on prosocial preferences can enhance our understanding of what mechanisms underlie healthcare professionals' 'altruism'. This could not only increase our understanding of healthcare professionals' prosocial preferences but also guide recruitment strategies in future.

Selection. While knowledge from the above can be used to develop new approaches to recruitment campaigns, selection tools to address these preferences are needed. Patterson et al. (2016) have provided a detailed exploration of SJTs in medical education and selection and how they can be used to assess such values. In addition, psychometric tools could be used that focus on selection criteria like, compassion, politeness, fairness, reciprocity that have not traditionally been used in medical selection.

Key among these might be tools based on Haidt's (2007; See also Graham et al., 2011, 2012) moral foundations and Schwartz's (Schwartz, 1992, 2012) values. Haidt (2007) defines five moral foundations (Table 12.1) that include the traditional caring and reciprocity but also include group loyalty, authority and purity. All relate to altruism and all have relevance for medicine and healthcare professionals. These foundations can be grouped into two higher order domains that reflect '*Egalitarianism*' (Harm–Care and Fairness–Reciprocity)

Table 12.1 Haidt's Moral Foundations

Foundation	Definition	Higher-order concept
Harm-care	A moral reaction triggered by others' needs and distress, it is linked to both compassion for the victim as well as anger at perpetrators of unfairness, and embedded within evolutionary kin selection section theory	Egalitarianism
Fairness-reciprocity	A moral reaction and behavior in response to others' acts of cooperation or defection, which is linked to emotions of gratitude, anger and guilt and based on evolutionary reciprocity models	Egalitarianism
Ingroup-loyalty	A moral reaction triggered by threats to the persons in-group based on pride at one's group and anger at traitors, it is linked to evolutionary theories of group selection	Order-traditionalism'
Authority-respect	A moral reaction triggered by the social status/ranking of the other person/people and linked to emotions of respect	Order-traditionalism'
Purity-sanctity	A moral reaction triggered by waste products, disease, and linked to disgust	Order-traditionalism'

and '*Order-Traditionalism*' (Ingroup–Loyalty, Authority–Respect and Purity–Sanctity) (see Graham et al., 2011).

Likewise, Shwartz's 10 values can be organized across two bipolar dimensions (1) '*openness-to-change*' vs '*conservation*' and (2) '*self-enhancement*' vs '*self-transcendence*'. The '*Openness-to-change*' vs '*conservation*' captures the balance and conflict between values of being independent and open to change (self-direction and stimulation) and resistance to change and order (security, conformity and tradition). The '*self-enhancement*' vs '*self-transcendence*' bipolar dimension contrasts welfare and caring for others (universalism and benevolence) with self-interest (power and achievement) which maps onto prosociality.[1] The NHS values focus primarily on *self-transcendence* and again these could be used in selection materials (see Chapter 11 for a review of values-based recruitment).

Although there is a strong case for selecting for prosocial traits and values, it is important to offer a cautionary note as there might be several 'dark-sides' associated with selecting on prosocial values such as empathy (see Ferguson, 2017 for a review). When selecting on traits like empathy, one needs to be careful not to select people high in psychopathy unintentionally as psychopathy is characterized by high cognitive empathy (i.e., understanding what others think—perspective-taking) but low on emotional empathy (i.e., feeling for others) (Blair 2005, 2008). Hyper-Empathy is another concern especially for medical professionals. Hyper-Empathy occurs when empathy is very extreme to the extent that an individual may care so much for others that they neglect themselves (Baron-Cohen, 2012) and thus is potentially harmful to the individual as negating one's own needs (e.g., eating well, emotional support, etc.) can result in physical and psychological distress. Moreover, some research suggests that increased feelings of pain may also be linked to empathy for others in pain (Singer et al., 2004; see Bernhardt & Singer, 2012; Engen & Singer, 2013; Frith & Singer, 2008; Lamm, Decety, & Singer, 2011; Singer & Frith, 2005; Singer & Kimecki, 2014; for reviews), be it a loved one or a stranger (Cheng, Chen, Lin, Chou, & Decety, 2010). Singer et al. (2004) also showed that such neural responses to observing pain in another are stronger in those who score higher in trait empathic concern (Singer et al., 2004).

Thus, a healthcare professional facing pain in others on a daily basis may have their pain areas overly activated, especially if they score high on trait emotional empathy.

Conclusions

Altruism/prosociality is a key for high-quality healthcare provision and a part of the professional identity of healthcare professionals. In selection into healthcare, a focus on altruism and prosociality in addition to academic attainment, may help to widen the applicant pool (especially in medicine) in addition to opening up new avenues for selection research using interdisciplinary approaches. The application of behavioral economic games offers fresh insights into understanding altruism and prosociality in healthcare professionals. Further research in this new and uncharted area promises fresh approaches to development of recruitment campaigns and selection tools. Beyond selection, further research in this area may also help inform future curriculum, education and training design.

Note

1. Hedonism sits across '*Openness-to-change*' and '*self-enhancement*' as it contains elements of both.

References

Andreoni, J. (1990). Impure altruism and donations to public goods: A theory of warm glow giving. *Economic Journal, 100,* 464–4877.

Andreoni, J., & Rao, J. M. (2011). The power of asking: How communication affects selfishness, empathy and altruism. *Journal of Public Economics, 95,* 513–520.

Baron-Cohen, S. (2012). Autism, Empathizing-Systematizing (E-S) theory, and pathological altruism. In B. Oakley, A. Knafo, G. Madhava, & D.

S. Wilson (Eds.), *Pathological altruismi* (pp. 345–348). Oxford: Oxford University Press.

Batson, C. D. (1991). *The altruism question: Toward a social-psychological answer* (pp. 1–257). Hillsdale, NJ: Erlbaum.

Berg, J., Dickhaut, J., & McCabe, K. (1995). Trust, reciprocity and social history. *Games and Economic Behavior, 10,* 122–142.

Bernhardt, B. C., & Singer, T. (2012). The neural basis of empathy. *Annual review of neuroscience, 35,* 1–23.

Blair, R. J. P. (2005). Responding to the emotions of others: Dissociating form of empathy through the study of typical and psychiatric populations. *Consciousness and Cognition, 14,* 698–718. https://doi.org/10.1016/jconcog.2005.06.004.

Blair, R. J. P. (2008). Fine cuts of empathy and the amygdale: Dissociable deficits in psychopathy and autism. *Quarterly Journal of Experimental Psychology, 61,* 157–170. https://doi.org/10.1080/1740210701508855.

Brownell, A. K. W., & Côté, L. (2001). Senior residents' views on the meaning of professionalism and how they learn about it. *Academic Medicine, 76*(7), 734–737.

Bshary R., & Bergmüller, R. (2008). Distinguishing four fundamental approaches to the evolution of helping. *Journal of Evolutionary Biology, 21,* 405–420.

Burks, D. J., & Kobus, A. M. (2012). The legacy of altruism in health care: The promotion of empathy, prosociality and humanism. *Medical Education, 46,* 317–325.

Cheng, Y., Chen, C., Lin, C. P., Chou, K. H., & Decety, J. (2010). Love hurts: An fMRI study. *NeuroImage, 51,* 923–929. https://doi.org/1016/j.neuroimage.2010.02.047.

Chestnut, D. H. (2017). On the road to professionalism. *Anesthesiology: The Journal of the American Society of Anesthesiologists, 126*(5), 780–786.

Eliason, B. C., Guse, C., & Gottlieb, M. S. (2000). Personal values of family physicians, practice satisfaction, and service to the underserved. *Archives of Family Medicine, 9,* 228–232.

Engel, C. (2011). Dictator games: A meta study. *Experimental Economics, 14,* 583–610.

Engen, H. G., & Singer, T. (2013). Empathy circuits. *Current opinion in neurobiology, 23*(2), 275–282.

Fehr, E., & Fischbacher, U. (2004). Third-party punishment and social norms. *Evolution and Human Behavior, 25,* 63–87.

Fehr, E., & Gachter, S. (2002). Altruistic punishment in humans. *Nature, 415,* 137–140.

Ferguson, E. (2015). Mechanisms of altruism approach to blood donor recruitment and retention: A review and future directions. *Transfusion Medicine, 25,* 211–226. https://doi.org/10.1111/tme.12233.

Ferguson, E., Buttery, A., Miles, G., Tatalia, C., Clarke, D. D., Lonsdale, A. J., Baxendale, B., & Lawrence, C. (2014). Self and peer assessed non-technical skills in medical education: Effects of emotions and rater bias. *BMC Medical Education, 14,* 240. https://doi.org/10.1186/s12909-014-0240-y.

Ferguson, E., Farrell, K., & Lawrence, C. (2008). Blood donation is an act of benevolence rather than altruism. *Health Psychology, 27,* 327–336. https://doi.org/10.1037/0278-6133.27.3.327.

Ferguson, E., & Flynn, N. (2016). Moral relativism as a disconnect between behavioural and experienced warm glow. *Journal of Economic Psychology, 56,* 163–175. https://doi.org/10.1016/j.jeop.2016.06.002.

Ferguson, E., James, D., & Madely, L. (2002). Factors associated with success in medical school: Systematic review of the literature. *British Medical Journal, 324,* 952–957. https://doi.org/10.1136/bmj.324.7343.952.

Ferguson, E., James, D., O'Hehir, F., & Sanders, A. (2003). A pilot study of the roles of personality, references and personal statements in relation to performance over the 5 years of a medical degree. *British Medical Journal, 326,* 429–431. https://doi.org/10.1136/bmj.326.7386.429.

Ferguson, E., James, D., Yates, J., & Lawrence, C. (2012). Predicting who applies to study medicine: Implication for diversity in UK medical schools. *Medical Teacher, 34,* 382–391.

Ferguson, E., & Lawrence, C. (2018). It's only fair: Blood donors are more sensitive to violations of fairness norms than non-donors—Converging psychometric and ultimatum game evidence. *Vox Sanguinis* (in press).

Ferguson, E., Semper, H., Yates, J., Fitzgerald, J. E., Skatova, A., & James, D. (2014). The 'dark side' and 'bright side' of personality: When too much conscientiousness and too little anxiety are detrimental to the acquisition of medical knowledge and skill. *PLoS One, 9,* 2, article e8860. https://doi.org/10.1371/journal.pone.0088606.

Ferguson, E., Taylor, M., Keatley, D., Flynn, N., & Lawrence, C. (2012). Blood donors' helping behavior is driven by warm glow more evidence for the blood donor benevolence hypothesis. *Transfusion, 52,* 2189–2200. https://doi.org/10.1111/j.1537-2995.2011.03557.x.

Ferguson, E., Zhao, K., O'Carroll, R. E., & Smillie, L, D. (2018). Costless and costly pro-sociality: Correspondence among personality traits, economic preferences, and real world pro-sociality. *Social Psychology and Personality Science* (in press).

Flood, M. M. (1958). Some experimental games. *Management Science, 5*(1), 5–26.

Frith, C. D., & Singer, T. (2008). The role of social cognition in decision making. *Philosophical Transactions of the Royal Society of London B: Biological Sciences, 363*(1511), 3875–3886.

Forsythe, R., Horowitz, J. L., Savin, N. E., & Sefton, M. (1994). Fairness in simple bargaining experiments. *Games and Economic Behavior, 6,* 347–369.

Graham, J., Haidt, J., Koleva, S., Motyl, M., Iyer, R., Wojcik, S. P., & Ditto, P. H. (2012). *Moral Foundation Theory: The Pragmatic validity of moral pluralism.* http://www-bcf.usc.edu/~jessegra/papers/GHKMIWD.inpress.MFT.AESP.pdf.

Graham, J., Nosek, B. A., Haidt, J., Iyer, R., Koleva, S., & Ditto, P. H. (2011). Mapping the moral domain. *Journal of Personality and Social Psychology, 101,* 366–385.

Güth, W., Schmittberger, R., & Schwarze, B. (1982). An experimental analysis of ultimatum bargaining. *Journal of Economic Behavior & Organization, 3*(4), 367–388.

Haidt, J. (2007). The new synthesis in moral psychology. *Science, 316,* 998–1002.

Hallsworth, M., Chadborn, T., Sallis, A., Sanders, M., Berry, D., Greaves, F., …, Davisd, S. C. (2016). Provision of social norm feedback to high prescribers of antibiotics in general practice: A pragmatic national randomized controlled trial. *Lancet, 387,* 1743–1752. https://doi.org/10.1016/50140-6736(16)00215-4.

Jones, R. (2002). Declining altruism in medicine. *British Medical Journal, 324,* 624–625.

Kahneman, D., Knetsch, J. L., & Thaler, R. H. (1986). Fairness and the assumptions of economics. *Journal of Business, 59*(4), S285–S300.

Lamm, C., Decety, J., & Singer, T. (2011). Meta-analytic evidence for common and distinct neural networks associated with directly experienced pain and empathy for pain. *Neuroimage, 54*(3), 2492–2502.

Leliveld, M. C., van Dijk, E., & van Beest, I. (2012). Punishing and compensating others at your own expense: The role of empathic concern on reactions to distributive injustice. *European Journal of Social Psychology, 42*(2), 135–140.

List, J. A. (2007). On the interpretation of giving in dictator games. *Journal of Political Economy, 115,* 482–493.

Lotz, S., Okimoto, T. G., Schlösser, T., & Fetchenhauer, D. (2011). Punitive versus compensatory reactions to injustice: Emotional antecedents to third-party interventions. *Journal of Experimental Social Psychology, 47*(2), 477–480. https://doi.org/10.1016/j.jesp.2010.10.004.

Ma, L., Tunney, R., & Ferguson, E. (2017). Does gratitude enhance prosociality: A meta-analytic review. *Psychological Bulletin, 143,* 601–635. https://doi.org/10.1037/bul0000103.

McManus, I. C., Powis, D. A., Wakeford, R., Ferguson, E., James, D. K., & Richards, P. (2005). Why intellectual aptitude test ate not useful for selecting UK medical students but A-levels could once more be effective. *British Medical Journal, 331,* 555–559.

McManus, I. C., Woolf, K., Darce, J., Paice, E., & Dewberry, C. (2013). The academic backbone: Longitudinal continues in educational achievement from secondary school and medical school to MRCP(UK) and the specialist register in UK medical students and doctors. *BMC Medicine, 11,* 242. https://doi.org/(10.1186/1741-7015-11-242).

Milinski, M., Semmann, D., Bakker, T. C., & Krambeck, H. J. (2001). Cooperation through indirect reciprocity: Image scoring or standing strategy?. *Proceedings of the Royal Society of London B: Biological Sciences, 268*(1484), 2495–2501.

Nagal, T. (1970). *The possibility of altruism.* London: Oxford University Press.

Nelissen, R. M., & Zeelenberg, M. (2009). Moral emotions as determinants of third-party punishment: Anger, guilt and the functions of altruistic sanctions. *Judgment and Decision making, 4*(7), 543.

Nowak, M. A. (2006). Five rules for the evolution of cooperation. *Science, 314*(5805), 1560–1563.

Patterson, F., & Ferguson, E. (2007). *Selecting for medical education and training.* Edinburgh: Association for the Study of Medical Education (ASME).

Patterson, F., Ferguson, E., Lane, P., Farrell, K., Martlew, J., & Wells, A. (2000). A competency model of general practice: Implications for selection, training and development. *British Journal of General Practice, 50,* 188–193.

Patterson, F., Ferguson, E., Lane, P., & Norfolk, T. (2005). A new selection system to recruit GPRS. *British Medical Journal, 330,* 711–714.

Patterson, F., Ferguson, E., & Thomas, S. (2008). Using job analysis to identify core and specific competencies for three secondary care specialties: Implications for selection and recruitment. *Medical Education, 42,* 1195–1204.

Patterson, F., Prescott-Clements, L., Zibarras, L., Edwatds, H., Kerrin, M., & Cousans, F. (2016). Recruiting for values in healthcare: A preliminary review of the evidence. *Advances in Health Sciences and Education, 21,* 859–881.

Powis, D., James, D., & Ferguson, E. (2007). Demographic and socio-economic associations with UCAS tariff scores in applicants to medical school. *Medical Education, 41,* 242–249.

Rice, T. (2013). The behavioral economics of health and health care. Annual *Review of Public Health, 34*, 4341–447. https://doi.org/10.1146/annrev-pubhealth-031912-114353.

Roth, A., Sonmer, T., & Unver, M. U. (2004). Kidney exchange. *Quarterly Journal of Economics, 119,* 457–488.

Schwartz, S. H. (1992). Universals in the content and structure of values: Theoretical advances and empirical tests in 20 counties. *Advances in Experimental Social Psychology, 25,* 17–22.

Schwartz, S. H. (2012). An overview of Schwartz theory of basic values. *Online Readings in Psychology and Culture, 22,* 11.

Singer, T., & Frith, C. (2005). The painful side of empathy. *Nature neuroscience, 8*, 845–846. https://doi.org/10.1038/nn0705-845.

Singer, T., & Klimecki, O. M. (2014). Empathy and compassion. *Current Biology, 24*(18), R875–R878.

Singer, T., Seymour, B., O'Doherty, J., Kaube, H., Dolan, R. J., & Frith, C. (2004). Empathy for pain involves the affective but not sensory components of pain. *Science, 303*, 1157–1161. https://doi.org/10.1038/narure04271.

Sober, E., & Wilson, D. S. (1998). *Unto others: The evolution and psychology of unselfish behaviour* (pp. 1–39). Cambridge: Harvard University Press.

Steinberg, D. (2010). Altruism in medicine: Its definition, nature, and dilemmas. *Cambridge Quarterly of Healthcare Ethics, 19*(2), 249–257.

van Prooijen, J. W. (2010). Retributive versus compensatory justice: Observers' preference for punishing in response to criminal offenses. *European Journal of Social Psychology, 40*(1), 72–85.

West, S. A., Mouden, C. E., & Gardner, A. (2011). Sixteen common misconceptions about the evolution of cooperation in humans. *Evolution and Human Behavior, 32,* 231–262.

Yamagishi, T., Horita, Y., Takagishi, H., Shinda, M., Tanida, S., & Cook, K. S. (2009). The private rejection of unfair offers and emotional commitment. *Proceedings of the National Academy of Science, 106*, 11520–11523. www.pnas.org/cgi/doi/10.1073/pnas.0900636106.

Zhao, K., Ferguson, E., & Smillie, L. (2017a). Politeness and compassion differentially predict adherence to fairness norms and interventions to norm violation. *Scientific Reports, 7,* 3415. https://doi.org/10.1038/s41598-017-02952-1.

Zhao, K., Ferguson, E., & Smillie, L. (2017b). Individual differences in good manners rather than compassion predict fair allocations in wealth in the dictator game. *Journal of Personality, 85,* 244–256. https://doi.org/10.1111/jopy.12237.

Zhao, K., & Smillie, L. D. (2015). The role of interpersonal traits in social decision making: Exploring sources of behavioral heterogeneity in economic games. *Personality and Social Psychology Review, 19,* 277–302. https://doi.org/10.1177/1088868314553709.

Zhao, K., Smillie, L., & Ferguson, E. (2016). Prosocial personality traits differentially predict egalitarianism, generosity, and reciprocity in economic games. *Frontiers in Psychology, 7,* 1137. https://doi.org/10.3389/fpsyg.2016.01137.

13

Reflections on the Future Challenges for Researchers and Practitioners in Selection for Healthcare

Fiona Patterson and Lara Zibarras

Our book presents new insights in selection research in healthcare including the evidence for different selection methods, the key issues regarding the design of selection systems and broader challenges regarding recruitment processes. We bring together a collection of international case material that demonstrates some of these issues in practice. In this chapter, we summarise emerging findings, synthesize key learnings and use this as a platform to offer topics for future research.

F. Patterson
Work Psychology Group, Derby, UK
e-mail: f.patterson@workpsychologygroup.com

L. Zibarras (✉)
Department of Psychology, City, University of London, London, UK
e-mail: Lara.Zibarras.1@city.ac.uk

F. Patterson and L. Zibarras (eds.), *Selection and Recruitment in the Healthcare Professions*, https://doi.org/10.1007/978-3-319-94971-0_13

Summary of Findings

The first part of our book reviews evidence for different selection methods where the field has matured over the past decade with good-quality research evidence emerging to guide practitioners. Historically, selection (especially in medicine) has relied heavily on previous academic achievement to select. The evidence is now clear that many other skills and attributes are required beyond academic ability for an individual to be successful in a career within healthcare.

Regarding *Aptitude Tests* (Chapter 2), the evidence is variable, so we suggest that the quality and appropriateness of each tool needs to be judged separately. Some tests focus on fluid intelligence (e.g. general IQ) whilst others focus on crystallized abilities (e.g. scientific knowledge) and so recruiters must decide what type of test best fits their strategic goals and selection policy. In addition, a key question is whether recruiters wish to select those with the greatest aptitude for being a successful student or whether the main goal is to select those with the greatest aptitude to become competent practitioners. A key issue here is defining what is meant by a 'competent healthcare practitioner' (outlined in Chapter 6).

Various *Personality Traits* (Chapter 3) are shown to be linked to a range of in-training outcomes including those relating to well-being and performance. Again, there is a plethora of different personality assessment tools and each needs to be judged in its own right. Research developments in this area show that personality assessment can potentially aid selection practices, although great care needs to be taken in how it is used. For example, recent research shows that applicants can engage in substantial response distortion in completing personality assessments in medical selection (Anglim, Bozic, Little, & Lievens, 2018). Therefore, evidence suggests that personality assessments should only be used alongside other selection tools, such as to guide questioning in interviews regarding one's behavior, for example. In linking selection to educational interventions, information from accurate personality assessment can be used to help develop a richer dialogue regarding educational and training needs early in the curriculum.

Situational Judgement Tests (Chapter 4) are now being used across the globe to assess non-academic personal attributes for recruitment in healthcare. The evidence for validity is generally positive and SJTs have been shown to be less susceptible to sub-group differences than other tools, especially regarding socioeconomic status. The construct validity of SJTs has been questioned over time and we now understand that as SJTs are a measurement method (and there is no one single type of test), the construct validity (and reliability) can vary significantly depending on the specific tool. Although SJTs can be relatively costly to design, they can be machine-marked and delivered online, producing cost savings in high-volume selection.

Due to their improved reliability and validity over traditional interviews, *Structured Interviews and Multiple-Mini Interviews* (Chapter 5) are increasingly being used in a healthcare context. MMIs are the most structured type of interview and typically comprise six or more interview stations, which broadens the sampling of performance to enhance reliability. Interviews create the opportunity for an interaction with applicants, although this can be resource-intensive to deliver when they are face-to-face interviews. New developments in technology are exploring ways in which the efficiency can be significantly improved (e.g. asynchronous video interviewing, see Case Study 13.2 in this chapter). Candidates generally prefer interviews to other methods.

Far less research has explored issues in the selection systems design; and in our book, the evidence for the cornerstone of selection, *Role Analysis* studies (Chapter 6) is reviewed. Few studies have explored how adopting *Modular Approaches to Selection System Design* could help recruiters and researchers innovate in future (Chapter 7). Here, researchers are encouraged to investigate how different combinations of selection methods can lead to new hybrid selection procedures and impact on key selection outcomes such as validity, adverse impact and applicant perceptions. In turn, very little is known about how to best weight and sequence selection methods in a selection process to achieve the desired goal and further research is required in this area.

Candidate perceptions (Chapter 8) is an increasingly important consideration. This chapter explores why this is the case, particularly in a healthcare context. Research shows that negative reactions can result in the loss of good applicants from the selection process, legal challenges and reduce the quality of the applicant pool. The chapter also explores practical tips for ensuring that applicants leave the process feeling positive about their experience.

Very little research has explored the issues surrounding access to *Coaching* (Chapter 9), yet when tests are used to make selection decisions, it has become increasingly common for candidates to use commercial coaching services to improve their score. This chapter explores the issues raised by the coaching industry and the extent to which it is problematic in this context.

Widening Access to the healthcare professions (especially medicine) is a long-standing and now burgeoning issue, and yet, evidence-based practical guidance in how best to design selection systems to address this issue is still lacking (Chapter 10). There remains a significant gap between political directives and policy enactment within medical education, especially to increase diversity and widen participation; and further research is required to guide practitioners in future.

Since more emphasis is being placed on how best to select for important non-academic attributes in the healthcare professions (beyond academic ability), both theory developments and case material is presented on *Values-based recruitment* on this topic in Chapter 11. Through the case material presented, values-based recruitment is one example where UK government policy directives have directly influenced all recruitment processes, as all UK healthcare educational programmes must now ensure that an individual's values are assessed as part of selection. As time unfolds, it will be important to evaluate the extent to which this policy directive has impacted the workforce. In addition, for anyone entering a career within healthcare, it is argued that *Altruism* and *Prosociality* are important requirements (Chapter 12) which should be encompassed within approaches to selection and recruitment, which in turn might positively impact widening access. Here, new theoretical insights from interdisciplinary research are presented and approaches to selection are reviewed using new paradigms from behavioral economics.

Implications for Future Policy and Practice

As the field of selection and recruitment has significantly advanced over the past decade, there is currently an increasing use of more 'evidence-based' approaches to selection in practice. However, it remains notable that many continue to use selection methods that have little or no research evidence supporting them (e.g. personal statements, references) and as such there remains a substantial gap between research and practice. Reflecting on the issues presented in our book, it is clear that more work is required to translate existing research findings into practice. In this respect, there is still much to be discovered to offer clear practical guidance for those involved in designing and implementing selection systems in healthcare. Our authors have provided practical case examples in our book wherever possible, but further work in interpreting the latest research into practical and policy guidance is urgently needed. Moreover, it is clear that there is no 'one best way' as choices in selection process design are heavily influenced by a multitude of different contextual factors and stakeholder requirements.

As a first step in this journey, we must first understand how policy makers consume and use research evidence to guide future policy directives. Below we present a UK case example (Case Study 13.1) of how the regulator, the General Medical Council (GMC) and the UK Medical Schools Council (the representative body for UK medical schools and forum for schools to provide expert opinion on areas of medical education) have used research evidence to guide future policy on widening participation in selection for medicine. A key message is for researchers to translate their results into 'hard-hitting' statistics that can be readily understood by a broad audience in order to impact policy and practice.

Case Study 13.1: How Do Policy Makers Use Research? A Selection Case Study

Clare Owen (UK Medical Schools Council) and Terence Stephenson (General Medical Council, UK).

The best policy development is driven by evidence. Whilst regulators like the General Medical Council (GMC) and representative bodies such as the Medical Schools Council (MSC) are subject to numerous policy drivers, including the needs and wants of government and other stakeholders, they also have a responsibility to ensure that they respond to these drivers in an evidence-based way. The development of policy relating to the selection of medical students in the UK is a good example of this.

In 2012, the GMC looked at its data on selection methods and found that medical schools were selecting students in a variety of ways. At the same time, the UK government began to focus on widening participation.

The GMC commissioned a research team to explore selection and widening participation. They found that although there were a variety of selection processes being used to select medical students, there was no evidence base to justify this variation. It also found differing approaches to widening participation.

As a response to this research report the MSC, as the representative body for UK medical schools, set up the Selecting for Excellence project to look at selection with a focus on widening participation. The recommendations of the Selecting for Excellence project are being taken forward by the MSC Selection Alliance (MSCSA). Some examples of the way research have shaped this policy development include:

- *Multiple Mini-Interviews*—A report by Cleland, Patterson, Dowell, & Nicholson in 2014 recommended that MSC should work with medical schools to facilitate the sharing of MMI items and the building of an evidence base as to the effectiveness of different forms of MMI items. MSCSA took the first step towards actioning this recommendation when it held a collaborative MMI station writing workshops.
- *Contextual admissions*—Contextual admissions is a process whereby an application is considered in the light of the individual applicant's context; for example, their socio-economic background or the type of school they attended. Research by Cleland et al. in 2015 found that 'a combination of several weak contextual admissions markers does not automatically improve reliability and accuracy'. Instead they recommended that medical schools look at an individual's performance in relation to the average academic attainment of the school they attended. MSCSA has a data monitoring group that is looking at contextual measures to see if there is a relationship between this cohort of students and other widening participation measures.

Conclusions

- Research is an important tool in ensuring that policy development is evidenced based.
- Research can be used to legitimize recommendations and increase the acceptability of policy development for stakeholders.
- What policy makers need from research are 'hard-hitting statistics' and actions that could be implemented both in the short term as well as the medium term.

The 2018 Ottawa Consensus Statement on Selection and Recruitment

At the time of writing this book, there has recently been a new Ottawa consensus statement published on selection and recruitment to the healthcare professions (referred to in Chapter 1; see Patterson et al., 2018 for the full statement). The statement was devised as part of an international collaboration between experts in selection. Reflecting the available evidence at the time, the previous consensus statement (Prideaux et al., 2011) focused largely on the quality of different selection methods. The updated statement reflects progression within the field, to also consider new issues including: selection philosophies and policies; methodological concerns (beyond psychometric issues); social accountability, diversity and fairness; new evaluation frameworks and developments in theory.

Many of the issues discussed in the 2018 statement resonate with the research findings presented by our authors in our book and our authors provide a detailed analysis of various selection methods and issues in recruitment. The consensus statement also acknowledges that there exists a gap between research and practice and with the key recommendations provided as a guide to future work required to address these issues (see Table 13.1 and Patterson et al., 2018 for the full paper).

Key Challenges for Future Research

Having reflected on the evidence presented, we propose seven key challenges as priority topics for future research and debate (acknowledging that this list is not exhaustive), linked to implications for policy and practice. We also present additional case material for our readers to explore the issues.

Table 13.1 Ottawa 2018 consensus statement on selection and recruitment recommendations (Patterson et al., 2018)

1.	Use **validated taxonomies of desirable behaviors** that indicate success as a healthcare practitioner to judge the quality of selection, which are contextualized and relevant across stages of training
2.	Develop **more sophisticated research designs and methodologies to evaluate the validity of selection practices**, using multi-site high quality data sets, that take differences into context and content of selection practices into account
3.	Consider the opportunities and challenges of using **complex big data approaches to evaluate selection policies and practices linked to health outcomes**
4.	Explore ways in which **social accountability** agendas of universities support **social inclusion**, address **workforce issues**, and navigate *government and institutional policy* issues while including the **patient perspective**
5.	Methods of selection must ensure **fairness** and **accountability** for all candidates. Research is required to explain why there is significant **variation** in differing contexts with respect to approaches to address **diversity and widening access**. In addition, more robust evidence is required to evaluate the effectiveness of **outreach, targeting strategies, preparation programmes** and other means to **widening access**
6.	Research is required to better understand the role that selection and recruitment practices might play, in influencing the **high migration rates** of health profession graduates from many developing countries to those in the developed world
7.	The opportunities and challenges of enacting **large scale, nationally coordinated** approaches to selection should be compared and contrasted with **local arrangements** for selection and recruitment in different contexts
8.	Consider working with economists in policy planning that uses **econometric evaluation and cost benefit analysis** of the infrastructure required for delivering selection processes, selection methods, decision-making and reporting in a range of contexts internationally
9.	Use **interdisciplinary theoretical frameworks** to facilitate the future development of both selection policy and practice using appropriate methodologies which are sensitive to local contextual priorities.
10.	Investigate systematic approaches that can ensure a **greater translation of selection research evidence into policies and practice**

Challenge 1. Healthcare is a Rapidly Changing Environment; How Should Selection Criteria be Defined in Future?

In Chapter 6, Kerrin, Morley, Flaxman, Mossop and Fleming explore the proposition that selection design should involve future-oriented role analysis studies and the use of evidence from validation studies to continually improve accuracy and fairness in developing selection criteria. They recommend using multi-source, multi-method approaches and show how previous research has tended to focus on a single job role to define selection criteria. Given that healthcare is increasingly delivered in multi-professional teams, researchers should explore more sophisticated role analysis methods that more adequately account for the contingencies and temporal dynamics of how healthcare workers operate within highly complex organizations. It is also clear that improvements in technology will dramatically change the way in which healthcare is delivered in future and role analysis and work design studies must account for such complex human–machine interactions to understand how healthcare workers can optimize such advances.

We also note that many of the current selection criteria used do not necessarily reflect the competency domains that will be required of clinicians in future, such as resilience, flexibility, use of technology, creativity and innovation (Patterson & Zibarras, 2017). Here, role analysis research findings can also be linked to educational interventions and curriculum design in future.

Challenge 2: Technology and Social Media will Fundamentally Change the Way Selection is Delivered and Perceived in Future

More research is urgently required to understand how technology and social media will influence the quality and delivery of different selection methods and recruitment systems. Similarly, research could explore how machine learning can be used to evaluate selection decisions and systems (see Chapter 2, Kelly, Tiffin, & Mwandigha). Although it is likely that the use of enhanced technology in selection will improve efficiency, a key question is whether this will lead to better validity of selection decisions.

To illustrate some of the issues, we present case material where the use of technology can be viewed as beneficial to both candidates and to healthcare educators and trainers. In Case Study 13.2, *The NHS Leadership Academy's usage of Asynchronous Video Interviewing*, we explore the extent to which technology has been useful in this context. It is likely that these kinds of technologies will be increasingly used in the future in healthcare selection. The use of technology or web-based selection may have significant impact in the way selection is conducted, and also candidate perceptions since personal contact with organizational representatives will be established much later in the selection process (explored in Chapter 8, Zibarras). Although web-based technologies may speed up the application and selection process, this may also result in expectations of reduced response times from candidates which may not be realistic in healthcare education and training. However, it is also important to consider the potential risk of adverse impact (negatively influencing widening access) since certain groups of candidates may not have access to the speed of Internet access required to complete online selection tests (Konradt et al., 2013). Similarly, lack of invigilation of test-takers may result in applicants cheating, or possibly generate a perceived sense of 'unfairness' amongst applicants. Finally, organizations need to be aware of issues around privacy or confidentiality due to the transition of personal data (via tests and/or web-based interviews).

The rise of social media may also significantly impact selection processes in the future. Many employers outside of the healthcare professions currently using social networking sites to research job candidates, and this trend is likely to continue. From the candidate's perspective, this may be an invasion of privacy, and concerns may also be raised in terms of how information is collected, obtained and then stored. However, from an organization's perspective, social media can also pose a challenge: recently Virgin Media conducted a "rejected candidate" survey in which they found that 18% of applicants were customers. In the survey, they found that 7500 applicants (6%) switched to a competitor due to a poor recruitment experience, which resulted in £4.4m in lost revenue (https://www.fastcompany.com/3058571/how-your-companys-lame-hiring-process-is-losing-you-customers). Whilst in healthcare it might not be so easy to "switch provider", the rise of social media has enabled negative publicity to quickly 'go viral'.

Case Study 13.2: The NHS Leadership Academy's Usage of Asynchronous Video Interviewing

Joy Redmund, Head of Research at Sonru

The Aspiring Chief Executive program prepares current NHS directors with the potential to become chief executives within 12–18 months. An asynchronous video interview was used, where the candidate is guided through a recorded and structured interview process, but the candidate is alone (asynchronous means you conduct the interview without the interviewer being present). This technology was used for two main reasons. Firstly, to accommodate a geographically disparate and incredibly busy candidate pool and secondly, to accommodate the many senior stakeholders who are geographically widely dispersed. Applications were received from staff currently working in the NHS at director level from locations throughout the UK, mainly England from the North East to the South West.

Stages of the Selection Process:

- **Stage 1: Online application—from applicants throughout the UK**
- **Stage 2: Video interview**
- **Stage 3: Selection center**

Results

There were three key findings:

(1) <u>Flexibility for Applicants:</u> The flexibility offered to candidates to complete a video interview in their own time was crucial given both their location and the demands of their current roles. Candidates of this level are not clustered in one geographic region—they are in similar situations and roles right across the country. Furthermore, given that these applicants work in exceptionally busy director posts, the asynchronous video interview enabled them to fit this initial stage of the recruitment process in with their diaries and time commitments.
According to Rob Farace, National Resourcing Manager at NHS Leadership Academy: *"It can be so difficult to schedule interviews with candidates that don't typically work 9–5 hours. For example, an applicant will be running an essential hospital service and would find it difficult to just take a day off to attend a short screening interview".*

(2) <u>Flexibility for Assessors:</u> In terms of the stakeholders, lots of people wanted to see the candidates and the limitations of physically fitting up to 10 "interviewers" from throughout the UK in a room along with the adverse candidate experience effects made asynchronous video interviewing a very attractive solution.
"If we didn't use video interviewing, we would have interviewed candidates face-to-face, which would be nightmarish to coordinate

so many candidates' and interviewers' schedules not to mention the time constraints of recruiting that amount of candidates within two months."
Rob Farace, National Resourcing Manager, NHS Leadership Academy

(3) Cost Savings: *"The cost of using the video interviewing was nominal compared to coordinating and conducting preliminary face-to-face interviews with thirty candidates and over ten interviewers.*

Overview of the Benefits of Asynchronous Video Interviewing

- Accommodated disparate candidates and multiple assessors in terms of locations and schedules.
- Screening and filtering out unsuitable candidates during the early stages.
- Enabled NHS to select excellent candidates.
- Eliminated the hassles of scheduling and conducting face-to-face interviews.
- Cost-effective solution for a national and niche recruitment drive.
- Team and candidate buy-in.

Conclusion

Asynchronous video interviewing has had a positive impact on not just the selection process but also the employer brand. As one candidate concludes: *"An intriguing system; I can see how it makes for a very efficient interview service, cutting out vast amounts of travel time and so on"*.

Challenge 3. In Judging the Quality of Selection Decisions, How can we Solve the Criterion Problem?

There is relatively little research investigating the quality of selection methods and systems in healthcare education and training other than the prediction of exam performance. Whilst these are clearly important markers in a trainee's education, they are constructed within a *maximal* performance assessment paradigm (i.e. the best one can do within a specified period), whereas less attention has been given to important markers of *typical* performance (how one performs day-to-day). Important personal attributes such as resilience, integrity and teamwork are rarely directly measured in licensing exams which naturally focus on clinical knowledge and clinical skills. This is especially problematic when researchers are attempting to explore the criterion-related validity of measures of non-academic attributes. That said, recent research is emerging that examines the quality of selection methods using a variety of outcome measures such as multi-source feedback, patient satisfaction and educational supervisor ratings (Naidoo, Lopes, Patterson, Mead, & MacLeod, 2017). It is clear however that each of these types of outcome measures have their own challenges which imply that multiple outcome criteria should be considered in future, where researchers should also consider the convergent and discriminant validity of different selection methods. Practically, conducting good quality, longitudinal multi-site validation studies is difficult and there are calls for the use of more sophisticated interdisciplinary research designs beyond linear, regression-based approaches (see the 2018 Ottawa consensus statement for a review, Patterson et al., 2018) which potentially underestimate the complexities of selection system design. Similarly, validation studies have yet to link selection to long-term health outcomes, so this debate links with the overall purpose of selection: are we selecting for the 'best' versus trying to solve workforce issues (see also Challenge 7 below)?

Challenge 4. Practical Solutions to Adequately Address Widening Access, Diversity and Differential Attainment Remain Elusive

Widening access and diversity in selection is not a new topic—recruiters have been dealing with this issue for more than a century. So why are practical solutions that make the difference not yet available? We argue that selection system design requires radically different approaches in future to adequately address diversity issues.

Regarding widening access, given that there exists unequal access to good quality education across the globe, using prior academic achievement as the primary screening method means that those from less privileged backgrounds are significantly less likely to be selected.

If a (healthcare) school's mission is to increase diversity and improve widening participation, then the evidence clearly signals that selection systems need to be fundamentally re-designed. Traditional approaches to selection system design should be revisited. For example, recruiters could use SJTs as the primary screening tool (which are shown to be far less susceptible to adverse impact for socioeconomic status) and thus 'select out' on the basis on non-academic attributes, and subsequently 'select in' based on academic indicators (i.e. rank applicants on academic readiness in the latter parts of the selection system). It may be that some academically able individuals are fundamentally unsuited to a career in healthcare based on their professional attributes and values, and as such should be removed early in the selection process. Such propositions are in line with the research presented in Chapter 11 exploring values-based recruitment which highlights the importance of compassionate care giving from healthcare professionals (Edwards, Kinirons, & Patterson). Most (if not all) healthcare selection systems employ two or more selection methods, yet there remains a dearth of evidence regarding the optimal weightings of each stage and/or selection method. In Chapter 7, Lievens and Corstjens suggest how modular approaches to selection systems design could help systematically unpick the practical implications of different approaches to screening candidates, to help guide practitioners in future.

In Chapter 10, Cleland, Alexander and Nicholson present research and case material to significantly advance our understanding of widening access in relation to social (class) inequality. To date, the evidence to guide practitioners accurately is still in a very early stage of development, and Cleland et al. set out key priorities for future research. Much less is known about how to address differential attainment regarding ethnicity issues; a comprehensive *causal* explanation for substantial differences has yet to be offered (although this phenomenon is not unique to assessment for selection; see Woolf, Potts, & MacManus, 2011; Patterson, Tiffin, Lopes, & Zibarras, 2018). To address this ongoing knowledge gap, there is a need for increased research focus on the role of selection methods in promoting (or indeed prohibiting) diversity and inclusion within the healthcare professions.

Challenge 5. We Know Little of how the Political and Cultural Context in Which Selection Occurs, Acts to Shape Selection Policy and Recruitment Practices Internationally

Patterson, Lievens, Kerrin, Zibarras, and Carette (2012) suggested that the *political* validity of selection system design is an important consideration. This notion refers to all levels of acceptance of selection criteria and methods by a broad range of stakeholders. A recent systematic review of stakeholder perceptions of selection practices shows that organizational justice perceptions are especially influential in acceptability of different selection methods (Kelly, Patterson, O'Flynn, Mulligan, & Murphy, 2018). This topic is also reviewed in detail in the 2018 Ottawa consensus statement on selection and recruitment (Patterson et al., 2018). As the authors in this book have demonstrated, the reactions of applicants and recruiters are important, as are reactions from wider stakeholders, including government, regulatory bodies and the public, which play an important role in decision-making at policy level. However, relatively little research attention has been paid to important purposes of selection such as: (i) a '*public relations*' function (applicant experiences of an recruiter's selection procedure will influence their views of the organization/the role in general); (ii) a function of establishing a viable *psychological contract* between the recruiter and those who are appointed; (iii) and a function of exposing applicants to the *culture* of the organization and profession (e.g. Wanous, Poland, Premack, & Davis, 1992). In relation to the latter, Anderson's review (2001) highlights the role of selection methods initiating a pre-entry socialization process, a concept termed '*socialization impact*'. It is proposed that selection methods commence a pre-entry socialization process (Anderson & Ostroff, 1997; Feldman, 1976; Wanous, 1992) and do not merely act as neutral predictors of subsequent job performance. Rather, they unavoidably influence candidates' reactions, expectations, attitudes, career expectations and even subsequent job behavior. Future research should explore these issues within the healthcare professions which is a high stakes selection setting for all incumbents.

We propose that selection is a multi-faceted, socio-political process, and evaluation frameworks in future need to reflect this complexity. In Case Study 13.3, Stegers-Jaeger, Wouters and Schripsema, describe how a lottery system for medical school admissions is seen as politically acceptable within the Netherlands and how selection policy and practices are shaped by the national context and culture.

Case study 13.3: Selection Practices in The Netherlands

Karen Stegers-Jager[1], Anouk Wouters[2,3] & Nienke Schripsema[4]

[1]Assistant Professor, Institute of Medical Education Research Rotterdam, Erasmus University Medical Center, Rotterdam, The Netherlands
[2]Postdoc Researcher, Research in Education, VUmc School of Medical Sciences, Amsterdam, The Netherlands
[3]LEARN! Research Institute for Learning and Education, Faculty of Psychology and Education, VU University Amsterdam, Amsterdam, The Netherlands
[4]Institute for Medical Education, University Medical Center Groningen/ University of Groningen

Between 2000 and 2017, there were two routes for entry into Dutch medical schools: a national lottery system (weighted for pre-university grades) and (voluntary) school-specific selection procedures, usually consisting of a combination of academic and non-academic selection criteria. Medical schools were free to choose their selection criteria, provided that at least two criteria were used. This multi-process system enabled several natural experiments. In the early years, a maximum of 50% of students were admitted via the school-specific procedures. Following early positive findings, the government steadily increased this to the current 100%.

The co-existence of school-specific selection and lottery has led to several globally applicable "lessons learned" (Stegers-Jager, 2018):

1. Selection procedure participants outperform non-participants in preclinical training, suggesting a 'participation effect' of the voluntary process. This effect, however, seems to be mediated by the design of the selection procedure and curriculum (Schripsema et al., 2017).
2. Engaging in pre-university extracurricular activities (e.g. paid and unpaid jobs in health care, experience in management and organization) is associated with lower dropout rates and better pre-clinical and clinical performance. A success factor for assessing these activities during selection seems to be a sufficiently structured judgment process (Stegers-Jager, 2018).

3. Curriculum-sample selection, which measures applicants' performance on authentic tasks resembling the early years at medical school, should be considered when aiming to select students who fit that curriculum best (de Visser et al., 2017).
4. When using contextualized instruments such as SJTs, it is crucial to tailor them to the local context and to think carefully about the appropriate scoring method (De Leng et al., 2017). Placing SJT scenarios in health care settings where shortages of physicians may be expected, such as geriatrics, appears to be related to higher scores among candidates who are interested in working in those health care settings (Schripsema, van Trigt, Borleffs, & Cohen-Schotanus, 2017).
5. The better performance and motivation of selected students compared to lottery-admitted students reported in early Dutch studies was not confirmed in more recent research (Wouters, Croiset, Schripsema, et al., 2017a). This might be explained by the higher selection ratio due to a higher proportion of selected students per school (from 50 to 100%). According to the Taylor–Russell model, the additional value of selection decreases automatically when the selection ratio increases without changes in the number of suitable applicants (Niessen & Meijer, 2016). A second possible explanation is that applicants change their behavior to meet the known admission criteria. For example, applicants may participate in extracurricular activities not because they "want to", but because they feel they "have to" to get into medical school (Lucieer, Stegers-Jager, Rikers, & Themmen, 2016).
6. Using non-academic selection criteria may help to increase the diversity of the medical student population (Stegers-Jager, Steyerberg, Lucieer, & Themmen, 2015), but the effect depends on the type of instrument, its weighting and the selection ratio. However, inequalities in access to preparatory activities may cause self-selection among students without a "medical network" (Wouters, Croiset, Isik, & Kusurkar, 2017).

Recently, there have been calls in the Netherlands and abroad to replace medical school selection systems with a lottery. The main problem with a lottery is that applicants cannot influence the admission decision, which can lead to negative stakeholder reactions. A combination of targeted selection (e.g. on vocational interests or student background) and unweighted lottery among the suitable applicants might be "fairer" and increase student diversity.

Challenge 6. The Design of Future Evaluation Studies Must Better Acknowledge that Selection is a Complex, Multi-level, Dynamic Phenomenon

As acknowledged in Chapter 1, selection research in healthcare has tended to focus largely on reliability and in future greater attention should be paid to establishing the predictive and construct validity of selection systems. It was also acknowledged that establishing the validity of a selection system presents many methodological, conceptual and practical problems. As such, the process of assessing the validity of selection methods is complex and can (and in many cases, *should*) take many years. As a result, assessing the quality of selection methods and systems is an expensive process, and can often be over-simplified which reduces how informative and applicable data collected can be. More high-quality, large-scale, international, longitudinal research which takes account of the many variables impacting on the quality of selection methods and systems is required to gain a more sophisticated understanding of these issues in future.

While empirical and methodological advancements in our understanding of selection are essential, it is also important to ensure that the field progresses theoretically (see Cleland, Patterson, & Hanson, 2018; Patterson et al., 2018). Research which focuses on advancing our understanding of existing phenomenon is required to better understand the concepts and approaches we are already using in the field (for reference, see Chapter 12).

Challenge 7. Research is Urgently Required to Inform How Best to Attract and Recruit to Healthcare Specialties Where There are Workforce Shortages, Linking Results to Health Outcomes

Much previous research has tended to focus solely on selection issues rather than tackling broader issues relating to attraction and recruitment. This topic is now especially relevant as in many parts of the globe, postgraduate selection can be problematic as in various specialties there are significant workforce shortages (e.g. nursing, GP, Psychiatry;

see also Kiolbassa et al., 2011 and Tolhurst & Stewart, 2005). Furthermore, this issue is often compounded in certain contexts where workforce shortages can be especially acute in remote and rural locations (e.g. Lu, Hakes, Bai, Tolhurst, & Dickinson, 2008).

Some argue that the purpose of selection policies should be reviewed if ultimately selection policy does not align with sufficient service provision to meet healthcare needs in future (see Gorman, 2018). A key question is to what extent can admissions policies address these issues in future? We have already noted the practical difficulties in conducting validation studies in selection research and so a future challenge is to find ways to link selection policy to important health outcomes. This will require far more sophisticated data processing methodologies to deal with such complexities than has been used previously in selection research. Regarding how recruitment policies are formulated, in many parts of the globe, recruitment tends to be based on a meritocratic philosophy (i.e. those applicants scoring most highly on aptitude tests and prior attainment should be awarded a post), but how can the conflict be resolved between selections systems based on a meritocracy versus those designed to address workforce shortages in some specialties and communities? In this respect an important topic that remains relatively untouched in previous research concerns attraction and recruitment, especially for postgraduate selection.

In exploring the issues, in Box 13.1 we present a snapshot of research in the attraction literature and deal specifically with medical specialty choice for general practice.

Box 13.1: Issues in Attraction and Recruitment for General Practice (Tom Kinirons, Work Psychology Group)

Kiolbassa et al. (2011) aimed to identify some of the influencing factors in specialty choice in Germany with particular attention being paid to General Practice (GP). This was to address the shortage of young physicians in a variety of medical specialties in Germany. Their findings suggest that the most influential factors in career choice were individual factors rather than occupational factors. Individual factors refer to personal ambition, future perspective and work-life balance while occupational factors may refer to variety in job, job-related ambition, etc. They found that individual aspects along with 'patient orientation' were more important than any other occupational factors in influencing medical students to choose a career as a GP. Overall, this study provides evidence that students who intend on entering GP differ from those entering other specialties in terms of patient-orientation, personal ambition, future perspective and work-life balance. The researchers suggest that improving the job conditions of general practice in terms of family compatibility and work-life balance could help increase the attractiveness of the career. They also propose that there is the potential to make these influencing factors more evident at early points in medical school.

Deutsch et al. (2015) also aimed to investigate the factors related to GP career choice in Germany. In this observational study, the researchers found that there were six student-associated variables that were independently related to GP as a career choice; age, having family or friends in GP, consideration of GP as a career at matriculation, preference for working in rural areas, valuing the prospect of seeing a wide variety of patients and valuing doctor-patient relationships. In addition, in terms of curriculum during training, there were a number of significant associations with GP as a career choice; a specific pre-clinical GP elective, a GP clerkship and a GP clinical rotation. Furthermore, this piece of research found strong evidence that female participants' work-related values were more congruent with the values of those who decide on GP as a career choice. These findings are in line with a range of previous research investigating the factors that influence choosing a career in GP including previous studies in Germany, Switzerland and Finland (Buddeberg-Fischer, Stamm, Buddeberg & Klaghofer, 2008; Kiolbassa et al., 2011; Kuikka et al., 2012). In addition, findings in this area of research suggest that exposure to and experience in practice-orientated curricular activities can have a profound influence on the choice of GP as a career (Bennett & Phillips, 2010; Bland, Meurer & Maldonado, 1995) with Deutsch et al. (2015) findings supporting this premise.

Positive role models and the opportunity to dismiss negative views and create more accurate views on the field have all been linked to an increase in attraction to GP as a career (Burack et al., 1997; Kuikka et al., 2012; Musham & Chessman, 1994). However, there is the potential that there is an element of self-selection bias taking place in that those who choose to take GP electives are already attracted to it as a career prospect. According to Wesnes, Aasland, and Baerheim (2012) and Biggs, Schmittling, Bieck, Crosley, and Pugno (2011), universities that have a GP department and a strong GP curriculum have, on average, a higher number of graduates choosing to become GPs.

With this knowledge, how can we improve/increase the attractiveness of GP as a career choice? Deutsch et al. (2015) propose that having an increased awareness regarding the characteristics that may make someone more or less likely to become a GP can assist in devising interventions to increase the attractiveness of GP as a career. Suggestions include a practice-oriented GP curriculum both at the early and later stages of medical school. In addition, they also suggest that the provision of the academic institutionalization of GP as a specialty could improve recruitment problems.

In conclusion, although historically research into selection for healthcare education and practice has painted a picture of quantity over quality, this landscape has changed significantly, and key insights are now emerging to guide further enquiry and to influence future policy and practice internationally. That said, there are many complex challenges ahead and several areas of uncharted territory to explore which makes selection and recruitment thought-provoking topics for further research. This book is intended as a platform to promote further debate between colleagues across the globe on these issues.

References

Anderson, N. (2001). Towards a theory of socialization impact: Selection as pre-entry socialization. *International Journal of Selection and Assessment, 9*(1–2), 84–91.

Anderson, N., & Ostroff, C. (1997). Selection as socialization. *International Handbook of Selection and Assessment, 13*, 413–440.

Anglim, J., Bozic, S., Little, J., & Lievens, F. (2018). Response distortion on personality tests in applicants: Comparing high-stakes to low-stakes medical settings. *Advances in Health Sciences Education, 23*(2), 311–321.

Bennett, K. L., & Phillips, J. P. (2010). Finding, recruiting, and sustaining the future primary care physician workforce: A new theoretical model of specialty choice process. *Academic Medicine, 85*(10), S81–S88.

Biggs, W. S., Schmittling, G. T., Bieck, A. D., Crosley, P. W., & Pugno, P. A. (2011). Entry of US medical school graduates into family medicine residencies: 2010–2011 and 3-year summary. *Family Medicine, 43*(9), 625–630.

Bland, C. J., Meurer, L. N., & Maldonado, G. (1995). Determinants of primary care specialty choice: A non-statistical meta-analysis of the literature.

Buddeberg-Fischer, B., Klaghofer, R., Stamm, M., Siegrist, J., & Buddeberg, C. (2008). Work stress and reduced health in young physicians: Prospective evidence from Swiss residents. *International Archives of Occupational and Environmental Health, 82*(1), 31–38.

Burack, J. H., Irby, D. M., Caline, J. D., Ambrozy, D. M., Ellsbury, K. E., & Stritter, F. T. (1997). A study of medical students' specialty-choice pathways: Trying on possible selves. *Academic Medicine, 72*, 534–541.

Cleland, J., Patterson, F., & Hanson, M. (2018). To what extent are selection and widening access complex and wicked problems? *Medical Education* (in press).

Cleland, J. A., Patterson, F., Dowell, J., & Nicholson, S. (2014). *How can greater consistency in selection between medical schools be encouraged? A mixed-methods programme of research that examines and develops the evidence base.* A project commissioned by the Selecting for Excellence Group (SEEG) and published at http://www.medschools.ac.uk/SiteCollectionDocuments/Selecting-for-Excellence-research-Professor-Jen-Cleland-et-al.pdf. Accessed November 2017.

De Leng, W. E., Stegers-Jager, K. M., Husbands, A., Dowell, J. S., Born, M. P., & Themmen, A. P. N. (2017). Scoring method of a situational judgment test: Influence on internal consistency reliability, adverse impact and correlation with personality? *Advances in Health Sciences Education: Theory and Practice, 22*(2), 243–265.

Deutsch, T., Lippmann, S., Frese, T., & Sandholzer, H. (2015). Who wants to become a general practitioner? Student and curriculum factors associated with choosing a GP career—A multivariable analysis with particular consideration of practice-orientated GP courses. *Scandinavian Journal of Primary Health Care, 33*(1), 47–53.

de Visser, M., Fluit, C., Fransen, J., Latijnhouwers, M., Cohen-Schotanus, J., & Laan, R. (2017). The effect of curriculum sample selection for medical school. *Advances in Health Sciences Education: Theory and Practice, 22*(1), 43–56.

Feldman, D. C. (1976). A contingency theory of socialization. *Administrative Science Quarterly*, 433–452.

Gorman, D. (2018). Matching the production of doctors with national needs. *Medical Education, 52*, 103–113.

Kelly, M. E., Patterson, F., O'Flynn, S., Mulligan, J., & Murphy, A. W. (2018). A systematic review of stakeholder views of selection methods for medical schools admission. *BMC Medical Education, 18*(1), 139.

Kiolbassa, K., Miksch, A., Hermann, K., Loh, A., Szecsenyi, J., Joos, S., et al. (2011). Becoming a general practitioner—Which factors have most impact on career choice of medical students? *BMC Family Practice, 12*(1), 25.

Konradt, U., Warszta, T., & Ellwart, T. (2013). Fairness Perceptions in Web-Based selection: Impact on applicants' pursuit intentions, recommendation intentions, and intentions to reapply. *International Journal of Selection and Assessment, 21*(2), 155–169.

Kuikka, L., Nevalainen, M. K., Sjöberg, L., Salokekkilä, P., Karppinen, H., Torppa, M., …, Pitkälä, K. H. (2012). The perceptions of a GP's work among fifth-year medical students in Helsinki, Finland. *Scandinavian Journal of Primary Health Care, 30*(2), 121–126.

Lu, D. J., Hakes, J., Bai, M., Tolhurst, H., & Dickinson, J. A. (2008). Rural intentions: Factors affecting the career choices of family medicine graduates. *Canadian Family Physician, 54*(7), 1016–1017.

Lucieer, S. M., Stegers-Jager, K. M., Rikers, R. M., & Themmen, A. P. N. (2016). Non-cognitive selected students do not outperform lottery-admitted students in the pre-clinical stage of medical school. *Advances in Health Sciences Education: Theory and Practice, 21*(1), 51–61.

Musham, C., & Chessman, A. (1994). Changes in medical students' perceptions of family practice resulting from a required clerkship. *Family Medicine, 26*(8), 500–503.

Naidoo, S., Lopes, S., Patterson, F., Mead, H. M., & MacLeod, S. (2017). Can colleagues', patients' and supervisors' assessments predict successful completion of postgraduate medical training? *Medical Education, 51*(4), 423–431.

Niessen, A. S., & Meijer, R. R. (2016). Selection of medical students on the basis of non-academic skills: Is it worth the trouble? *Clinical Medicine, 16,* 339–342.

Patterson, F., Lievens, F., Kerrin, M., Zibarras, L., & Carette, B. (2012). Designing selection systems for medicine: Implications for the political validity of high stakes selection methods. *International Journal of Selection and Assessment, 20*(4), 486–496.

Patterson, F, Roberts, C., Hanson, M. D., Hampe, W., Eva, K., Ponnamperuma, G., …, Cleland, J. (2018). The Ottawa 2018 consensus statement on selection and recruitment in the healthcare professions. *Medical Teacher* (in press).

Patterson, F., Tiffin, P., Lopes, S., & Zibarras, L. (2018). Unpacking the dark variance of differential attainment on examinations in overseas graduate. *Medical Education* (in press).

Patterson, F., & Zibarras, L. D. (2017). Selecting for creativity and innovation potential: Implications for practice in healthcare education. *Advances in Health Sciences Education, 22*(2), 417–428.

Prideaux, D., Roberts, C., Eva, K., Centeno, A., Mccrorie, P., Mcmanus, C., …, Wilkinson, D. (2011). Assessment for selection for the health care professions and specialty training: Consensus statement and recommendations from the Ottawa 2010 Conference. *Medical Teacher, 33*(3), 215–223.

Schripsema, N. R., van Trigt, A. M., Borleffs, J. C. C., & Cohen-Schotanus, J. (2017). Impact of vocational interests, previous academic experience, gender and age on situational judgement test performance. *Advances in Health Sciences Education: Theory and Practice, 22*(2), 521–532.

Schripsema, N. R., van Trigt, A. M., Lucieer, S. M., Wouters, A., Croiset, G., Themmen, A. P. N., …, Cohen-Schotanus, J. (2017). Participation and selection effects of a voluntary selection process. *Advances in Health Sciences Education: Theory and Practice, 22*(2), 463–476.

Stegers-Jager, K. M. (2018). Lessons learned from 15 years of non-grades-based selection for medical school. *Medical Education, 52*(1), 86–95.

Stegers-Jager, K. M., Steyerberg, E. W., Lucieer, S. M., & Themmen, A. P. N. (2015). Ethnic and social disparities in performance on medical school selection criteria. *Medical Education, 49*(1), 124–133. https://doi.org/10.1111/medu.12536.

Tolhurst, H., & Stewart, M. (2005). Becoming a GP—A qualitative study of the career interests of medical students. *Australian Family Physician, 34*(3), 204.

Wanous, J. P. (1992). *Organizational entry: Recruitment, selection, orientation, and socialization of newcomers* (2nd ed.). Reading, MA: Addison-Wesley.

Wanous, J. P., Poland, T. D., Premack, S. L., & Davis, K. S. (1992). The effects of met expectations on newcomer attitudes and behaviors: A review and meta-analysis. *Journal of Applied Psychology, 77*(3), 288.

Wesnes, S. L., Aasland, O., & Baerheim, A. (2012). Career choice and place of graduation among physicians in Norway. *Scandinavian Journal of Primary Health Care, 30*(1), 35–40.

Woolf, K., Potts, H. W. W., & MacManus, I. C. (2011). Ethnicity and academic performance in UK trained doctors and medical students: Systematic review and meta-analysis. *British Medical Journal, 342*, d901. https://doi.org/10.1136/bmj.d901.

Wouters, A., Croiset, G., Isik, U., & Kusurkar, R. A. (2017). Motivation of Dutch high school students from various backgrounds for applying to study medicine: A qualitative study. *British Medical Journal Open, 7*(5), e014779.

Wouters, A., Croiset, G., Schripsema, N. R., Cohen-Schotanus, J., Spaai, G. W. G., Hulsman, R. L., & Kusurkar, R. A. (2017). A multi-site study on medical school selection, performance, motivation and engagement. *Advances in Health Sciences Education: Theory and Practice, 22*(2), 447–462.

Glossary

Abstract reasoning The ability for lateral thinking skills or fluid intelligence to quickly identify patterns, logical rules and trends in new data, integrate this information and apply it to solve problems.

Academic attainment The highest degree of education an individual has completed.

Acceptability The quality of being accepted, tolerated or allowed.

Adverse impact Refers to employment practices that appear neutral but have a discriminatory effect on a protected group. Adverse impact may occur in hiring, promotion, training and development, transfer, layoff, and even performance appraisals.

Aptitude tests A test designed to assess what an individual is capable of doing or to predict what a person is able to learn or do given the right education and instruction. It represents an individual's level of competency to perform a certain type of task.

Artificial intelligence (AI) Refers to intelligence demonstrated by machines, in contrast to the natural intelligence (NI) displayed by humans and other animals.

Assessment center (AC) A combination of tasks and activities that tests an individual's wide range of skills to assess the suitability for a job.

Assessment criteria See selection criteria.

F. Patterson and L. Zibarras (eds.), *Selection and Recruitment in the Healthcare Professions*, https://doi.org/10.1007/978-3-319-94971-0

Assessor load The level of effort being used in the working memory of an assessor during a selection stage.

Asynchronous video interviewing A new form of interview in which the applicant is guided through a structured interview process, which the applicant does on their own and not at the same time as the interviewer.

Attrition The gradual reduction of the size of a workforce by not replacing personnel lost through retirement or resignation.

Augmented reality (AR) A technology that superimposes a computer-generated image on a user's view of the real world.

Behavioral indicator A specific description of a effective behavior; can be positive or negative.

Behavior modelling The act of showing employees how to do something and guiding them through the process of imitating the modeled behavior.

Behavioral Consistency Theory Theory underpinning SJTs and other methodologies. Theory proposes that future behavior is likely to be consistent with past behavior.

Big Five Personality Factors A model based on common language descriptors of personality. The five broad personality traits described by the theory are extraversion, agreeableness, openness, conscientiousness, and neuroticism.

Biomedical Admissions Test (BMAT) An aptitude test used as part of the admissions process for Medicine, Biomedical Sciences and Dentistry in some universities in the United Kingdom, Singapore, Spain, Malaysia, Thailand, and the Netherlands.

BME Black and Minority Ethnic.

Calibration The comparison of performance on a test with a reference standard.

California Personality Inventory (CPI) A self-report inventory created by Harrison G. Gough and currently published by Consulting Psychologists Press. It is designed to assess social communication and interpersonal behavior.

CanMEDS Canadian Medical Education Directives for Specialists.

Closed-ended response format Multiple-choice or forced-choice response formats in which possible response options are predetermined and prompts are frequently used.

Cognitive ability Refers to the capacity of individuals to process information and carry out certain tasks.

Cognitive ability tests A measure of an individual's reasoning skills in interpreting written information and reports, using figures, data and statistics and understanding abstract or logical symbols.

Cognitive load Refers to the effort being used in the working memory; the total amount of mental activity imposed on working memory.

Collective engagement A learning process that involves multiple parties coming together in multiple interactions for the purpose of exchanging ideas and knowledge.

Commercial coaching A form of coaching which focuses on a specific test (usually used for selection purposes) with the aim of improving test scores, regardless of whether or not the underlying skill or ability measured by the test is improved.

Common method variance This is variance that is attributable to the measurement method, rather than to the constructs the measures are assumed to represent.

Competency The specific behavior patterns (including knowledge, skills and abilities) a job holder is required to demonstrate in order to perform the relevant job tasks with competence.

Competency framework Defines the KSAOs needed for each individual role within an organization.

Computer Adaptive Testing (CAT) A form of computer-based test that adapts to the examinee's ability level.

Consensus scores Scores that are awarded when test takers' ratings resemble the ratings provided by a reference group.

Construct What is being measured (or aims to be measured) by a given methodology.

Construct validity An indication of the extent to which the test or procedure measures the construct that it is intended to measure (such as empathy, clinical expertise).

Content validity The extent to which a measure represents all facets of a given construct.

Contextual admissions The use of additional information such as school performance data and socioeconomic markers so as to provide context for a candidate's university application and achievement.

Contextualization The extent to which test stimuli are embedded in a detailed and realistic context.

Cost-benefit analysis A systematic process for calculating and comparing benefits and costs of a decision, in order to estimate the strengths and weaknesses of alternative measures.

Criterion validity The extent to which a predictor measure (e.g. a selection test score) is correlated to a criterion measure (e.g. work performance). High predictive validity indicates that a selection measure gives an accurate indication of candidates' future performance on the criterion.

Criterion-related validity (concurrent) A form of criterion-related validity in which data on the predictor and criterion are obtained at the same time. High correlations between predictor and criterion scores indicate concurrent validity.

Criterion-related validity (predictive) This is the extent to which a predictor measure (e.g. a selection test score) is correlated to a criterion measure (e.g. work performance). High predictive validity indicates that a selection measure gives an accurate indication of candidates' future performance on the criterion.

Critical incident technique (CIT) A set of procedures used for collecting direct observations of human behavior that have critical significant and meet methodically defined criteria.

Crystallized intelligence Basic scientific knowledge.

Dental Admissions Test (DAT) A multiple-choice standardized exam taken by potential dentists in the United States and Canada. Its four sections are: Survey of the Natural Sciences, Perceptual Ability, Reading Comprehension, and Quantitative Reasoning.

Didactic learning environment A learning environment that follows a consistent scientific approach or educational style.

Differential item functioning A statistical characteristic of an item that shows the extent to which the item might be measuring different abilities for members of separate subgroups.

Diligent syndrome A tendency to be attentive and good with details, orderly, rational, careful and well organized.

Distributive justice Perceptions of equal and fair outcomes for different people.

Diversity To understand that each individual is unique and recognizing our individual differences. These can include: race, ethnicity, gender, sexual orientation, socio-economic status, age, physical abilities, religious beliefs, political beliefs or other ideologies.

Domain-based knowledge Valid knowledge used to refer to an area of human endeavor.

Dynamic Development Model (DDM) A conceptualization of job demands as dynamic rather than static.

Dynamic testing A learning environment is created within the test itself.

Effect size A simple way of quantifying the difference between two groups.

Emotional Intelligence (EI) A set of characteristics and styles that is thought to enable a person to utilize intellect, emotion and awareness of other people in their day-to-day behavior.

Enculturation The process by which a culture that is already established teaches an individual the accepted norms and values of that culture.

Equal opportunities All people, regardless of their group membership, are given a fair chance to succeed during selection and in the workplace.

Error variance The proportion of variance in a set of scores that is due to extraneous variables and measurement.

Face validity The selection tool content appears relevant to the target role (determined by the applicants).

Factor analysis A statistical technique used to identify key factors that underlie relationships between variables.

Fairness Equal opportunity of job applicants when applying for a newly released post or the accuracy of a set of test results.

Faith validity 'Blind' faith that a selection method works because someone plausible said so.

Feasibility Capable of being accomplished or brought about; possible.

Flexner Report A book-length study of medical education in the United States and Canada, written by Abraham Flexner and published in 1910 under the aegis of the Carnegie Foundation. Many aspects of the present-day American medical profession stem from the Flexner Report and its aftermath.

Fluid intelligence Mental processing, reasoning and decision making without testing underlying background knowledge.

g component See cognitive ability.

General Certificate of Education Advanced Level (A-level) A subject-based qualification conferred as part of the General Certificate of Education, as well as, a school leaving qualification offered by the educational bodies in the United Kingdom.

General mental ability Also referred to as intelligence or cognitive ability and refers to the capacity of individuals to process information and use the information to behave effectively (including the capacity to learn from experience).

Generalizability The extent to which findings (from a study) can be extended to the those in natural settings (ecological validity).

Generalizability study (G-study) The extension of research findings and conclusions from a study conducted on a sample population to the population at large. While the dependability of this extension is not absolute, it is statistically probable.

Generalizability theory Refers to a statistical framework for conceptualizing, investigating, and designing reliable observations. It is used to determine the reliability (i.e., reproducibility) of measurements under specific conditions.

Grade inflation (1) Grading leniency: the awarding of higher grades than students deserve, which yields a higher average grade given to students (2) The tendency to award progressively higher academic grades for work that would have received lower grades in the past.

Grade Point Average (GPA) An internationally recognized calculation used to find the average result of all grades achieved for a course. It is calculated by dividing the total amount of grade points earned by the total amount of credit hours attempted.

Graduate Medical School Admissions Test (GAMSAT) Developed and administered by the Australian Council for Educational Research, GAMSAT has been used since 1995. It has three sections: (1) reasoning in humanities and social sciences; (2) written communication and (3) reasoning in biological and physical sciences.

Graphology The study of handwriting with the intention of inferring a person's character.

Haidt's Moral Foundation (2007) Five moral foundations described by Haidt (2007); caring reciprocity, group loyalty, authority and purity. These can be grouped into two higher order domains; Egalitarianism and Order-Traditionalism.

Health Science Reasoning Test (HSRT) Used since 1994, the HSRT is a multiple choice test designed and administered by Insight Assessment, specifically for use in health professions. An overall critical thinking score and five subscale scores are reported: inference, induction, deduction, analysis, and evaluation.

Hogan Development Survey Describes the dark side of personality—qualities that emerge in times of increased strain and can disrupt relationships, damage reputations and derail an individual's chances of success. By assessing dark-side personality, you can recognize and mitigate performance risks.

Honesty tests A form of personality test designed to assess an applicant's tendency to be honest, dependable and trustworthy.

Implicit Trait Policy (ITP) Suggested beliefs about causal relations between personality traits and behavioral effectiveness.

Incremental Validity The extent to which adding another predictor (i.e. selection method) can increase the predictive power of the selection process.

Indigenous communities Communities that have a historical continuity with pre-invasion and pre-colonial socieites that developed on their territories.

Individual differences How people are similar and how they differ in their thinking, feeling and behavior.

Intercultural awareness An awareness of both one's own culture and another culture and involves the ability to stand back from one's own point of view to take other's cultural values, beliefs and perceptions into account along with our own.

Internal consistency A statistical measure based on the correlations between different items on the same test (or the same subscale on a larger test). It measures whether several items that propose to measure the same general construct produce similar scores.

Inter-rater reliability A form of reliability testing which involves correlating scores given by a range of different assessors i.e. the same candidate should receive similar scores from different raters.

Job analysis Procedures (there is more than one way to do a job analysis) for producing systematic information about jobs, including the nature of the work performed, position in the organization and relationships of the job holder with other people.

Job demands All physical, psychological, social or organizational aspects of a job that require continuous physical and/or psychological (i.e.: cognitive or emotional) effort.

Job description A document that describes the general tasks, or other related duties and responsibilities of a position. It may specify the functionary to whom the position reports, specifications such as the qualifications or skills needed by the person in the job and a salary range.

Knowledge skills, abilities and other characteristics (KSAOs) The job-related knowledge, skills, abilities and other characteristics than an applicant/candidate must have to perform successfully in the prospective position.

Latent construct A construct that is theoretical in nature and therefore cannot be observed or measured directly e.g. personality.

Learning style The preferential way in which an individual (student) absorbs, processes, comprehends and retains information.

Mechanisms of Altruism (MOA) The means by which people engage in altruistic behaviors e.g. blood donation.

Medical College Admission Test (MCAT) A standardized admissions exam for prospective medical students in the United States, Australia, Canada and Caribbean Islands.

Meritocratic selection A concept where people achieve or are selected on the basis of their merits or abilities rather than because of their money or social position.

Meta-analysis A statistical technique for aggregating data from a number of different studies in order to establish overall trends.

Modular assessment A form of assessment whereby courses or qualifications are split into different units with an assessment at the end of each unit.

Moss test A combination of true/false and multiple choice questions. It was designed to measure scientific vocabulary, pre-medical information, memory for verbal content of a medical nature, recall of names of parts on an anatomical diagram, reading comprehension, and logical reasoning.

Multiple mini-interview (MMI) An interview format that uses multiple short assessments, that are independent of each other, typically in a timed circuit, to obtain an aggregate score of candidates' soft skills.

National Health Service (NHS) The government-funded medical and health care services available to UK residents.

Non-verbal reasoning Involves the ability to understand and analyze visual information and solve problems using visual reasoning.

Norm-referencing Scoring performance in a relative fashion.

Numerical reasoning A test which requires the test taker to answer questions using facts and figures presented in statistical tables.

Open-ended response format A response format which allows for a free text response.

Organizational attractiveness The appeal of an organization to prospective employees.

Organizational culture The norms, beliefs and values, specific to an organization, that combine to give an organization a distinctive character.

Organizational justice theory The theory that refers to perceptions of fairness relating to the selection process.

Performance management The activities and set of processes that aim to both maintain and improve performance in line with an organization's objectives.

Person specification The person specification is a description of the qualifications, skills, experience, knowledge and other attributes (selection criteria) which a candidate must possess to perform the job duties. The specification should be derived from the job description and forms the foundation for the recruitment process.

Personality assessment Personality assessment involves the administration, scoring and interpretation of empirically supported measures of personality traits and styles.

Personality inventory A type of questionnaire designed to reveal the respondent's personality traits.

Personality profiling A means of measuring an individual's personality in a particular situation. It is not a measure of intelligence or ability—but of behavior.

Personality traits Distinguishing qualities or characteristics of an individual; they are an individual's habitual patterns of behavior, temperament and emotion.

Person-oriented specialty An area of study that has an orientation towards people.

Pharmacy College Admission Test (PCAT) A multiple-choice standardized exam for potential pharmacy students in the United States. It consists of five subtests: Writing, Biological Processes, Chemical Processes, Critical Reading, and Quantitative Reasoning.

Piloting Testing a scheme or project before introducing it more widely.

Political validity An indication of the extent to which various stakeholders and stakeholder groups (such as employers, parents, government departments, society, the regulator) consider the tool(s) to be appropriate and acceptable for use in selection.

Political validity The acceptance of selection practices by a range of stakeholders. This includes the reactions of applicants and recruiters, along with reactions from wider stakeholders, such as government, regulatory bodies and the general public, which play an important role in decision-making at policy level.

Predictive power The ability of a given theory to allow us to make predictions about the natural world.

Predictive validity See criterion validity.

Pre-entry socialization The process involved in gathering information regarding the role or organization during the selection and/or recruitment phase.

Pre-screening See shortlisting.

Prioritization task To rank tasks in order of importance.

Procedural justice Perceptions regarding the extent to which a selection process is well designed (e.g. job-related, appropriate level etc.).

Procedural learning The acquisition of a skill through repeated performance and practice.

Propensity scoring A form of scoring which involves identifying a set of covariates likely to influence outcomes, then estimating the probability of each participant has of being influenced by these covariates and removing these effects.

Prosocial behavior A social behavior that benefits other people or society as a whole (e.g., helping, sharing, donating, co-operating, and volunteering).

Psychological contract The unwritten set of expectations of the employment relationship; separate from the formal employment contract.

Psychometric tests Standardized procedures (often using pen and paper or delivered online), embodying a series of questions (items) designed to assess key cognitive or personality dimensions. Must have acceptable levels of validity and reliability to be of value.

Quantitative reasoning The application of basic mathematics skills to the analysis and interpretation of real-world quantitative information, in the context of a discipline or an interdisciplinary problem to draw conclusions.

Quasi-experimental design An experimental design that does not involve random assignment.

Randomized trials A study in which people are allocated at random to receive one of several different interventions.

Range restriction/restriction of range The case in which observed sample data is not available across the entire range of interest.

Rank-ordering Refers to the scale that gives respondents a set of simultaneous items and asks them to put the items in some form of order.

Reliability An indicator of the consistency which a test or procedure provides. It is possible to quantify reliability to indicate the extent to which a measure is free from error.

Reliability—parallel forms A measure of reliability obtained by administering different versions of an assessment tool (both versions must contain items that probe the same construct, skill, knowledge base, etc.) to the same group of individuals.

Response evaluation consistency The level of standardization that evaluators adopt to evaluate test-takers' responses.

RIASEC model RIASEC is also called John Holland's Six Types of Personality and stands for realistic, investigative, artistic, social, enterprising and conventional.

Robustness The ability to withstand or overcome adverse conditions or rigorous testing.

Role design A consideration of the tasks involved in a role and how these are to be performed.

Rule-consciousness The extent (high or low level) to which an individual is dutiful and conforms to the rules.

Scalability An attribute that describes the ability of a process, network, software or organization to grow and manage increased demand; the capacity to be changed in size or scale.

Scholastic Aptitude Test (SAT) A standardized test used across the United States for college admissions.

Schwartz's values (1992) Schwartz's (1992) 10 values which are organized across two bipolar dimensions; openness-to-change vs. conservation and self-enhancement vs. self-transcendence.

Score inflation The increase in a student's scores on tests or other assessments without any increase in learning. This can be caused by a flawed testing design or process or by educators inadvertently or unintentionally inflating scores.

Selection bias Selection bias is the bias introduced by the selection of individuals, groups, or data for analysis in such a way that proper randomization is not achieved, thereby ensuring that the sample obtained is not representative of the population intended to be analyzed.

Selection center An assessment process that involves multiple selection methods and multiple assessors to rate a candidate's performance on several job-relevant competencies.

Selection criteria A set of standards that job applicants need to meet.

Selection method The methods for selecting an individual that determine whether or not a candidate is suitable for the job.

Selection process Refers to the steps involved in choosing an individual who has the appropriate skills and qualifications to fill a current or future job opening. The first stage of the selection process typically involves carrying out an analysis of the job itself to identify the key elements or dimensions involved in it.

Selection ratio Indicates the number of positions available compared to the number of candidates who apply to that job. For example, 20 candidates for every post would give a ratio of 1:20.

Self-awareness The capacity to know and understand one's own characteristics, motives, and values.

Self-report questionnaires A method in which respondents read the question and select a response by themselves, without researcher interference. It usually involves asking a respondent about their feelings, attitudes, and beliefs.

Semi-structured interview A method of research used most often in the social sciences; the interviewer in a semi-structured interview generally has a framework of themes to be explored in an open manner.

Shadow education Activities that fall outside of formal education.

Shortlisting A reduced list of candidates for some situation that has been cut down from a larger list.

Simulation-based training A virtual medium through which various types of skills can be acquired. Training simulations can be used in a variety of genres.

Situational judgement tests (SJT) A selection test that requires candidates to decide how they would behave in response to a situation described in the test. Often the test would also require the candidates to give details of the reasoning that led their decision.

Social desirability The tendency of some respondents to report an answer in a way they deem to be more socially acceptable than would be their "true" answer. This is typically done to project a favorable image of themselves and to avoid receiving negative evaluations.

Social inclusion The act of making all groups of people within a society feel valued and important.

Social mobility The movement of people within or between layers or tiers in a social system which values status characteristics.

Socialization The process of learning to behave in a way that is acceptable to society.

Socialization impact The role of selection methods in initiating the pre-socialization process.

Sociodemographic factors Characteristics of a population such as age, race, ethnicity, and language.

Socioeconomic diversity A mixture/combination of different income levels, social backgrounds and in some cases, racial and ethnic backgrounds.

Socioeconomic status An economic and sociological measure of a person's work experience and of their or their family's economic and social position in relation to others based on education, occupation, and income.

Stakeholder A party of interest in an organization that can either have an effect on the organization or can be affected by it, e.g., investors, employees, customers.

Standardization Consistency and objectivity of how tests are administered and scored. In order to compare one person to another on a test, it is important that they take the test under the same conditions and the same scoring procedure is applied to both.

State anxiety An unpleasant emotional arousal in face of threatening demands or dangers.

Structured behavioral interviews A style of interview in which candidates are asked to describe actual past behaviors that relate to the job for which they are being interviewed.

Structured situational interviews A style of interview in which candidates are asked hypothetical, job-oriented questions.

Subject matter expert (SME) A person who is an authority in a particular area or topic.

Summative assessment To evaluate student learning at the end of an instructional unit, by comparing it against some standard or benchmark. Summative assessments are often high stakes, which means that they have a high point value.

Systematic review A systematic review summarizes the results of available carefully designed healthcare studies (controlled trials) and provides a high level of evidence on the effectiveness of healthcare interventions.

Technique-oriented specialty An area of study that has an orientation towards techniques and instruments.

Test familiarization A form of coaching that can be self-led which involves familiarizing oneself with test content and structure.

Test-retest reliability A form of reliability testing which involves correlating the reliability of the test after various sittings of the test, i.e., the reliability should be similar each time the test is taken.

Trait Activation Theory (TAT) The process by which individuals express their traits when presented with trait-relevant situational cues.

Trait anxiety Refers to relatively stable individual differences between people, in the tendency to perceive stressful situations as dangerous or threatening and to respond to such situations with elevations in the intensity of their state anxiety.

Turnover intention A measurement of whether a business' or organization's employees plan to leave their positions or whether that organization plans to remove employees from positions. It may be a voluntary or involuntary process.

UK Clinical Aptitude Test (UKCAT) An admissions test used by a consortium of UK Universities for their medical and dental degree programs.

Under-represented minority (URM) African Americans, Native Americans, and Latin Americans who have historically comprised a minority of the population in the United States.

United Nations Educational Scientific and Cultural Organisation (UNESCO) A specialized agency of the United Nations that promotes international collaboration in educational, scientific, and cultural reform.

Validation Studies Works consisting of research using processes by which the reliability and relevance of a procedure for a specific purpose are established.

Value internalization The acceptance of a set of values, established by others, through socialization.

Values-based recruitment An approach to recruitment that helps to attract and select students, trainees, and employees, whose personal values and behaviors align with the business/organization hiring. Recruiting people for their values and behaviors.

Variance The expectation of the squared deviation of a random variable from its mean. It measures how far a set of (random) numbers are spread out from their average value.

Verbal reasoning The ability to comprehend and reason using concepts expressed through words. A verbal reasoning test is a form of aptitude test used by interviewers to find out how well a candidate can assess verbal logic, and how successfully they can extract the correct meaning from complex written information.

Virtual reality (VR) A computer-generated scenario that simulates experience.

Widening access The movement to 'widen access' to those who have not traditionally participated in Higher Education; driven by each country's historical and current social issues.

Index

F. Patterson and L. Zibarras (eds.), *Selection and Recruitment in the Healthcare Professions*, https://doi.org/10.1007/978-3-319-94971-0

FSC
www.fsc.org
MIX
Papier | Fördert
gute Waldnutzung
FSC® C083411

Kolibri 360 GmbH
Ferdinand-Jühlke-Straße 7
99095 Erfurt, Deutschland
produktsicherheit@kolibri360.de